TAKING SIDES

Clashing Views on

Economic Issues

FOURTEENTH EDITION

D1056533

TAKING SIDES

Clashing Views on

Economic Issues

FOURTEENTH EDITION

Selected, Edited, and with Introductions by

Frank J. Bonello
University of Notre Dame

Isobel Lobo
Benedictine University

 **Higher Education**

Boston   Burr Ridge, IL   Dubuque, IA   New York   San Francisco   St. Louis
Bangkok   Bogotá   Caracas   Kuala Lumpur   Lisbon   London   Madrid   Mexico City
Milan   Montreal   New Delhi   Santiago   Seoul   Singapore   Sydney   Taipei   Toronto

Higher Education

TAKING SIDES: CLASHING VIEWS ON ECONOMIC ISSUES, FOURTEENTH EDITION

Published by McGraw-Hill, a business unit of The McGraw-Hill Companies, Inc., 1221 Avenue of the Americas, New York, NY 10020. Copyright © 2010 by The McGraw-Hill Companies, Inc. All rights reserved. Previous edition(s) 2008, 2006, 2004. No part of this publication may be reproduced or distributed in any form or by any means, or stored in a database or retrieval system, without the prior written consent of The McGraw-Hill Companies, Inc., including, but not limited to, in any network or other electronic storage or transmission, or broadcast for distance learning.

Some ancillaries, including electronic and print components, may not be available to customers outside the United States.

Taking Sides® is a registered trademark of The McGraw-Hill Companies, Inc.
Taking Sides is published by the **Contemporary Learning Series** group within the McGraw-Hill Higher Education division.

1 2 3 4 5 6 7 8 9 0 DOC/DOC 0 9

MHID: 0-07-352730-0
ISBN: 978-0-07-352730-7
ISSN: 1094-7612

Managing Editor: *Larry Loeppke*
Senior Managing Editor: *Faye Schilling*
Senior Developmental Editor: *Jade Benedict*
Editorial Coordinator: *Mary Foust*
Production Service Assistant: *Rita Hingtgen*
Permissions Coordinator: *Shirley Lanners*
Senior Marketing Manager: *Julie Keck*
Marketing Communications Specialist: *Mary Klein*
Marketing Coordinator: *Alice Link*
Senior Project Manager: *Jane Mohr*
Design Specialist: *Tara McDermott*
Cover Graphics: *Rick D. Noel*

Compositor: Macmillan Publishing Solutions
Cover Image: © The McGraw-Hill Companies, Inc./Doug Sherman

Library of Congress Cataloging-in-Publication Data

Main entry under title:
 Taking Sides: Clashing Views on Economic Issues/Selected, Edited, and with Introductions by Frank J. Bonello—14th edition

 Includes bibliographical references and index.
 1. United States—Economic policy—1971–1981. 2. United States—Economic policy—1981–1993. 3. United States—Economic policy—1993–.
 I. Bonello, Frank J., comp.
        338.9′22

www.mhhe.com

Clashing Views on

Economic Issues

FOURTEENTH EDITION

Frank J. Bonello
University of Notre Dame

Isobel Lobo
Benedictine University

Advisory Board

Preface

> Where there is much desire to learn, there of necessity will be much arguing.
>
> –John Milton (1608–1674), English poet and essayist

Presented here are 20 debates on important economic issues, which are designed to stimulate critical thinking skills and initiate lively and informed discussion. These debates take economic theory and show how it is applied to current real-world public policy decisions, the outcomes of which will have an immediate and personal impact. How these debates are resolved will affect our taxes, jobs, wages, educational systems, and so on; in short, they will shape the society in which we live.

The goal throughout each of the 14 editions of *Taking Sides: Clashing Views on Economic Issues* has been to select issues that reveal something about the nature of economics itself and something about how economics relates to current everyday newspaper headlines and television news stories on public policy concerns. To assist the reader, we begin each issue with an issue introduction, which sets the stage for the debate as it is argued in the "yes" and "no" selections. Each issue concludes with a postscript that briefly reviews the arguments and makes some final observations. The introduction and postscript do not preempt what is the reader's own task: to achieve a critical and informed view of the economic issue at stake. Certainly, the reader should not feel confined to adopt one or the other of the positions presented. The views presented should be used as starting points, and the suggestions for further reading in the each issue postscript offer additional resources on the topic. Internet site addresses (URLs) have been provided at the beginning of each unit, which should also prove useful as resources for further research. At the back of the book is a listing of all the contributors to this volume, which provides information about the economists, policymakers, political leaders, and commentators whose views are presented here.

Changes to this edition This new edition of *Taking Sides* represents a considerable revision. Of the 20 issues, seven are completely new and three represent updates. Thus, as the journey into the new millennium continues, this substantially revised book will help us understand the implications of a changing set of economic issues that were not part of our world just a few years ago. The new issues are: "Is OSHA Working Effectively to Protect the Safety of Construction Workers?" (issue 3); "Should Unemployment Benefits Be Extended?" (issue 9); "Is a Fair Trade Policy Superior to a Free Trade Policy?" (issue 13); "Is Loan Mitigation the Answer to the Housing Foreclosure Problem?" (issue 14); "Will Biofuels Like Ethanol Reduce U.S. Dependence on Foreign Oil?" (issue 15); "Is the Inequality in U.S. Income Distribution Surging?" (issue 19); and "Is the Treasury's $700 Billion Bailout the Solution to the Credit Crisis?" (issue 20).

The updated issues involve health care policy, consumer credit, and education policy: "Are Health Savings Accounts Working Effectively?" (issue 5); "Do American Consumers Need a Credit Card Bill of Rights?" (issue 10); and education policy "Do the Testing and Accountability Elements of the No Child Left Behind Act Prevent a Proper Cost-Benefit Evaluation?" (issue 18).

As this edition goes to press, the U. S. economy is in the middle of a recession that began, according to the National Bureau of Economic Research, in December 2007. Of course, the recession, caused by the bursting of the housing bubble and the ensuing credit crisis, has affected our selection of issues. Three of the issues directly relate to the recession: issue 9 on the extension of unemployment benefits, issue 14 on loan mitigation, and issue 20 on the Treasury's attempt to resolve the credit crisis with a $700 billion bailout.

It should also be noted that over time there has been a shift in sources for the issue selections, with a greater reliance on congressional hearings. For example, see the new issues on the safety of construction workers, the extension of unemployment benefits, and loan mitigation as well as the revised issues on health savings accounts and the need for a credit card bill of rights. Several factors explain this increasing use of congressional testimony. One factor is our continuing concern that the issues we include have direct and immediate policy consequences. Another is the fact that congressional hearings are typically structured so that alternatives, views, and recommendations are presented.

As with all of the previous editions the issues in the fourteenth edition can be used in any sequence. Although the organization of the book loosely parallels the sequence of topics found in a standard introductory economics textbook, you can pick and choose which issues to read first, since they are designed to stand alone. Unit 3, "The World Around Us," is structured to allow coverage of a broader set of problems society faces in an ever-changing world.

A word to the instructor An *Instructor's Resource Guide with Test Questions* (multiple choice and essay) is available from the publisher. A general guidebook, *Using Taking Sides in the Classroom,* which discusses methods and techniques for integrating the pro/con approach into any classroom setting, is also available. An online version of *Using Taking Sides in the Classroom* and a correspondence service for *Taking Sides* adopters can be found at http://www.mhcls .com/usingts/

Taking Sides: Clashing Views on Economic Issues is only one title in the Taking Sides series. If you are interested in seeing the table of contents for any of the other titles, please visit the Taking Sides Web site at http://www.mhcls .com/takingsides/

Acknowledgments Friends and readers across the United States and Canada have offered helpful comments and suggestions. As always, their suggestions were welcomed and have markedly enhanced the quality of this edition of *Taking Sides*. If as you read this book you are reminded of an essay that could be included in a future edition. We hope that you will drop either of us a note at either Bonello.1@nd.edu or lLobo@ben.edu. We very much appreciate your interest and help, and we are always pleased to hear from you.

We are most appreciative of the encouragement and effort that the staff of McGraw-Hill Contemporary Learning Series have expanded in expediting this edition of *Taking Sides*, especially Jade Benedict, Developmental Editor. To all those we owe a huge debt, many thanks, and none of the blame for any shortcomings that remain in this edition of *Taking Sides*.

Frank J. Bonello
University of Notre Dame
Isobel Lobo
Benedictine University

This book is dedicated to Frank Bonello's children and grandchildren (John, David, Michael, Amanda, and Jack) and to Isobel Lobo's parents.

Contents In Brief

Contents

UNIT 1 MICROECONOMIC ISSUES 1

Issue 1. Are Profits the Only Business of Business? 2

Free-market economist and Nobel Laureate Milton Friedman contends that the sole responsibility of business is to increase its profits. Philosopher Robert Almeder maintains that if capitalism is to survive, it must act in socially responsible ways that go beyond profit making.

Issue 2. Are CEOs Paid What They Are Worth? 20

Ira T. Kay, businessman and author, defends current CEO pay practices. He argues that "Empirical studies show that executive compensation has closely tracked corporate performance," and that rejecting pay-for-performance will hurt both workers and stockholders. Edgar Woolard, Jr., former CEO and chairman of Dupont, describes four myths regarding the compensation received by corporate business leaders. Dismissing the myths, he believes no one but CEOs get "paid excessively when they fail."

Issue 3. Is OSHA Working Effectively to Protect the Safety of Construction Workers? 34

Assistant Secretary of Labor and OSHA head Foulke states that his agency is committed to protecting employees, that it has a multi-faceted approach to reducing construction-related accidents, and that it has a strong, targeted enforcement program. Union official Mark Ayers believes that OSHA is failing to improve the safety and health of construction workers, and he calls for several changes, including an increase in OSHA enforcement activities.

Health care administrator Mark McClellan believes that the Part D drug benefit is the most important new addition to Medicare in its history, providing millions of Americans with better benefits "at a significantly lower cost than originally estimated." Cato Institute senior fellow Jagadeesh Gokhale believes that Medicare's Part D drug benefit is "bad and shortsighted economic policy." He believes this program will, among other things, increase private drug prices, impose higher fiscal burdens on future generations, and reduce national saving and investment.

The American Benefits Council, a national trade association, believes that "HSAs are working as intended" for the vast majority of the 6.1 million Americans covered by "HAS-eligible plans." Linda J. Blumberg, Urban Institute research associate, identifies a number of problems associated with medical care and argues that "HSAs are not the solutions to these pressing national concerns."

The U.S. Department of Health and Human Services (HHS) argues that although the United States has a health care system that "is the envy of the world," it is a system that is to be brought to its knees by aggressive attorneys who force the medical community to practice costly "defensive medicine." Jackson Williams, legal counsel for the watchdog group Public Citizen, charges that the position taken by HHS is factually "incorrect, incomplete, or misleading" and even contradicted by other governmental agencies.

University of Michigan Professor Rebecca Blank supports an extension of unemployment, arguing that the time to extend the time period for unemployment benefits is in the early stages of an economic slowdown. American Enterprise Institute Research Fellow Alex Brill argues against a simple extension of the benefit period, in part because it "could likely lead to higher unemployment and slower growth in the United States."

Travis Plunkett, Legislative Director for the Consumer Federation of America, argues that creating a credit cardholder's bill of rights would have a number of beneficial effects, including the elimination of abusive pricing. John Carey, Chief Administrative Officer of Citi Cards, admits that there is broad dissatisfaction with the credit card industry but asserts that a credit cardholder's bill of rights will create more problems than it will solve.

Economics instructor D. W. MacKenzie believes that eliminating minimum wage laws would "reduce unemployment and improve the efficiency of markets for low productivity labor." He also believes that the "economic case for a living wage is unfounded." Economist Jeannette Wicks-Lim stresses the ripple effects of minimum and living wage laws; these effects increase the "effectiveness" of minimum and living wage laws as "antipoverty strategies."

Columnist Steven Malanga believes the influx of unskilled immigrants into the U.S. economy has imposed large costs on the larger society, including job loss by native workers and lower investment in labor-saving technology. More importantly, he argues that this immigration has increased utilization of the "vast U.S. welfare and social-services apparatus." Diana Furchtgott-Roth, senior fellow at the Hudson Institute and director of Hudson's Center for Employment Policy, and a former chief economist at the U.S. Department of Labor, observes that annual immigration is "a tiny fraction of our labor force," and immigrant laborers are "complements, rather than substitutes for native born Americans." She also cites a National Academy of Sciences study that concluded that foreign-born households are no more likely to use "welfare" than native-born households.

UNIT 3   THE WORLD AROUND US   245

Former chief economist of the World Bank, Joseph E. Stiglitz, argues that trade liberalization can make everyone worse off when markets are not perfect. Furthermore, "free trade" agreements protect special interests in the advanced industrial countries. Stiglitz maintains that the United States should move toward fairer trade and should manage trade liberalization better so that the rich and the poor in all countries share the benefits of trade. Gary Hufbauer, senior fellow at the Peterson Institute for International Economics, claims that free trade, when properly implemented with market reforms, "can lift the lives of hundreds of millions of people." Free trade "pays off" for the United States and "is not some sort of 'gift' to foreign countries." He is critical of political rhetoric in the United States on halting or opting out of trade agreements, including NAFTA.

Mortgage Bankers Association official David Kittle, after reviewing the cost of foreclosure and loan mitigation options, presents data to back his assertion that loan mitigation is working. Center for Responsible Lending policy counsel Julia Gordon stresses both the direct costs and the spillover costs of foreclosures and believes that voluntary loan modifications "have done little to stem the overwhelming tide of foreclosures."

Deputy Assistant U.S. Trade Representative John M. Melle outlines the benefits of NAFTA and concludes that the three NAFTA countries "have not only become better customers for each other but better neighbors, more committed partners, and effective colleagues in a wide range of trade-related international organizations." Sandra Polaski, director of the Trade, Equity and Development Project, argues that NAFTA has produced negative effects in all three countries, including contributing to wage inequality in the United States. But the largest negative effects have been felt by the rural poor in Mexico: They "have borne the brunt of the adjustment to NAFTA and been forced to adapt without adequate government support."

Chairman of the Education and Labor Committee of the United States House of Representatives, California Democrat George Miller states that schools and students are not making enough progress and significant changes must be made to the law so that its goals may be achieved. "America needs and must have an educational law that insists on accountability with high expectations and high-quality assessments; that closes the achievement gap; and helps all children to learn." Deputy Secretary, U.S. Department of Education, Raymond Simon states that NCLB is working for students. Simon believes that there is consensus for a limited number of changes. He claims that NCLB's insistence on scientifically based research and the gathering and using of reliable data has been one of its major successes.

Economist James M. Cypher believes that the U.S. economy is currently experiencing the largest shift in the distribution of income and wealth since the late nineteenth century, with the share of income of the poorest 90 percent of the population falling from 67 percent in 1970 to 52 percent in 2000. Hudson Institute Scholar Diana Furchtgott-Roth does not deny that income inequality is rising but argues that by considering alternative measures of income and recognizing demographic changes, the shifts in income distribution are not a cause for alarm.

President George W. Bush maintains that the rescue will reduce the risk
posed by troubled assets and allow banks to resume credit flows to
families and businesses. Newt Gingrich contends that the bailout will
become a long-term mess and that there is a nonbureaucratic solution to
the multiple crises affecting the economy.

Correlation Guide

The *Taking Sides* series presents current issues in a debate-style format designed to stimulate student interest and develop critical thinking skills. Each issue is thoughtfully framed with an issue summary, an issue introduction, and a postscript. The pro and con essays—selected for their liveliness and substance—represent the arguments of leading scholars and commentators in their fields.

Taking Sides: Clashing Views on Economic Issues, 14/e is an easy-to-use reader that presents issues on important topics such as *CEO compensation, health savings accounts, and income distribution.* For more information on *Taking Sides* and other *McGraw-Hill Contemporary Learning Series* titles, visit www.mhcls .com.

This convenient guide matches the issues in **Taking Sides: Economic Issues, 14/e** with the corresponding chapters in two of our best-selling McGraw-Hill Economic textbooks by Frank/Bernanke and McConnell/Brue.

Taking Sides: Economics, 14/e	Principles of Economics, 4/e by Frank/Bernanke	Economics, 17/e by McConnell/Brue
Issue 1: Are Profits the Only Business of Business?	**Chapter 9:** Monopoly, Oligopoly, and Monopolistic Competition	**Chapter 16:** Economic Growth **Chapter 27:** Rent, Interest, and Profit
Issue 2: Are CEOs Paid What They Are Worth?	**Chapter 18:** Wages and Unemployment	**Chapter 26:** Wage Determination
Issue 3: Is OSHA Working Effectively to Protect the Safety of Construction Workers?	**Chapter 13:** Labor Markets, Poverty, and Income Distribution	**Chapter 34:** Labor Market Institutions and Issues
Issue 4: Is the New Medicare Part D Drug Benefit Good Health Care Policy?	**Chapter 14:** The Environment, Health, and Safety	**Chapter 33:** The Economics of Health Care
Issue 5: Are Health Savings Accounts Working Effectively?	**Chapter 14:** The Environment, Health, and Safety	**Chapter 33:** The Economics of Health Care
Issue 6: Is it Time to Reform Medical Malpractice Litigation?	**Chapter 14:** The Environment, Health, and Safety	**Chapter 33:** The Economics of Health Care
Issue 7: Is Wal-Mart Good for the Economy?	**Chapter 9:** Monopoly, Oligopoly, and Monopolistic Competition	**Chapter 19:** Consumer Behavior and Utility Maximization

Taking Sides: Economics, 14/e	Principles of Economics, 4/e by Frank/Bernanke	Economics, 17/e by McConnell/Brue
Issue 8: Should Social Security be Changed to Include Personal Retirement Accounts?	**Chapter 15:** Public Goods and Tax Policy	**Chapter 28:** Government and Market Failure
Issue 9: Should Unemployment Benefits Be Extended?	**Chapter 18:** Wages and Unemployment	**Chapter 34:** Labor Market Institutions and Issues
Issue 10: Do American Consumers Need a Credit Card Bill of Rights?	**Chapter 20:** Saving, Capital Formation, and Financial Markets	**Chapter 28:** Government and Market Failure
Issue 11: Should Minimum Wage and Living Wage Laws Be Eliminated?	**Chapter 18:** Wages and Unemployment	**Chapter 28:** Government and Market Failure
Issue 12: Do Unskilled Immigrants Hurt the Economy?	**Chapter 19:** Economic Growth	**Chapter 34:** Labor Market Institutions and Issues
Issue 13: Is a Fair Trade Policy Superior to a Free Trade Policy?	**Chapter 28:** International Trade and Capital Flows	**Chapter 35:** International Trade
Issue 14: Is Loan Mitigation the Answer to the Housing Foreclosure Problem?	**Chapter 20:** Saving, Capital Formation, and Financial Markets	**Chapter 28:** Government and Market Failure
Issue 15: Will Biofuels Like Ethanol Reduce U.S. Dependence on Foreign Oil?	**Chapter 15:** Public Goods and Tax Policy	**Chapter 31:** Agriculture: Economics and Policy
Issue 16: Are Spending Cuts the Right Way to Balance the Federal Government's Budget?	**Chapter 16:** Spending, Income, and GDP **Chapter 19:** Economic Growth	**Chapter 14:** Interest Rates and Monetary Policy **Chapter 16:** Economic Growth
Issue 17: Has the North American Free Trade Agreement Benefited the Economies of Canada, Mexico and the United States?	**Chapter 28:** International Trade and Capital Flows	**Chapter 36:** Exchange Rates, the Balance of Payments, and Trade Deficits
Issue 18: Do the Testing and Accountability Elements of the No Child Left Behind Act Prevent a Proper Cost-Benefit Evaluation?	**Chapter 15:** Public Goods and Tax Policy	
Issue 19: Is the Inequality in U.S. Income Distribution Surging?	**Chapter 13:** Labor Markets, Poverty, and Income Distribution	**Chapter 32:** Income Inequality and Poverty
Issue 20: Is the Treasury's $700 Billion Bailout the Solution to the Credit Crisis?	**Chapter 20:** Saving, Capital Formation, and Financial Markets **Chapter 21:** The Financial System, Money, and Prices **Chapter 24:** Stabilizing the Economy: The Role of the Federal Reserve	**Chapter 28:** Government and Market Failure

Introduction

Economics and Economists: The Basis for Controversy

"I think that Capitalism, wisely managed, can probably be more efficient for attaining economic ends than any alternative system yet in
sight, but that in itself it is in many ways extremely objectionable."

—Lord John Maynard Keynes, *The End of Laissez-Faire* (1926)

Although more than 80 years have passed since Lord Keynes penned these
lines, many economists still struggle with the basic dilemma he outlined. The
paradox rests in the fact that a free-market system is extremely efficient. It is
purported to produce more at a lower cost than any other economic system.
But in producing this wide array of low-cost goods and services, problems arise.
These problems—most notably a lack of economic equity and economic
stability—concern some economists.

If the problems raised and analyzed in this book were merely the product
of intellectual gymnastics undertaken by "egg-headed" economists, then we
could sit back and enjoy these confrontations as theoretical exercises. Unfortunately, we are not afforded that luxury. The essays contained in this book
touch each and every one of us in tangible ways. They are real-world issues.
One set of issues deals with "microeconomic" topics. (We refer to these issues
as "micro" problems not because they are small problems, but because they
deal with small economic units, such as households, firms, or individual industries.) An example here is government assistance for seniors in their purchases
of prescription drugs. Another set focuses upon "macroeconomic" topics, such
as the minimum and living wages, topics with impacts on the whole economy,
on many industries. A third set of issues deals with matters that do not fall
neatly into the macroeconomic or microeconomic classifications, including
two issues relating to the international aspects of economic activity.

The range of issues and disagreements raises a fundamental question:
Why do economists disagree? One explanation is suggested by Lord Keynes'
1926 remark. How various economists will react to the strengths and weak-
nesses found in an economic system will depend upon how they view the relative importance of efficiency, equity, and stability. These are central terms, and
we will define them in detail in the following pages. For now the important
point is that some economists may view efficiency as overriding. In other
cases, the same economists may be willing to sacrifice the efficiency generated
by the market in order to ensure increased economic equity and/or increased
economic stability.

Given this discussion of conflict, controversy, and diversity, it might
appear that economists rarely, if ever, agree on any economic issue. We would

be most misleading if we left the reader with this impression. Economists rarely challenge the internal logic of the theoretical models that have been developed and articulated by their colleagues. Rather, they will challenge either the validity of the assumptions used in these models or the value of the ends these models seek to achieve. For example, it is most difficult to discredit the internal logic of the microeconomic models employed by the "free-market economist." These models are elegant, and their logical development is most persuasive. However, these models are challenged. The challenges typically focus upon such issues as the assumption of functioning, competitive, markets and the desirability of perpetuating the existing distribution of income. In this case, those who support and those who challenge the operation of the market agree on a large number of issues. But they disagree most assuredly on a few issues that have dramatic implications.

This same phenomenon of agreeing more often than disagreeing is also true in the area of economic policy. In this area, where the public is most acutely aware of differences among economists, these differences are not generally over the kinds of changes that will be brought about by a particular policy. Again, the differences more typically concern the timing of the change, the specific characteristics of the policy, and the size of the resulting effect or effects. For example, a recent survey found that 85 percent of economists agree that the United States should eliminate tariffs and other trade restrictions (see "Do Economists Agree on Anything? Yes!" by Robert Whaples, *The Economists' Voice*, November 2006, available at http://www.bepress.com/ev/vol3/iss9/).

Economists: What Do They Represent?

Newspaper, magazine, and TV commentators all use handy labels to describe certain members of the economics profession. What do the headlines mean when they refer to the "Chicago School," the "Keynesians," the "Institutional Economists," or the "Radical Economists"? What do these individuals stand for? Since these labels are used throughout this book, we feel obliged to identify the principal groups or camps in our profession. Let us warn you that this can be a misleading venture. Some economists, perhaps most economists, defy classification. They drift from one camp to another, selecting a gem of wisdom here and another there. These are practical men and women who believe that no one camp has all the answers to all the economic problems confronting society.

Recognizing this limitation, four major groups of economists can be identified. These groups are differentiated on the basis of two criteria: how they view efficiency relative to equity and stability, and what significance they attach to imperfectly competitive market structures. Before describing the views of the four groups on these criteria, it is essential to understand the meaning of certain terms to be used in this description.

Efficiency, equity, and stability represent goals for an economic system. An economy is efficient when it produces those goods and services which people want and does so without wasting scarce resources. Equity in an economic sense has several dimensions. It means that income and wealth are distributed according to accepted principles of fairness, that those who are unable to care for themselves receive adequate care, and that mainstream economic activity is open to all persons. Stability is viewed as the absence of sharp ups and downs in business activity, in prices, and in employment. In other words, stability is marked by steady increases in output, little inflation, and low unemployment.

When the term "market structures" is used, it refers to the number of buyers and sellers in the market and the amount of control they exercise over price. At one extreme is a perfectly competitive market where there are so many buyers and sellers that no one has any ability to influence market price. One seller or buyer obviously could have great control over price. This extreme market structure, which we call pure monopoly, and other market structures that result in some control over price are grouped under the broad label of imperfectly competitive markets. That is, imperfect competition is a situation where the number of market participants is limited and, as a consequence, the participants have the ability to influence price. With these terms in mind, we can begin to examine the various schools of economic thought.

Free-Market Economists

One of the most visible groups of economists and perhaps the easiest group to identify and classify is the "free-market economists." In general, this is also the group of economists that persons have in mind when they speak of conservative economists. These economists believe that the market, operating freely without interferences from government or labor unions, will generate the greatest amount of well-being for the greatest number of people.

Economic efficiency is one of the priorities for free-market economists. In their well-developed models, consumer sovereignty—consumer demand for goods and services—guides the system by directly influencing market prices. The distribution of economic resources caused by these market prices not only results in the production of an array of goods and services which are demanded by consumers, but this production is undertaken in the most cost-effective fashion. The free-market economists claim that at any point, some individuals must earn incomes that are substantially greater than those of other individuals. They contend that these higher incomes are a reward for greater efficiency or productivity and that this reward-induced efficiency will result in rapid economic growth that will benefit all persons in the society. They might also admit that a system driven by these freely operating markets will be subject to occasional bouts of instability (slow growth, inflation, and unemployment). However, they maintain that government action to eliminate or reduce this periodic instability will only make matters worse. Consequently, government, according to the free-market or conservative economist, should play a minor role in the economic affairs of society.

Although the models of free-market economists are dependent upon functioning, competitive markets, the lack of these competitive markets in the real world does not seriously jeopardize their position. First, they assert that large firms are necessary to achieve low per-unit costs; that is, a single large firm may be able to produce a given level of output with fewer scarce resources than a large number of small firms. Second, they suggest that the benefits associated with the free operation of markets are so great compared to government intervention that even a "second best solution" of imperfectly competitive markets still yields benefits far in excess of government intervention.

These advocates of the free market have been given various labels over time. The oldest and most persistent label is "classical economists." This is because the classical economists of the eighteenth century, particularly Adam Smith, were the first to point out the virtues of the market. Smith captured the essence of the system with the following words:

> Every individual endeavors to employ his capital so that its produce may be of greatest value. He generally neither intends to promote the public interest nor knows how much he is promoting it. He intends only his own security, only his own gain. And he is in this led by an invisible hand to promote an end that was no part of his intention. By pursuing his own interest he frequently promotes that of society more effectively than when he really intends to promote it.
>
> —Adam Smith, *The Wealth of Nations* (1776)

Liberal Economists

Another significant group of economists in the United States can be classified as liberal economists. "Liberal" in this instance refers to the willingness to intervene in the free operation of the market. These economists share with the free-market economists a great respect for the market. However, the liberal economist does not believe that the explicit and implicit costs of a freely operating market should or can be ignored. Rather, the liberal maintains that the costs of an uncontrolled marketplace are often borne by those in society who are least capable of bearing them: the poor, the elderly, and the infirm. Additionally, liberal economists maintain that the freely operating market sometimes results in economic instability (i.e., in bouts of inflation, unemployment, and slow or negative growth).

Consider for a moment the differences between free-market economists and liberal economists at the microeconomic level. Liberal economists take exception to the free market on two grounds. First, these economists find a basic problem with fairness in the marketplace. Since the forces of consumer spending drive the market, there are those who through no fault of their own (they may be aged, young, infirm, physically or mentally handicapped) may not have the wherewithal to participate in the economic system. Second, the unfettered marketplace does not and cannot handle spill-over effects or what are known as "externalities." These are the third-party effects that may occur as a result of some action. Will a firm willingly compensate its neighbors for the pollutants it pours into the nearby lake? Will a truck driver willingly drive at an appropriately safe speed and in the process reduce the highway accident rate? Liberal economists think not. These economists are therefore willing to have the government intervene in these and other similar cases.

The liberal economists' role in macroeconomic issues is more readily apparent. Ever since the failure of free-market economics during the Great Depression of the 1930s, Keynesianism (still another label for liberal economics) has become widely known. In his 1935 book *The General Theory of Employment, Interest, and Money,* Lord John Maynard Keynes laid the basic groundwork for this school of thought. Keynes argued that the history of freely operating market economies was marked by periods of recurring recessions, sometimes very deep recessions, which we call depressions. He maintained that government intervention through its fiscal policy—government tax and spending power—could eliminate, or at least soften, these sharp reductions in economic activity and as a result move the economy along a more stable growth path. Thus, for the Keynesians, or liberal economists, one of the "extremely objectionable" aspects of a free-market economy is its inherent instability.

Liberal economists are also far more concerned about the existence of imperfections in the marketplace than are their free-market counterparts. They reject the notion that imperfect competition is an acceptable substitute for competitive markets. These economists may agree that the imperfectly competitive firms can achieve some savings because of their large size and efficiency, but they assert that since there is little or no competition the firms are not forced to pass these cost savings on to consumers. Thus, liberal economists, who in some circles are labeled "antitrusters," are willing to intervene in the market in two ways. In some cases, they are prepared to allow some monopolies, such as public utilities, to exist, but they contend that government must regulate these monopolies. In other cases, they maintain that there is no justification for monopolies and they are prepared to invoke the powers of antitrust legislation to break up existing monopolies and/or prevent the formation of new monopolies.

The Mainstream Critics and Radical Reform Economists

There are two other groups of economists that we must identify. One group can be called mainstream critics. Included in this group are individuals like Thorstein Veblen (1857–1929) and his critique of conspicuous consumption and John Kenneth Galbraith (1908–2006) and his views on industrial structure. One reasonably cohesive group of mainstream critics are the post-Keynesians. They are post-Keynesians because they believe that as the principal economic institutions have changed over time, they have remained closer to the spirit of Keynes than the liberal economists. As some have suggested, the key aspect of Keynes as far as the post-Keynesians are concerned is his assertion that "expectations of the future are not necessarily certain." On a more practical level post-Keynesians assert, among other things, that the productivity of the economic system is not significantly affected by changes in income distribution, that the system can still be efficient without competitive markets, that conventional fiscal policies cannot control inflation, and that "incomes policies" are the means to an effective and equitable answer to the inflationary dilemma. (This characterization of post-Keynesianism is drawn from Alfred S. Eichner's "Introduction" in *A Guide to Post-Keynesian Economics,* White Plains: M.E. Sharpe, Inc., 1978).

The fourth and last group can be called radical reformist economists. Many in this group trace their ideas to the nineteenth-century philosopher-economist Karl Marx and his most impressive work, the three volumes of *Das Kapital*. As with the other three groups of economists, there are subgroups of radical reform economists. One subgroup, which may be labeled contemporary Marxists, is best represented by those who have published their research over the years in the *Review of Radical Political Economy*. These economists examine issues that have been largely ignored by mainstream economists, issues such as war, sexism, racism, imperialism, and civil rights. In their analyses of these issues, they borrow from and refine the work of Marx. In the process, they emphasize the role of class in shaping society and the role of the economy in determining class structures. Moreover, they see a need to encourage explicitly the development of some form of democratic socialism, for only then will the greatest good for the greatest number be ensured.

We must warn you to use these labels with extreme care. Our categories are not hard and fast. There is much grayness around the edges and little that is black and white in these classifications. This does not mean, however, that they have no value. It is important to understand the philosophical background of the individual authors. This background does indeed color and shade their work.

Before we conclude this section, it deserves to be noted again that economists are pragmatic, they are responsive to evidence and events. Perhaps the best current example is that of Alan Greenspan, who served as chairman of the Federal Reserve System from 1987 into 2006. Greenspan is best described as a conservative economist and a strong supporter of free markets. He has been quoted as saying, "I do have an ideology. My judgment is that free competitive markets are by far the unrivaled way to organize economies. We have tried regulation, none meaningfully worked." But the events that unfolded with the bursting of the housing bubble and the credit crisis had a strong impact on Greenspan's thinking and his views on deregulation: In congressional testimony in late October 2008 (*Hearings on The Financial Crisis and the Role of Federal Regulators,* House of Representatives, Committee on Oversight and Government Reform October 23, 2008) Greenspan said, "The crisis has turned out to be much broader than anything I could have imagined. I made a mistake in presuming that the self interest of organizations, specifically banks and others, was such that they were best capable of protecting their own shareholders." To rectify the problems Greenspan, in this same testimony, called for regulatory action in the "areas of fraud, settlement, and securitization."

Summary

It is clear that there is no shortage of economic problems. These problems demand solutions. At the same time there is no shortage of proposed solutions. In fact, the problem is often one of oversupply. The 20 issues included in this volume will acquaint you or, more accurately, reacquaint you with some of these problems. And, of course, there are at least two proposed solutions for each of the problems. Here we hope to provide new insights regarding the alternatives available and the differences and similarities of these alternative remedies.

If this introduction has served its purpose, you will be able to identify common elements in the proposed solutions to the different problems. For example, you will be able to identify the reliance on the forces of the market advocated by free-market economists as the remedy for several economic ills. This introduction should also help you understand why there are at least two proposed solutions for every economic problem; each group of economists tends to interpret a problem from its own philosophical position and to advance a solution that is grounded in that same philosophical framework.

Our intention, of course, is not to connect persons to one philosophic position or another. We hope instead to generate discussion and promote understanding. To do this, each of us must see not only a proposed solution, we must also be aware of the foundation that supports that solution. With greater understanding, meaningful progress in addressing economic problems can be achieved.

Internet References . . .

The Dismal Scientist

The Dismal Scientist provides, on a subscription basis, economic data, analysis, and forecasts on a variety of topics.

http://www.dismal.com

Economist.com

The Web edition of *The Economist* is available free to subscribers to the print edition or for an annual fee to those who wish to subscribe online. A selection of articles is available free to those who want to explore this publication.

http://www.economist.com

The Policy Action Network

The site offers timely information and analysis of national policy in the form of a virtual magazine. It also provides links to the home pages of a number of liberal organizations and publications.

http://www.movingideas.org

Resources for Economists on the Internet

This guide to economic resources on the Internet is sponsored by the American Economic Association. It is an excellent starting point for anyone who wants to do research on economic topics. It has many Web links.

http://rfe.org

Statistical Resources on the Web: Comprehensive Economics

This site provides links to a wide variety of economic data at the city, state, country, and global level.

http://www.lib.umich.edu/govdocs/stecon.html

WebEc: WWW Resources in Economics

This site is a virtual library that categorizes free information in economics available on the World Wide Web.

http://www.helsinki.fi/WebEc

Internet Resources for Economists

This site offers a number of links to economic blogs, classic works, textbooks, data sources, journals, etc.

http://www.oswego.edu/~economic/econweb.htm

Microeconomic Issues

*E*conomic decisions made at the microeconomic level affect our lives in a variety of important ways. Public and private actions determine what goods and services are produced as well as the prices we pay for them. The actions also affect our incomes and even our health. In this unit, we examine the profit decisions of business, the pay of business leaders, job safety, the prices the elderly have to pay for drugs, health savings accounts, and reform of medical malpractice litigation.

- Are Profits the Only Business of Business?
- Are CEOs Paid What They Are Worth?
- Is OSHA Working Effectively to Protect the Safety of Construction Workers?
- Is the New Medicare Part D Drug Benefit Good Health Care Policy?
- Are Health Savings Accounts Working Effectively?
- Is It Time to Reform Medical Malpractice Litigation?

ISSUE 1

Are Profits the Only Business of Business?

YES: Milton Friedman, from "The Social Responsibility of Business Is to Increase Its Profits," *The New York Times Magazine* (September 13, 1970)

NO: Robert Almeder, from "Morality in the Marketplace: Reflections on the Friedman Doctrine," in Milton Snoeyenbos, Robert Almeder, and James Humber, eds., *Business Ethics,* rev. ed. (Prometheus Press, 1998)

ISSUE SUMMARY

YES: Free-market economist and Nobel Laureate Milton Friedman contends that the sole responsibility of business is to increase its profits.

NO: Philosopher Robert Almeder maintains that if capitalism is to survive, it must act in socially responsible ways that go beyond profit making.

Every economic society—whether it is a traditional society in Central Africa, a fossilized planned economy such as Cuba's, or a wealthy capitalist society such as those found in North America, Western Europe, and the Pacific Rim—must address the basic economic problem of resource allocation. These societies must determine *what* goods and services they can and will produce, *how* these goods and services will be produced, and *for whom* these goods and services will be produced.

The *what, how,* and *for whom* questions must be answered because of the problem of scarcity. Even if a given society were indescribably rich, it would still confront the problem of scarcity—in the case of a rich society, "relative scarcity." It might have all the resources it needs to produce all the goods and services it would ever want, but it could not produce all these things simultaneously. Thus, even a very rich society must set priorities and produce first those goods and services with the highest priority and postpone the production of those goods and services with lower priorities. If time is of the essence, this society would determine *how* these goods and services should be produced. And

2

since this wealthy society cannot produce all it wants instantly, it must also determine *for whom* the first bundle of goods and services will be produced.

Few, if any, economic societies are indescribably rich. On the other hand, there are many examples of economic societies that face grinding deprivation daily. In these societies and in all the societies that fall between poverty and great affluence, the *what, how,* and *for whom* questions are immediately apparent. Somehow these questions must be answered.

In some societies, such as the Amish communities of North America, the answers to these questions are found in tradition: Sons and daughters follow in their parents' footsteps. Younger generations produce *what* older generations produced before them. The methods of production—the horsedrawn plow, the hand-held scythe, the use of natural fertilizers—remain unchanged; thus, the *how* question is answered in the same way that the *for whom* question is answered—by following historic patterns. In other societies, such as self-sustaining religious communities, there is a different pattern of responses to these questions. In these communities, the "elder" of the community determines *what* will be produced, *how* it will be produced, and *for whom* it will be produced. If there is a well-defined hierarchical system, it is similar to one of the former stereotypical command economies of Eastern Europe.

Although elements of tradition and command are found in the industrialized societies of Western Europe, North America, and Japan, the basic answers to the three questions of resource allocation in these countries are determined by profit. In these economic societies, *what* will be produced is determined by what will yield the greatest profit. Consumers, in their search for maximum satisfaction, will bid for those goods and services that they want most. This consumer action drives the prices of these goods and services up, which, in turn, increases producers' profits. The higher profits attract new firms into the industry and encourage existing firms to increase their output. Thus, profits are the mechanism that ensures that consumers get what they want. Similarly, the profit-seeking behavior of business firms determines *how* the goods and services that consumers want will be produced. Since firms attempt to maximize their profits, they select those means of production that are economically most efficient. Lastly, the *for whom* question is also linked to profits. Wherever there is a shortage of goods and services, profits will be high. In the producers' attempts to increase their output, they must attract factors of production (land, labor, and capital) away from other economic activities. This bidding increases factor prices or factor incomes and ensures that these factors will be able to buy goods and services in the open marketplace.

Both Milton Friedman and Robert Almeder recognize the merits of a profit-driven economic system. They do not quarrel over the importance of profits. But they do quarrel over whether or not business firms have obligations beyond making profits. In the following selection, Friedman holds that the *only* responsibility of business is to make profits and that anyone who maintains otherwise is "preaching pure and unadulterated socialism." In the second selection, Almeder, who is clearly not a "socialist," contends that business must act in socially responsible ways "if capitalism is to survive."

YES

Milton Friedman

The Social Responsibility of Business Is to Increase Its Profits

When I hear businessmen speak eloquently about the "social responsibilities of business in a free-enterprise system," I am reminded of the wonderful line about the Frenchman who discovered at the age of 70 that he had been speaking prose all his life. The businessmen believe that they are defending free enterprise when they declaim that business is not concerned "merely" with profit but also with promoting desirable "social ends; that business has a social conscience" and takes seriously its responsibilities for providing employment, eliminating discrimination, avoiding pollution and whatever else may be the catchwords of the contemporary crop of reformers. In fact they are— or would be if they or anyone else took them seriously—preaching pure and unadulterated socialism. Businessmen who talk this way are unwitting puppets of the intellectual forces that have been undermining the basis of a free society these past decades.

The discussions of the "social responsibilities of business" are notable for their analytical looseness and lack of rigor. What does it mean to say that "business" has responsibilities? Only people can have responsibilities. A corporation is an artificial person and in this sense may have artificial responsibilities, but "business" as a whole cannot be said to have responsibilities, even in this vague sense. The first step toward clarity in examining the doctrine of the social responsibility of business is to ask precisely what it implies for whom.

Presumably, the individuals who are to be responsible are businessmen, which means individual proprietors or corporate executives. Most of the discussion of social responsibility is directed at corporations, so in what follows I shall mostly neglect the individual proprietor and speak of corporate executives.

In a free-enterprise, private-property system, a corporate executive is an employee of the owners of the business. He has direct responsibility to his employers. That responsibility is to conduct the business in accordance with their desires, which generally will be to make as much money as possible while conforming to the basic rules of the society, both those embodied in law and those embodied in ethical custom. Of course, in some cases his employers may have a different objective. A group of persons might establish a corporation for an eleemosynary purpose—for example, a hospital or a school. The manager of such a corporation will not have money profit as his objective but the rendering of certain services.

In either case, the key point is that, in his capacity as a corporate executive, the manager is the agent of the individuals who own the corporation or establish the eleemosynary institution, and his primary responsibility is to them.

Needless to say, this does not mean that it is easy to judge how well he is performing his task. But at least the criterion of performance is straightforward, and the persons among whom a voluntary contractual arrangement exists are clearly defined.

Of course, the corporate executive is also a person in his own right. As a person, he may have many other responsibilities that he recognizes or assumes voluntarily—to his family, his conscience, his feelings of charity, his church, his clubs, his city, his country. He may feel impelled by these responsibilities to devote part of his income to causes he regards as worthy, to refuse to work for particular corporations, even to leave his job, for example, to join his country's armed forces. If we wish, we may refer to some of these responsibilities as "social responsibilities." But in these respects he is acting as a principal, not an agent; he is spending his own money or time or energy, not the money of his employers or the time or energy he has contracted to devote to their purposes. If these are "social responsibilities," they are the social responsibilities of individuals, not of business.

What does it mean to say that the corporate executive has a "social responsibility" in his capacity as businessman? If this statement is not pure rhetoric, it must mean that he is to act in some way that is not in the interest of his employers. For example, that he is to refrain from increasing the price of the product in order to contribute to the social objective of preventing inflation, even though a price increase would be in the best interests of the corporation. Or that he is to make expenditures on reducing pollution beyond the amount that is in the best interests of the corporation or that is required by law in order to contribute to the social objective of improving the environment. Or that, at the expense of corporate profits, he is to hire "hard-core" unemployed instead of better-qualified available workmen to contribute to the social objective of reducing poverty.

In each of these cases, the corporate executive would be spending someone else's money for a general social interest. Insofar as his actions in accord with his "social responsibility" reduce returns to stockholders, he is spending their money. Insofar as his actions raise the price to customers, he is spending the customers' money. Insofar as his actions lower the wages of some employees, he is spending their money.

The stockholders or the customers or the employees could separately spend their own money on the particular action if they wished to do so. The executive is exercising a distinct "social responsibility," rather than serving as an agent of the stockholders or the customers or the employees, only if he spends the money in a different way than they would have spent it.

But if he does this, he is in effect imposing taxes, on the one hand, and deciding how the tax proceeds shall be spent, on the other.

This process raises political questions on two levels: principle and consequences. On the level of political principle, the imposition of taxes and the expenditure of tax proceeds are governmental functions. We have established elaborate constitutional, parliamentary and judicial provisions to control these functions, to assure that taxes are imposed so far as possible in accordance with the preferences and desires of the public—after all, "taxation without representation" was one of the battle cries of the American Revolution. We have a system of checks and balances to separate the legislative function of imposing taxes and enacting expenditures from the executive function of collecting taxes and administering expenditure programs and from the judicial function of mediating disputes and interpreting the law.

Here the businessman—self-selected or appointed directly or indirectly by stockholders—is to be simultaneously legislator, executive and jurist. He is to decide whom to tax by how much and for what purpose, and he is to spend the proceeds—all this guided only by general exhortations from on high to restrain inflation, improve the environment, fight poverty and so on and on.

The whole justification for permitting the corporate executive to be selected by the stockholders is that the executive is an agent serving the interests of his principal. This justification disappears when the corporate executive imposes taxes and spends the proceeds for "social" purposes. He becomes in effect a public employee, a civil servant, even though he remains in name an employee of a private enterprise. On grounds of political principle, it is intolerable that such civil servants—insofar as their actions in the name of social responsibility are real and not just window-dressing—should be selected as they are now. If they are to be civil servants, then they must be selected through a political process. If they are to impose taxes and make expenditures to foster "social" objectives, then political machinery must be set up to guide the assessment of taxes and to determine through a political process the objectives to be served.

This is the basic reason why the doctrine of "social responsibility" involves the acceptance of the socialist view that political mechanisms, not market mechanisms, are the appropriate way to determine the allocation of scarce resources to alternative uses.

On the grounds of consequences, can the corporate executive in fact discharge his alleged "social responsibilities"? On the one hand, suppose he could get away with spending the stockholders' or customers' or employees' money. How is he to know how to spend it? He is told that he must contribute to fighting inflation. How is he to know what action of his will contribute to that end? He is presumably an expert in running his company—in producing a product or selling it or financing it. But nothing about his selection makes him an expert on inflation. Will his holding down the price of his product reduce inflationary pressure? Or, by leaving more spending power in the hands of his customers, simply divert it elsewhere? Or, by forcing him to produce less because of the lower price, will it simply contribute to shortages? Even if he could answer these questions, how much cost is he justified in imposing on his stockholders, customers and employees for this social purpose? What is the appropriate share and what is the appropriate share of others?

And, whether he wants to or not, can he get away with spending his stockholders', customers' or employees' money? Will not the stockholders fire him? (Either the present ones or those who take over when his actions in the name of social responsibility have reduced the corporation's profits and the price of its stock.) His customers and his employees can desert him for other producers and employers less scrupulous in exercising their social responsibilities.

This facet of "social responsibility" doctrine is brought into sharp relief when the doctrine is used to justify wage restraint by trade unions. The conflict of interest is naked and clear when union officials are asked to subordinate the interest of their members to some more general social purpose. If the union officials try to enforce wage restraint, the consequence is likely to be wildcat strikes, rank-and-file revolts and the emergence of strong competitors for their jobs. We thus have the ironic phenomenon that union leaders—at least in the U.S.—have objected to Government interference with the market far more consistently and courageously than have business leaders.

The difficulty of exercising "social responsibility" illustrates, of course, the great virtue of private competitive enterprise—it forces people to be responsible for their own actions and makes it difficult for them to "exploit" other people for either selfish or unselfish purposes. They can do good—but only at their own expense.

Many a reader who has followed the argument this far may be tempted to remonstrate that it is all well and good to speak of government's having the responsibility to impose taxes and determine expenditures for such "social" purposes as controlling pollution or training the hard-core unemployed, but that the problems are too urgent to wait on the slow course of political processes, that the exercise of social responsibility by businessmen is a quicker and surer way to solve pressing current problems.

Aside from the question of fact—I share Adam Smith's skepticism about the benefits that can be expected from "those who affected to trade for the public good"—this argument must be rejected on grounds of principle. What it amounts to is an assertion that those who favor the taxes and expenditures in question have failed to persuade a majority of their fellow citizens to be of like mind and that they are seeking to attain by undemocratic procedures what they cannot attain by democratic procedures. In a free society, it is hard for "good" people to do "good," but that is a small price to pay for making it hard for "evil" people to do "evil," especially since one man's good is another's evil.

I have, for simplicity, concentrated on the special case of the corporate executive, except only for the brief digression on trade unions. But precisely the same argument applies to the newer phenomenon of calling upon stockholders to require corporations to exercise social responsibility (the recent G.M. crusade, for example). In most of these cases, what is in effect involved is some stockholders trying to get other stockholders (or customers or employees) to contribute against their will to "social" causes favored by the activists. Insofar as they succeed, they are again imposing taxes and spending the proceeds.

The situation of the individual proprietor is somewhat different. If he acts to reduce the returns of his enterprise in order to exercise his "social responsibility," he is spending his own money, not someone else's. If he wishes to spend his money on such purposes, that is his right, and I cannot see that there is any objection to his doing so. In the process, he, too, may impose costs on employees and customers. However, because he is far less likely than a large corporation or union to have monopolistic power, any such side effects will tend to be minor.

Of course, in practice the doctrine of social responsibility is frequently a cloak for actions that are justified on other grounds rather than a reason for those actions.

To illustrate, it may well be in the long-run interest of a corporation that is a major employer in a small community to devote resources to providing amenities to that community or to improving its government. That may make it easier to attract desirable employees, it may reduce the wage bill or lessen losses from pilferage and sabotage or have other worthwhile effects. Or it may be that, given the laws about the deductibility of corporate charitable contributions, the stockholders can contribute more to charities they favor by having the corporation make the gift than by doing it themselves, since they can in that way contribute an amount that would otherwise have been paid as corporate taxes.

In each of these—and many similar—cases, there is a strong temptation to rationalize these actions as an exercise of "social responsibility." In the present climate of opinion, with its widespread aversion to "capitalism," "profits," the "soulless corporation" and so on, this is one way for a corporation to generate goodwill as a by-product of expenditures that are entirely justified in its own self-interest.

It would be inconsistent of me to call on corporate executives to refrain from this hypocritical window-dressing because it harms the foundations of a free society. That would be to call on them to exercise a "social responsibility"! If our institutions, and the attitudes of the public, make it in their self-interest to cloak their actions in this way, I cannot summon much indignation to denounce them. At the same time, I can express admiration for those individual proprietors or owners of closely held corporations or stockholders of more broadly held corporations who disdain such tactics as approaching fraud.

Whether blameworthy or not, the use of the cloak of social responsibility, and the nonsense spoken in its name by influential and prestigious businessmen, does clearly harm the foundations of a free society. I have been impressed time and again by the schizophrenic character of many businessmen. They are capable of being extremely far-sighted and clear-headed in matters that are internal to their businesses. They are incredibly short-sighted and muddleheaded in matters that are outside their businesses but affect the possible survival of business in general. This short-sightedness is strikingly exemplified in the calls from many businessmen for wage and price guidelines or controls or income policies. There is nothing that could do more in a brief period to destroy a market system and replace it by a centrally controlled system than effective governmental control of prices and wages.

The short-sightedness is also exemplified in speeches by businessmen on social responsibility. This may gain them kudos in the short run. But it helps to strengthen the already too prevalent view that the pursuit of profits is wicked and immoral and must be curbed and controlled by external forces. Once this view is adopted, the external forces that curb the market will not be the social consciences, however highly developed, of the pontificating executives; it will be the iron fist of Government bureaucrats. Here, as with price and wage controls, businessmen seem to me to reveal a suicidal impulse.

The political principle that underlies the market mechanism is unanimity. In an ideal free market resting on private property, no individual can coerce any other, all cooperation is voluntary, all parties to such cooperation benefit or they need not participate. There are no "social" values, no "social" responsibilities in any sense other than the shared values and responsibilities of individuals. Society is a collection of individuals and of the various groups they voluntarily form.

The political principle that underlies the political mechanism is conformity. The individual must serve a more general social interest—whether that be determined by a church or a dictator or a majority. The individual may have a vote and a say in what is to be done, but if he is overruled, he must conform. It is appropriate for some to require others to contribute to a general social purpose whether they wish to or not.

Unfortunately, unanimity is not always feasible. There are some respects in which conformity appears unavoidable, so I do not see how one can avoid the use of the political mechanism altogether.

But the doctrine of "social responsibility" taken seriously would extend the scope of the political mechanism to every human activity. It does not differ in philosophy from the most explicitly collectivist doctrine. It differs only by professing to believe that collectivist ends can be attained without collectivist means. That is why, in my book "Capitalism and Freedom," I have called it a "fundamentally subversive doctrine" in a free society, and have said that in such a society, "there is one and only one social responsibility of business—to use its resources and engage in activities designed to increase its profits so long as it stays within the rules of the game, which is to say, engages in open and free competition without deception or fraud."

Robert Almeder

NO

Morality in the Marketplace: Reflections on the Friedman Doctrine

Introduction

In seeking to create a climate more favorable for corporate activity, International Telephone and Telegraph allegedly contributed large sums of money to "destabilize" the duly elected government of Chile. Even though advised by the scientific community that the practice is lethal, major chemical companies reportedly continue to dump large amounts of carcinogens and mutagens into the water supply of various areas and, at the same time, lobby strongly to prevent legislation against such practices. General Motors Corporation, other automobile manufacturers, and Firestone Tire and Rubber Corporation have frequently defended themselves against the charge that they knowingly and willingly marketed a product that, owing to defective design, had been reliably predicted to kill a certain percentage of its users and, moreover, refused to recall promptly the product even when government agencies documented the large incidence of death as a result of the defective product. Finally, people often say that numerous advertising companies happily accept, and earnestly solicit, accounts to advertise cigarettes knowing full well that as a direct result of their advertising activities a certain number of people will die considerably prematurely and painfully. Most recently, of course, American Tobacco Companies have been charged with knowingly marketing a very addictive product known to kill untold numbers in slow, painful and costly deaths while the price of the stock of these companies has made fortunes for the shareholders. We need not concern ourselves with whether these and other similar charges are true because our primary concern here is with what might count as a justification for such corporate conduct were it to occur. There can be no question that such corporate behavior sometimes occurs and is frequently legal, or at least not illegal. The question is whether corporate behavior should be constrained by nonlegal or moral considerations. If so, to what extent and how could it be done? As things presently stand, it seems to be a dogma of contemporary capitalism rapidly emerging throughout the world that the sole responsibility of business is to make as much money as is *legally* possible. But the interesting question is whether this view is rationally defensible.

Sometimes, although not very frequently, corporate executives will admit to the sort of behavior depicted above and then proceed proximately to justify such behavior in the name of their responsibility to the shareholders or owners (if the shareholders are not the owners) to make as much profit as is legally possible. Thereafter, less proximately and more generally, they will proceed to urge the more general utilitarian point that the increase in profit engendered by such corporate behavior begets such an unquestionable overall good for society that the behavior in question is morally acceptable if not quite praiseworthy. More specifically, the justification in question can, and usually does, take two forms.

The first and most common form of justification consists in urging that, as long as one's corporate behavior is not illegal, the behavior will be morally acceptable because the sole purpose of being in business is to make a profit; and the rules of the marketplace are somewhat different from those in other places and must be followed if one is to make a profit. Moreover, proponents of this view hasten to add that, as Adam Smith has claimed, the greatest good for society in the long run is achieved not by corporations seeking to act morally, or with a sense of social responsibility in their pursuit of profit, but rather by each corporation seeking to maximize its own profit, unregulated in that endeavor except by the laws of supply and demand along with whatever other laws are inherent to the competition process. This, they say, is what has made capitalist societies the envy of the world while ideological socialisms sooner or later fail miserably to meet deep human needs. Smith's view, that there is an invisible hand, as it were, directing an economy governed solely by the profit motive to the greatest good for society in the long run,[1] is still the dominant motivation and justification for those who would want an economy unregulated by any moral concern that would, or could, tend to decrease profits for some *alleged* social or moral good.

Milton Friedman, for example, has frequently asserted that the sole moral responsibility of business is to make as much profit as is legally possible; and by that he means to assert that attempts to regulate or restrain the pursuit of profit in accordance with what some people believe to be socially desirable ends are in fact *subversive* of the common good because the greatest good for the greatest number is achieved by an economy maximally competitive and unregulated by moral rules in its pursuit of profit.[2] So, on Friedman's view, the greatest good for society is achieved by corporations acting legally, but with no further regard for what may be morally desirable; and this view begets the paradox that, *in business*, the greatest good for society can be achieved only by acting without regard for morality, at least in so far as moral rules are not reflected in the legal code. Moreover, adoption of this position constitutes a fairly conscious commitment to the view that while one's personal life may well need moral governance beyond the law, when pursuing profit, it is necessary that one's corporate behavior be unregulated by any moral concern other than that of making as much money as is legally possible; curiously enough, it is only in this way that society achieves the greatest good. So viewed, it is not difficult to see how a corporate executive could sincerely and consistently adopt rigorous standards of morality in his or her personal life and yet feel quite comfortable in abandoning those standards in the pursuit of profit. Albert Carr, for example, likens the conduct of business to that of playing poker.[3] As Carr would have it, moral busybodies who insist on corporations acting morally might do just as well to censure a good bluffer in poker for being deceitful. Society, of course, lacking a perspective such as Friedman's and Carr's, is only too willing to view such behavior as strongly hypocritical and fostered by an unwholesome avarice.

The second way of justifying, or defending, corporate practices that may appear morally questionable consists in urging that even if corporations were to take seriously the idea of limiting profits because of a desire to be moral or more responsible to social needs, then corporations would be involved in the unwholesome business of selecting and implementing moral values that may not be shared by a large number of people. Besides, there is the overwhelming question of whether there can be any non-questionable moral values or noncontroversial list of social priorities for corporations to adopt. After all, if ethical relativism is true, or if ethical nihilism is true (and philosophers can be counted upon to argue agressively for both positions), then it would be fairly silly of corporations to limit profits for what may be a quite dubious reason, namely, for being moral, when there are no clear grounds for doing it, and when it is not too clear what would count for doing it. In short, business corporations could argue (as Friedman has done)[4] that corporate actions in behalf of society's interests would require of corporations an ability to clearly determine and rank in noncontroversial ways the major needs of society; and it would not appear that this could be done successfully.

Perhaps another, and somewhat easier, way of formulating this second argument consists in urging that because moralists and philosophers generally fail to agree on what are the proper moral rules (if any), as well as on whether we should be moral, it would be imprudent to sacrifice a clear profit for a dubious or controversial moral gain. To authorize such a sacrifice would be to abandon a clear responsibility for one that is unclear or questionable.

If there are any other basic ways of justifying the sort of corporate behavior noted at the outset, I cannot imagine what they might be. So, let us examine these two modes of justification. In doing this, I hope to show that neither argument is sound and, moreover, that corporate behavior of the sort in question is clearly immoral if anything is immoral—and if nothing is immoral, then such corporate behavior is clearly contrary to the long-term interest of a corporation. In the end, we will reflect on ways to prevent such behavior, and on what is philosophically implied by corporate willingness to act in clearly immoral ways.

The "Invisible Hand"

Essentially, the first argument is that the greatest good for the greatest number will be, and can only be, achieved by corporations acting legally but unregulated by any moral concern in the pursuit of profit. As we saw earlier, the evidence for this argument rests on a fairly classical and unquestioning acceptance of Adam Smith's view that society achieves a greater good when each person is allowed to pursue her or his own self-interested ends than when each person's pursuit of self-interested ends is regulated in some way or another by moral rules or concern. But I know of no evidence Smith ever offered for this latter claim, although it seems clear that those who adopt it generally do so out of respect for the perceived good that has emerged for various modern societies as a direct result of the free enterprise system and its ability to raise the overall standard of living of all those under it.

However, there is nothing inevitable about the greatest good occurring in an unregulated economy. Indeed, we have good inductive evidence from the age of the Robber Barons that unless the profit motive is regulated in various ways (by statute or otherwise) untold social evil can, and *will*, occur because of the natural tendency of the system to place ever-increasing sums of money in ever-decreasing numbers of hands as a result of the nature of competition unregulated. If all this is so, then so much the worse for all philosophical attempts to justify what would appear to be morally questionable corporate behavior on the grounds that corporate behavior, unregulated by moral concern, is necessarily or even probably productive of the greatest good for the greatest number. Moreover, a rule utilitarian would not be very hard pressed to show the many unsavory implications to society as a whole if society were to take seriously a rule to the effect that, if one acts legally, it is morally permissible to do whatever one wants to do to achieve a profit. We shall discuss some of those implications of this rule below before drawing a conclusion.

The second argument cited above asserts that even if we were to grant, for the sake of argument, that corporations have social responsibilities beyond that of making as much money as is legally possible for the shareholders, there would be no noncontroversial way for corporations to discover just what these responsibilities are in the order of their importance. Owing to the fact that even distinguished moral philosophers predictably disagree on what one's moral responsibilities are, if any, it would seem irresponsible to limit profits to satisfy dubious moral responsibilities.

For one thing, this argument unduly exaggerates our potential for moral disagreement. Admittedly, there might well be important disagreements among corporations (just as there could be among philosophers) as to a priority ranking of major social needs; but that does not mean that most of us could not, or would not, agree that certain things ought not be done in the name of profit even when there is no law prohibiting such acts. Doubtless, there will always be a few who would do most anything for a profit; but that is hardly a good argument in favor of their having the moral right to do so rather than a good argument showing that they refuse to be moral. In sum, it is difficult to see how this second argument favoring corporate moral nihilism is any better than the general argument for ethical nihilism based on the variability of ethical judgments or practices; and apart from the fact that it tacitly presupposes that morality is a matter of what we all in fact would, or should, accept, the argument is maximally counterintuitive (as I shall show) by way of suggesting that we cannot generally agree that corporations have certain clear social responsibilities to avoid certain practices. Accordingly, I would now like to argue that if anything is immoral, a certain kind of corporate behavior is quite immoral although it may not be illegal.

Murder for Profit

Without caring to enter into the reasons for the belief, I assume we all believe that it is wrong to kill an innocent human being for no other reason than that doing so would be more financially rewarding for the killer than if he were to earn his livelihood in some other way. Nor, I assume, should our moral feeling on this matter change depending on the amount of money involved. Killing an innocent baby for fifteen million dollars would not seem to be any less objectionable than killing it for twenty cents. It is possible, however, that a self-professing utilitarian might be tempted to argue that the killing of an innocent baby for fifteen million dollars would not be objectionable if the money were to be given to the poor; under these circumstances, greater good would be achieved by the killing of the innocent baby. But, I submit, if anybody were to argue in this fashion, his argument would be quite deficient because he has not established what he needs to establish to make his argument sound. What he needs is a clear, convincing argument that raising the standard of living of an indefinite number of poor persons by the killing of an innocent person is a greater good for all those affected by the act than if the standard of living were not raised by the killing of an innocent person. This is needed because part of what we mean by having a basic right to life is that a person's life cannot be taken from him or her without a good reason. If our utilitarian cannot provide a convincing justification for his claim that a greater good is served by killing an innocent person in order to raise the standard of living for a large number of poor people, then it is hard to see how he can have the good reason that he needs to deprive an innocent person of his or her life. Now, it seems clear that there will be anything but unanimity in the moral community on the question of whether there is a greater good achieved in raising the standard of living by killing an innocent baby than in leaving the standard of living alone and not killing an innocent baby. Moreover, even if everybody were to agree that the greater good is achieved by the killing of the innocent baby, how could that be shown to be true? How does one compare the moral value of a human life with the moral value of raising the standard of living by the taking of that life? Indeed, the more one thinks about it, the more difficult it is to see just what would count as objective evidence for the claim that the greater good is achieved by the killing of the innocent baby. Accordingly, I can see nothing that would justify the utilitarian who might be tempted to argue that if the sum is large enough, and if the sum were to be used for raising the standard of living for an indefinite number of poor people, then it would be morally acceptable to kill an innocent person for money.

These reflections should not be taken to imply, however, that no utilitarian argument could justify the killing of an innocent person for money. After all, if the sum were large enough to save the lives of a large number of people who would surely die if the innocent baby were not killed, then one would as a rule be justified in killing the innocent baby for the sum in question. But this situation is obviously quite different from the situation in which one would attempt to justify the killing of an innocent person in order to raise the standard of living for an indefinite number of poor people. It makes sense to kill one innocent person in order to save, say, twenty innocent persons; but it makes no sense at all to kill one innocent person to raise the standard of living of an indefinite number of people. In the latter case, but not in the former, a comparison is made between things that are incomparable.

Given these considerations, it is remarkable and somewhat perplexing that certain corporations should seek to defend practices that are in fact instances of killing innocent persons for profit. Take, for example, the corporate practice of dumping known carcinogens into rivers. On Milton Friedman's view, we should not regulate or prevent such companies from dumping their effluents into the environment. Rather we should, if we like, tax the company after the effluents are in the water and then have the tax money used to clean up the environment.[5] For Friedman, and others, the fact that so many people will die as a result of this practice seems to be just part of the cost of doing business and making a profit. If there is any moral difference between such corporate practices and murdering innocent human beings for money, it is hard to see what it is. It is even more difficult to see how anyone could justify the practice and see it as no more than a business practice not to be regulated by moral concern. And there are a host of other corporate activities that are morally equivalent to deliberate killing of innocent persons for money. Such practices number among them contributing funds to "destabilize" a foreign government, selling cigarettes while knowing that they are highly addictive killers of innocent people, advertising cigarettes, knowingly marketing children's clothing having a known cancer-causing agent, and refusing to recall (for fear of financial loss) goods known to be sufficiently defective to directly maim or kill a certain percentage of their unsuspecting users because of the defect. On this latter item, we are all familiar, for example, with convincingly documented charges that certain prominent automobile and tire manufacturers will knowingly market equipment sufficiently defective to increase the likelihood of death as a direct result of the defect, and yet refuse to recall the product because the cost of recalling and repairing would have a greater adverse impact on profit than if the product were not recalled and the company paid the projected number of predictably successful suits. Of course, if the projected cost of the predictably successful suits were to outweigh the cost of recall and repair, then the product would be recalled and repaired, but not otherwise.

In cases of this sort, the companies involved may admit to having certain marketing problems or a design problem, and they may even admit to having made a mistake; but, interestingly enough, they do not view themselves as immoral or as murderers for keeping their product in the market place when they know people are dying from it, people who would not die if the defect were corrected.

The important point is not whether in fact these practices have occurred in the past, or occur even now; there can be no doubt that such practices have occurred and continue to occur. Rather the point is that when companies act in such ways as a matter of policy, they must either not know what they do is murder (i.e., unjustifiable killing of an innocent person), or knowing that it is murder, seek to justify it in terms of profit. And I have been arguing that it is difficult to see how any corporate manager could fail to see that these policies amount to murder for money, although there may be no civil statute against such corporate behavior. If so, then where such policies exist, we can only assume that they are designed and implemented by corporate managers who either see nothing wrong with murder for money (which is implausible) or recognize that what they do is wrong but simply refuse to act morally because it is more financially rewarding to act immorally.

Of course, it is possible that corporate executives would not recognize such acts as murder. They may, after all, view murder as a legal concept involving one non-corporate person or persons deliberately killing another non-corporate person or persons and prosecutable only under existing criminal statute. If so, it is somewhat understandable how corporate executives might fail, at least psychologically, to see such corporate policies as murder rather than as, say, calculated risks, tradeoffs, or design errors. Still, for all that, the logic of the situation seems clear enough.

Conclusion

In addition to the fact that the only two plausible arguments favoring the Friedman doctrine are unsatisfactory, a strong case can be made for the claim that corporations *do* have a clear and noncontroversial moral responsibility not to design or implement, for reasons of profit, policies that they know, or have good reason to believe, will kill or otherwise seriously injure innocent persons affected by those policies. Moreover, we have said nothing about wage discrimination, sexism, discrimination in hiring, price fixing, price gouging, questionable but not unlawful competition, or other similar practices that some will think businesses should avoid by virtue of responsibility to society. My main concern has been to show that because we all agree that murder for money is generally wrong, and since there is no discernible difference between that and certain corporate policies that are not in fact illegal, then these corporate practices are clearly immoral (that is, they ought not to be done) and incapable of being morally justified by appeal to the Friedman doctrine since that doctrine does not admit of adequate evidential support. In itself, it seems sad that this argument needs to be made and, if it were not for what appears to be a fairly strong commitment within the business community to the Friedman doctrine in the name of the unquestionable success of the free enterprise system, the argument would not need to be stated.

The fact that such practices do exist—designed and implemented by corporate managers who, for all intents and purposes, appear to be upright members of the moral community—only heightens the need for effective social prevention. Presumably, of course, any company willing to put human lives into the profit and loss column is not likely to respond to moral censure. Accordingly, I submit that perhaps the most effective way to deal with the problem of preventing such corporate behavior would consist in structuring legislation such that senior corporate managers who knowingly concur in practices of the sort listed above can effectively be tried, at their own expense, for murder, rather than censured and fined a sum to be paid out of corporate profits. This may seem a somewhat extreme or unrealistic proposal. However, it seems more unrealistic to think that aggressively competitive corporations will respond to what is morally necessary if failure to do so could be very or even minimally profitable. In short, unless we take strong and appropriate steps to prevent such practices, society will be reinforcing a destructive mode of behavior that is maximally disrespectful of human life, just as society will be reinforcing a value system that so emphasizes monetary gain as a standard of human success that murder for profit could be a corporate policy if the penalty for being caught at it were not too dear.

Fortunately, a number of states in America have enacted legislation that makes corporations subject to the criminal code of that state. This practice began to emerge quite strongly after the famous Pinto case in which an Indiana superior court judge refused to dismiss a homicide indictment against the Ford Motor Company. The company was indicted on charges of reckless homicide stemming from a 1978 accident involving a 1973 Pinto in which three girls died when the car burst into flames after being slammed in the rear. This was the first case in which Ford, or any other automobile manufacturer, had been charged with a criminal offense. The indictment went forward because the state of Indiana adopted in 1977 a criminal code provision permitting corporations to be charged with criminal acts. At the time, incidentally, twenty-two other states had similar codes. At any rate, the judge, in refusing to set aside the indictment, agreed with the prosecutor's argument that the charge was based not on the Pinto design fault, but rather on the fact that Ford had permitted the car "to remain on Indiana highways knowing full well its defects." The fact that the Ford Motor Company was ultimately found innocent of the charges by the jury is incidental to the point that the increasing number of states that allow corporations to fall under the criminal code is an example of social regulation that could have been avoided had corporations and corporate managers not followed so ardently the Friedman doctrine.

In the long run, of course, corporate and individual willingness to do what is clearly immoral for the sake of monetary gain is a patent commitment of a certain view about the nature of human happiness and success, a view that needs to be placed in the balance with Aristotle's reasoned argument and reflections to the effect that money and all that it brings is a means to an end, and not the sort of end in itself that will justify acting immorally to attain it. What that beautiful end is and why being moral allows us to achieve it, may well be the most rewarding and profitable subject a human being can think about. Properly understood and placed in perspective, Aristotle's view on the nature and attainment of human happiness could go a long way toward alleviating the temptation to kill for money.

In the meantime, any ardent supporter of the capitalistic system will want to see the system thrive and flourish; and this it cannot do if it invites and demands government regulation in the name of the public interest. A *strong* ideological commitment to what I have described above as the Friedman doctrine is counterproductive and not in anyone's long-range interest because it is most likely to beget an ever-increasing regulatory climate. The only way to avoid such encroaching regulation is to find ways to move the business community into the long-term view of what is in its interest, and effect ways of both determining and responding to social needs before society moves to regulate business to that end. To so move the business community is to ask business to regulate its own modes of competition in ways that may seem very difficult to achieve. Indeed, if what I have been suggesting is correct, the only kind of enduring capitalism is humane capitalism, one that is at least as socially responsible as society needs. By the same token, contrary to what is sometimes felt in the business community, the Friedman doctrine, ardently adopted for the dubious reasons generally given, will most likely undermine capitalism and motivate an economic socialism by assuring an erosive regulatory climate in a society that expects the business community to be socially responsible in ways that go beyond just making legal profits.

In sum, being socially responsible in ways that go beyond legal profit making is by no means a dubious luxury for the capitalist in today's world. It is a necessity if capitalism is to survive at all; and, presumably, we shall all profit with the survival of a vibrant capitalism. If anything, then, rigid adherence to the Friedman doctrine is not only philosophically unjustified, and unjustifiable, it is also unprofitable in the long run, and therefore, downright subversive of the long-term common good. Unfortunately, taking the long-run view is difficult for everyone. After all, for each of us, tomorrow may not come. But living for today only does not seem to make much sense either, if that deprives us of any reasonable and happy tomorrow. Living for the future may not be the healthiest thing to do; but do it we must, if we have good reason to think that we will have a future. The trick is to provide for the future without living in it, and that just requires being moral.[6]

This paper is a revised and expanded version of "Morality in the Marketplace," which appears in Business Ethics *(revised edition) eds. Milton Snoeyenbos, Robert Almeder and James Humber (Buffalo, N.Y.: Prometheus Press, 1992) 82–90, and, as such, it is a revised and expanded version of an earlier piece "The Ethics of Profit: Reflections on Corporate Responsibility," which originally appeared in* Business and Society *(Winter 1980, 7–15).*

Notes

1. Adam Smith, *The Wealth of Nations,* ed. Edwin Canaan (New York: Modern Library, 1937), p. 423.

2. See Milton Friedman, "The Social Responsibility of Business Is to Increase Its Profits," in *The New York Times Magazine* (September 13, 1970), pp. 33, 122–126 and "Milton Friedman Responds," in *Business and Society Review* no. 1 (Spring 1972), p. 5ff.

3. Albert Z. Carr, "Is Business Bluffing Ethical?" *Harvard Business Review* (January–February 1968).

4. Milton Friedman in "Milton Friedman Responds," in *Business and Society Review* no. 1 (Spring 1972), p. 10.

5. Ibid.

6. I would like to thank J. Humber and M. Snoeyenbos for their comments and criticisms of an earlier draft.

POSTSCRIPT

Are Profits the Only Business of Business?

Friedman dismisses the pleas of those who argue for socially responsible business action on the grounds that these individuals do not understand the role of the corporate executive in modern society. Friedman points out that the executives are responsible to the corporate owners, and if the corporate executives take a "socially responsible" action that reduces the return on the owners' investment, they have spent the owners' money. This, Friedman maintains, violates the very foundation of the American political-economic system: individual freedom. If the corporate executives wish to take socially responsible actions, they should use their own money; they should not prevent the owners from spending their money on whatever social actions they might wish to support.

Almeder argues that some corporate behavior is immoral and that defense of this immoral behavior imposes great costs on society. He likens corporate acts such as advertising cigarettes, marketing automobiles that cannot sustain moderate rear-end collisions, and contributing funds to destabilize foreign governments to murdering innocent children for profit. He argues that society must not condone this behavior but, instead, through federal and state legislation, must continue to impose regulations upon businesses until businesses begin to regulate themselves.

Perhaps no single topic is more fundamental to microeconomics than the issue of profits. Many pages have been written in defense of profits; see, for example, Milton and Rose Friedman's *Free to Choose: A Personal Statement* (Harcourt Brace Jovanovich, 1980). A classic reference is Frank H. Knight's *Risk, Uncertainty, and Profits* (Kelly Press, 1921). Friedrich A. Hayek, the author of many journal articles and books, is a guru for many current free marketers. There are a number of other books and articles, however, that are highly critical of the Friedman-Knight-Hayek position, including Christopher D. Stone's *Where the Law Ends: Social Control of Corporate Behavior* (Harper & Row, 1975). Others who challenge the legitimacy of the notion that markets are morally free zones include Thomas Mulligan, "A Critique of Milton Friedman's Essay 'The Social Responsibility of Business Is to Increase Its Profits,'" *Journal of Business Ethics* (1986); Daniel M. Hausman, "Are Markets Morally Free Zones?" *Philosophy and Public Affairs* (Fall 1989); and Andrew Henley, "Economic Orthodoxy and the Free Market System: A Christian Critique," *International Journal of Social Economics* (vol. 14, no. 10, 1987).

ISSUE 2

Are CEOs Paid What They Are Worth?

YES: Ira T. Kay, from "Don't Mess With CEO Pay," *Across the Board* (January/February 2006)

NO: Edgar Woolard, Jr., from "CEOs Are Being Paid Too Much," *Across the Board* (January/February 2006)

ISSUE SUMMARY

YES: Ira T. Kay, businessman and author, defends current CEO pay practices. He argues that "Empirical studies show that executive compensation has closely tracked corporate performance," and that rejecting pay-for-performance will hurt both workers and stockholders.

NO: Edgar Woolard, Jr., former CEO and chairman of Dupont, describes four myths regarding the compensation received by corporate business leaders. Dismissing the myths, he believes no one but CEOs get "paid excessively when they fail."

Perhaps the strongest argument for market economies rests on their ability to produce an efficient allocation of resources. There may be cases in which markets fail to produce these efficient outcomes, but these instances of market failure, as in the case of public goods or goods that involve positive or negative externalities, should be infrequent. In the process of producing these efficient outcomes, markets will also produce inequalities. Indeed, most people are willing to accept unequal outcomes because of the resulting efficiencies. In taking this position, these individuals distinguish between equality of outcomes from equality of opportunities; the former is accepted so long as the latter exists.

These abstract notions of inequality of outcomes become more real when we consider some of the actual differences in incomes and earnings. Take first the differences in the distribution of household income. In 2005 the poorest 20 percent of households in the United States received 3.4 percent of total household income while the richest 20 percent of households received more than 15 times as much, about 50 percent of total household income (there were 114 million households in 2005). The figures are perhaps even more striking if we consider the difference in the earnings of those working at the minimum wage and those who serve as the heads of the country's largest companies. The current federal minimum wage is $5.15 an hour, a level set by Congress in 1996. This translates into a yearly income of $10,300 (assuming the individual works 40 hours a week for 50 weeks per year). This compares with an estimated 2005 total compensation package of $13.5 million for the average chief executive of a Standard and Poor's 500 company (The Corporate Library's 2006 CEO Pay Survey, The Corporate Library, September 29, 2006). And while the federal minimum wage has not changed since 1996, the just-cited study estimated the change in average total executive compensation between 2004 and 2005 at 16.4 percent.

Some people do more than simply complain that executive compensation is excessive; they have taken legal action to take away a part of that compensation. Perhaps the most famous of these cases involves Eliot Spitzer, who before being elected governor of the state of New York served as its attorney general, and Richard Grasso, former president of the New York Stock Exchange (NYSE). The charge is that Mr. Grasso's $187.5 million pay package was excessive and that he must return a portion of his pay to the NYSE. At the time of this writing the outcome of this case has not been determined.

Although almost everyone would agree that a chief executive of a business should be paid more than the average employee of that business, the issue is one of how much more. Are the executives, in fact, worth the pay represented by the $13.5 million figure cited above? Ira T. Kay admits that there are abuses in executive compensation, but argues that in most cases CEOs really earn all that they get. Edward Woolard, Jr., takes the opposite position. He believes that CEO pay is excessive, and it is time to get the system of executive compensation back under control.

YES

Ira T. Kay

Don't Mess with CEO Pay

For years, headlines have seized on dramatic accounts of outrageous amounts earned by executives—often of failing companies—and the financial tragedy that can befall both shareholders and employees when CEOs line their own pockets at the organization's expense. Images of lavish executive lifestyles are now engraved in the popular consciousness. The result: public support for political responses that include new regulatory measures and a long list of demands for greater shareholder or government control over executive compensation.

These images now overshadow the reality of thousands of successful companies with appropriately paid executives and conscientious boards. Instead, fresh accusations of CEOs collecting huge amounts of undeserved pay appear daily, fueling a full-blown mythology of a corporate America ruled by executive greed, fraud, and corruption.

This mythology consists of two related components: the myth of the failed pay-for-performance model and the myth of managerial power. The first myth hinges on the idea that the link between executive pay and corporate performance—if it ever existed—is irretrievably broken. The second myth accepts the idea of a failed pay-for-performance model and puts in its service the image of unchecked CEOs dominating subservient boards as the explanation for decisions resulting in excessive executive pay. The powerful combination of these two myths has captured newspaper headlines and shareholder agendas, regulatory attention and the public imagination. . . .

Fueling the Fiction

. . . In recent years, dozens of reporters from business magazines and the major newspapers have called me and specifically asked for examples of companies in which CEOs received exorbitant compensation, approved by the board, while the company performed poorly. Not once have I been asked to comment on the vast majority of companies—those in which executives are appropriately rewarded for performance or in which boards have reduced compensation or even fired the CEO for poor performance.

I have spent hundreds of hours answering reporters' questions, providing extensive data and explaining the pay-for-performance model of executive compensation, but my efforts have had little impact: The resulting stories feature the same anecdotal reporting on those corporations for which the process has gone awry. The press accounts ignore solid research that shows that annual pay for most executives moves up and down significantly with the company's performance, both financial and stock-related. Corporate wrong-doings and outlandish executive pay packages make for lively headlines, but the reliance on purely anecdotal reporting and the highly prejudicial language adopted are a huge disservice to the companies, their executives and employees, investors, and the public. The likelihood of real economic damage to the U.S. economy grows daily.

For example, the mythology drives institutional investors and trade unions with the power to exert enormous pressure on regulators and executive and board practices. The California Public Employees' Retirement System—the nation's largest public pension fund—offers a typical example in its Nov. 15, 2004, announcement of a new campaign to rein in "abusive compensation practices in corporate America and hold directors and compensation committees more accountable for their actions."

The AFL-CIO's website offers another example of the claim that managerial power has destroyed the efficacy of the pay-for-performance model: "Each year, shocking new examples of CEO pay greed are made public. Investors are concerned not just about the growing size of executive compensation packages, but the fact that CEO pay levels show little apparent relationship to corporate profits, stock prices or executive performance. How do CEOs do it? For years, executives have relied on their shareholders to be passive absentee owners. CEOs have rigged their own compensation packages by packing their boards with conflicted or negligent directors."

The ROI of the CEO

As with all modern myths, there's a grain of truth in all the assumptions and newspaper stories. The myths of managerial power and of the failed pay-for-performance model find touchstones in real examples of companies where CEOs have collected huge sums in cash compensation and stock options while shareholder returns declined. . . .

These exceptions in executive pay practices, however, are now commonly mistaken for the rule. . . . Never mind that these same CEOs stand at the center of a corporate model that has generated millions of jobs and trillions of dollars in shareholder earnings. Worse, using CEOs as scapegoats distracts from the real causes of and possible solutions for inequality.

The primary determinant of CEO pay is the same force that sets pay for all Americans: relatively free—if somewhat imperfect—labor markets, in which companies offer the levels of compensation necessary to attract and retain the employees who generate value for shareholders. Part of that pay for most executives consists of stock-based incentives. A 2003 study by Brian J. Hall and Kevin J. Murphy shows that the ratio of total CEO compensation to production workers' average earnings closely follows the Dow Jones Industrial Average. When the Dow soars, the gap between executive and non-executive compensation widens. The problem, it seems, is not that CEOs receive too much performance-driven, stock-based compensation, but that non-executives receive too little.

The key question is not the actual dollar amount paid to a CEO in total compensation or whether that amount represents a high multiple of pay of the average worker's salary but, rather, whether that CEO creates an adequate return on the company's investment in executive compensation. In virtually every area of business, directors routinely evaluate and adjust the amounts that companies invest in all inputs, and shareholders directly or indirectly endorse or challenge those decisions. Executive pay is no different.

Hard Realities

The corporate scandals of recent years laid bare the inner workings of a handful of public companies where, inarguably, the process for setting executive pay violated not only the principle of pay-for-performance but the extensive set of laws and regulations governing executive pay practices and the role of the board. But while I condemn illegal actions and criticize boards that reward executives who fail to produce positive financial results, I know that the vast majority of U.S. corporations do much better by their shareholders and the public. I have worked directly with more than a thousand publicly traded companies in the United States and attended thousands of compensation-committee meetings, and I have *never* witnessed board members straining to find a way to pay an executive more than he is worth.

In addition, at Watson Wyatt I work with a team of experts that has conducted extensive research at fifteen hundred of America's largest corporations and tracked the relationship between these pay practices and corporate performance over almost twenty years. In evaluating thousands of companies annually, yielding nearly twenty thousand "company years" of data, and pooling cross-sectional company data over multiple years, we have discovered that for both most companies and the "typical" company, there is substantial pay-for-performance sensitivity. That is, high performance generates high pay for executives and low performance generates low pay. Numerous empirical academic studies support our conclusions.

Our empirical evidence and evidence from other studies have produced the following key findings:

1. Executive pay is unquestionably high relative to low-level corporate positions, and it has risen dramatically over the past ten to fifteen years, faster than inflation and faster than average employee pay. But executive compensation generally tracks total returns to shareholders—even including the recent rise in pay.
2. Executive stock ownership has risen dramatically over the past ten to fifteen years. High levels of CEO stock ownership are correlated with and most likely the cause of companies' high financial and stock-market performance.
3. Executives are paid commensurate with the skills and talents that they bring to the organization. Underperforming executives routinely receive pay reductions or are terminated—far more often than press accounts imply.

4. CEOs who are recruited from outside a company and have little influence over its board receive compensation that is competitive with and often higher than the pay levels of CEOs who are promoted from within the company.
5. At the vast majority of companies, even extraordinarily high levels of CEO compensation represent a tiny fraction of the total value created by the corporation under that CEO's leadership. (Watson Wyatt has found that U.S. executives receive approximately 1 percent of the net income generated by the corporations they manage.) Well-run companies, it bears pointing out, produce significant shareholder returns and job security for millions of workers. . . .

Why CEOs Are Worth the Money

The huge gap between the realities of executive pay and the now-dominant mythology surrounding it has become even more evident in recent years. Empirical studies show that executive compensation has closely tracked corporate performance: Pay rose during the boom years of the 1990s, when U.S. corporations generated huge returns, declined during the 2001–03 profit slowdown, and increased in 2004 as profits improved. The myth of excessive executive pay continued to gain power, however, even as concrete, well-documented financial realities defied it.

The blind outrage over executive pay climbed even during the slowdown, as compensation dropped drastically. During this same period, in the aftermath of the corporate scandals, Congress and the U.S. regulatory agencies instituted far-reaching reforms in corporate governance and board composition, and companies spent millions to improve their governance and transparency. But the critics of executive pay and managerial power were only encouraged to raise their voices.

It might surprise those critics to learn that CEOs are not interchangeable and not chosen by lot; they are an extremely important asset to their companies and generally represent an excellent investment. The relative scarcity of CEO talent is manifested in many ways, including the frenetic behavior of boards charged with filling the top position when a CEO retires or departs. CEOs have significant, legitimate, market-driven bargaining power, and in pay negotiations, they use that power to obtain pay commensurate with their skills. Boards, as they should, use their own bargaining power to retain talent and maximize returns to company shareholders.

Boards understand the imperative of finding an excellent CEO and are willing to risk millions of dollars to secure the right talent. Their behavior is not only understandable but necessary to secure the company's future success. Any influence that CEOs might have over their directors is modest in comparison to the financial risk that CEOs assume when they leave other prospects and take on the extraordinarily difficult task of managing a major corporation, with a substantial portion of their short- and long-term compensation contingent on the organization's financial success. . . .

Properly designed pay opportunities drive superior corporate performance and secure it for the future. And most importantly, many economists argue, the U.S. model of executive compensation is a significant source of competitive advantage for the nation's economy, driving higher productivity, profits, and stock prices.

Resetting the Debate

Companies design executive pay programs to accomplish the classic goals of any human-capital program. First, they must attract, retain, and motivate their human capital to perform at the highest levels. The motivational factor is the most important, because it addresses the question of how a company achieves the greatest return on its human-capital investment and rewards executives for making the right decisions to drive shareholder value. Incentive-pay and pay-at-risk programs are particularly effective, especially at the top of the house, in achieving this motivation goal. . . .

A long list of pressures, including institutional-investor pushback, accounting changes, SEC investigations, and scrutiny from labor unions and the media, are forcing companies to rethink their executive-compensation programs, especially their stock-based incentives. The key now is to address the real problems in executive compensation without sacrificing the performance-based model and the huge returns that it has generated. Boards are struggling to achieve greater transparency and more rigorous execution of their pay practices—a positive move for all parties involved.

The real threat to U.S. economic growth, job creation, and higher living standards now comes from regulatory overreach as proponents of the mythology reject market forces and continue to push for government and institutional control over executive pay. To the extent that the mythology now surrounding executive pay leads to a rejection of the pay-for-performance model and restrictions on the risk-and-reward structure for setting executive compensation, American corporate performance will suffer.

There will be more pressure on boards to effectively reduce executive pay. This may meet the social desires of some constituents, but it will almost surely cause economic decline, for companies and the U.S. economy. We will see higher executive turnover and less talent in the executive suite as the most qualified job candidates move into other professions, as we saw in the 1970s, when top candidates moved into investment banking, venture-capital firms, and consulting, and corporate performance suffered as a result.

Our research demonstrates that aligning pay plans, incentive opportunities, and performance measures throughout an organization is key to financial success. Alignment means that executives and non-executives alike have the opportunity to increase their pay through performance-based incentives. As new regulations make it more difficult to execute the stock-based elements of the pay-for-performance model, for example, by reducing broad-based stock options, we will see even less alignment between executives' compensation and the pay packages of the rank-and-file. We are already witnessing the unintended consequences of the new requirement for stock-option expensing as companies cut the broad-based stock-option plans that have benefited millions of workers and given them a direct stake in the financial success of the companies for which they work.

Instead of changing executive pay plans to make them more like pay plans for employees, we should be reshaping employee pay to infuse it with the same incentives that drive performance in the company's upper ranks. A top-down regulatory approach to alignment will only damage the entire market-based, performance-management process that has worked so well for most companies and the economy as a whole. Instead of placing artificial limits on executive pay, we should focus squarely on increasing performance incentives and stock ownership for both executive and non-executive employees and rewarding high performers throughout the organization, from top to bottom. Within the context of a free-market economy, equal opportunity—not income equality by fiat—is the goal. . . .

In some ways, the decidedly negative attention focused on executive pay has increased the pressure that executives, board members, HR staffs, and compensation consultants all feel when they enter into discussions about the most effective methods for tying pay to performance and ensuring the company's success. The managerial-power argument has contributed to meaningful discussions about corporate governance and raised the level of dialogue in boardrooms. These are positive developments.

When the argument is blown into mythological proportions, however, it skews thinking about the realities of corporate behavior and leads to fundamental misunderstandings about executives, their pay levels, and their role in building successful companies and a flourishing economy. Consequently, the mythology now surrounding executive compensation leads many to reject a pay model that works well and is critical to ongoing growth at both the corporate and the national economic level. We need to address excesses in executive pay without abandoning the core model, and to return the debate to a rational, informed discussion. And we can safely leave Marie Antoinette out of it.

CEOs Are Being Paid Too Much

There's a major concern out there for all of us. I personally am extremely saddened by the loss of the respect that this country's corporate leaders have experienced. We've had a double blow in the last ten years or so. The first one we know way too much about—the fraud at Enron, Tyco, Adelphia, WorldCom, and many others.

The CEOs say there were a few rotten apples in that barrel, and maybe that's the answer—but there are a hell of lot more rotten apples than I would have ever guessed. But that's just the base of one of the issues that has eroded the trust and confidence in American business leaders.

The second one is the perception of excess compensation received by CEOs getting worse year by year. And if directors agree, they can be the leaders in making a very important change. I'd like to deal with it by describing several myths about compensation and trying to undermine them.

Myth #1: CEO Pay by Competition

The first is the myth that CEO pay is driven by competition—and to that I say "bull." CEO pay is driven today primarily by outside consultant surveys, and by the fact that many board members have bought into the concept that your CEO has to be at least in the top half, and maybe in the top quartile. So we have the "ratchet, ratchet, ratchet" concept. We all understand it well enough to know that if everybody is trying to be in the top half, everybody is going to get a hefty increase every year. If Bill and Sally get an increase in their total compensation, I have to get an increase so that I will stay in the top half.

How can we change that?

In 1990, we addressed this issue at DuPont. I became CEO in 1989, and I was concerned about what was evident even then. A 1989 *Business Week* article talked about executive pay—who makes the most and are they worth it: Michael Eisner, $40 million in 1988; Ross Johnson, $20 million; and others. I don't know Eisner, but I know that even fifteen years later he's one of the most criticized CEOs in the country.

What we did at DuPont was go to a simple concept: internal pay equity. I went to the board and the compensation committee and said, "We're going to look at the people who run the businesses, who make decisions on prices and new products with guidance from the CEO—the executive vice presidents—and we're going to set the limit of what a CEO in this company can be paid at 1.5 times the pay rate for the executive vice president—50 percent."

That to me seemed equitable. It had been anywhere from 30 to 50 percent in the past. I said, "Let's set it at 50 percent, and we're not going to chase the surveys." And this is the way DuPont has done it ever since. I think we have tweaked it up a little bit since then, but using a multiple still is the right way to go.

Board members can do this by suggesting that the HR and compensation people look at what's happened to internal pay equity, and seriously consider going in that direction. That will solve this problem in a great way.

Myth #2: Compensation Committees Are Independent

I give a "double bull" to this one. It could be that committees are becoming more independent, but over the last fifteen years they certainly haven't been.

Let me describe how it works: The compensation committee talks to an outside consultant who has surveys that you could drive a truck through and that support paying anything you want to pay. The consultant talks to the HR vice president, who talks to the CEO. The CEO says what he'd like to receive—enough so he will be "respected by his peers." It gets to the HR person, who tells the consultant, and the CEO gets what he's implied he deserves. The members of the compensation committee are happy that they're independent, the HR person is happy, the CEO is happy, and the consultant gets invited back next year.

There are two ways to change that as well. Here's the first one. When John Reed came back to the New York Stock Exchange to try to clean up the mess after Dick Grasso, he made the decision—which I admire him for—that the board was going to have its own outside consultant, one who was not going to be allowed to talk to internal people—not to the HR vice president, not to the CEO.

I'm the head of the comp committee at the NYSE, and when I talk with our outside consultant, he gives us his ideas of what he thinks the pay package ought to be. Then, with the consultant there, I talk to the compensation committee, and we make a decision. I talk to the HR vice president to see if he has any other thoughts, but the committee is totally independent.

The other way to change things is to truly insist on pay-for-performance, which everyone likes to talk about but no one does. Boards pay everybody in the top quartile whether they have good performance or bad performance—or even if they're about to be fired.

Well, I was on a board fifteen years ago, and four CEOs were on the compensation committee, and for two consecutive years, we gave the CEO and the executives there no bonus, no salary increase, and modest stock options, because their performance was lousy those years. After that, they did extremely well, and we paid them extremely well. That's how pay-for-performance should work.

Myth #3: Look How Much Wealth I Created

This one is really a joke. It was born in the 1980s and '90s during the stock-market bubble, when all CEOs were beating their chest about how much wealth they were creating for shareholders. And I'd look to the king, Jack Welch. Jack's the best CEO of the last fifty years, and I've told him this. But he likes to say, "I created $400 billion worth of wealth." No, Jack—no, you didn't. He said that when GE's stock was at 60, but when the bubble burst it went to 30, and it's in the low 30s now. So he created $150 to $200 billion.

But besides the actual figure, there are two things wrong with his claim. Now, I don't care how much money Jack Welch made. God bless him; I think he's terrific. But what did it do? It set a new level for CEO pay based on the stock-market bubble; all the other CEOs were saying, "Look how much wealth I created."

So you've got this more recent high level of executive pay, and then you've got the ratcheting effect in the system. Those things have to change.

Myth #4: Severance for Failing

The last one is the worst of all. Any directors who agree to give these huge severance pay packages to CEOs who fail—Philip Purcell of Morgan Stanley got $114 million, Carly Fiorina of Hewlett-Packard got $20 million—why are you doing that? No one else gets paid excessively when they fail. They get fired; they get fair severance.

All of this is killing the image of CEOs and corporate executives. When it comes to our image, we're in the league with lawyers and politicians. I don't want to be there, and I don't think you do either. We need the respect of our employees and the general public. And there's a lot of skepticism about leaders in politics and in churches and in the military—but we can't have it in the business community, because we're the backbone of the market system that has made this country great and created so many opportunities for people. We can't be seen as either dishonest or greedy.

What can you do about it?

Some of you CEOs need to show leadership and say, "We're going to do internal pay equity." It's easy to get the data, and then you can decide what you think is fair and how much you think the CEO contributes versus the other business leaders who make their companies so strong.

Compensation committees need to seriously consider implementing internal pay equity. Pay only for outstanding performance. Quit giving people money just because Bill and Sally are getting it. Consider going to an independent consultant that deals only with the board while you deal with HR and the CEO.

Last, take a look at stock-option packages. Not just for one year but the mega-grants that built up in the 1980s and '90s. If you've given huge stock-option packages for the last five years, look at their value. There's nothing in the Bible that says that you have to give increased stock options every year. Give a smaller grant; give a different kind of grant; put some kind of limits on.

There are many ways to do it, but it's important to get the system back under control. It's important for our image, for our reputation, for integrity, for trust, and for our leadership in this country.

POSTSCRIPT

Are CEOs Paid What They Are Worth?

Ira T. Kay begins his defense of executive compensation by noting the common misperception that the high level of pay is undeserved. He believes this misperception rests on two myths. The first is that the pay-for-performance model no longer works as an explanation of executive compensation. The second myth is that executives control their own boards of directors and in this way determine their own compensation. He feels that these myths, which are fueled by the media's reporting of exceptional cases, may be damaging to the economy because various groups including institutional investors and trade unions exert pressure to change the pay-for-performance model. But the fact is, Kay maintains, the cases of abuse are the exception and not the rule. He then offers five key findings from various studies of executive compensation. One of these findings is that "Executives are paid commensurate with the skills and talents that they bring to the organization." He concludes by asserting that the real issue is how to spread the pay-for-performance model from the executive suite to all levels of the corporation.

Edgar Woolard, Jr., also considers some myths. He lists four. First, there is the myth that executive pay is determined by competition. He believes that in reality consultants pay a major role is setting the pay of business leaders. The second myth is that compensation committees, in the first instance, setting executive pay are independent. Woolard argues that over the last 15 years these committees have, in fact, not gotten more independent. The third myth holds that executive pay is tied to the wealth created by the executive. Woolard points to the fact that the rise in stock prices through the 1990s was a general phenomenon, not determined by the actions of business leaders but in large part the result of a stock market bubble. The last myth is that severance packages given to executives who have failed are fair. Instead, the opposite is true: The one group who gets excess severance pay is executives. Based on reality rather than myth, it is important to get the executive compensation system back under control.

There is a growing literature on executive compensation. The popular press certainly reports on the pay of corporate heads, sometimes as part of the business news and other times from the perspective that the pay is excessive or undeserved. For an example of the former, see "An Early Christmas at Lehman," by Randall Smith (*Wall Street Journal,* December 6, 2006). For an example of the latter, see "While Shares Fell, Viacom Paid Three $160 Million" (*New York Times*, April 16, 2005). Other articles include "Special Report: CEO Pay 'Business as Usual'" (*USA Today*, March 30, 2005) and "The True Measure of a CEO" by James O'Toole (*Across the Board*, September/October 2005). The issue has attracted the attention of various public officials, including Congressman Barney Frank, who serves on the House Committee on Financial Services: His views are expressed in "The Problem of Executive Compensation" at http://www.house.gov/banking_democrats/ExecCompProblems.html. The views of labor as represented by the AFL-CIO can be found at http://www.aflcio/corporatewatch/paywatch/pay/. For a more complete and critical analysis of executive compensation see *Pay Without Performance* by Lucian Benchuk and Jesse Fried (Harvard University Press, 2005).

ISSUE 3

Is OSHA Working Effectively to Protect the Safety of Construction Workers?

YES: Edwin G. Foulke, Jr., from Statement to the Subcommittee on Workforce Protections of the House Committee on Education and Labor (June 24, 2008)

NO: Mark H. Ayers, from Testimony before the Subcommittee on Workforce Protections of the House Committee on Education and Labor (June 24, 2008)

ISSUE SUMMARY

YES: Assistant Secretary of Labor and OSHA head Foulke states that his agency is committed to protecting employees, that it has a multi-faceted approach to reducing construction-related accidents, and that it has a strong, targeted enforcement program.

NO: Union official Mark Ayers believes that OSHA is failing to improve the safety and health of construction workers, and he calls for several changes, including an increase in OSHA enforcement activities.

President Richard M. Nixon signed the Occupational Safety and Health Act into law on December 29, 1970. Among other things, this legislation created the Occupational Safety and Health Administration, or OSHA. According to OSHA, which is housed in the U.S. Department of Labor, its mission is to "assure safe and healthful working conditions for working men and women." Currently, it attempts to fulfill its mission with a three-pronged strategy: (i) strong and effective enforcement, (ii) outreach, education, and compliance assistance, and (iii) partnerships and cooperative programs. To do this, during fiscal year 2007, OSHA had 2,150 employees (including 1,100 inspectors) and an appropriation of $490 million.

In an attempt to assess the effectiveness of OSHA, evaluation can follow either a macro or a micro approach. With the former, the assessment involves data on workplace fatalities and injuries over time. OSHA, using this approach, states that since its inception it has helped to cut workplace fatalities by more than 60 percent and occupational injury and illness rates by 40 percent. Moreover, this was accomplished over a period when U.S. employment increased from 56 million employees at 3.5 million worksites to more than 135 million employees at 8.9 million worksites. The macro critics respond in at least two different ways. One is that even more progress could have been achieved if OSHA had been more aggressive in issuing regulations and more aggressive in their enforcement. The other criticism involves cost-benefit analysis; that is, the costs, measured in terms of both tax dollars and additional costs that were eventually passed on to consumers, far exceeded the benefits. Reworded, the second criticism simply argues that greater or similar benefits could have been achieved with the same or lower costs.

But the issue as presented here involves a micro approach, specifically the impact that OSHA has had on the construction industry. According to the U.S. Bureau of Labor Statistics, the construction industry was the second most dangerous industry in 2007, accounting for 1,178 of 5,488 fatalities, or 21 percent of the total number of fatal occupational injuries in 2007. When the analysis shifts from industries to occupations, the same pattern emerges with construction and extraction occupations ranking second in fatal occupational injuries with 21 percent (1,152 of 5,488).

While occupational safety in the construction industry is not typically on the minds and lips of most Americans, several incidents during 2008 served to highlight the dangers to these workers and spurred inquiries into the effectiveness of OSHA in protecting the construction workers. The first incident was a widely publicized collapse of a construction crane in New York City in mid-March that killed four construction workers and injured 17. This was followed by another construction crane accident, some 10 days later in Miami, that killed two workers and injured five others. The next fatal accident occurred on May 1 in Annapolis, Maryland, when a single worker lost his life while he was in the process of dismantling a crane. On May 31, a construction worker in Las Vegas was crushed to death while he was working on a moving crane. The frequency of these accidents and their high visibility led to the congressional hearings on the effectiveness of OSHA in improving safety in the construction industry.

In his testimony, Assistant Secretary Foulke takes the affirmative and defends his agency. He admits that even one fatality is too many, but argues that OSHA has been aggressive in efforts to improve construction worker safety. Union official Ayers believes that employers and OSHA both share responsibility for construction worker safety, but they are both failing to do what is needed.

YES

Edwin G. Foulke, Jr.

Statement to the Subcommittee on Workforce Protections Hearing

To accomplish its mission of saving lives and reducing injuries and illnesses, OSHA utilizes a balanced approach which includes: 1) strong, fair, and effective enforcement; 2) safety and health standards and guidance; 3) training and education; and 4) cooperative programs, compliance assistance and outreach. The Occupational Safety and Health Act (the OSH Act) enacted by Congress in 1970 stipulates that employers are ultimately responsible for providing a safe and healthful work environment. OSHA has a critical role in helping employers with their responsibilities, and utilizes all components incorporated in its balanced approach.

Since 2001, as part of its strong enforcement program, OSHA proposed more than three-quarters of a billion dollars in penalties for safety and health violations and made 64 criminal referrals to the Department of Justice, which represents more than 30 percent of all criminal referrals in the history of OSHA and more than any previous Administration. In Fiscal Year (FY) 2008, of the almost 57,000 violations issued so far, 80 percent have been categorized as serious, willful, repeat or failure-to-abate, the highest percentage ever recorded by the agency. We are also effectively targeting our inspections – 78 percent of the worksites we inspected had violations. Our approach is working. All three key indicators – injury, illness and fatality rates – are all at the lowest levels in the nation's history. Most importantly, the overall fatality rate in construction has declined by 18 percent since 2001. These achievements highlight the Administration's commitment and success in protecting the safety and health of the nation's workforce.

Even with all these achievements, OSHA recognizes that there are still safety and health concerns to be addressed at workplaces, including construction sites. We must remember that a successful construction project is one that is done safely and without loss of life. One fatality is one too many.

According to data from the Bureau of Labor Statistics (BLS) Current Population Survey, employment in the construction industry averaged approximately 11.9 million in 2007, with approximately 16 percent of the total classified as unincorporated self-employed. Since FY 2003, 78 percent of all OSHA fatality investigations in the construction industry have been conducted on companies with 25 or fewer employees. According to the National Institute for

U.S. House of Representatives, June 24, 2008, excerpted.

Occupational Safety and Health (NIOSH), 80 percent of the construction businesses have fewer than 10 employees. Construction is dangerous work which requires constant vigilance against hazards such as falls from elevated positions; trenching and excavations; confined spaces; scaffolding; electrocution and exposure to dust and noise. The dangers in construction work are well known and the challenge for OSHA is to use the best mix of enforcement, outreach, education, and cooperative programs to address construction workplace hazards.

Another challenge presented to OSHA by the construction industry is the nature of this industry. Unlike other workplaces that have permanent and ongoing operations, the work performed at construction sites is highly dynamic, often involving dozens of different employers at a single construction site, whether it is a large industrial project or a residential home. It is in this complex and challenging worksite that OSHA works with employers, employees, and their representatives to improve safety and health.

OSHA is familiar with these challenges and in response, has a multi-faceted approach to reducing construction-related accidents and preventing exposures to health hazards. OSHA focuses on the four most common causes of occupational fatalities in the construction industry: falls; "struck by"; "crushed by"; and electrocutions. In addition to a strong, targeted enforcement program, OSHA continues to revise and update its standards, create meaningful compliance assistance resources, and provide outreach, education and training. OSHA is committed to protecting employees by identifying hazards, citing employers when standards are violated, and educating stakeholders on ways to reduce the hazards associated with construction work across the country. OSHA also helps employers to provide safer working environments by engaging in a balanced approach of enforcement and outreach to key stakeholders to collaborate on important safety and health issues.

OSHA: Strong Enforcement Program for Construction

Strong enforcement of safety and health standards is a component of our effective approach on construction safety. In FY 2007, approximately 51 percent of total OSHA inspections, both federal and State Plan inspections, were conducted in the construction industry. More than 67 percent of all federal and about 74 percent of State Plan construction inspections were programmed inspections. In FY 2007, OSHA issued 74,816 citations just in the construction industry. Since 2001, OSHA has issued 256 significant enforcement cases – those with penalties of at least $100,000 – in the construction industry. As these statistics show, OSHA enforcement is strong and enforcement of our safety and health standards is a top priority of the agency.

OSHA has addressed the top four causes of fatalities found in its Integrated Management Information System in several ways. The agency has been aggressive in issuing citations and penalties for violations of the standards that address these key hazards. In FY 2007, for fall protection violations, we issued

24,358 citations for a total of $33.5 million in penalties; for struck-by and crushed-by, we issued 3,317 citations for a total of $9.1 million in penalties; for electrical violations, we issued 3,566 citations for a total of $2.4 million in penalties.

Enhanced Enforcement Program

In addition to our standard enforcement efforts, OSHA has created other enforcement mechanisms to focus on those companies that ignore their obligations under the OSH Act. The Enhanced Enforcement Program (EEP) complements the agency's targeted approach to enforcement by addressing employers who, despite OSHA's enforcement and outreach efforts, ignore their obligations to provide a safe and healthful work environment. The program looks at an employer's national inspection history, not just the violations at a single facility, to determine whether failure to comply with OSHA safety and health standards is a problem at one facility or job site, or systemic throughout the entire company. If an employer meets the criteria for EEP, it will be subject to much greater enforcement scrutiny from OSHA, which may ultimately result in court enforcement of citations or criminal referrals. This program has been used in the construction industry to focus resources on companies that fail to adequately protect their employees. There were 1,189 EEP construction cases, which represents almost half of all OSHA EEP cases. After four years of implementation, OSHA revised the EEP program to focus greater enforcement emphasis on those employers that have a history of violations with OSHA (including history with the State Plans). The revised program became effective on January 1, 2008.

Special Emphasis Programs

OSHA conducts National, Regional, and Local Emphasis Programs (NEPs, REPs, and LEPs) that target particular hazards or industries such as trenching, amputations, and refining. These programs combine enforcement and outreach efforts to address a particular safety and health issue. OSHA has completed a number of successful emphasis programs focused on such topics as fall hazards in construction, mobile crane operations, bridge and tunnel construction, silica and road hazards, falls relating to scaffolding, and energized power lines.

Hexavalent Chromium

OSHA promulgated a standard on exposures to hexavalent chromium on February 29, 2006 which reduced the permissible exposure limit (PEL). Construction employees are primarily exposed to hexavalent chromium during the welding/cutting of stainless steel, removing paint from existing structures such as bridges, and during refractory restoration.

Portland Cement

OSHA implemented new Portland Cement Inspection Procedures at construction sites as part of its settlement of a legal challenge to the new Hexavalent Chromium Standard by the Building and Construction Trades Department, AFL-CIO, Laborers' International Union of North America, and International Brotherhood of Teamsters.

Preventing Falls

In 2001, OSHA issued a new steel erection standard that modified a provision to allow the use of nets instead of a fully planked floor. Specifically, the new provision provides that the employer has the option of either maintaining a fully planked/decked floor or maintaining nets, every two stories. In 2002, stakeholders asked OSHA to permit the use of 100 percent fall protection instead of using planking or nets. They argued that planking is not effective fall protection and that 100 percent tie-off is safer than allowing connectors and deckers to work without personal fall protection above a planked floor. In response, OSHA issued a compliance policy stating that, if an employer used 100 percent fall protection, including for connectors and deckers, the failure to comply with this provision would be considered *de minimis*. . . .

Preventing Construction "Struck By" Accidents

An OSHA NEP addressing roadway work zone safety was created after the success of a local initiative that began in OSHA's Parsippany, New Jersey office. This collaborative program brings together state transportation and police authorities, as well as local unions, in cross-training efforts to improve hazard identification and correction at highway job sites. The success of this approach is reflected in New Jersey; OSHA data indicates that where 8–12 employees were being killed in roadway work zones annually, the number of work zone fatalities there was reduced to one in 2007. . . .

In addition, OSHA is conducting a study of struck-by accidents to determine patterns and root causes.

Trenching Initiative Is Successful

The OSHA Trenching Initiative, which was begun in 2003, has proven to be successful. The trenching initiative is a large-scale effort to raise awareness of trenching hazards and basic trench safety practices. Working through cooperative programs such as the American Pipeline Contractors Association, and with other stakeholders, 500,000 Trenching Quickcards, 50,000 Trenching Posters, and NIOSH's CD *Trench Safety Awareness Training* have been distributed. Most of these training and education materials, such as the Quickcards, are designed specifically for use by the many small contractors that are engaged in trenching work. OSHA data indicates that the Initiative has helped to reduce the annual number of trenching and excavation related fatalities by 46 percent.

Preventing Electrocutions in Construction

A National Strategic Partnership between OSHA and the Electrical Transmission and Distribution Construction Contractors, trade associations, and International Brotherhood of Electrical Workers was originally signed in August 2004 and continues today. The partners represent the interests of more than 70 percent of the industry. The partnership's tri-level leadership (CEO's, corporate safety, employees/supervisors) harnesses industry expertise with that of OSHA to make significant progress towards the Partnership's goals: reduction of fatalities through data analysis, training, and best practice development/implementation. . . .

Unprecedented Levels of Hispanic Outreach Activities

OSHA continues to make workplace safety and health for Hispanic employees a priority. The agency has a Diverse Workforce Issues Group that focuses on outreach, training and education issues through various means, including the OSHA – Mexican Embassy Letter of Agreement (LOA), several construction alliances, including alliances with the International Association of Foundation Drilling, the American Pipeline Contractors Association, the American Society of Safety Engineers, the National Association of Home Builders, and the Roadway Work Zone Safety and Health Partners, and OSHA's On-site Consultation Program. There is active participation by our stakeholders, including foreign consulates, industry, professional associations, organized labor, community faith-based organizations, and small business employers to address the safety and health issues for this hard to reach segment of the work force. . . .

Training for Construction Employees: OSHA Construction Outreach Training Program

The OSHA Outreach Training Program is a "train-the-trainer" program in which trainers who successfully complete the required OSHA Training Institute trainer course are authorized to conduct 10- and 30-hour training programs in construction and to give cards provided by the OSHA Training Institute to their students. This "train-the-trainer" program is OSHA's primary initiative for training employees in the basics of occupational safety and health hazard recognition and avoidance.

The OSHA Construction Outreach Training Program is a voluntary program. However, its considerable growth has been driven through industry groups such as the building trades, contractors, employer associations, and specific companies. The endorsement by these groups has resulted in the requirement of the training as a condition of employment for their employees or members. Over 1.6 million construction participants have been trained by these trainers since 2004.

OSHA Cooperative Programs

OSHA makes use of a variety of effective cooperative programs which engages various stakeholders such as employers, organizations, organized labor, and others to improve safety and health in the construction industry. The agency's cooperative programs include Alliances, Strategic Partnerships, Voluntary Protection Programs (VPP), and On-Site Consultation programs to name a few.

OSHA's VPP has 113 construction participants across the nation. There are 146 Strategic Partnerships with construction companies which account for more than 80 percent of all partnerships. OSHA's newest program, OSHA Challenge, "A Roadmap to Safety and Health Excellence," has 72 participants. . . .

I want to make it clear, however, that, while the agency offers technical assistance to employers to help them comply with OSHA standards as well as recognize employers for implementing exemplary safety and health management systems, *compliance with OSHA safety and health standards is not voluntary. There is no such term or practice as "voluntary compliance."*

Pending Rulemakings

OSHA recognizes that a dynamic industry requires that we continuously evaluate regulations and standards. The following four items on OSHA's current regulatory agenda are particularly applicable to the construction industry.

Cranes:
Several recent fatal crane accidents have highlighted the importance of crane safety. OSHA estimates that there are approximately 96,000 construction cranes in use each year in the United States. The recent crane accidents in New York, Miami, and Annapolis involved tower cranes. According to OSHA accident investigation data, in the period from 2000 to 2007, there were a total of 20 incidents involving tower cranes which resulted in 10 fatalities.

OSHA is proactively engaged to improve crane safety. The Administration is in the final stages of preparing a proposed rule to update and improve its current construction cranes and derricks standard. The rule is being developed through a negotiated rulemaking process which provides opportunities for all stakeholders to provide input.

The cranes and derricks proposed rule will comprehensively address the hazards associated with the use of cranes and derricks in construction, including tower cranes. Developing the proposal is a complex, large-scale project which requires diligent and thoughtful considerations of all the technical issues. Pursuant to statutory requirements, OSHA has completed the regulatory flexibility analysis, small business review, paperwork burden analysis, and economic impact analysis of the proposed rule.

In addition to rulemaking, OSHA is highly engaged in a number of activities designed to heighten awareness of best practices and the construction hazards associated with crane use. OSHA's regional offices have established Alliances and partnerships, participated in numerous training activities, and provided information and training as part of proactive outreach programs. . . .

Finally, OSHA compliance officers inspect employer compliance with the OSHA construction crane standard as part of their inspections of construction sites. OSHA has detailed requirements for crane safety, which employers are required to follow. The requirements of the current crane standard include operational safety; a general requirement for employers to inspect construction cranes prior to each use; an annual inspection that must be "thorough" and documented, and that defects or deficiencies discovered in any inspection be repaired before the crane may be used; and requirements that employers conduct tower crane inspections prescribed by the manufacturer. Currently, there is no federal program under which OSHA is specifically charged with inspecting all construction cranes. Nor does OSHA currently require certification for crane operators.

After the March 2008 tower crane collapse in New York City, OSHA increased inspections of large construction sites there, since those are the sites where cranes are most likely to be used. Similarly, the State Plan partner, New York-OSHA, staff increased outreach efforts to address crane safety. OSHA's National Office deployed an engineering expert to the accident sites in New York and Miami as part of the agency's on-going investigations of those accidents.

Power Generation, Transmission, and Distribution:
On June 15, 2005, OSHA published a proposed rule to revise the general industry and construction standards for electric power generation, transmission, and distribution work and for electrical protective equipment. Public comments were received, hearings were held, and the final posthearing briefs were due on July 14, 2006. . . .

Confined Spaces:
Fatality and injury data, OSHA enforcement experience, and advice from OSHA's Advisory Committee for Construction Safety and Health indicate that the existing construction standard for confined spaces does not adequately protect construction employees in confined spaces from atmospheric and physical hazards. The existing construction standard only requires employers to instruct their employees about confined-space hazards, and comply with other OSHA construction standards that address confined-space hazards. On November 28, 2007, the agency issued a proposed rule for confined spaces in construction that is estimated to prevent 6 fatalities and 900 injuries. . . .

We are currently analyzing the public comments that were submitted and have scheduled a hearing for July 22, 2008.

Hearing Loss in Construction:
OSHA is continuing work on a new hearing conservation rule for construction. The current requirement requires employers to implement an effective hearing conservation program but contains no details on what such a program must include. . . .

Some of the issues under study that have added to the complexity of promulgating a rule include the seasonal nature of many construction jobs, the high employee turnover rate on many construction worksites, the temporary nature of many construction worksites, and the amount of noise generated by some commonly used construction equipment.

OSHA is committed to enhancing construction safety, to continuing to provide employers and employees with safety information, and to ensuring that worksites comply with existing safety regulations. I assure the subcommittee that construction safety is a top priority for OSHA and that we are striving to ensure that all employees return safely to their families and friends at the end of every work day.

Mark H. Ayers  **NO**

Testimony before the Subcommittee on Workforce Protections Hearing

My name is Mark Ayers, and I am the president of the Building and Construction Trades Department of the AFL-CIO. I am a 36 year member of the IBEW, the International Brotherhood of Electrical Workers, and have served in various leadership positions prior to being elected as president of the Building Trades Department last year.

My organization, which I will refer to as "the Department," is composed of 13 international/national unions representing 2.5 million construction workers in the United States and Canada. The Department and its affiliated unions have a long history of improving working conditions for construction workers – both union and non-union alike. In fact, many of our organizations were founded over 100 years ago for that very purpose.

Introduction

I am here today to address the safety and health of all construction workers in this country: union and non-union alike. All of these workers enjoy the right, under federal and state law, to a safe and healthful workplace. Yet, many continue to die, incur injuries, and/or become ill due to exposure to dangerous substances on the job.

You have convened this hearing because of the critical point at which we find ourselves in today. We appreciate your concern. After 20 years of steady improvement in construction safety and health, we suddenly find ourselves in the midst of a safety and health crisis.

While the safety and health of construction workers has long been a priority of the Department, it's the alarming number of construction worker deaths that have occurred in Las Vegas – 12 workers have died in just 16 months – that brings us here today. These deaths, along with the dramatic collapse of two tower cranes in New York City and other recent crane incidents in cities across the nation that have killed and injured construction workers, bystanders and even first responders, have drawn the media's attention to the dangerous nature of construction work.

U.S. House of Representatives, June 24, 2008.

Of course, this is not a new subject for those of us in the building trades. While we mourn the loss of every one of these workers, we know that by the end of this day, another four construction workers may lose their lives. And tomorrow, another two. And the next day, maybe six.

We know this because an average of four workers are killed every day on U.S. construction sites. Yes, in our nation we lose, on average, four construction workers a day, some 1,200 to 1,500 workers each year. That's 10 times the number of firefighters who are killed each year, 10 times the number of law enforcement officers killed in the line of duty each year, and 20 times the number of miners who are killed each year. And, for every worker killed, several hundred workers are seriously injured. If the carnage that takes place in the construction industry happened in any other industry there would be a national outcry. Yet, the only way we seem to be able to get attention to this huge problem is when a crisis hits, like the one we are faced with now. Think about it. It is an absolute outrage.

Construction worker deaths usually do not get front-page coverage. For the most part, they are usually single incidents – like an electrocution in New Jersey, a fall in Texas, a trench collapse in South Carolina, or a bulldozer rolling over on its operator in California. But let me tell you, they don't go unnoticed by other workers in the construction community. We know what it's like to lose a friend, and to see his or her family suffer.

In 2006, 1,239 construction workers were killed on the job, or died as a result of their injuries. Construction workers make up only 8 percent of the U.S. workforce, but account for more than 22 percent of all work-related deaths.

In 2006, according to BLS reports, 412,900 construction workers experienced injury or illness, of which 153,200 cases were serious enough to require days away from work. However, recent studies show the BLS survey may miss half to two-thirds of all injuries due to underreporting. Moreover, the misclassification of workers as independent contractors means many more injuries are unaccounted for, since self-employed workers aren't covered by OSHA or the BLS survey.

Less than 2.5 percent of the cases are from a work-related illness, but please don't let this low percentage fool you. Unfortunately, hundreds or even thousands of construction workers are being exposed at this very moment to an array of substances, such as asbestos, hexavalent chromium and silica, to name a few, that will cause disease years from now.

The sad fact is that we as an industry and as a nation really have no idea how many construction workers die each day from disease resulting from job site exposures. Moreover, family members, including children, have often been exposed to these harmful substances as well.

Those of us intimately involved in construction safety and health know that these deaths, injuries and illnesses are, by and large, all preventable. The outrageous number of fatalities in Las Vegas combined with crane incidents in New York and elsewhere has brought attention to the issue. Now that we have the attention of the media, the public, and, most importantly, the United States Congress, it's time that we talk about the construction industry as a whole and what needs to be done about it.

Describing the Problems

Workers falling to their deaths in the construction industry are not unique to the Vegas strip. Falls are the leading cause of death in our industry. They make up about one-third of all construction deaths. Fatal falls from rooftops are the most common, followed by falls from scaffolding and ladders. Fatal falls from girders, attributed to some of the deaths in Las Vegas, make up only 8 percent of fall fatalities.

Workers who walk the iron have the highest rate of death among all other occupations in construction. Fortunately, due to a focused effort by all industry partners, death rates during steel erection have steadily declined over the years. That is a positive example of what can be done to improve safety and health conditions when there is a firm commitment to it.

It was the Department's commitment to improving safety and health conditions in the construction industry that almost 20 years ago led it to create our own non-for-profit institute-CPWR: The Center for Construction Research and Training. CPWR is nationally, and even internationally, recognized as a leading organization in the field on construction safety and health research and training. Through its partnerships with NIOSH, NIEHS, and DOE, CPWR has developed an impressive network of over 30 collaborating organizations, including universities, as part of its national construction safety and health research and training center. Since 1990, the CPWR has been a major participant in the NIOSH construction initiative.

CPWR currently has over 25 construction safety and health research projects underway, mostly involving development of specific interventions for hazards, such as falls and electrocutions. CPWR has developed and delivers an array of construction safety and health training courses to thousands of construction workers every year. CPWR also publishes the Construction Chart Book, now in its 4th edition, a copy of which will be submitted with my written statement. The Chart Book compiles everything there is to know about the U.S. construction industry and its workers based on the national data available to us. It goes into great depth about what we know about construction industry fatalities, injuries, illnesses, and hazards.

As president of the Department, I also serve as president of CPWR. I'm extremely proud of the accomplishments of CPWR over the years. It's one of the most successful public-private partnerships in the construction industry, or any industry for that matter when it comes to occupational safety and health. The National Academy of Sciences reviewed the NIOSH construction program last year. While the Academy's final report has not yet been released, I'm confident that it will point to CPWR's national construction center as a key element of the NIOSH construction research program.

Through the work of CPWR and others we have *characterized the problem* and advanced the *state of knowledge* about construction safety and health significantly over the last two decades. In areas where we have had special emphasis efforts, such as preventing falls and electrocutions, we have seen significant progress over the past 20 years. Unfortunately, that progress in now beginning to be reversed.

Why is the progress being reversed? Research entities can produce useful information, and unions can push for, and even bargain for safety and health provisions as part of the collective bargaining, but both as a legal and practical matter, employers are ultimately responsible for the safety and health of employees, and Occupational Safety & Health Administration (OSHA) is responsible for enforcing construction safety and health laws. In our opinion, both are failing us at this time.

Recommendations

In our opinion, five major actions are urgently needed at this time:

1. We need an OSHA temporary emergency standard requiring that all workers in the industry are trained and certified in accordance with the basic 10-hour OSHA safety and health training program.
2. We need OSHA to promulgate a crane safety standard.
3. OSHA needs to increase enforcement activities.
4. We need a dedicated Construction Occupational Safety and Health Administration, just like we have a dedicated Mine Safety and Health Administration.
5. We need to increase NIOSH's funding for construction safety and health research consistent with the recommendations of the soon-to-be-released National Academies Review.

Two weeks ago over 6,000 construction workers walked off the Las Vegas City Center project after the sixth construction fatality. In negotiations between the general contractor and local construction unions, it was agreed that CPWR would put in place a system to train all site workers at City Center, and the adjacent Cosmopolitan project, in the OSHA 10-hour training program. Our estimate is that approximately two-thirds of the workers on both sites, or roughly 5,000 workers, have not had the basic OSHA 10-hour hazard awareness training. Why? The basic training is voluntary and until now, the contractors did not require it on the site.

This is not unique to these two projects in Vegas, and it brings me to my first point about what needs to be done as a general rule in the construction industry. OSHA needs to promulgate a construction training standard, making it mandatory for every construction worker to have, at a minimum, the basic 10-hour safety and health hazardous awareness training. We've seen several states enact legislation requiring this training, and it's time a rule is enacted at the national level. Surely, requiring that workers engaged in this very hazardous industry have basic safety and health training is not asking for too much.

We also need to take serious steps to change the safety and health culture on construction sites, so everyone participating in the construction process – from the owner to the general contractor and subcontractors to the workers – understands the premium placed on working safely. As a first step in achieving this objective, we call on OSHA to require every construction project to have a written safety program and plan that clearly spells out the safety and health requirements of the site, the respective roles of the OWNER, contractors, subcontractors and employees, and the systems for identifying and minimizing hazards.

Also on the issue of standards, in 2004, a group of labor, industry, and government safety and health professionals reached a consensus on a standard for crane and derrick safety in the construction industry. After four years, OSHA has indicated its plans to publish the standard for public comment in August 2008. OSHA must live up to this commitment, promulgate a final rule, and enforce the new standard.

OSHA enforcement is particularly problematic in construction, due to the transient nature of our industry. About 80% of U.S. construction industry employers have 10 employees or fewer, and over 2 million workers in the U.S. construction industry are classified, or should I say misclassified, as self-employed or independent contractors. OSHA needs to be more innovative in its targeted enforcement activities; compliance operations need to be focused on those issues and violations that are known killers in the construction industry; OSHA needs to redirect the resources allocated to compliance assistance and alliances to enforcement; and OSHA penalties for serious and willful violations need to be enhanced so that there are serious consequences for serious violations of the law, particularly in cases of worker fatalities.

Although there is value in forming partnerships to encourage workplace safety, in my estimation the extensive resources OSHA has devoted to alliances simply means the agency is spending its money on contractors that are already performing at a relatively high level, rather than reaching those medium to small employers that are willingly or unwillingly putting their workers in harm's way.

According to 2006 data, there were a total of 876,229 construction establishments in the United States. In 2007, OSHA data indicates there were 49,666 construction inspections (combining Federal OSHA and State Plans), meaning that it would take OSHA an average of 17.6 years to inspect each construction establishment once. I don't know of many construction projects that last 17.6 years, and I venture to guess that there are thousands of employers in our industry that will never see an OSHA compliance officer.

One has to ask what good are construction industry standards if they are not enforced. Funding is certainly a critical issue, and the Department has long been a proponent of OSHA's budget. However, I am of the mind that, no matter how much funding is appropriated, our current system may simply not work for this industry. I'm sure there are members of this Committee more familiar with the legislative history than I am, but I think we should explore the need for a dedicated Construction Occupational Safety and Health Administration, just like we have a dedicated Mine Safety and Health Administration. In the short term, we need a stronger Construction Directorate Office within OSHA, one that is willing to work with all industry stakeholders, and not just with a selected few.

From before the OSH Act, it has been recognized that the construction industry is different from other industries in many critical aspects. It is very large, and it is very transient and mobile. The worksites are temporary, with many different employers and trades working on them simultaneously. The recognition of the need for special OSHA approaches for this industry also goes back a long way. The Secretary of Labor's Advisory Committee on Construction Safety and Health existed before the OSH Act and was continued after OSHA to make sure that OSHA's rules were responsive to the needs of the industry. In 1994, OSHA established a dedicated Directorate of Construction to make its operations more attuned to the needs of the industry. Both of these have been valuable resources, but they are not enough.

The Building Trades Department and CPWR are committed to improving safety and health conditions for all construction workers. We will continue to develop joint safety and health initiatives with our employers, associations, and owners. We have enjoyed a longstanding partnership with NIOSH, and we have made tremendous strides. Congress needs to increase NIOSH funding for construction safety and health research consistent with the recommendations of the soon-to-be-released National Academies Review.

Twenty years ago there was no research being performed on construction safety and health. Congress corrected that and began to dedicate funding for construction safety and health research at the National Institute for Occupational Safety and Health. By 1995 the budget had increased to $12.1 million, which has remained unchanged in 13 years thereafter. As a consequence, the amount of funding available after adjusting of inflation has significantly eroded the funding. It is today equal to $1 per construction industry worker. That does not say much for the priority that Congress places on construction safety and health.

While it's not our responsibility under the law, it's our obligation as trade unionists and industry leaders to make sure construction workers' rights to a safe and healthy workplace are honored. We can do better. We have to do better.

POSTSCRIPT

Is OSHA Working Effectively to Protect the Safety of Construction Workers?

Former Assistant Secretary of Labor for the Occupational Safety and Health Administration (OSHA) Edwin G. Foulke, Jr., begins his testimony by briefly reviewing the mission and history of OSHA. He then proceeds to describe two of the challenges OSHA faces when it attempts to carry out its mission in the context of the construction industry. First, while the construction industry is large, construction companies are small with few employees. Second, "the work performed at construction sites is highly dynamic, often involving dozens of different employees at a single site." He indicates that OSHA has taken a "multi-faceted approach" to meet these challenges: (i) it focuses on the four most common causes of fatalities in the industry; (ii) it is involved in almost continuous revision and updating of standards; (iii) it is committed to the creation of "meaningful compliance assistance resources"; and (iv) it provides outreach, education, and training. Foulke then makes a series of arguments to support his position that "construction safety is a top priority for OSHA." First, OSHA has a strong enforcement program for construction: in fiscal year 2007 about half of total OSHA inspections were conducted in the construction industry. Second, OSHA has revised its Enhanced Enforcement Program to put more emphasis on employers with a history of violations. Third, OSHA has created a series of special programs to deal with issues such as "fall hazards in construction, mobile crane operations, bridge and tunnel construction, silica and road hazards, falls relating to scaffolding, and energized power lines."

AFL-CIO Building and Construction Trade Department (BCTD) president Mark Ayers starts his testimony by reviewing recent construction worker deaths, including 12 such deaths in Las Vegas. He proceeds to offer more data to support his assertion that the number of construction deaths is "an absolute outrage." Here he notes that on average four construction workers die on the job each day. This is more than 10 times the number of firefighters and 10 times the number of law enforcement officers who are killed in the line of duty. He then describes some of the actions that BCTD has taken to improve construction worker safety, including the creation of the Center for Construction Research and Training. These actions have lead to progress, but Ayers believes that this progress has been reversed. To get things moving in the appropriate direction again, he believes "five major actions are urgently needed at this time." They are (i) OSHA needs to issue a temporary emergency standard requiring all construction workers be trained and certified in accordance with the basic 10-hour OSHA safety and health training program; (ii) OSHA needs to "promulgate a crane safety standard"; (iii) OSHA needs to increase its enforcement activities; (iv) there is a need to create a "dedicated Construction Occupational Safety and Health Administration"; and (v) there is a need for increased funding for construction safety and health research.

For a brief statement of OSHA's mission values and vision see http://www. osha.gov/as/opa/missionposter.html. For more detailed information about OSHA see http://www.osha.gov/Publications/all_about_OSHA.pdf. OSHA's *Fact Book,* which is "intended to report the progress of the Agency's safety and programs and responsibilities," is available at http://www.osha.gov/as/opa/OSHAfact-book-stohler .pdf. For more information about the BCTD see http://www.buildingtrades.org/. The hearings at which Ayers and Foulke testified contain testimony from others, including Robert LiMandri, Building Commissioner for New York City, and Mike Kallmeyer of Denier Electric.

ISSUE 4

Is the New Medicare Part D Drug Benefit Good Health Care Policy?

YES: Mark McClellan, from "Generic Drugs and the Medicare Prescription Drug Benefit," Testimony to the Senate Special Committee on Aging (September 21, 2006)

NO: Jagadeesh Gokhale, from "An Evaluation of Medicare's Prescription Drug Policy," Testimony to the Committee on Homeland Security and Government Affairs Subcommittee on Federal Financial Management, Government Information, and International Security (September 20, 2005)

ISSUE SUMMARY

YES: Health care administrator Mark McClellan believes that the Part D drug benefit is the most important new addition to Medicare in its history, providing millions of Americans with better benefits "at a significantly lower cost than originally estimated."

NO: Cato Institute senior fellow Jagadeesh Gokhale believes that Medicare's Part D drug benefit is a "bad and shortsighted economic policy." He believes this program will, among other things, increase private drug prices, impose higher fiscal burdens on future generations, and reduce national saving and investment.

Medicare came into existence on July 30, 1965, when President Lyndon B. Johnson signed Public Law 98-97. This law amended the Social Security Act by adding Title XVIII, which created Medicare. Medicare can be described, very simply, as a program to provide medical care to the elderly. Generally speaking, persons over age 65 and getting Social Security benefits automatically qualify for Medicare. Public Law 98-97 also added Title XIX or Medicaid, a program designed to help the poor obtain medical care. Thus, this law, by extending the ability of elderly and the poor to obtain medical care, constituted a critical component of President Johnson's Great Society program.

At its creation, Medicare consisted of two major parts. Part A is an insurance program that covers inpatient hospital care, skilled nursing care, and other services. Part B is described as a medical services insurance program and covers physician services, outpatient hospital services, certain home health services, and durable medical equipment. At the end of 2003 Medicare covered 41 million people with annual costs of approximately $280 billion, or about 2.7 percent of U.S. gross domestic product.

On December 8, 2003, President George W. Bush signed the Medicare Prescription Drug Improvement and Modernization Act. This legislation has been described as the most significant change in Medicare since its creation. In particular, it established Part D of Medicare, which is intended to fill an important gap in Medicare's coverage by providing some assistance to seniors for their purchases of prescription drugs. The importance of prescription drugs in modern medicine can hardly be overstated. There are drugs to prevent conception, drugs to promote conception, drugs to battle HIV, drugs to lower cholesterol, and most recently drugs to prevent cancer. The drug industry is large with U.S. sales of approximately $235 billion in 2004, and growing rapidly with 2004 sales over 8 percent higher than 2003.

Part D was designed to relieve a problem for many seniors: the high cost of prescription drugs that are essential to living well, and in some cases, essential simply to living. Part D, or the Medicare Prescription Drug Coverage, began on January 1, 2006. The program, which covers both brand-name and generic drugs, is voluntary. The enrollee must select a drug insurance program from a number offered by a variety of different vendors (the number varies from state to state). The enrollee pays a monthly premium for a basic benefit package (one estimate of the average monthly premium in 2006 was about $35). In addition, the enrollee pays an annual deductible up to $250 (for 2006). There is coinsurance as well. For 2006 the coinsurance was set at 25 percent of the covered drugs between $251 and $2,250; 100 percent of the cost of the covered drugs between $2,251 and $5,100 (this is the so-called donut hole); and 5 percent of the covered drugs above $5,101. The U.S. Department of Health and Human Services estimates that about 53 percent of Medicare beneficiaries now have Part D coverage, 37 percent have some other type of drug coverage, but 10 percent remain without any coverage. Most recent estimates place the cost to the federal government of the program at $30 billion for 2006 and $48 billion for 2007.

This then provides some background on the issue. The debate as framed here considers the broad consequences of Part D. Mark McClellan emphasizes the large number of persons who benefit from the program, while Jagadeesh Gokhale raises concerns about those who do not have drug insurance and future costs.

YES

Mark McClellan

Generic Drugs and the Medicare Prescription Drug Benefit

Chairman Smith, Senator Kohl, distinguished committee members, thank you for the opportunity to provide you with information on how the new Medicare prescription drug benefit (Part D) is helping to encourage generic drug utilization and lower the cost of prescription drugs for people with Medicare, the Medicare program, and taxpayers. I appreciate your interest in this topic, but more importantly, Members of Congress from both parties have been a key part of this massive grassroots education effort put in place to help Medicare beneficiaries select a plan that best fits their needs. Members of Congress have supported and participated in enrollment events sponsored by CMS and our thousands of partners throughout the country, sent flyers to their constituents, and spoken extensively to the public about the value of this new benefit. With the recent launch of this fall's *My Health. My Medicare.* campaign, I expect that this partnership will continue as we begin to drive greater awareness and use of the enhanced preventive benefits and coverage options for 2007.

Improvements made to the drug benefit in 2007 will continue to help beneficiaries save money, in part by increasing awareness about the value of generic drugs. There are a number of tools available to consumers to help them evaluate their options for the new plan year, including enhancements for the Drug Plan Finder, the *Medicare & You Handbook,* and personalized assistance through our 1-800-Medicare call centers and the State Health Insurance Assistance Programs (SHIP). As we change our focus from that of a payer of health benefits to one that promotes steps to stay well and reduce health care costs, we will be educating beneficiaries and partners about the preventive benefits offered in Medicare.

The Part D benefit is the most important new coverage to be added to the Medicare program in its more than 40-year history. It is critical to preventing and managing chronic disease, treating illness, preserving quality of life, and delivering modern medical care in the 21st century. Comprehensive prescription drug coverage is also a key element of our ongoing efforts to transform the emphasis in Medicare from simply paying bills when people get sick to paying for high quality, prevention-oriented care that allows

U.S. Senate, September 21, 2006.

people with Medicare to live healthier lives while avoiding preventable healthcare costs.

Thanks to the enactment of the new Medicare prescription drug benefit, tens of millions of Americans are now getting better benefits from Medicare than ever before and at a significantly lower cost than originally projected. Strong competition in 2006 and well-informed beneficiary choices have resulted in significant savings over what had been previously estimated. Current estimates of the cost of the drug benefit indicate that beneficiaries and the Federal government will be saving tens of billions of dollars more, over the next five years, than had been anticipated just a year ago. Notably, the average Part D premium for 2006, now estimated to be less than $24, is about 35 percent lower than had been projected a year ago. Beneficiaries, the Federal government and the states are all benefiting from lower costs and will continue doing so next year. And even greater savings are ahead in 2007. Based in part on the strong competitive bids for 2007, average premiums will again be around $24 for beneficiaries, and the vast majority of beneficiaries will have access to Medicare drug plans that have lower premiums than those in 2006. In addition, costs to taxpayers may be even lower in 2007 than 2006 because lower bid amounts mean that the Federal government's costs will be commensurately lower.

The utilization of generic drugs has played an important role in the low costs and expected further cost reductions in the drug benefit. Due in part to increasing generic drug availability, strong competition in the prescription drug marketplace has led to slower rates of growth in overall prescription drug spending. Also, the availability of excellent coverage of generic drugs in the Part D drug benefit, as well as personalized information and support to help beneficiaries find out about how they can save using generics, have been important contributors to costs that are much lower than expected. Continuing to promote greater reliance on generics when available among Medicare beneficiaries is an important strategy to keep the new drug benefit affordable over the long term.

Generics Are Widely Available at Low Cost

With ever increasing generic drug availability, more and more Americans are seeing the value of generics and using them to help save money on their prescription drug costs. Roughly three-quarters of the drugs currently listed in the Food and Drug Administration's Orange Book currently have generic counterparts. According to the Generic Pharmaceutical Association (GPhA), U.S. generic pharmaceutical sales increased 10 percent between 2003 and 2004 and amounted to $22.3 billion in 2005; the generic share of the pharmaceutical market is expected to grow by roughly 13 percent in 2006. This growing availability of generics is well accounted for in Medicare Part D, with all stand-alone prescription drug plans and Medicare Advantage Prescription Drug plans (MA-PDs) offering comprehensive, low-cost access to generic pharmaceuticals in 2006. In addition, all Medicare beneficiaries eligible for Medicare Part D had access to at least one prescription drug plan with some coverage in the gap in 2006, including coverage of generics during the gap. And in 2007, even more plans will offer coverage of generics in the gap.

Equally important, and again as a result of strong competition, the cost of generic drugs in the United States is very low and they are relatively widely used. The FDA notes that generic drugs typically cost 50–70 percent less than their brand-name counterparts. Further, prices for generic drugs in the U.S. are much lower than in many other countries. For example, a study by the National Opinion Research Center at the University of Chicago reported that people living in Canada pay 37 percent more for generic drugs than people in the U.S.[1] In addition, generic drugs are more widely used in the U.S. than in other countries, providing further drug cost savings. For example, during 2005, in terms of value, generic drugs accounted for less than 10 percent of the market in Austria, Belgium, Finland, France, Ireland, Italy, Portugal and Spain.[2]

The Medicare prescription drug benefit is reinforcing these trends. Generic drug prices for people with Medicare can be even lower due to the excellent coverage available through Part D. Medicare plans encourage the use of generics with tiered formularies, under which generic drug co-pays are typically far lower than co-pays for brand alternatives. Some Part D plans even offer generics for a $0 copay. As a result of very low prices and information and support for beneficiaries on how they personally can save by using generic versions of their medicines, Medicare Part D has resulted in increased use of generic drugs by Medicare beneficiaries.

The benefits of generic drug use by the Medicare population is clear, and generic drug availability for Medicare beneficiaries will be increasing further, leading to additional savings. The GPhA has indicated that "blockbuster" name-brand pharmaceuticals coming off patent are valued at $22 billion in 2006, $27 billion in 2007, and $29 billion in 2008. For example, Zocor, a cholesterol lowering drug and one of the nation's top sellers, just recently came off patent. An anti-depressant, Zoloft, recently came off patent as well. The patent for a high blood pressure medicine, Norvasc, expires next year, and Advair, an asthma fighter, loses its patent protection in 2008. All told, between 2006 and 2009, there will be a significant number of patent expirations, opening the way for cheaper, generic alternatives.

Under the Medicare Part D program, prescription drug plans are able to add to their formularies at any time, making it simple to pass along to beneficiaries and taxpayers the savings offered by new generics as they become available. CMS takes its role as public health educator seriously; and we are committed to helping health care providers and people with Medicare to understand the value of generics.

Generic Utilization on the Rise

As more widely used branded prescription drugs go off patent and more generics become available, we expect to continue to see generic utilization rise. This will help provide additional savings on prescriptions for beneficiaries, as well as for the Medicare program. In fact, early evidence shows that CMS and its partners' efforts to promote generic utilization are paying off. There are early indications Medicare beneficiaries enrolled in Part D are relying on generics to a greater extent than the U.S. population as a whole. We would expect this utilization trend to continue, as more and more beneficiaries realize the significant savings available by switching to generic drugs.

Nationwide, among all payers, the proportion of generic usage by prescriptions dispensed stands at 51.9 percent. Data recently gathered by CMS show that generic usage among all types of Part D plans was 60.1 percent during the first two quarters of 2006. Notably, Medicare Advantage plans offering drug coverage have achieved an even higher generic utilization rate. We attribute this to their longer experience with providing low-cost drug coverage to the Medicare beneficiaries they serve, and greater experience and ability to help provide well-coordinated, low-cost care for beneficiaries. In addition, many Part D plans are increasing the growth rate of generic utilization at a faster rate than the overall market. One large plan sponsor's generic utilization rate has grown at three times that of the national market.

This is very good news for beneficiaries and for the program. It means that beneficiaries have access to and are using lower-cost alternatives offered by their plans. It also means that our efforts to educate beneficiaries about the cost-saving potential of therapeutic alternatives have been successful and that pharmacists and physicians have the information they need to help beneficiaries make choices about their medications.

The benefit of greater reliance on generics or, in many cases, less expensive brand-name drugs that are equally effective for the same condition and appropriate for the beneficiary is well documented. According to an ongoing CMS analysis of negotiated price discounts available to illustrative beneficiaries under Medicare Part D, when compared to retail prices, such beneficiaries would see savings of up to 74 percent if they joined one of a broad range of lower-cost Part D plans and then switched to generics.[3] When such beneficiaries, who are taking a brand name drug for which there are cheaper brand name drugs that treat the same condition and are clinically appropriate, switch to those cheaper alternatives, their savings increase to 82 percent for the lowest-cost plan and up to 75 percent for a range of low-cost plans. A number of external reports have comparable findings. For example, Consumers Union found that beneficiaries with common chronic conditions who switch to generic or other therapeutically equivalent medications can save between $2,300 and $5,300 a year.[4] These individual savings can add up to billions of dollars in savings across the beneficiary population as a whole.

Similarly, the Pharmaceutical Care Management Association (PCMA) released a study earlier this year indicating that Medicare drug plans offer significant price discounts compared to what beneficiaries would pay without coverage.[5] A recent follow-up PCMA study found that beneficiaries can maximize the already-significant savings noted above by switching to lower-cost medications, such as generics.[6]

Education Helps Beneficiaries Save

Beneficiary and partner education has been an essential component of our strategy to increase the utilization of generic drugs among Medicare beneficiaries, to help them get the most out of their prescription drug coverage. The personalized attention that people found so helpful in making decisions about the new drug benefit has become part of routine business for CMS, and we are going to continue to build on it to ensure that beneficiaries have what they need to make informed choices.

Immediately after the MMA was signed into law in 2003, CMS devised a comprehensive strategy for successful implementation of the Part D benefit by its January 1, 2006 effective date. Educating people with Medicare about the design and availability of the new drug benefit, and developing information and resources to assist them in evaluating numerous plan options were and continue to be among CMS' highest priorities.

Beginning in the fall of 2005, CMS launched a major initiative to educate beneficiaries about Part D, putting into place an outreach and education partnership comprised of more than 20,000 local and national organizations. Forty thousand volunteers staffed more than 50,000 Part D enrollment events across the country. Today, more than 38 million Medicare beneficiaries—over 90 percent of people with Medicare—have prescription drug coverage either through Part D directly, an employer plan that is supported through Part D, or another equivalent source, and satisfaction rates with the Part D prescription drug plans' coverage are very high—over 80 percent.

Improvements for 2007

CMS has a new and more comprehensive approach to beneficiary outreach called *My Health, My Medicare*, which exemplifies the transformation of CMS from an entity which simply pays the bills, to one that promotes quality health care, that provides personalized support to help each of our beneficiaries stay well and lower their health care costs. We have been working to transform our approach at the agency to assisting beneficiaries in achieving this goal over the past few years. As a part of this approach, CMS has developed and enhanced many tools available to provide beneficiaries enrolled in Part D the information they need to achieve maximum savings on their prescription drugs. One of these key tools is the *Medicare & You Handbook* that beneficiaries will receive in October. This year, the Handbook will highlight the preventive services available to people with Medicare, including a wide range of screening services. It has also been revised to enhance information on the benefits of using generic drugs, and to address potential beneficiary concerns about switching from brand name drugs to generics. Additionally, during our outreach events and through our extensive partner network, we are advising beneficiaries that asking their doctor or pharmacist about the generics or lower cost brand name alternatives available for their prescription drug needs can help them delay reaching the coverage gap. This strategy is supported by a recent PCMA study, which found that beneficiaries who use more generic drugs may be able to delay by an average of 74 days or even avoid the coverage gap.[7]

In addition to outreach through partners and special events, CMS developed and maintains a comprehensive resource that beneficiaries can use to find lower-cost drugs covered by their plan: the "Drug Plan Finder" available at . . . . Beneficiaries can use the Plan Finder to search for lower cost alternatives available under a specific plan. When beneficiaries enter their drug regimen in the Plan Finder, the system defaults to provide them information about lower cost generic drugs when they are available, including personalized information on the specific additional estimated savings. In addition, the Plan Finder provides a link to a page that highlights the benefits of generic alternatives. Millions of people have already accessed this site to find information on their options and to help make important choices about their drug coverage based on their preferences. Even beneficiaries who choose a plan with no coverage in the gap can use the Plan Finder to access and compare prices negotiated by their plan on both generics and branded drugs.

In an effort to improve our many resources for beneficiaries, we have made enhancements to the Medicare Drug Plan Finder for 2007. In addition to including call center performance, complaint information and other plan performance information, it will be tightly integrated with the updated Medicare Coverage Options tool, making it easy for people to get personalized comparisons of their health plan choices along with their drug plan options. Users will be able to get estimates for their total annual health costs, and month to month estimated costs, incorporating the latest information on discounted drugs.

Plans, Pharmacists and Physicians Help Beneficiaries Save

In a competitive Part D market with proactive consumers who receive the support they need, Medicare drug plans have shown that competition leads to attractive plan options at competitive prices. Promoting generic utilization through education or by offering coverage for generics through the coverage gap helps plans stay competitive and saves beneficiaries and taxpayers money. This increased availability of plans with some coverage in the gap is good news for beneficiaries, who in 2006 overwhelmingly opted for benefit packages offering predictable coverage this year through features such as gap coverage, fixed co-pays and zero deductibles.

Physicians and pharmacists are important partners in helping beneficiaries get the most from their prescription drug coverage, and CMS truly appreciates their leadership in assisting so many beneficiaries to use their coverage effectively. CMS, Part D plans, pharmacists and physicians are all helping beneficiaries achieve even greater cost savings by educating them about lower-cost alternatives and their money saving potential. CMS has worked closely with physicians to ensure they have the tools and knowledge they need to help their Medicare patients. Among these key tools is a feature on . . . called the Formulary Finder that allows doctors to link directly to a plan's formulary through the Web. Additionally, it is possible for physicians to use handheld and web based clinical reference tools, to access all Medicare Part D formularies, which are being made available for free. This means that any physicians using this approach will have quick access to formulary information, enabling them to make a decision about the potential of a lower-cost prescription while a beneficiary is in their office.

As an important element of Part D implementation, CMS supported the launch of the Pharmacy Quality Alliance (PQA), in partnership with pharmacy organizations, health plans, employers, consumers and many others. This strong and extensive alliance will focus primarily on developing strategies for defining and measuring pharmacy performance. A key step that PQA has taken is to develop an initial set of metrics to measure quality based on available pharmacy claims data. Included in these metrics is an evaluation of generic efficiency and formulary management. More specifics on the results of these evaluations will be available in the fall, and will help CMS promote best practices in pharmacy care—including generic utilization—for the Medicare population and more broadly.

Looking Ahead

Notwithstanding the many successes and high satisfaction with the Part D benefit in 2006, we are confident that even better things are coming in 2007 as a result of strong competition and enhanced benefit choices. More plans will be offering coverage in the gap, and lower-cost options will be available for most beneficiaries everywhere. Additional enhanced plan options enable beneficiaries to obtain more stable monthly costs throughout the year. And, with the average bids for 2007 almost 10 percent lower than in 2006, Part D will have lower Federal costs, making the program more stable and affordable over time. These cost savings are due in no small part to tough plan negotiation for lower drug prices and effective use of generics that cost much less than the drugs seniors may have used in the past.

Conclusion

Chairman Smith and Senator Kohl, thank you again for inviting me to speak with you today about generic drug utilization and how we can work to continue providing a high quality, low cost prescription drug benefit for Medicare beneficiaries. The drug benefit provides important new coverage for people with Medicare, and generic alternatives serve as an important and safe way to save a lot of money for both beneficiaries and the Medicare program.

CMS is working hard to make sure that everyone with Medicare has the tools and knowledge to make the most of their Medicare coverage. This means receiving high quality benefits at the lowest possible cost. We will continue to work to meet the health needs of beneficiaries by building on the strong partnerships that are helping to make the Medicare prescription drug program a success.

Notes

1. Understanding Variations in International Drug Prices. National Opinion Research Center (NORC) at the University of Chicago and Georgetown University. July 2006.

2. See . . .

3. CMS Office of Policy, Analysis of Savings Available Under Medicare Prescription Drug Plans, June 20, 2006.

4. "Helping Medicare Beneficiaries Lower Their Out-of-Pocket Costs Under the New Prescription Drug Benefit," Consumer's Union, December 14, 2005. As CMS has noted, beneficiaries should discuss any therapeutic changes with their physician and pharmacist, and the personalized information we provide can help inform those discussions.

5. "Medicare Drug Discounts Real & Holding Steady," Pharmaceutical Care Management Association, February 7, 2006.

6. "Potential Beneficiary Savings Associated with Generics & Mail-Service Pharmacies for Five Conditions Chronic to Seniors," Pharmaceutical Care Management Association, September 7, 2006.

7. Pharmaceutical Care Management Association, "Potential Beneficiary Savings Associated with Generics & Mail-Service Pharmacies For Five Conditions Common to Seniors," September 7, 2006.

Jagadeesh Gokhale  **NO**

An Evaluation of Medicare's Prescription Drug Policy

Chairman Coburn, Senator Carper, members of the Committee, thank you for the opportunity to testify on the Medicare Prescription Drug Program. I feel very honored by it.

I especially appreciate this opportunity because no policy issue appears more vital than how to preserve the efficient operation of health care markets to pay for our growing health care needs. It is well known that designing policies to improve health-care market efficiency is difficult. But it is not yet widely appreciated how huge Medicare's future financial shortfall is. The Medicare Prescription Drug Improvement and Modernization Act of 2003 (MMA) substantially increases that shortfall and is likely to worsen the operation of markets for prescription drugs and drug insurance. As such it deserves urgent reconsideration—a view that is shared by many health care experts and policymakers including, I suspect, by members of this Committee.

MMA offers prescription drug coverage to all retirees. The new law will benefit seniors on the whole but will exert several negative economic effects:

Five issues stand out:

- Government intervention is usually justified when private markets fail. With 75 percent of retirees already having prescription drug coverage and 90 percent having access to prescription drugs prior to MMA, this market did not exhibit the symptoms of "market failure." Indeed, passage of MMA is likely to cause market failure by displacing the private market's provision of drug insurance.
- MMA will improve access to prescription drugs for poorer retirees— both those who are and those who are not currently covered under Medicaid. Well-to-do retirees will also benefit in general but some may experience higher out-of-pocket costs if they lose their private drug coverage and are forced to enroll into Medicare Part D. This law, therefore, appears designed to first displace the private market followed by sustained pressure on Congress to liberalize the MMA's benefit formula over time.
- MMA will influence prescription drug prices in the private market as the share of government-subsidized purchasers expands. Theoretical reasoning and empirical studies suggest that private drug prices would increase with additional government-subsidized patients entering the

U.S. Senate, September 20, 2005.

market. Most of the burden of this increase will fall on workers by making employer-provided health insurance or private plans more expensive. That will reduce younger workers' likelihood of employment, cause lower wage growth, increase conversion from full- to part-time jobs, and reduce work effort.

- MMA makes a large addition to the already considerable financial shortfall in the rest of Medicare. Unresolved, this shortfall will grow larger and impose higher fiscal burdens on future generations, further eroding their productivity and work incentives.

- MMA will change workers' and younger generations' perceptions about the need to save for health-care expenses during retirement. Studies show that expansion in government entitlement obligations leads to higher consumption and reduces national saving and investment—delivering a further negative impact on future worker productivity and output.

MMA was hastily passed without a proper evaluation of its short- and long-term cost and it lacks appropriate measures to control spending escalations. That means future Congresses may be induced to regulate the actions of pharmacies, drug manufacturers, employers, and plan providers with regard to drug pricing and spending per person on prescription drugs. Such regulations would be counterproductive because they would restrict prescription drug supply, generate illegal prescription drug sales, and reduce the quality of prescription drug coverage for everyone—and not just for retirees.

If MMA cannot be repealed, a financially and economically sensible course would be to scale it back to a sustainable level by providing coverage only to those seniors who are under financial pressure on account of their prescription drug expenses. That effort needs to be combined with restoring the rest of Medicare to financial sustainability.

II. Pre-MMA Prescription Drug Coverage of Retirees

Prior to MMA's enactment, Medicare Parts A and B provided no limits on out-of-pocket costs and did not insure retirees against outpatient prescription drug expenses.

The vast majority of retirees (75 percent) had prescription drug coverage under private plans: Employer supplemental health coverage (33 percent), Medicaid and state drug programs (17 percent), Medicare + Choice Plans (15 percent), Medigap policies with prescription drug coverage (2 percent) or other sources (8 percent). New retirees were guaranteed access to 10 alternative Medigap plans, three of which covered prescription drugs.

Some retirees, however, faced financial pressure on account of their prescription drug costs: Estimates as of 2000 suggest that average out of pocket costs for retirees in poor health took up about 44 percent of their incomes. Low-income single women not covered under Medicaid spent about 52 percent of their incomes on health expenses, on average.

Enrollment into Medigap plans including prescription drug coverage has been quite low. Such plans impose spending caps and so do not cover catastrophic expenses. Their high premiums, deductibles and cost-sharing requirements make them expensive and their availability varies widely by geographic area. Premium inflation among plans with prescription drug coverages has been very rapid. The plans also provided first-dollar coverage that discouraged prudent use of services and prescription drugs.

These features made Medigap policies inferior to employer supplemental coverage, which generally had low co-insurance requirements, no separate spending caps for prescription drugs, and drug prices after negotiated discounts. Employer plans also do not provide first-dollar coverage, thus promoting prudent use of health services including prescription drugs.

III. MMA, the Drug Market, and Retiree Prescription Drug Coverage

Drug treatments are becoming standard practice treating chronic conditions. Greater intensity of use of existing drugs and the development of new and more effective, but also more expensive, drugs have increased the entire population's dependence on drugs therapies. Higher drug development costs and higher demand for drug treatments have caused drug prices to grow rapidly.

1. Is There "Market Failure" in the Prescription Drug Marketplace?

Data (cited earlier) show that a significant share of retirees already had access to prescription drugs and drug insurance. About 90 percent of seniors reported taking at least 1 prescription drug. Thus, MMA represents an increase in government intervention in prescription drug and drug insurance markets where there was no prior market failure.

Whether the provision of a good or service is financed by the government or through private markets makes a large difference to whether the economy's scarce resources are allocated efficiently. Efficient allocation of resources implies their use in meeting the most important needs first—as signaled by peoples' willingness to pay.

It is well known that government intervention replaces resource allocation through competitive forces by allocation through fiat. Because the government does not maximize profits, federal price setting and resource allocation decisions are not based on market signals of efficient resource use. The usual result is a loss in economic efficiency. That will happen to the prescription drug and drug insurance markets because of MMA.

That does not necessarily mean that market outcomes are fully acceptable. If there is considerable inequality of wealth or of needs among individuals, market operation will provide goods and services to the rich, whereas the poor will be unable to make their demands effective. Because such outcomes may be socially unacceptable, government intervention could be justified—but only at the margin—to assist those in need of subsidies because of economic misfortunes.

A study based on 2003 data indicates that only 25 percent of retirees reported forgoing medications due to high costs. The most vulnerable categories of retirees on account of prescription drug expenses are those without any drug insurance (50 percent spending $100 or more on prescription drugs), those in low-income groups (34 percent spending more than $100 per month) and those with three or more chronic conditions (42 percent spending more than $100 per month).

It is usually difficult to demarcate the appropriate extent of government intervention on account of wealth inequality. MMA clearly oversteps all reasonable limits, however, because it provides a broad drug subsidy to all retirees regardless of their economic status, previous access to prescription drug coverage, and prescription drug needs.

MMA's generosity will significantly worsen the economy's ability to allocate resources efficiently—directly by reducing the size of the private market, increasing drug prices, imposing larger than necessary tax burdens on current and future productive citizens, and indirectly by reducing their ability and willingness to save and invest for the future.

2. Who Will Benefit From MMA?

Dual eligible beneficiaries—those eligible for both Medicaid and Medicare coverage—will now receive drug coverage through Medicare. The lowest income beneficiaries among them will receive premium and cost-sharing subsidies as well—and would have to pay out-of-pocket only for nominal drug co-payments. Low-income cost-sharing support would be phased out for families with higher income and assets.

Dual beneficiaries will not lose the value of their coverage. Indeed, their drug coverage is likely to become more generous under Medicare Part D compared to Medicaid—especially as state budget problems increase the likelihood of stricter future cost containment measures under Medicaid. Several states already regulate the number of prescriptions filled per period, the number of allowable refills, size of dosages, and drug dispensing frequencies etc. These limitations will be disallowed when dual-eligible beneficiaries are shifted to Medicare Part D—making their prescription drug coverage more valuable.

Many states facing budget pressures are likely to increase their cost-sharing requirements in the future making Medicaid benefits less valuable. Hence, taxpayer costs of covering dual eligibles' drug insurance may be higher under Medicare Part D because Medicaid savings "clawed back" by the federal government are likely to be smaller than the actual costs saved.

In addition, MMA will benefit seniors with poor health and considerable dependence on costly prescription drugs—including those who purchase Medigap plans offering prescription drug coverage. As mentioned earlier, such plans' premiums, deductibles, and cost-sharing requirements can amount to thousands of dollars. In contrast, Medicare Part D's co-insurance rates are only 5 percent beyond expenditures exceeding $5,100. For example, under Medigap plan J, retirees must spend $6,250 out of pocket to attain the maximum benefit of $3,000 (implying total annual health care spending of $9,250). In contrast,

Medicare Part D's cost-sharing formula would pick-up $5,059 of spending up to $9,250 leaving the beneficiary better off by $2,058 per year.

Medicare Part D will also benefit those retirees who choose to purchase Medigap plans without prescription drug coverage because they face restrictive choices among available plans. Such purchasers constitute the vast majority of Medigap clients.

3. Some Retirees May Pay More in the Long-Term

Generally, employer provided retiree health coverage is broad, includes comprehensive drug coverage, requires low co-pay and co-insurance rates, and does not impose separate caps on drug expenses. In contrast, Medicare Part D premium, deductible, and co-insurance costs will be substantial for those with drug expenses up to $5,100 per year. Hence, during the short-term many retirees may choose to remain under employer-provided prescription drug insurance.

Over the long-term, however, MMA is likely to induce employers and other private providers to restrict or eliminate retiree drug coverage. Those covered under such plans would then be forced to sign up for Medicare Part D and could face larger out-of-pocket costs—unless they qualify for additional low-income subsidies. This is likely to increase political pressure to shrink or eliminate the "donut-hole" in the benefit formula. That, in turn, could prompt yet more seniors to drop their private coverage and enroll into Medicare Part D, increasing the program's already high overall costs.

Thus, although retirees as a whole would gain considerably, on net, from the implementation of MMA, some retirees may become worse off over the long-term if employers cut costs by dropping retiree drug coverage. That means some of MMA's benefit won't stay with retirees but flow through to employers. Employers' overall gains could be limited, however, as prescription drug usage expands and drug prices increase. Those effects would increase the cost of providing health care insurance to workers.

IV. MMA's Impact on the Private Drug Market

The government already subsidizes prescription drug use by Medicaid patients. The federal subsidy is provided through the states' Medicaid programs. States possess set drug reimbursement rates within but must adhere to federally specified upper-payment limits. Drug reimbursement rates to providers, however, must be set to ensure drug provision consistent with the provision of other complementary medical services within each state. Rates must also ensure that comparable service levels [are] available to those eligible for Medicaid in all states.

Drug prices and federal and state drug spending under Medicaid has escalated recently because of increased drug use and availability of new, effective, but more expensive drugs for replacing traditional medical treatments. Because prices of established drugs are not allowed to rise by more than the Consumer Price Index, manufacturers have set high initial prices for drugs that are technically "new" but work very much like older versions already on the market.

The entry of sizable additional government-subsidized patients (retirees) in the drug market means either that drug manufacturers must ramp up drug production or substitute sales to Medicare in place of sales to private purchasers including drug exports.

Some studies have estimated that post-MMA increases in drug demand would be small. But they assume that those who already purchase prescription drugs will not change their use of prescription drugs. That assumption defies past experience.

Those who lack coverage today would increase their drug usage as they obtain insurance against out-of-pocket costs. So also would those with very high dependence on prescription drugs because MMA reduces their cost-sharing expenses. In addition, MMA is likely to reduce state restrictions on drug usage for dual-eligibles—whose drug costs would now be met through Medicare Part D. And doctors will hesitate less in prescribing drugs now that their retiree patients have acquired access to a new "third party" payer.

As mentioned earlier, drug usage intensity is likely to increase as MMA expands retiree budgets for prescription drugs. Consequently, the demand for drugs is likely to increase considerably and will likely cause higher-than-projected program outlays.

If manufacturers can increase drug production without significant additional costs it may be feasible to accommodate the additional demand without significant price increases. However, in a competitive marketplace where manufacturers must accept the highest price offers first, pharmacies and, in turn, the federal government may have to increase offer prices to manufacturers to obtain additional drug supplies for their new Medicare patients. In that case, prices charged in the private market must also increase and the size of the private drug market must become smaller. Thus, theoretically, an increase in the drug market share of government patients would increase drug prices and shrink the private drug market.

This theoretical expectation is supported by empirical evidence on the relationship between the government's share in particular drug markets and the private market prices of those drugs. A study covering 200 drugs during 1997 and 2001 found that government participation in the drug market through Medicaid significantly increased drug prices faced by non-government payers. An increase in the government's market share by 10 percent was found to be associated with a 10 percent increase in the drug's price. This finding remains true despite the addition of several controlling factors such as drug therapeutic classes, the existence of generics, the number of close substitutes, and the time since the drug's first introduction.

Considering Medicaid's market share in the top 200 drugs, the study suggests that private-market drug prices would have been lower by 13.3 percent, on average, in the absence of Medicaid. Greater intensity of drug use by retirees would, therefore, imply yet higher prescription drug prices. Thus, with federal drug insurance guaranteed to all retirees, the higher drug prices will negatively impact workers through employer-sponsored or privately provided health plans. As a consequence, employers may seek to cut back on wages, reduce workers' health-care coverage, increase health-insurance premiums, or convert full-time jobs to part-time positions that do not provide health benefits.

Another recent study documents that higher health insurance costs are taking a heavy toll on workers. Each 10 percent hike in health insurance costs reduces the likelihood of being employed by 1.6 percent, and cuts hours worked by 1 percent. Workers whose health insurance is maintained are forced to accept smaller wage gains: A 10 percent increase in premiums is offset by a 2.3 percent decrease in wages.

The prior study also demonstrates that the government's drug rebate program operated for Medicaid—that limits established drugs' price increases to no more than the Consumer Price Index—leads to larger manufacturer incentives to introduce new drugs with slight performance enhancements but with initial prices set at much higher levels to compensate for the federal drug rebate program.

V. MMA's Financial Implications for Workers and Future Generations

CMS estimates that Medicare Part D's unfunded obligation (future outlays less enrollee premiums and cost-sharing) is zero. However, CMS assumes that Congress will continue to authorize general revenue transfers to Medicare Part D as and when needed to bridge the gap between outlays and enrollee premiums. In present discounted value, total future general-revenue infusions required are estimated at $18.2 trillion. That is, Medicare Part D promises to provide net benefits to current and future generations of retirees to the tune of $18.2 trillion in excess of the premiums they will pay for enrollment into Medicare Part D.

According to CMS, Medicare's Parts A and B combined are estimated to require total financial infusions of almost $50 trillion in present value to meet benefit costs under current laws. MMA's enactment has, therefore, increased Medicare's fiscal burden on current and future taxpayers to $68.1 trillion. The additional charge on federal general revenues from the new drug program is significantly higher than Social Security's future financial shortfall—estimated by Social Security's Trustees to be $11.2 trillion.

An $18.2 trillion figure is better understood as a share of the present value of GDP from which it must be financed. According to CMS's projections, that share equals 1.9 percent. That is, MMA commits 1.9 percent of all future GDP to funding seniors' drug coverage.

Because, the entire GDP is not (and will never be) subject to taxes, it is more instructive to compare MMA's general revenue charge to the present value of the future income tax base from which all federal general receipts are drawn. Unfortunately, there is no official estimate of the present value of the income tax base. However, if future taxable (personal and corporate) income averages about 55 percent of GDP—its current ratio—Medicare Part D's $18.2 trillion charge on general revenues would equal 3.5 percent of the present value of the income tax base.

Because Medicare Part D is not financed out of a dedicated revenue sources, it is impossible to know when the implied fiscal burden—either higher taxes or federal spending cuts—would be imposed. It is also impossible to know how this fiscal burden will be distributed across different income groups and across living and future generations.

The calculation of MMA's fiscal burden above involves a critical assumption: That GDP and the tax base will remain unchanged despite the imposition of higher taxes or spending cuts. However, higher taxes will adversely impact work incentives and spending cuts may degrade critical economic infrastructure, both of which would adversely affect productivity. Thus, financing the $18.2 trillion charge on general revenues is likely to require an income tax-rate increase exceeding 3.5 percentage points because the "feedback" effect of financing MMA benefits through higher taxes on national output would reduce future national output.

VI. The Impact of MMA on National Saving

The difference between what current generations earn by way of income each year and their annual consumption determines how many resources are saved and invested. The more current generations consume, the less is available for investment. The $18.2 trillion estimate of the present value of Part D benefit encompasses the entire future without a time limit. That is, it includes benefits that will accrue to future generations.

Unborn generations, obviously, do not consume out of current income. The impact of Medicare Part D's net benefit on current consumption depends on the share of it accruing to those alive today. The Medicare program's Trustees' have estimated that federal general revenue infusions into Medicare Part D will equal $8.7 trillion through the year 2079. Of this, $6.7 trillion will be on account of those alive today. That is, today's retirees and workers (those aged 15 and older) can, under MMA, expect to receive from the federal government $6.7 trillion dollars on net by way of prescription drug coverage.

As the drug law is implemented and as today's generation's expectations regarding their drug benefits become firmer, they will perceive an improvement in their total wealth position. Their natural response to higher perceived wealth would be to increase their consumption. As a consequence, national saving would decline.

Evidence from survey data confirms that retirees increase their consumption in response to receipt of additional entitlement benefits. Figure 1 [omitted] shows consumption indices by age derived from the Consumer Expenditure Surveys for four periods: 1960–61, 1972–73, 1984–87 and 1987–90. In each period, the consumption per capita of all age groups is shown relative to the consumption of a contemporaneous 30-year-old person—whose consumption index is set equal to 1 in each of the four periods.

The figure shows that consumption per capita of 70-year-olds in 1960–61 fell short of 30-year-olds' consumption per capita in the same period by 29 percent. However, by 1987–90, 70-year-olds consumed 18 percent more per capita than 30-year-olds in the same period. More recent data also show the same pattern of increasing consumption levels by retirees relative to the consumption of their younger contemporaries.

One of the most important elements driving the change in relative consumption patterns by age appears to be the change in the pattern of resource ownership by age. The expansion of federal benefits by way of growing Social Security and Medicare outlays have transferred resources from workers to retirees during the past four decades. That process is continuing today with liberalized Social Security benefits and the enactment of new entitlement benefits—such as Medicare Part D.

Those transfers have increased retirees' command over resources relative to those available to younger generations. Figure 2 [omitted] shows total resource indices by age for the same four periods, where total resources include current net worth per capita and present values per capita of life-time earnings, pensions, and government transfers from all programs.

Figure 2 shows that retirees' had more resources at their disposal compared to their younger counterparts' resources in 1987–90 than did retirees in 1961–62. The passage of MMA will continue the trend of increasing retiree resources relative to those of workers and younger generations. As a result, consumption by retirees is likely to increase and national saving will continue to decline.

How large would be the impact of MMA's cross-generation resource redistribution on saving? A Congressional Budget Office study reviewed academic literature on this question and concluded that for every $1 increase in federal unfunded entitlement obligations, current national saving declines by between 0 and 50 cents.

That range indicates the considerable uncertainty surrounding such estimates. However, it suggests that the best estimate of the MMA's impact on national saving is negative. Taking the mid-point of the range of estimates, national saving may be expected to cumulatively decline by $1.7 trillion by the time today's workers achieve retirement age. That is, by 2079, the national capital stock would erode by $1.7 trillion and future Americans' income and living standards would decline correspondingly.

MMA subsidizes retirees' prescription drug expenses but will probably lead to considerable economic inefficiency. It will improve prescription drug coverage for low-income seniors who were previously covered under Medicaid. It is also likely to benefit low-income seniors without Medicaid coverage and those with high drug expenses. It will also provide a substantial subsidy for those seniors previously covered against drug expenses under a Medigap policy. However, out-of-pocket costs of those seniors previously covered under an employer-provided prescription drug plan are likely to increase as employers increase their premiums to soak up the subsidy or reduce, possibly drop, their coverage completely leaving retirees to foot MMA's premiums and cost-sharing expenses.

MMA will increase the share of government-subsidized patients in the market for prescription drugs. That is likely to shrink the share of privately purchased drugs via higher drug prices. The adverse impact will mostly be on workers as the cost of employer provided health insurance plans increases. That will trigger lower employment, slower wage growth, reduced hours worked, and conversion of more full-time jobs to part-time jobs.

MMA's long-term costs represent a massive addition to the already steep fiscal burdens implicit in current Medicare Part A and Part B policies. This massive cost must eventually be met via tax increases or cuts in other federal spending such as defense, infrastructure, education, social welfare programs, R&D and so on. Meeting future health-care needs as projected under current policies through tax increases alone appears infeasible as higher tax burdens erode work incentives, lower employment, reduce national output and the tax base—requiring yet higher tax rates to draw the necessary revenues.

Past experience indicates that redistributing sizable amounts of resources from workers and future generations toward retirees will erode national saving and investment, and increase our dependence on foreign savings. Implementing MMA will induce a similar intergenerational redistribution of resources, causing higher consumption by retirees and reducing national saving. This is likely to further reduce worker productivity and exacerbate the output-reducing effects of higher taxes.

Overall, MMA is a bad and shortsighted economic policy. This program needs to be re-evaluated and recalibrated from its current focus on covering all retirees regardless of their health-care costs and ability to pay for prescription drugs. It should be refocused on those retirees who most need financial support against prescription drug expenses.

POSTSCRIPT

Is the New Medicare Part D Drug Benefit Good Health Care Policy?

Mark McClellan begins his testimony before the Senate Special Committee on Aging by asserting that Medicare's Part D is "critical to preventing and managing chronic disease, treating illness, preserving quality of life, and delivering modern medical care in the twenty-first century." He gives the new program high marks for at least three reasons. First, the costs of the program, including insurance premiums and cost to taxpayers, have been lower than expected; for example, premiums for 2006 were about 35 percent lower than initially expected. The reasons for the lower cost include greater use of generic drugs and strong competition within the drug marketplace. Second, drug coverage has been extended, either through Part D, an employer drug plan, or some equivalent source, to 90 percent of Medicare beneficiaries. Third, those participating in Part D are happy with their drug plans: "satisfaction rates with the Part D prescription drug plans' coverage are very high—over 80 percent." Although improvements can be made in the program, it is a high-quality, low-cost benefit for Medicare beneficiaries.

In his Senate testimony Jagadeesh Gokhale argues for the repeal of the Medicare Prescription Drug Program (MMA) or at least a significant recalibration "from its current focus on covering all retirees." Gokhale rests his position on what he sees as five major negative effects of MMA. First, the new program is likely to displace the private market in the provision of drug insurance. Second, as the government program expands, there will be demands that Congress provide ever increasing benefits. Third, with government-subsidized patients entering the market, private drug prices will increase. Fourth, Part D will generate a significant increase in Medicare deficits. Fifth, there will be lower saving and investment because Part D will change worker and younger people's "perceptions about the need to save for health-care expenses during retirement." In short, MMA is bad policy.

The literature on MMA and Part D can be divided into two parts. One part of the literature tries to explain this complex piece of legislation and the various drug insurance plans that it has created. One place to start in looking for this information is the U.S. Department of Health and Human Resources Prescription Drug Coverage site: http://www.medicare.gove/pdphome .asp. Another site is provided by the U.S. Pharmacist at http://www.uspharamacist .com/index.asp?page=ce/105381/default.in. The second part of the literature concentrates on evaluations of MMA and Part D. The best single source of alternative assessments involves testimony given by several individuals before the House Committee on Ways and Means on June 14, 2006. This can be accessed at http://waysandmeans.house.gov/hearings.asp.

ISSUE 5

Are Health Savings Accounts Working Effectively?

YES: **American Benefits Council**, from "Statement before the Subcommittee on Health of the House Committee on Ways and Means" (May 14, 2008)

NO: **Linda J. Blumberg**, from "Testimony before the Subcommittee on Health of the House Committee on Ways and Means" (May 14, 2008)

ISSUE SUMMARY

YES: The American Benefits Council, a national trade association, believes that "HSAs are working as intended" for the vast majority of the 6.1 million Americans covered by "HSA-eligible plans."

NO: Linda J. Blumberg, Urban Institute research associate, identifies a number of problems associated with medical care and argues that "HSAs are not the solutions to these pressing national concerns."

Evaluations of the health care sector of the U.S. economy usually take one of two approaches. In one approach, analysts and commentators point to the advances in health care produced by the U.S. economy: miracle drugs, path breaking surgical procedures, new diagnostic machinery, and so on. This approach suggests that American medicine is the best in the world. The second approach takes a cost–benefit position and yields a less optimistic assessment. The analysts and commentators using this approach note that the United States spends more on health care than any other country in the world, an estimated 15 percent of gross domestic product. But the results are considered mediocre at best: 36 countries have both lower infant mortality rates and higher life expectancy than the United States (see GeographyIQ at http://www.geographyiq.com/index.htm).

While the analysts and commentators may be undecided about the right approach for the evaluation of the health care sector, most would agree that the sector does not operate as efficiently as it should. In particular, they point to health insurance and the extensive use of third-party payment of health expenses, arguing that even with deductibles and coinsurance, there is little incentive for the typical health care consumer to "comparison shop." In short, there would be a bigger bank for the medical buck if health care consumers had more incentive to spend their health care dollars in the same way they spend their dollars on housing, on automobiles, and on computers—seeking out low-cost providers and using medical health care resources only when they are needed. The question, then, is how to create these incentives and induce greater efficiency in the health care sector.

The Bush administration promotes one answer: health savings accounts (HSAs). These accounts were created on December 8, 2003, when President Bush signed the Medicare Prescription Drug, Improvement, and Modernization Act. How do HSAs work? First, a consumer must purchase an inexpensive health insurance plan that has a high deductible. Then the consumer can open an HSA account at a financial institution, contributing a particular amount to the account. Initially the limit on the amount that could be contributed to an HSA was 100 percent of the insurance's deductible. This was changed in 2006, and in 2008 the cap was $5,800 for family policies and $2,900 for a single person. These contributions are done on a tax-preferred basis. Withdrawals from the account are tax-exempt if they are spent on out-of-pocket medical expenses, and unused funds can be rolled over from one year to the next. If the money is withdrawn from an HSA and not spent on medical expenses, it is subject to income tax and a 10 percent penalty. The tax and penalty do not apply for persons 65 and older. As described by the U.S. Treasury:

> You own and control the money in your HSA. Decisions on how to spend the money are made by you without relying on a third party or a health insurer. You will also decide what types of investments to make with the money in your account in order to make it grow.

The debate on HSAs did not end with their creation in 2003. This issue examines alternative evaluations of the effectiveness of HSAs and suggestions for change. The American Benefits Council supports HSAs, while Linda J. Blumberg offers a number of criticisms.

YES

Statement before the Subcommittee on Health of the House Committee on Ways and Means

The American Benefits Council (the "Council") appreciates the opportunity to submit this written statement to the Subcommittee regarding the increasing utilization and effectiveness of health savings accounts ("HSAs") and high deductible health plans ("HDHPs"). The Council is a national trade association representing principally Fortune 500 companies and other organizations that either sponsor or administer health and retirement benefit plans covering more than 100 million Americans.

HSAs are a fairly new health coverage option for American families, having been established by Congress in 2003 as part of the Medicare Modernization Act. Nevertheless, for millions of Americans, HSAs have already become an important tool in securing essential health coverage for themselves and their families. Early data from the Government Accounting Office ("GAO") and other third parties is encouraging, indicating that HSAs are working as intended for the vast majority of Americans who use them. HSA/HDHP arrangements can provide vital "first-dollar" medical coverage for accountholders (and their spouses and qualifying dependents), while utilizing important cost-sharing principles to help lower health coverage costs generally for individuals and employers alike. It is critical that we allow this important new health care option to fully develop and that we permit comprehensive data to be collected on the role it can play in providing quality health care at an affordable price. Any actions to apply new restrictions or burdens on this option would be premature and would risk eliminating a health care tool already being successfully used by millions of Americans.

The following is a summary of our comments:

- Health savings accounts have become an increasingly important tool for millions of Americans in securing lower cost, high-quality medical coverage. Recent data compiled by GAO indicates that an estimated 6.1 million Americans were covered by HSA/HDHP arrangements as of January 2008.

U.S. House of Representatives, May 14, 2008, excerpts.

- Early data and testimony before the Subcommittee on May 14, 2008, indicate that the vast majority of HSAs include comprehensive "first-dollar" preventive care coverage and that HSAs can succeed in reducing health care costs for American families, while also resulting in increased wellness and quality of care.
- Recent data strongly indicates that participants have sufficient HSA assets to meet actual out-of-pocket expenses under HDHPs, and (i) HSA withdrawals are being used principally for current-year qualified medical expenses, and (ii) HSAs, rather than being used primarily by high-income individuals as a tax shelter, are being used by individuals at a broad range of income levels. For example, one survey found that 45% of all HSA enrollees in 2005 had annual incomes of $50,000 or less, and there are good reasons to believe that this percentage may be even higher today.
- Current rules regarding HSA substantiation are consistent with the treatment afforded other special purpose accounts and health tax provisions. As discussed below, there are *numerous* instances under the Internal Revenue Code ("Code") where amounts withdrawn from a special purpose account are *not* subject to mandatory third-party FSA-like substantiation rules. Similarly, the general approach toward health expenditures under federal tax law does *not* require third-party substantiation for an individual to obtain a specific income tax deduction or other tax-favored treatment.
- Imposing third-party substantiation requirements on HSAs is not appropriate, will increase costs for HSA accountholders and limit options for health coverage at a time when such options should be expanded. The Council urges members of the Subcommittee, and members of Congress more generally, to oppose the imposition of third-party substantiation requirements on HSAs, such as the requirements included in H.R. 5719 (the "Taxpayer Assistance and Simplification Act of 2008").

HSAs Are an Increasingly Important Component to Many American Families' Health Coverage

Recent data compiled by GAO indicates that the number of Americans covered by HSA-eligible plans increased from 438,000 in September 2004 to an estimated 6.1 million in January 2008.[1] This represents a 1,400% increase in their use in just over three years. Moreover, a recent study by America's Health Insurance Plans ("AHIP") found that HSA-usage increased by 35% in the 12-month period from January 2007 to January 2008.[2] American families and workers are indisputably turning to HSAs in increasing numbers to help control their ever-rising health coverage costs.

Early data also indicates that the increased use of HSAs is broad-based. Specifically, recent survey data by AHIP indicates that of those individuals covered by HSAs, 30% were in the small group market, 45% in the large group market, and 25% in the individual market.[3] In addition, it is very significant that the greatest growth in the HSA/HDHP market is in the small plan market, where health care coverage has been a constant public policy challenge.[4]

HSAs Can Reduce Health Costs and Improve Quality of Care

In this era of ever-rising health care costs – costs that continue to well outpace general inflation as measured by the Consumer Price Index ("CPI") – American workers and their employers continue to look for ways to help rein in these costs without negatively affecting health standards and quality of care. As Michael Chernew, Professor of Health Care Policy for Harvard Medical School, testified, cost sharing can reduce excess utilization and health expenditures generally, and HSA/HDHP coverage utilizes certain cost-sharing principles like upfront deductibles and copayments to help reduce excess utilization.[5]

Testimony from Wayne Sensor, CEO of Alegent Health, also provides a first-hand example of how HSA/HDHP coverage can both reduce costs *and* lead to increased health standards and quality of care. Specifically, Mr. Sensor testified that "there is a significantly higher level of engagement among those participants [in one of our HSA plans]." He stated that HSA participants "consume more preventive care than any other plan we offer," and that "[m]ore than 45% of HSA participants completed their health risk assessments, compared to just 16% in our PPO plan." On top of all of this, he noted that "[f]rom 2006 to 2007, the cost trend in our two HSA plans declined a full 15%!"[6]

Mr. Sensor's testimony is supported by findings from another study performed by HealthPartners. This study found that the cost of care for participants in HSAs and health reimbursement arrangements ("HRAs") was 4.4% lower than for those individuals with traditional low-deductible coverage.[7] The study also found that the cost savings did not impair the standard of care and that the utilization of preventive care services and medication for chronic illness was equivalent to that of individuals covered under more traditional low-deductible plans.

Data Indicates HSA/HDHP Coverage Utilizes Important "First-Dollar" Preventive Care Coverage

As Mr. Sensor's first-hand experience at Alegent Health demonstrates, HSA/HDHP coverage, if structured correctly, can achieve its intended result – providing quality care to Americans and their families at reduced costs. One component of successful HSA/HDHP coverage appears to be the inclusion of "first-dollar" preventive care coverage. A survey by AHIP last year showed that recommended preventive care is covered on a "first-dollar" basis by the vast majority of HSA/HDHP products.[8] Overall, the survey found that 84% of HSA/HDHP plans purchased in the group and individual markets provide "first-dollar" coverage for preventive care. Specifically, nearly all HSA plans purchased in the large group market (99%) and small group market (96%) provide "first-dollar" coverage, while 59% of HSA/HDHP policies sold on the individual market include such coverage.[9]

The AHIP survey also found that among those HSA/HDHP policies offering "first-dollar" coverage for preventive care, 100% provide coverage for adult and child immunizations, well-baby and well-child care, mammography, Pap tests, and annual physical exams. Nearly 90% of the policies provide "first-dollar" coverage for prostate screenings and more than 80% offer "first-dollar" coverage for colonoscopies.[10]

Early Data Strongly Indicates That Participants Have Sufficient HSA Assets to Meet Actual Out-of-Pocket Expenses Under HDHPs

AHIP's most recent census data indicates that HSA enrollees had an average account balance for 2007 of approximately $1,380 and withdrew on average $1,080 to reimburse qualified medical expenses, including those expenses not otherwise covered under their HDHP.[11] Additionally, early findings indicate that many employers are contributing substantial amounts to their employees' HSAs. Specifically, GAO reports that of those small and large employers that made contributions to HSAs in 2007, the average annual contribution totaled $806.[12]

The Council views these early findings as very encouraging. One criticism of HSAs has been that accountholders cannot contribute a sufficient amount to an HSA on an annual basis to meet their actual out-of-pocket expenses. This is due in large part to the fact that the maximum HSA contribution limit is almost certainly significantly less than the plan's maximum out-of-pocket limit (for example, for 2008, the maximum HSA contribution limit was $2,800 for self-only coverage and $5,900 for family coverage, but the maximum out-of-pocket limit for HDHPs was $5,600 and $11,200, respectively). Notwithstanding this fact, the data indicates that American families have been able to utilize their HSAs to effectively meet their out-of-pocket liability under the HDHP. This is very welcome news as it suggests that HSA/HDHPs meet both the cost and coverage needs of the average American family.

Data Indicates That HSAs Are *Not* being Used As Tax Shelters by High-Income Individuals

The early data from GAO and AHIP is also encouraging for another reason. Contrary to concerns by some that HSAs would be used primarily by high-income individuals as an IRA-like retirement savings vehicle, the data indicates that HSAs are being used by both lower- and higher-income individuals principally to meet current year health costs.

With respect to the specific income levels of those individuals who are currently utilizing HSAs, available data for the 2005 tax year indicates that nearly 50% of all HSA enrollees had annual incomes of less than $60,000. Specifically, the recent GAO report indicates that 41% of HSA tax filers for 2005 had annual incomes below $60,000.[13] Similarly, a survey by eHealthInsurance, an online broker of health insurance policies, found that 45% of all HSA enrollees in 2005 had annual incomes of $50,000 or less.[14] The same survey found that 41% of HSA purchasers were not covered by health insurance during the preceding six months.[15]

Notably, the findings for the 2005 tax year may fail to accurately reflect current trends in HSA usage and may, in fact, understate the percentage of low- and middle-income HSA enrollees. This is because, as part of the Medicare Modernization Act, Congress allowed participants in early HSA-like accounts, called Medical Savings Accounts ("MSAs"), to convert these accounts into HSAs. Because MSAs generally were only available to self-employed individuals and small business owners – persons who on average would likely have higher incomes than the average American worker – the data for 2005 may well underestimate the number of low- and middle-income individuals who are currently enrolled in HSA/HDHP coverage.

Recent data from AHIP indicates that for 2007, HSA enrollees withdrew on average 80% of their annual contributions to reimburse current-year qualified medical expenses. Moreover, the GAO report states that "average contributions and average withdrawals generally increased with both income and age."[16] Thus, although higher-income individuals on average contributed more to their HSAs in a given year, they also withdrew more contributions during the same year. These early findings, when taken together, are very encouraging because they indicate that that HSAs are *not* being used primarily by higher-income individuals as a retirement savings vehicle or tax-shelter, but rather are being used by both lower- and higher-income individuals to obtain essential current-year health care coverage.

Lastly, some have pointed to the early data indicating that all HSA account balances are not "spent down" on an annual basis (as is frequently the case with FSAs given the "use-it-or-lose-it" rule) as evidence that HSAs are being used inappropriately as a tax savings vehicle. Such critiques fail to recognize the mechanics of HSA/HDHP coverage in light of the statutory contribution limits and potential out-of-pocket expenses. As noted above, in the vast majority of instances, the HSA participant's potential out-of-pocket exposure under the related HDHP can be as much as 200% of the maximum HSA annual contribution. Thus, to the extent that accountholders do not withdraw all of their HSA contributions in the same year (*i.e.*, as necessary to meet health expenditures), this should be viewed as positive from a public policy perspective. This is because any remaining account balance at year-end will help ensure that accountholders have sufficient HSA assets to meet potential out-of-pocket expenses under the HDHP plan in later years.

Available Data Indicates That HSA Monies Are Being Used for Qualified Medical Expenses

The early data, as compiled by GAO, suggests that amounts withdrawn from HSAs are being used by accountholders for qualified medical expenses. The GAO report states that "[o]f the HSA funds that were withdrawn in 2005, about 93 percent were claimed for qualified medical expenses."[17] Moreover, recent statements by a Treasury Department representative before the Ways and Means Committee indicate that 8.4% of all HSA accountholders list at least some of their HSA distributions as nonqualified taxable distributions.[18]

Under current rules, amounts withdrawn from HSAs that are not used for qualified medical expenses are subject to substantial negative tax consequences. Specifically, such amounts are subject to income tax at the accountholder's marginal tax rate as well as an additional 10% penalty tax. To the extent that an accountholder fails to accurately report taxable withdrawals, he or she would likely also be subject to various accuracy-related penalties and additions for the underpayment of income tax, as well as related interest.

The early data indicates that accountholders are using their HSAs as intended – primarily to reimburse qualified medical expenses not otherwise covered under the HDHP. Moreover, where amounts are withdrawn and are not used to reimburse qualified medical expenses, the data indicates that accountholders are correctly reporting such amounts as subject to income taxation under the current rules.

Current Rules Regarding HSA Substantiation Are Consistent with Other Special Purpose Accounts and Health Tax Provisions

Some persons have suggested that the treatment of HSAs under federal tax law – specifically the lack of a third-party substantiation requirement – is unparalleled and otherwise unique to HSAs. Such assertions are not correct. There are *numerous* instances under the Code where amounts withdrawn from a special purpose account are *not* subject to mandatory third-party FSA-like substantiation rules, such as with respect to withdrawals from 529 college saving plans or withdrawals from IRAs *in connection with a qualifying first-time home purchase.* . . .

With respect to the treatment of medical expenses more generally under federal tax law, it is HRAs and FSAs – rather than HSAs – that are in fact the exception to the rule. This is because, as with HSAs, the general approach towards health expenditures under federal tax law does not require that a taxpayer obtain third-party substantiation of qualifying medical expenses in order to obtain a specific income tax deduction or other tax-favored treatment.

One example of this can be found under Code section 162(l), which allows self-employed persons to take an above-the-line deduction for qualified medical care. In order to avail oneself of the deduction under this provision, the self-employed individual must certify on his or her annual income tax return the amount that he or she paid for qualified health insurance during the respective tax year. As with HSAs, no third-party substantiation is required under federal tax law, although the taxpayer remains subject to accuracy-related penalties and additions under federal tax law. . . .

Imposing Third-Party Substantiation Requirements on HSAs Will Increase Costs and Limit Americans' Options for Health Care Coverage

. . . At a time when Americans continue to struggle to afford their health care coverage and/or secure appropriate coverage, imposing third-party substantiation rules would impose additional costs and burdens on HSA providers and accountholders. These additional costs could operate to limit the attractiveness and efficacy of HSAs.

Americans' options for health coverage need to be expanded at this time, not limited, and imposing third-party substantiation could negatively affect the use and/or effectiveness of HSAs. Moreover, given the relative newness of HSAs generally and the encouraging early data indicating that such substantiation is unnecessary, the Council opposes the imposition of third-party substantiation rules in connection with HSAs.

Conclusion

HSAs were never intended to be a comprehensive answer to all of America's health care problems. Rather, HSAs were designed to be one important option for American families seeking lower-cost but high-quality comprehensive coverage. As the GAO report makes clear, for a significant percentage of American families, HSAs have become an integral part of their health coverage and, thus, should not be curtailed at this time.

More than ever before, Americans need good health coverage options. For a significant segment of American families, HSA/HDHP coverage meets this need by providing lower-cost, high-quality coverage. Moreover, as noted above, early data is encouraging and suggests that for the vast majority of HSA participants, HSA/HDHP coverage is operating as intended by Congress. But early data is just that – "early." It is critical, therefore, that we allow this new health care option to develop without additional burdens or restrictions. The Council believes that there is no justification for changes that could curtail the use and/or effectiveness of HSAs. Otherwise, we risk taking away from millions of American families a vital tool in securing affordable, quality health care coverage.

Notes

1. *Health Savings Accounts (HSAs) and Consumer Driven Health Care: Cost Containment or Cost-Shift? Hearing Before the Subcomm. on Health of the H. Comm. on Ways and Means, 110th Cong.* (2008) (statement of John E. Dicken, Director of Health Care, Government Accountability Office).

2. *Health Savings Accounts (HSAs) and Consumer Driven Health Care: Cost Containment or Cost-Shift? Hearing Before the Subcomm. on Health of the H. Comm. on Ways and Means, 110th Cong.* (2008) (statement of America's Health Insurance Plans) (hereinafter ("AHIP").

3. *See* AHIP, *supra.*

4. *See* Id.

5. *Health Savings Accounts (HSAs) and Consumer Driven Health Care: Cost Containment or Cost-Shift? Hearing Before the Subcomm. on Health of the H. Comm. on Ways and Means, 110th Cong.* (2008) (statement of Michael E. Chernew, Ph.D., Professor of Health Care Policy, Harvard Medical School).

6. *Health Savings Accounts (HSAs) and Consumer Driven Health Care: Cost Containment or Cost-Shift? Hearing Before the Subcomm. on Health of the H. Comm. on Ways and Means, 110th Cong.* (2008) (statement of Wayne Sensor, CEO, Alegent Health).

7. *Consumer Directed Health Plans Analysis*, HealthPartners, October 2007.

8. *See* AHIP, *supra.*

9. *See* Id.

10. *Id.*

11. *See* Id. *See also Health Savings Accounts: Participation Increased and Was More Common among Individuals with Higher Incomes*, GAO-08-474R (April 2008), at 8 (stating that in 2005, the average HSA contribution was $2,100, with the average withdrawal being approximately $1,000).

12. *See* Id at 9 (*citing* Kaiser Family Foundation and Health Research and Educational trust, *Employer Health Benefits: 2007 Annual Survey* (Menlo Park, Calif., and Chicago, Ill.: 2007). It should also be noted that in a study conducted by Mercer during the same period which covered only large employers, the average contribution was $626. *Id.* at 9.

13. *Id.* at 6.

14. *See* AHIP, *supra* (citing eHealthInsurance survey findings).

15. *See* Id.

16. *See* GAO, *supra*, at 8.

17. *See* Id at 9.

18. *April 9, 2008 Mark-up of H.R. 5719 by the Subcomm. on Health of the H. Comm. on Ways and Means, 110th Cong.* (2008) (comment by Thomas Reeder, Benefits Tax Council, Dept. of Treasury) (as reported by Congressional Quarterly).

Linda J. Blumberg  **NO**

Testimony before the Subcommittee on Health of the House Committee on Ways and Means

. . . Thank you for inviting me to share my views on Health Savings Accounts (HSAs) and their implications for cost containment and the distribution of health care financing burdens. The views I express are mine alone and should not be attributed to the Urban Institute, its trustees, or its funders.

In brief, my main points are the following:

- The related issues of a large and growing number of uninsured Americans and the escalating cost of medical care create problems of limited access to necessary medical care for millions of Americans, financial hardship for many households, and severe budgetary pressures on the public health care safety net as well as on federal and state government. However, HSAs are not the solutions to these pressing national concerns.
- HSAs provide additional subsidies to the people most likely to purchase health insurance even in the absence of no subsidy at all—those with high incomes. As income and marginal tax rates increase, the value of the tax exemption associated with contributions to HSAs and the interest, dividends, and capital gains earned on HSA balances grows as well. Because most of the uninsured have low incomes and get little or no value from tax exemptions, the subsidies are very poorly targeted for expanding coverage.
- Because of the highly skewed nature of health care spending—the highest-spending 10 percent of the population accounts for 70 percent of total health expenditures—cost containment strategies that do not deal substantially with the high users of health care services will not have a significant effect on overall spending. . . .
- To the extent that high-deductible plans raise costs for higher-cost users, their use of medical services may fall. But there are no provisions to help these patients choose the services most important to their health, so reductions in care could lead to expensive, catastrophic health consequences in the long run. Moreover, patients' ability to compare health care providers on the basis of cost and quality is extremely limited. As a consequence, high-deductible plans and HSAs have a limited ability to make patients better value shoppers.

U.S. House of Representatives, May 14, 2008, excerpts.

- Because high-deductible plans with or without HSAs place greater financial burdens on frequent users of medical care than do comprehensive policies (policies with lower out-of-pocket maximums and possibly broader sets of covered benefits), they tend to attract healthier enrollees. This selection can raise costs for the less healthy. The higher-cost insured population remaining in comprehensive coverage will tend to see their premiums rise as the healthy peel off into high-deductible/HSA plans. Unless the costs of these high users of care are spread more broadly by manipulating premiums across plan types or through regulation or subsidization, this dynamic will make coverage less affordable for those with the greatest medical needs.
- Despite lower premiums compared with comprehensive plans, high-deductible/HSA plans have so far failed to attract many low-income uninsured individuals and families. In addition to the fact that they get little tax benefit, they often do not have assets to cover the high deductibles—and have decided that they are better off remaining uninsured. The "one size fits all" high-deductible policy under the HSA legislation is flawed since, for example, a $2,200 deductible could be financially ruinous for a low-income family, while the same deductible could have virtually no cost-containment impact for a high-income family.
- Roughly half of those with HSA-compatible, high-deductible policies do not open HSAs (GAO 2008), despite the tax advantages of doing so. Two-thirds of employers offering single coverage through high-deductible/HSA combinations report making no contribution to the HSAs of their workers (Kaiser Family Foundation/Health Research and Education Trust 2007). As a consequence, low-income or high health-care-need workers with no choice of coverage but a high–deductible/HSA plan are likely to be exposed to much larger out-of-pocket financial burdens than they would be under a comprehensive policy, since employers are not, by and large, offsetting these higher deductibles with cash contributions to HSAs. Presented with the option of making varying contributions to HSAs as a function of worker income or health status, employers are highly unlikely to do so.
- At present, the legal use of HSAs is far more tax favored than is any other health or retirement account. Contributions, earnings, and withdrawals for HSAs can be tax free, if spending is health related. However, there is no mechanism in place, other than being subjected to a general tax audit, to verify that spending out of HSA balances is actually being done for medical purposes. Medical Flexible Spending Accounts (FSAs), a much more widely used tax-advantaged account for paying out-of-pocket medical costs, do have verification mechanisms in place that add very little to the costs of the plans. H.R. 5917 would prevent the illegal use of HSAs as a general tool of tax evasion.

Background

Between 2000 and 2006, employer-based health insurance premiums grew by 86 percent, compared with 20 percent for worker earnings and 18 percent for overall inflation (Kaiser Family Foundation and Health Research and Educational Trust 2006). By 2006, the number of uninsured had increased to 18 percent of the total nonelderly population in the United States, and a third of the nonelderly population with incomes below 200 percent of the federal poverty level were uninsured (Holahan and Cook 2007). Health Savings Accounts have been one approach some policymakers have embraced to addressing these dual and growing problems.

While high-deductible plans have been available in the nongroup market for many years, the 2003 Medicare Prescription Drug, Improvement, and Modernization Act (MMA) included provisions to provide a generous tax incentive for certain individuals to seek out high-deductible health insurance policies with particular characteristics. . . .

Individuals (and families) buying these policies either through their employers or independently in the private nongroup insurance market can make tax-deductible contributions into an HSA. Funds deposited into the accounts are deducted from income for tax purposes, and any earnings on the funds accrue tax free, and are not taxed as long as they are used to cover medical costs. Contributions can be made by employers, individuals, or both. In 2006, Congress removed the requirement that annual deposits into HSAs be capped at the level of the plan's deductible, and instead provided a fixed statutory limit for annual contributions. . . .

HSAs were intended to encourage more cost-conscious spending by placing more of the health care financing burden on the users of services, as opposed to having them incorporated in the shared financing inherent in insurance coverage.

What Makes HSAs Attractive?

As a consequence of the structure of the tax subsidy and the shift of health care spending to out-of-pocket costs, these accounts are most attractive to high-income people and those with low expected health care expenses. The tax subsidy provided for HSA participants is greatest for those in the highest marginal tax bracket and is of little or no value to those who do not owe income tax. Clemans-Cope (forthcoming) demonstrated that 70 percent of the nonelderly uninsured have family incomes below 200 percent of the federal poverty level, and that only 16 percent of uninsured adults fall into the 20 percent or greater marginal tax bracket. A $5,800 HSA contribution, the maximum permitted under the law, would generate a tax reduction of $2,030 to a household in the top income tax bracket. The value of the tax benefit would be less than half as much for a moderate-income family. And it would be worth much less if the family could not afford to contribute very much into the account. For those whose incomes are so low that they have no income tax liability, the subsidy is worth nothing. However, HSA contributions made by an employer, as opposed to by an individual, will decrease even a low-income worker's payroll tax liability, resulting in a modest tax savings.

Higher-income individuals are also better able to cover the costs of a high deductible, should significant medical expenses be incurred. Jacobs and Claxton (2008) showed that uninsured households have substantially lower assets than do the insured. As a consequence, high-deductible policies are unlikely to provide the uninsured with sufficient financial access to medical care in the event of illness or injury.

Additionally, those who do not expect to have much in the way of health expenses will be attracted to HSAs by the ability to accrue funds tax free that they can use for a broad array of health-related expenses that are not reimbursable by insurance (e.g., non-prescription medications, eyeglasses, cosmetic surgery). Those without substantial health care needs may also be attracted to HSAs because they can be effectively used as an additional IRA, with no penalty applied if the funds are spent for non-health-related purposes after age 65. Young, healthy individuals may even choose to use employer contributions to their HSAs for current non-health-related expenses, after paying a 10 percent penalty and income taxes on the funds—a perk unavailable to those enrolled in traditional comprehensive insurance plans.

These expectations have been borne out in the enrollment experience of HSAs (United States General Accountability Office [US GAO] 2008). The GAO analysis found that the average adjusted gross income of HSA participants was about $139,000 in 2005, compared with $57,000 for all other tax filers. They also found that average contributions to HSAs were more than double the average withdrawals, suggesting that either HSA participants were not high users of medical services or they used these accounts purely as investment vehicles—or both.

The incentive structure and the findings strongly indicate that HSAs and their associated tax subsidies are health care spending vehicles that are poorly targeted to the population most in need—the low-income and those with above average medical needs.

The Cost Containment Implications of the Health Care Spending Distribution

The distribution of health care spending is highly skewed, meaning a small percentage of the population accounts for a large share of total health care spending. The top 10 percent of health care spenders spend 70 percent of health care dollars, while the bottom 50 percent of spenders account for only 3 percent of those dollars (Berk and Monheit 2001). As a consequence, significantly decreasing health care spending will require substantially lowering the spending associated with high users of medical services, ideally, while not decreasing quality of care. However, the high-deductible/HSA plan approach is not well designed for lowering the spending of the high-cost population in a manner that does not negatively affect their health.

Cost savings can be manifested through two mechanisms: a decline in the amount of services per episode of care due to an increase in marginal price, or a decline in the number of episodes of care due to an increase in the average price. For those who are generally healthy and would not have annual spending that exceeded the high deductibles associated with HSA compatible plans, the increased marginal price of out-of-pocket medical care could have some impact on their use (Newhouse 1993, 2004). Incentives to curtail unnecessary services are strongest for these individuals. However, our analysis of the Medical Expenditure Panel Survey – Household Component showed that only 3 percent of total health care spending is attributable to those who spend below the minimum required deductibles. Consequently, there is little room for systemwide cost savings among this population since their spending accounts for so little of the overall expenditures.

For those who are unhealthy and who, with comprehensive insurance coverage, would spend above these higher deductibles, a number of scenarios are possible. Those who do not face significantly higher out-of-pocket maximums relative to their previous plan would not have any additional cost containment incentives. Those who face significantly higher out-of-pocket maximums under the new high-deductible/HSA plans would face a higher average price of medical care, and could reduce their spending as a consequence. However, research has demonstrated that the reductions in their spending would occur as a consequence of their reducing the number of episodes of their care, as opposed to reducing the cost of an episode once initiated (Newhouse 1993, 2004). In other words, they would decide not to initiate a contact with a medical professional for financial reasons, with potentially serious consequences for their health and for the long-term costs of their care. Two studies (Fronstin and Collins 2005; Davis et al. 2005) have found that HSA participants were more likely to report missed or delayed health services and not filling prescriptions due to cost. These problems were greater for those with lower incomes or worse health.

Paradoxically, high-cost individuals are not likely to curtail unnecessary services before reaching the high deductible, as might be desired. That is because the lion's share (80 percent) of health care spending for high-cost users of care is attributable to their spending that is incurred once those higher deductible levels are surpassed (Clemans-Cope forthcoming). . . .

While a number of studies have found that modest one-time savings of between 4 to 15 percent might be anticipated from conversion to high-deductible/HSA plans, they do not imply that such a change would have a significant impact on the rate of growth of medical spending. This is because medical spending growth is driven largely by the increased use of, and intensity of, technologies and services for people with high health care needs (Newhouse 2004). So while increased cost sharing can be used to lower the frequency of health care provider visits, it does not lower the costs per episode once an episode of care occurs.

Other, more promising avenues exist for achieving significant cost savings in our health care system. These include, among others,

- coordinated approaches to evaluation of cost-effectiveness and efficacy of new and existing technologies/procedures/medications combined with new regulatory and pricing strategies to target resources to the most cost-effective options;
- increasing the use of preventive care and chronic-care or high-cost case management strategies;
- payment reform and development of purchasing strategies that promote the consistent delivery of care in the most efficient and appropriate setting;

• administrative cost-saving strategies, including development of effective information technology infrastructure.

While many of these avenues require significant upfront investment in infrastructure, research, analysis, or experimentation, they are substantially more likely to yield systemwide savings without compromising access to and quality of care for the high-need population.

Implications of HSAs for the High Medical Need Population

The most significant premium savings accruing to high-deductible/HSA plan enrollees likely occur by altering the mix of individuals who purchase coverage of different types. By providing incentives for healthy individuals and groups to purchase HSA-compatible plans, insurance risk pools can be further segmented by health status. The average medical costs of those purchasing the HSA plans will be substantially lower if the high-risk population is left in more traditional comprehensive plans. As the average cost of those in the comprehensive plans increases, so does the premium associated with the coverage. In the extreme risk segmentation circumstance, premiums for comprehensive coverage may increase so much that maintaining that type of coverage is no longer financially viable. . . .

Without some type of intervention, by government or employers to spread health care risk more broadly, the practical effect of high-deductible/ HSA plans is that the most vulnerable populations (the sick and low-income) are left bearing a greater burden of their health expenses. The extent to which this is a preferred societal outcome should be explicitly debated, as it is the primary impact of a move toward high-deductible/HSA plans.

The Ability of Patients to Be Good Value Shoppers

Theoretically, placing a greater share of the health care financing burden on the individual users of health care should create incentives for greater price/quality comparisons and more cost-effective medical decisions. However, the ability of the patients to engage in such comparison shopping is extremely limited in the current private insurance context. As Ginsburg (2007) describes, effective comparison of services on price occurs only in the context of non-emergency care, services that are not complex, bundled prices for services, consistent quality across providers, and only after an appropriate diagnosis has been made. Situations that meet such criteria eliminate a great deal of the medical care within the system. In addition, confidentiality agreements between providers and insurers prevent the providers from being able to give patients actual prices, as opposed to ranges that are generally not useful for comparison purposes. Traditionally, patients have relied upon their insurers to guide their provider decisions by choosing an efficient provider network on their behalf.

Enforcement of HSA Legal Requirements

As noted earlier, spending by those under 65 years of age out of HSA accounts is tax advantaged only if that spending is for medical purposes. If HSA funds are used for nonmedical purposes, a nonelderly individual would be required to pay taxes on the withdrawal in addition to a 10 percent penalty. However, currently, there is no administrative mechanism in place to verify that spending from HSAs is in fact being used for medical purposes. Unless an individual HSA participant is subjected to an IRS audit, there are no checks on the type of spending being done. Given that any individual's likelihood of an audit is very low, this lack of verification creates an easy mechanism for evading taxes. This problem is amplified by the increase in allowable annual contributions to HSAs and the fact that such contributions can now exceed the associated insurance plan's annual deductible.

Flexible spending accounts (FSAs) are employment-related accounts that allow users to deposit pretax dollars into accounts that can then be drawn down during the year to pay for medical expenses. The permissible medical expenses are defined broadly, including out-of-pocket costs for care that is or is not part of the account-holder's insurance policy, just like HSAs. There are a number of differences between FSAs and HSAs (e.g., unused FSA balances are forfeited at the end of the year, they do not earn income, and they do not require health insurance plan participation), but the only relevant difference for this discussion is that withdrawals from FSAs are verified by the account administrators to be medical-related expenses that comply with the FSA law. . . .

The insurance industry complains that imposing such verification on HSAs would eliminate their cost saving potential by imposing new and onerous administrative costs. However, the administrative costs of FSAs, which would be directly comparable with that of HSAs for this purpose, are actually very low. In fact, overall FSA administrative costs, which include payment of claims (a function which HSAs already perform and is included in their current administrative costs) as well as verification of the appropriateness of claims, are about $5.25 per member per month ($63 per member per year).[1] However, much of the administrative tasks associated with FSAs are not applicable to HSAs, and the cost of adding adjudication of claims to the HSAs would be about $2 per member per month according to the third-party administrator of such plans that we contacted. If an additional cost of $24 per member would substantially reduce or eliminate the cost savings associated with HSAs, as some contend, then that is clear evidence that there is currently little to no cost savings associated with participating in those plans today.

Such an increment to administrative costs associated with these plans is clearly a very small price to pay to ensure that the law is being complied with and individuals are not using HSAs merely as a personal tax dodge.

Conclusion

HSAs are a highly tax-advantaged savings vehicle that is most attractive to people with high incomes and those with low expected use of health care services. As such, they are unlikely to significantly decrease the number of uninsured, who often have low incomes and neither benefit significantly from the tax advantages nor have the assets necessary to cover the large deductibles associated with the plans. Their ability to reduce systemwide spending is also very limited. The plans have the potential to increase segmentation of health care risk in private insurance markets, unless employers set premiums to offset the healthier selection into the plans or government subsidizes the higher costs associated with the remaining comprehensive coverage market.

To date, HSAs have been less popular than their advocates envisioned, making up only about 2 percent of the health insurance market (US GAO 2008). Thus, their negative ramifications on populations with high medical needs have probably been limited. However, efforts to expand enrollment in these plans through further tax incentives, for example, could place growing financial burdens on those least able to absorb them, leading to increasing effective barriers to medical care for the low income and the sick and potentially increasing the net number of uninsured.

References

Berk, Marc and Alan Monheit. 2001. "The Concentration of Health Expenditures Revisited," *Health Affairs*, 20:204–213.

Clemans-Cope, Lisa. Forthcoming. "Short- and Long-term Effects of Health Savings Accounts." Working paper prepared for The Urban Institute – Brookings Institution Tax Policy Center.

Davis, K., Doty, M. M. and Ho, A. 2005. "How High Is Too High? Implications of High-Deductible Health Plans." The Commonwealth Fund, April.

Fronstin, Paul and S. R. Collins. 2005. "Early Experience with High-Deductible and Consumer-Driven Health Plans: Findings from the EBRI/Commonwealth Fund Consumerism in Health Care Survey," Employee Benefit Research Institute and the Commonwealth Fund, December.

Ginsburg, Paul B. 2007. "Shopping For Price In Medical Care." *Health Affairs*, March/April; 26(2): w208–w216.

Holahan, John and Allison Cook. 2007. "Health Insurance Coverage in America: 2006 Data Update." Henry J. Kaiser Family Foundation. . . .

Jacobs, Paul D. and Gary Claxton. 2008. "Comparing the Assets of Uninsured Households to Cost Sharing Under High-Deductible Health Plans." *Health Affairs*. web exclusive, April 15 2008, pp. w214–w221.

Henry J. Kaiser Family Foundation/Health Research and Educational Trust (Kaiser/HRET) Survey of Employer-Sponsored Health Benefits, 2006. . . .

Henry J. Kaiser Family Foundation/Health Research and Educational Trust (Kaiser/HRET) Survey of Employer-Sponsored Health Benefits, 2007. . . .

Newhouse, J. P., 2004. "Consumer-Directed Health Plans and the RAND Health Insurance Experiment." *Health Affairs* Volume 23(6): 107–113.

Newhouse, J. P. and the Insurance Experiment Group. 1993. *Free for All? Lessons from the Rand Health Insurance Experiment.* Cambridge, MA: Harvard University Press.

United States Government Accountability Office (US GAO). 2008. Health Savings Accounts: Participation Increased and Was More Common Among Individuals with Higher Incomes. April 1. GAO-08-474R.

Note

1. From personal communication with third-party administrators providing administrative services for FSAs and consumer-directed health plans.

POSTSCRIPT

Are Health Savings Accounts Working Effectively?

In its statement in support of health savings accounts (HSAs), the American Benefits Council raises a number of points. First, HSAs are growing in importance, with coverage estimated at 6.1 million persons in January 2008. Moreover, between January 2007 and January 2008 the use of HSAs increased by 35 percent. Second, HSAs "can succeed in reducing health care costs" while improving "wellness and quality of care." Here, a study is cited that reported the cost of care was 4.4 percent lower for those with "HSAs and health reimbursement arrangements" compared to those with "traditional low deductible coverage." Third, HSAs are being used appropriately by "individuals at a broad range of income levels." Fourth, there are other special purpose accounts like HSAs that are not subject to mandatory third-party substantiation, and the American Benefits Council is against the imposition of such substantiation because of the costs it would create. For these and other reasons, the Council believes that for a number of American families HSAs have become an integral part of their health coverage. Thus, the Council is against any changes "that would curtail the use and/or effectiveness of HSAs."

Urban Institute research associate Linda J. Blumberg also raises a number of points in her testimony. First, and perhaps most importantly, HSAs are not the solution to critical health care problems including the growing number of uninsured Americans, limited access to medical care, and "severe budgetary pressure on the public health care safety net." Second, the tax exemptions associated with HSAs are poorly targeted: they are of "little or no value" to the uninsured with low incomes. Third, as currently structured, HSAs have a limited ability to make patients better value shoppers. Fourth, the tax benefits of HSAs are greater than those associated with any other health or retirement account, but there are no provisions to insure the spending of "HSA balances are actually being done for medical purposes." Blumberg concludes that HSAs are not as popular as HSA advocates believe and that efforts to expand their use may exacerbate a number of problems that currently prevail in the health care sector.

For more detail about the basic structure of HSAs, the U.S. Treasury provides ample information at its Web site http://www.ustreas.gov/offices/public-affairs/hsa/. An alternative source of similar information is presented in *The Pocket Guide to Health Savings Accounts* by Liv S. Fine and Tanya E. Karwaki from the Washington Policy Center at http://www.washingtonpolicy.org/HealthCare/HSAHowToGuidePocket2 .pdf. For the position of the Bush administration on HSAs see: http://www .whitehouse.gov/news/releases/2006/04/20060405-6.html. For more background and a number of additional evaluations, see the March 2006 issue of the *Congressional Digest*. Finally, there is the complete set of hearings before the Subcommittee on Health held on May 14, 2008. Besides Blumberg's testimony, there is testimony from John E. Dicken of the U.S. Government Accountability Office, Michael Chernew of Harvard Medical School, Judy Waxman of the National Women's Law Center, and Wayne Sensor of Alegent Health. Besides the submission from the American Benefits Council, there are submissions, among others, from the Consumers Union, America's Health Insurance Plans, the Council for Affordable Health Insurance, and the National Business Group on Health. The hearings are available at http://waysandmeans.house.gov/hearings .asp?formmode=detail&hearing=632.

ISSUE 6

Is It Time to Reform Medical Malpractice Litigation?

YES: U.S. Department of Health and Human Services, from "Confronting the New Health Care Crisis: Improving Health Care Quality and Lowering Costs by Fixing Our Medical Liability System" (July 24, 2002)

NO: Jackson Williams, from "Bush's Medical Malpractice Disinformation Campaign: A Rebuttal to the HHS Report on Medical Liability," A Report of Public Citizen's Congress Watch (January 2003)

ISSUE SUMMARY

YES: The U.S. Department of Health and Human Services (HHS) argues that although the United States has a health care system that "is the envy of the world," it is a system that is about to be brought to its knees by aggressive attorneys who force the medical community to practice costly "defensive medicine."

NO: Jackson Williams, legal counsel for the watchdog group Public Citizen, charges that the position taken by the HHS is factually "incorrect, incomplete, or misleading" and even contradicted by other governmental agencies.

The headline reads, "Princeton Senior Permanently Disabled." The newspaper story reveals that honor student John Francis slipped on the icy steps of the Harvey S. Firestone Memorial Library after the ice storm that swept through central New Jersey. Francis was rushed to Pokagon Hospital, where emergency surgery was required to repair his ruptured spleen. Unfortunately, Francis failed to recover his strength and vitality after the surgery. He visited the campus infirmary, where X-rays of the surgery site revealed a silhouette of a silver object in his abdominal cavity. When Francis took the X-rays to his surgeon, it was clear that a retractor had been left behind. That is not the end of this tragic story, however. During surgery to remove this foreign object, it was discovered that the retractor had caused the growth of flesh-eating bacteria: necrotizing fasciitis. The damage was severe indeed; this once avid tennis player is now permanently disabled. He will be confined to a wheelchair for the rest of his life.

The question that this news article raises is the fundamental question addressed in this issue. Francis has been irreversibly damaged by a medical mistake. The liability seems clear: someone left the retractor behind, and the presence of this foreign object has caused flesh-eating bacteria to grow and invade an otherwise healthy body.

So what is owed to Francis? Few would challenge a demand to be compensated for the explicit costs he incurred: the additional medical expenditures, his wheelchair, and perhaps the costs associated with the extra semester he will spend earning his undergraduate degree. Then there is the "gray area." What of his future employment? Although Francis can be gainfully employed, are his options now limited? If his options are limited, should he be compensated for the fact that he cannot become the tennis pro he wanted to be but must now resign himself to being a stockbroker? Is he entitled to receive compensation for the pain and suffering he will endure for the rest of his life?

It is important to note that "medical misadventures" are few and far between, given the number of medical procedures that occur annually in the United States. The U.S. medical care industry is universally regarded as the best in the world. Thousands and thousands of individuals each year undergo medical procedures in the United States. Since physicians are human, however, mistakes are made. The number of people who suffer the consequences of these mistakes is a tiny fraction of those who seek medical relief, but that number is not inconsequential. Some estimate that in 2003 alone, nearly 100,000 will die of a medical misstep. A surprising number of other surgical procedures will result in some foreign object being left behind the sutures; in fact, it is estimated that in 2003, some 1,500 retractors, gauze pads, sponges, etc., will be left behind. Consequently, Francis is not alone in facing the lifelong aftereffects of a surgery gone wrong.

In light of rapidly rising medical insurance rates, it is fair to ask what underlies those rate increases. The medical community and the medical insurance industry, backed by the George W. Bush administration, allege that jury awards for "pain and suffering" are excessive and unreasonable and that they undermine the foundations of the medical industry. Attorneys for those who are impacted by alleged medical misadventures respond that the skyrocketing medical insurance rates are not the result of jury awards and court settlements; rather, they can be traced to insurance companies that have been mismanaged and the recent decline in interest rates in the U.S. economy at large.

The following selections exhibit vastly different views as to why medical malpractice insurance rates are increasing. The U.S. Department of Health and Human Services points a finger at extreme jury awards in medical malpractice cases, arguing that these awards drive the price of malpractice insurance beyond the reach of some practitioners. As a result, these doctors must either increase their fees, which reduces accessibility, or they must begin to practice "defensive medicine"—prescribing redundant medicines, making unnecessary referrals to specialists, and recommending too many invasive procedures. Jackson Williams accuses the HHS of disinformation, concluding that medical malpractice insurance rates are rising not because of jury awards but because of poor management decisions on the part of insurance companies.

YES

U.S. Department of Health and Human Services

Confronting the New Health Care Crisis

American health care is the envy of the world, but with rapidly rising health care costs, reforms are needed to make high-quality, affordable health care more widely available. These include new approaches to making employer-provided coverage more affordable, new initiatives to help states expand Medicaid and S-CHIP [State Children's Health Insurance Program] coverage for lower-income persons, and new policies including health insurance credits for persons who do not have access to employer or public health insurance. A critical element for enabling all of these reforms to provide real relief, and to help all Americans get access to better and more affordable health care, is curbing excessive litigation.

Americans spend proportionately far more per person on the costs of litigation than any other country in the world. The excesses of the litigation system are an important contributor to "defensive medicine"—the costly use of medical treatments by a doctor for the purpose of avoiding litigation. As multimillion-dollar jury awards have become more commonplace in recent years, these problems have reached crisis proportions. Insurance premiums for malpractice are increasing at a rapid rate, particularly in states that have not taken steps to make their legal systems function more predictably and effectively. Doctors are facing much higher costs of insurance, and some cannot obtain insurance despite having never lost a single malpractice judgment or even faced a claim.

This is a threat to health care quality for all Americans. Increasingly, Americans are at risk of not being able to find a doctor when they most need one because the doctor has given up practice, limited the practice to patients without health conditions that would increase the litigation risk, or moved to a state with a fairer legal system where insurance can be obtained at a lower price.

This broken system of litigation is also raising the cost of health care that all Americans pay, through out-of-pocket payments, insurance premiums, and federal taxes. Excessive litigation is impeding efforts to improve quality of care. Hospitals, doctors, and nurses are reluctant to report problems and participate in joint efforts to improve care because they fear being dragged into lawsuits, even if they did nothing wrong.

From U.S. Department of Health and Human Services, Office of the Assistant Secretary for Planning and Evaluation, July 24, 2002, notes omitted.

Increasingly extreme judgments in a small proportion of cases and the settlements they influence are driving this litigation crisis. At the same time, most injured patients receive no compensation. Some states have already taken action to squeeze the excesses out of the litigation system. But federal action, in conjunction with further action by states, is essential to help Americans get high-quality care when they need it, at a more affordable cost.

Access to Care Is Threatened

There are a number of obstacles that limit access to affordable health care in this country, including lack of affordable insurance and an outdated Medicare program. We now face another—the litigation crisis that has made insurance premiums unaffordable or even unavailable for many doctors, through no fault of their own. This is making it more difficult for many Americans to find care, and threatening access for many more.

- Nevada is facing unprecedented problems in assuring quick access to urgently needed care. The University of Nevada Medical Center closed its trauma center in Las Vegas for ten days earlier this month [July 2002]. Its surgeons had quit because they could no longer afford malpractice insurance. Their premiums had increased sharply, some from $40,000 to $200,000. The trauma center was able to re-open only because some of the surgeons agreed to become county government employees for a limited time, which capped their liability for non-economic damages if they were sued. This is obviously only a temporary solution. If the Las Vegas trauma center closes again, the most severely injured patients will have to be transported to the next nearest Level 1 trauma center, five hours away. Access to trauma care is only one problem Nevada faces; access to obstetrics and many other types of care is also threatened.
- Overall, more than 10% of all doctors in Las Vegas are expected to retire, or relocate their practices by this summer. For example, Dr. Cheryl Edwards, 41, closed her decade-old obstetrics and gynecology practice in Las Vegas because her insurance premium jumped from $37,000 to $150,000 a year. She moved her practice to West Los Angeles, leaving 30 pregnant women to find new doctors.
- Dr. Frank Jordan, a vascular surgeon, in Las Vegas, left practice. "I did the math. If I were to stay in business for three years, it would cost me $1.2 million for insurance. I obviously can't afford that. I'd be bankrupt after the first year, and I'd just be working for the insurance company. What's the point?"
- Other states are facing the same problem. A doctor in a small town in North Carolina decided to take early retirement when his premiums skyrocketed from $7,500 to $37,000 per year. His partner, unable to afford the practice expenses by himself, may now close the practice, and work at a teaching hospital.
- Pennsylvania physicians are also leaving their practices. About 44 doctors at the height of their careers in Delaware County outside Philadelphia left the state in 2001 or stopped practicing medicine because of high malpractice insurance costs. . . .

Patient Safety Is Jeopardized

Because the litigation system does not accurately judge whether an error was committed in the course of medical care, physicians adjust their behavior to avoid being sued. A recent survey of physicians revealed that one-third shied away from going into a particular specialty because they feared it would subject them to greater liability exposure. When in practice, they engage in defensive medicine to protect themselves against suit. They perform tests and provide treatments that they would not otherwise perform merely to protect themselves against the risk of possible litigation. The survey revealed that over 76% are concerned that malpractice litigation has hurt their ability to provide quality care to patients.

Because of the resulting legal fear:

- 79% said that they had ordered more tests than they would, based only on professional judgment of what is medically needed, and 91% have noticed other physicians ordering more tests;
- 74% have referred patients to specialists more often than they belived was medically necessary;
- 51% have recommended invasive procedures such as biopsies to confirm diagnoses more often than they believed was medically necessary; and
- 41% said that they had prescribed more medications, such as antibiotics, than they would based only on their professional judgment, and 73% have noticed other doctors similarly prescribing excessive medications.

Every test and every treatment poses a risk to the patient, and takes away funds that could better be used to provide health care to those who need it.

Physicians' understandable fear of unwarranted litigation threatens patient safety in another way. It impedes efforts of physicians and researchers to improve the quality of care. As medical care becomes increasingly complex, there are many opportunities for improving the quality and safety of medical care, and reducing its costs, through better medical practices. According to some experts, these quality improvement opportunities hold the promise of not only significant improvements in patient health outcomes, but also reductions in medical costs of as much as 30%. . . .

However, these efforts and other efforts are impeded and discouraged by the lack of clear and comprehensive protection for collaborative quality efforts. Doctors are reluctant to collect quality-related information and work together to act on it for fear that it will be used against them or their colleagues in a lawsuit. Perhaps as many as 95% of adverse events are believed to go unreported. To make quality improvements, doctors must be able to exchange information about patient care and how it can be improved— what is the effect of care not just in one particular institution or of the care provided by one doctor—but how the patient fares in the system across all providers. These quality efforts require enhancements to information and reporting systems.

In its recent report, "To Err is Human," the Institute of Medicine (IOM) observed that, "[R]eporting systems are an important part of improving patient safety and should be encouraged. These voluntary reporting systems [should] periodically assess whether additional efforts are needed to address gaps in information to improve patient safety and to encourage health care organizations to participate in . . . reporting, and track the development of new reporting systems as they form."

However, as the IOM emphasized, fear that information from these reporting systems will be used to prepare a lawsuit against them, even if they are not negligent, deters doctors and hospitals from making reports. This fear, which is understandable in the current litigation climate, impedes quality improvement efforts. According to many experts, the "#1 barrier" to more effective quality improvement systems in health care organizations is fear of creating new avenues of liability by conducting earnest analyses of how health care can be improved. Without protection, quality discussions to improve health care provide fodder for litigants to find ways to assert that the status quo is deficient. Doctors are busy, and they face many pressures. They will be reluctant to engage in health care improvement efforts if they think that reports they make and recommendations they make will be thrown back at them or others in litigation. Quality improvement efforts must be protected if we are to obtain the full benefit of doctors' experience in improving the quality of health care.

The IOM Report emphasized the importance of shifting the inquiry from individuals to the systems in which they work: "The focus must shift from blaming individuals for past errors to a focus on preventing future errors by designing safety into the system." But the litigation system impedes this progress—not only because fear of litigation deters reporting but also because the scope of the litigation system's view is restricted. The litigation system looks at the past, not the future, and focuses on the individual in an effort to assess blame rather than considering how improvements can be made in the system. "Tort law's overly emotional and individualized approach . . . has been a tragic failure."

Health Care Costs Are Increased

The litigation and malpractice insurance problem raids the wallet of every American. Money spent on malpractice premiums (and the litigation costs that largely determine premiums) raises health care costs. Doctors alone spent $6.3 billion last year to obtain coverage. Hospitals and nursing homes spent additional billions of dollars.

The litigation system also imposes large indirect costs on the health care system. Defensive medicine that is caused by unlimited and unpredictable liability awards not only increases patients' risk but it also adds costs. The leading study estimates that limiting unreasonable awards for non-economic damages could reduce health care costs by 5–9% without adversely affecting quality of care. This would save $60–108 billion in health care costs each year. These savings would lower the cost of health insurance and permit an additional 2.4–4.3 million Americans to obtain insurance.

The costs of the runaway litigation system are paid by all Americans, through higher premiums for health insurance (which reduces workers' take home pay if the insurance is provided by an employer), higher out-of-pocket payments when they obtain care, and higher taxes.

The Federal Government—and thus every taxpayer who pays federal income and payroll taxes—also pays for health care, in a number of ways. It provides direct care, for instance, to members of the armed forces, veterans, and patients served by the Indian Health Service. It provides funding for the Medicare and Medicaid programs. It funds Community Health Centers. It also provides assistance, through the tax system, for workers who obtain insurance through their employment. The direct cost of malpractice coverage and the indirect cost of defensive medicine increases the amount the Federal Government must pay through these various channels, it is estimated, by $28.6–47.5 billion per year. If reasonable limits were placed on non-economic damages to reduce defensive medicine, it would reduce the amount of taxpayers' money the Federal Government spends by $25.3–44.3 billion per year. This is a very significant amount. It would more than fund a prescription drug benefit for Medicare beneficiaries *and* help uninsured Americans obtain coverage through a refundable health credit.

The Increasingly Unpredictable, Costly, and Slow Litigation System Is Responsible

Insurance premiums are largely determined by the expensive litigation system. The malpractice insurance system and the litigation system are inexorably linked. The litigation system is expensive, but, at the same time, it is slow and provides little benefit to patients who are injured by medical error. Its application is unpredictable, largely random, and standardless. It is traumatic for all involved.

Most victims of medical error do not file a claim—one comprehensive study found that only 1.53% of those who were injured by medical negligence even filed a claim. Most claims—57–70%—result in no payment to the patient. When a patient does decide to go into the litigation system, only a very small number recover anything. One study found that only 8–13% of cases filed went to trial; and only 1.2–1.9% resulted in a decision for the plaintiff.

Although most cases do not actually go to trial, it costs a significant amount of money to defend each claim—an average of $24,669. The most dramatic cost, however, is the cost of the few cases that result in huge jury awards. Even though few cases result in these awards, they encourage lawyers and plaintiffs in the hope that they can win this litigation lottery, and they influence every settlement that is entered into.

A large proportion of these awards is not to compensate injured patients for their economic loss—such as wage loss, health care costs, and replacing services the injured patient can longer perform (such as child care). Instead, much of the judgment (in some cases, particularly the largest judgments, perhaps 50% or more) is for non-economic damages. Awarded on top of compensation for the injured patient's actual economic loss, non-economic damages are said to be compensation for intangible losses, such as pain and suffering, loss of consortium, hedonic (loss of the enjoyment of life) damages, and various other theories that are imaginatively created by lawyers to increase the amount awarded.

Non-economic damages are an effort to compensate a plaintiff with money for what are in reality non-monetary considerations. The theories on which these awards are made however, are entirely subjective and without any standards. As one scholar has observed: "The perceived problem of pain and suffering awards is not simply the amount of money expended, but also the erratic nature of the process by which the size of the awards is determined. Juries are simply told to apply their 'enlightened conscience' in selecting a monetary figure they consider to be fair."

Unless a state has adopted limitations on non-economic damages, the system gives juries a blank check to award huge damages based on sympathy, attractiveness of the plaintiff, and the plaintiff's socio-economic status (educated, attractive patients recover more than others).

The cost of these awards for non-economic damages is paid by all other Americans through higher health care costs, higher health insurance premiums, higher taxes, reduced access to quality care, and threats to quality of care. The system permits a few plaintiffs and their lawyers to impose what is in effect a tax on the rest of the country to reward a very small number of patients who happen to win the litigation lottery. It is not a democratic process.

The number of mega-verdicts is increasing rapidly. The average award rose 76% from 1996–1999. The median award in 1999 was $800,000, a 6.7% increase over the 1998 figure of $750,000; and between 1999 and 2000, median malpractice awards increased nearly 43%. Specific physician specialties have seen disproportionate increases, especially those who deliver babies. In the small proportion of cases where damages were awarded, the median award in cases involving obstetricians and gynecologists jumped 43% in one year, from $700,000 in 1999 to $1,000,000 in 2000.

The number of million dollar plus awards has increased dramatically in recent years. In the period 1994–1996, 34% of all verdicts that specified damages assessed awards of $1 million or more. This increased by 50% in four years; in 1999–2000, 52% of all awards were in excess of $1 million. There have been 21 verdicts of $9 million or more in Mississippi since 1995— one of $100,000,000. Before 1995 there had been no awards in excess of $9,000,000.

These mega-awards for non-economic damages have occurred (as would be expected) in states that do not have limitations on the amounts that can be recovered. . . .

Mirroring the increase in jury awards, settlement payments have steadily risen over the last two decades. The average payment per paid claim increased from approximately $110,000 in 1987 to $250,000 in 1999. Defense expenses per paid claim increased by $24,000 over the same period.

The winning lottery ticket in litigation, however, is not as attractive as it may seem at first blush. A plaintiff who wins a judgment must pay the lawyer 30–40% of it, and sometimes even more. Lawyers, therefore, have an interest in finding the most attractive case. They develop a portfolio of cases and have an incentive to gamble on a big "win." If only one results in a huge verdict, they have had a good payday. Thus, they have incentives to pursue cases to the end in the hope of winning the lottery, even when their client would be satisfied by a settlement that would make them whole economically. The result of the contingency fee arrangement is that lawyers have few incentives to take on the more difficult cases or those of less attractive patients.

One prominent personal injury trial lawyer explained the secret of his success: "The appearance of the plaintiff [is] number one in attempting to evaluate a lawsuit because I think that a good healthy-appearing type, one who would be likeable and one that the jury is going to want to do something for, can make your case worth double at least for what it would be otherwise and a bad-appearing plaintiff could make the case worth perhaps half . . ."

For most injured patients, therefore, the litigation process, while offering the remote chance of a jackpot judgment, provides little real benefit, even for those who file claims and pursue them. Even successful claimants do not recover anything on average until five years after the injury, longer if the case goes to trial.

The friction generated by operating the system takes most of the money. When doctors and hospitals buy insurance (sometimes they are required to buy coverage that provides more "protection" than the total amount of their assets), it is intended to compensate victims of malpractice for their loss. However, only 28% of what they pay for insurance coverage actually goes to patients; 72% is spent on legal, administrative, and related costs. Less than half of the money that does go back to injured patients is used to compensate the patient for economic loss that is not compensated from other sources—the purpose of a compensation system. More than half of the amount the plaintiff receives duplicates other sources of compensation the patient may have (such as health insurance) and goes for subjective, non-economic damages (a large part of which, moreover, actually goes to the plaintiff's lawyer).

The malpractice system does not accurately identify negligence, deter bad conduct, or provide justice. The results it obtains are unpredictable, even random. The same study that found that only 1.53% of patients who were injured by medical error filed a claim also found, on the flip side, that most events for which claims were filed did not constitute negligence. Other studies show the same random results. "The evidence is growing that there is a poor correlation between injuries caused by negligent medical treatment and malpractice litigation."

Not surprisingly, most people involved in health care delivery on a day-to-day basis believe that the system does not accurately reflect the realities of health care or correctly identify malpractice. A recent survey indicated that 83% of physicians and 72% of hospital administrators do not believe the system achieves a reasonable result. . . .

Insurance Premiums Are Rising Rapidly

The cost of the excesses of the litigation system shows up in the cost of malpractice insurance coverage. Premiums have increased rapidly over the past several years. Experts believe we are seeing just the tip of what will happen this year and next. Rates have escalated rapidly for doctors who practice internal medicine, general surgery, and obstetrics/gynecology. The average increases ranged from 11% to 17% in 2000, were about 10% in 2001, but are accelerating rapidly. . . . A recent special report revealed that rate increases are averaging 20%.

However, these increases have varied widely across states, and some states have experienced increases of 30–75%, although there is no evidence that patient care had worsened. . . . [A] major contributing factor to the most enormous increases in liability premiums has been rapidly growing awards for non-economic damages in states that have not reformed their litigation system to put reasonable standards on these awards.

Among the states with the highest average medical malpractice insurance premiums are Florida, Illinois, Ohio, Nevada, New York, and West Virginia. These states have not reformed their litigation systems as others have. (Florida's caps apply only in limited circumstances. New York has prevented insurers from raising rates, and accordingly it is expected that substantial increases will be needed in 2003.) . . .

The effect of these premiums on what patients must pay for care can be seen from an example involving obstetrical care. The vast majority of awards against obstetricians involve poor outcomes at childbirth. As a result, payouts for poor infant outcomes account for the bulk of obstetricians' insurance costs. If an obstetrician delivers 100 babies per year (which is roughly the national average) and the malpractice premium is $200,000 annually (as it is in Florida), each mother (or the government or her employer who provides her health insurance) must pay approximately $2,000 merely to pay her share of her obstetrician's liability insurance. If a physician delivers 50 babies per year, the cost for malpractice premiums per baby is twice as high, about $4,000. It is not surprising that expectant mothers are finding their doctors have left states that support litigation systems imposing these costs.

In addition to premium increases for physicians, nursing home malpractice costs are rising rapidly because of dramatic increases in both the number of lawsuits and the size of awards. Nursing homes are a new target of the litigation system. Between 1995 and 2001, the national average of insurance costs increased from $240 per occupied skilled nursing bed per year to $2,360. From 1990 to 2001, the average size of claims tripled, and the number of claims increased from 3.6 to 11 per 1,000 beds.

These costs vary widely across states, again in relation to whether a state has implemented reforms that improve the predictability of the legal system. Florida ($11,000) had one of the highest per bed costs in 2001. Nursing homes in Mississippi have been faced with increases as great as 900% in the past two years. It has been recently reported that "nearly all companies that used to write nursing home liability [insurance] are getting out of the business." Since the costs of nursing home care are mainly paid by Medicaid and Medicare, these increased costs are borne by taxpayers, and consume resources that could otherwise be used to expand health (or other) programs.

Insurers Are Leaving the Market

The litigation crisis is affecting patients' ability to get care not only because many doctors find the increased premiums unaffordable but also because liability insurance is increasingly difficult to obtain at any price, particularly in nonreform states. Demonstrating and exacerbating the problem, several major carriers have stopped selling malpractice insurance.

- St. Paul Companies, which was the largest malpractice carrier in the United States, covering 9% of doctors, announced in December 2001 that it would no longer offer coverage to any doctor in the country.
- MIXX pulled out of every state; it will reorganize and sell only in New Jersey.
- PHICO and Frontier Insurance Group have also left the medical malpractice market.
- Doctors Insurance Reciprocal stopped writing group specialty coverage at the beginning of 2002.

States that had not enacted meaningful reforms (such as Nevada, Georgia, Oregon, Mississippi, Ohio, Pennsylvania, and Washington) were particularly affected. Fifteen insurers have left the Mississippi market in the past five years.

States With Realistic Limits on Non-Economic Damages Are Faring Better

The insurance crisis is less acute in states that have reformed their litigation systems. States with limits of $250,000 or $350,000 on non-economic damages have average combined highest premium increases of 12–15%, compared to 44% in states without caps on non-economic damages. . . .

As Table 1 shows, there is a substantial difference in the level of medical malpractice premiums in states with meaningful caps, such as California, Wisconsin, Montana, Utah and Hawaii, and states without meaningful caps.

In the early 1970s, California faced an access crisis like that facing many states now and threatening others. With bi-partisan support, including leadership from then Governor Jerry Brown and now Congressman Henry Waxman, then chairman of the Assembly's Select Committee on Medical Malpractice, California enacted comprehensive changes to make its medical liability system more predictable and rational. The Medical Injury Compensation Reform Act of 1975 (MICRA) made a number of reforms, including:

- Placing a $250,000 limit on non-economic damages while continuing unlimited compensation for economic damages.
- Shortening the time in which lawsuits could be brought to three years (thus ensuring that memories would still be fresh and providing some

Table 1

Malpractice Liability Rate Ranges by Specialty by Geography as of July 2001

	Cap in Non-Economic Damages	Low	High
INTERNISTS			
State Wide Data			
Wisconsin	$350,000	$5,000	$6,000
Montana	$250,000	5,300	7,000
Utah	$250,000	5,900	5,900
Hawaii	$350,000	6,800	6,800
Connecticut	No cap	6,200	15,800
Washington	No cap	7,100	9,000
Metropolitan Area Data			
California (Los Angeles area)	$250,000	$7,900	$13,000
Pennsylvania (Urban Philadelphia area)	No cap	10,700	11,800
Nevada (Las Vegas area)	No cap	11,600	15,800
Illinois (Chicagoland area)	No cap	16,500	28,100
Florida (Miami and Ft. Lauderdale areas)*	No cap	17,600	50,700
GENERAL SURGEONS			
State Wide Data			
Wisconsin (state wide)	$350,000	$16,000	$17,500
Montana (state wide)	$250,000	23,300	27,000
Utah (state wide)	$250,000	26,200	26,200
Hawaii (state wide)	$350,000	24,500	24,500
Connecticut (state wide)	No cap	26,200	45,800
Washington (state wide)	No cap	20,100	32,600
Metropolitan Area Data			
California (Los Angeles area)	$250,000	$23,700	$42,200
Pennsylvania (Urban Philadelphia area)	No cap	31,500	35,800
Nevada (Las Vegas area)	No cap	40,300	56,900
Illinois (Chicagoland area)	No cap	50,000	70,200
Florida (Miami and Ft. Lauderdale areas)*	No cap	63,200	126,600
OBSTETRICIANS/GYNECOLOGISTS			
State Wide Data			
Wisconsin (state wide)	$350,000	$23,800	$27,500
Montana (state wide)	$250,000	36,000	38,600
Hawaii (state wide)	$350,000	40,900	40,900
Utah (state wide)	$250,000	44,300	44,300
Connecticut (state wide)	No cap	45,400	64,800
Washington (state wide)	No cap	34,100	59,300

(continued)

Table 1 (Continued)

	Cap in Non-Economic Damages	Low	High
Metropolitan Area Data			
California (Los Angeles area)	$250,000	$46,900	$57,700
Pennsylvania (Urban Philadelphia area)	No cap	45,900	66,300
Nevada (Las Vegas area)	No cap	71,100	94,800
Illinois (Chicagoland area)	No cap	72,500	110,100
Florida (Miami and Ft. Lauderdale areas)*	No cap	108,000	208,900

Source: Medical Liability Monitor, Vol. 26, No. 10, October 2001: Shook, Hardy, Bacon, L.L.P., October 9, 2001.

*Florida imposes caps of $250,000–350,000 unless neither party demands binding arbitration or the defendant refuses to arbitrate.

> assurance to doctors that they would not be sued years after an event that they may well have forgotten).
> - Providing for periodic payment of damages to ensure the money is available to the patient in the future.

California has more than 25 years of experience with this reform. It has been a success. Doctors are not leaving California. Insurance premiums have risen much more slowly than in the rest of the country without any effect on the quality of care received by residents of California. Insurance premiums in California have risen by 167% over this period while those in the rest of the country have increased 505%. This has saved California residents billions of dollars in health care costs and saved federal taxpayers billions of dollars in the Medicare and Medicaid programs.

The President's Framework for Improving the Medical Liability System

Federal and state action is needed to address the impact of the medical liability crisis on health care costs and the quality of care.

Achieving a Fair, Predictable, and Timely Medical Liability Process

As years of experience in many states have proven, reasonable limits on the amount of non-economic damages that are awarded significantly restrain increases in the cost of malpractice premiums. These reforms improve the predictability of the medical liability system, reducing incentives for filing frivolous suits and for prolonged litigation. Greater predictability and more timely resolution of cases means patients who are injured can get fair compensation more quickly. They also reduce health care costs, enabling Americans to get more from their health care spending and enabling federal health programs to provide more relief. They improve access to care, by making insurance more affordable and available. They also improve the quality of health care, by avoiding unnecessary "defensive" treatments and enabling doctors to spend significantly more time focusing on patient care. Congress needs to enact legislation that would give all Americans the benefit of these reforms, eliminate the excesses of the litigation system, and protect patients' ability to get care.

The President [George W. Bush] supports federal reforms in medical liability law that would implement these proven steps for improving our health care system:

- Improve the ability of all patients who are injured by negligence to get quicker, unlimited compensation for their "economic losses," including the loss of the ability to provide valuable unpaid services like care for children or a parent.
- Ensure that recoveries for non-economic damages could not exceed a reasonable amount ($250,000).
- Reserve punitive damages for cases that justify them—where there is clear and convincing proof that the defendant acted with malicious intent or deliberately failed to avoid unnecessary injury to the patient—and avoid unreasonable awards (anything in excess of the greater of two times economic damages or $250,000).
- Provide for payment of a judgment over time rather than in one lump sum—and thus ensure that the money is there for the injured patient when needed.
- Ensure that old cases cannot be brought years after an event when medical standards may have changed or witnesses' memories have faded, by providing that a case may not be brought more than three years following the date or injury or one year after the claimant discovers or, with reasonable diligence, should have discovered the injury.
- Informing the jury if a plaintiff also has another source of payment for the injury, such as health insurance.
- Provide that defendants pay any judgment in proportion to their fault, not on the basis of how deep their pockets are.

The success of the states that have adopted reforms like these shows that malpractice premiums could be reduced by 34% by adopting these reforms. The savings to the Federal Government resulting from reduced malpractice premiums would be $1.68 billion.

Legislation such as H.R. 4600—a bill introduced by Congressman Jim Greenwood [R-Pennsylvania] with almost 100 bipartisan cosponsors—is now pending in Congress. Enactment of this legislation with improvements to ensure that its meaningful standards will apply nationally, will be a significant step toward the goals of affordable, high-quality health care for all Americans, and a fair and predictable liability system for compensating injured patients.

In addition, there are other promising approaches for compensating patients injured by negligence fairly and without requiring them to go through full-scale, time-consuming, and expensive litigation. Just as states like California have demonstrated the effectiveness of litigation reforms, they should also adopt and evaluate the impact of alternatives to litigation.

Early Offers is one innovative approach. This would provide a new set of balanced incentives to encourage doctors to make offers, quickly after an injury, to compensate the patient for economic loss, and for patients to accept. It would make it possible for injured patients to receive fair compensation quickly, and over time if any further losses are incurred, without having to enter into the litigation fray. Because doctors and hospitals would have an incentive to discover adverse events quickly in order to make a qualifying offer, it would lead to prompt identification of quality problems. The money that otherwise would be spent in conducting litigation would be recycled so that more patients get additional recovery, more quickly, with savings left over to the benefit of all Americans. It may also be possible to implement an administrative form of Early Offers as an option for care provided under federal health programs.

A second innovative approach involves strengthening medical review boards. Boards with special expertise in the technical intricacies of health care can streamline the fact-gathering and hearing process, make decisions more accurately, and provide compensation more quickly and predictably than the current litigation process. As with Early Offers, incentives are necessary for patients and health care providers to submit cases to the boards and to accept their decisions.

The Administration intends to work with states on developing and implementing these alternatives to litigation, so that injured patients can be fairly compensated quickly and without the trauma and expense that litigation entails.

Jackson Williams  **NO**

Bush's Medical Malpractice Disinformation Campaign

Introduction

The medical community continues to tout a report, *Confronting the New Health Care Crisis: Improving Health Care Quality and Lowering Costs by Fixing Our Medical Liability System,* issued by the Department of Health and Human Services [HHS] last summer [2002] as making an overwhelming case for medical liability "reform." In truth, a cursory examination of the report finds it to be a classic "clip job"—a collection of anecdotes, reports, and propaganda provided by lobbyists and stamped with the government's official imprimatur. The report cites such sources as Fox News Channel, Congressman Chip Pickering, and the Physician Insurers Association of America, the trade group leading the lobbying campaign. *It contains no new research nor any data generated by government health care experts or economists.*

A more intensive examination of the report shows that most of the "facts" it provides are incorrect, incomplete, or misleading; and that its conclusions are contradicted by those of other government agencies. . . .

The Bush Administration Says: "Access to Care Is Threatened"

"There are a number of obstacles that limit access to affordable health care in this country, including lack of affordable insurance and an outdated Medicare program. We now face another—the litigation crisis that has made insurance premiums unaffordable or even unavailable for many doctors, through no fault of their own. This is making it more difficult for many Americans to find care, and threatening access for many more. Dr. Cheryl Edwards, 41, closed her decade-old obstetrics and gynecology practice in Las Vegas because her insurance premium jumped from $37,000 to $150,000 a year. She moved her practice to West Los Angeles, leaving 30 pregnant women to find new doctors."

The Facts: Malpractice insurance costs are a minuscule part of a doctor's expenses and don't affect decisions about where to practice medicine.

From A Report of Public Citizen's Congress Watch by Jackson Williams, January 2003, pp. 1, 4–13, 15–18. Copyright © 2003 by Public Citizen. Reprinted by permission. Notes omitted.

- *There is a greater likelihood of doctors withdrawing from practice due to increases in their office rents or payroll costs than due to increases in malpractice insurance costs.* While there is a temporary spike in medical malpractice insurance rates due to insurance industry economics, it is necessary to look at the larger and longer-term picture. Specifically, while physicians spend about 3.2 percent of their gross income on medical malpractice costs, they spend 17 percent on payroll costs and 5.8 percent on office rent. According to the Medicare Payment Advisory Commission (MedPAC), the average increase in medical malpractice insurance rates last year was 4.4 percent. A doctor who stops practicing because of a malpractice insurance increase would be just as likely to retire due to increased health insurance costs for office staff, or because of increased rent for office space. If increased costs to doctors justify legislative action, they could also justify repeal of wages and hours laws or enactment of rent control laws.

- *Liability laws have no effect on a doctor's decision where to practice.* Even though damage awards are higher in more affluent states, those states still have more doctors. The District of Columbia has the highest average damage award and the most doctors. Idaho, with the fewest doctors, has the third lowest median damage award. While five of the states with the lowest per capita number of doctors have enacted caps on noneconomic damages, only three of the states with the highest number of doctors per capita have enacted them. According to the U.S. Chamber of Commerce, Iowa, Utah, and South Dakota rank 5th, 8th and 9th for "reasonable litigation environment," yet those states rank in the bottom ten in number of doctors. Only one state in the Chamber's legal climate top ten, Connecticut, also ranks in the top ten for doctors. California, whose damage caps supposedly drew Dr. Edwards from Las Vegas, did not add one additional doctor per 100,000 residents between 1990 and 1999, but the number of doctors per 100,000 residents increased in Nevada from 136 to 162 during that period.

- *Two factors explain almost all the variation in the number of doctors in a state: income level and urbanization.* Like anyone else, doctors want to live in places where they can earn high incomes, enjoy cultural and leisure activities, and send their children to good schools. Seven of the top ten states for doctors also rank in the top ten states in percentage of households earning $200,000 or more. Doctors want to live in areas with lots of affluent people—such areas are more likely to have the leafy suburbs, premium housing, clubs, and other amenities that doctors want. For every $1,000 increase in a state's median income for a four-person family, a state will have 2.3 more doctors per 100,000 residents. Doctors migrate to states on lists of "Best Places to Live": Forty of the top 100 cities with "strong arts, cultural programs, and higher education" were in the ten states with the highest per capita number of doctors, while there were none in the ten states with the lowest per capita number of doctors. Polled by the U.S. Chamber of Commerce, 41 percent of West Virginia doctors said that the inability of the state's poor resident to pay fees was responsible for the state's shortage of doctors, and 27 percent said that quality of life in the state was responsible.

- *There is no relationship between the level of increase in liability insurance premiums and the likelihood of discontinuing obstetric practice.* A recent study examined whether New York obstetricians facing higher premiums for obstetric liability insurance were more likely to discontinue practicing than physicians experiencing lower increases in premiums. The study found that the decrease in doctors practicing obstetrics was associated with the length of time since receiving a medical license in New York. This relationship "very likely represents the phenomenon of physicians retiring from practice or curtailing obstetrics as they age."

The Bush Administration Says: "Patient Safety Is Jeopardized"

"In its recent report, 'To Err is Human,' the Institute of Medicine (IOM) observed that, '[R]eporting systems are an important part of improving patient safety and should be encouraged. These voluntary reporting systems [should] periodically assess whether additional efforts are needed to address gaps in information to improve patient safety . . .' However, as the IOM emphasized, fear that information from these reporting systems will be used to prepare a lawsuit against them, even if they are not negligent, deters doctors and hospitals from making reports."

The Facts: Patient safety is enhanced by the tort system; it would be further enhanced by increased regulation of doctors.

- *The Administration's own Council of Economic Advisors said the opposite last year—the tort system increases patient safety.* Even the conservative appointees to the President's Council of Economic Advisors admit, "a patient purchasing a medical procedure, for example, may be unlikely to fully understand the complex risks, costs and benefits of that procedure relative to others. Such a patient must turn to a physician who serves as a 'learned intermediary,' though there remains the problem that the patient may also not be able to judge the skill of the physician from whom the procedure is 'purchased.' In such a case, the ability of the individual to pursue a liability lawsuit in the event of an improper treatment, for example, provides an additional incentive for the physician to follow good medical practice. Indeed, from a broad social perspective, this may be the least costly way to proceed—less costly than trying to educate every consumer fully. In a textbook example, recognition of the expected costs from the liability system causes the provider to undertake the extra effort or care that matches the customer's desire to avoid the risk of harm. This process is what economists refer to as 'internalizing externalities.' In other words, the liability system makes persons who injure others aware of their actions, and provides incentives for them to act appropriately."
- *Patient safety is at risk from medical providers' failure to commit to reducing medical errors.* In 1999 the Institute of Medicine released its report on patient safety in the U.S. The report estimated that between 44,000 and 98,000 Americans die annually as a result of preventable medical errors. The IOM recommended creation of a nationwide *mandatory*

reporting system of serious errors—those that result in death or serious harm—for hospitals, other institutional providers and ambulatory care systems. The IOM argued that such a system is necessary to hold providers accountable for maintaining safety and to implement safety systems that reduce the likelihood of such events occurring. IOM also recommended that health professional licensing conduct periodic re-examinations and re-licensing of doctors, nurses, and other key providers, based on both competence and knowledge of safety practices. Neither of these recommendations has been implemented, due to opposition from the medical community; nor are they mentioned in the HHS report.

- *Patient safety is also at risk from incompetent doctors.* Five percent of doctors are responsible for 54 percent of malpractice in the U.S., according to records in the National Practitioner Data Bank, maintained by HHS. An inquiry to this database, which covers malpractice judgments and settlements since September 1990, found that 5.1 percent of doctors (35,009) have paid two or more malpractice awards to patients. These doctors are responsible for 54 percent of all payouts reported to the Data Bank. Of these, only 7.6 percent have ever been disciplined by state medical boards. Even physicians who have made 5 payouts have been disciplined at only a 13.3 percent rate.

The Bush Administration Says: "Health Care Costs Are Increased"

"The litigation and malpractice insurance problem raids the wallet of every American. Money spent on malpractice premiums (and the litigation costs that largely determine premiums) raises health care costs. The litigation system also imposes large indirect costs on the health care system. Defensive medicine that is caused by unlimited and unpredictable liability awards not only increases patients' risk but it also adds cost . . . The leading study estimates that limiting unreasonable awards for noneconomic damages could reduce health care costs by 5–9% without adversely affecting quality of care. This would save $60–108 billion in health care costs each year."

The Facts: The Congressional Budget Office (CBO) says that limiting liability would have a negligible impact on health care costs.

- *In evaluating the impact of H.R. 4600, which would have severely limited the ability of patients to recover damages, the Congressional Budget Office projected only minimal savings.* This bill, which contained very stringent restrictions on patients' ability to recover damages, passed the U.S. House in 2002. CBO said: "The percentage effect of H.R. 4600 on overall health insurance premiums would be far smaller than the percentage impact on medical malpractice insurance premiums. Malpractice costs account for a very small fraction of total health care spending; even a very large reduction in malpractice costs would have a relatively small effect on total health plan premiums. In addition, some of the savings leading to lower medical malpractice premiums—those savings arising from changes in the treatment of collateral-source benefits—would represent a shift in costs from medical malpractice insurance to health insurance. Because providers of collateral-source benefits would be prevented from recovering their costs arising from the malpractice injury, some of the costs that would be borne by malpractice insurance under current law would instead be borne by the providers of collateral-source benefits. Most such providers are health insurers."

- *The Congressional Budget Office has rejected the "defensive medicine" theory.* CBO was asked to quantify the savings from reduced "defensive medicine" if Congress passed H.R. 4600. CBO declined, saying:

Estimating the amount of health care spending attributable to defensive medicine is difficult. Most estimates are speculative in nature, relying, for the most part, on surveys of physicians' responses to hypothetical clinical situations, and clinical studies of the effectiveness of certain intensive treatments. Compounding the uncertainty about the magnitude of spending for defensive medicine, there is little empirical evidence on the effect of medical malpractice tort controls on spending for defensive medicine and, more generally, on overall health care spending.

A small number of studies have observed reductions in health care spending correlated with changes in tort law, but that research was based largely on a narrow part of the population and considered only hospital spending for a small number of ailments that are disproportionately likely to experience malpractice claims. Using broader measures of spending, CBO's initial analysis could find no statistically significant connection between malpractice tort limits and overall health care spending. Although the provisions of H.R. 4600 could result in the initiation of fewer lawsuits, the economic incentives for individual physicians or hospitals to practice defensive medicine would appear to be little changed.

- *Overall tort expenditures are less than the cost of medical injuries.* Because so few medical injuries result in compensation to patients, the overall expenditures made for medical liability are far below the projected injury costs. The Institute of Medicine estimated the costs of preventable medical injuries in hospitals alone at between $17 billion and $29 billion a year. The Utah Colorado Medical Practice study estimated it at $20 billion. By contrast, the National Association of Insurance Commissioners reports that the total amount spent on medical malpractice insurance in 2000 was $6.4 billion. This is at least three to five times less than the cost of malpractice to society.
- *A leading actuary says the HHS report's numbers are "rubbish."* According to Robert Hunter, Director of Insurance for Consumer Federation of America, "The total cost of medical malpractice premiums is $6.4 billion (not just for doctors, as the report says, but for doctors, hospitals and other facilities). This represents about one-half of a percent of total health care expenses. In other words, if an outright ban were placed on medical malpractice lawsuits the total savings would be about $6 billion. The idea that a cap of any kind can save $60 to $108 billion is pure rubbish. How in the world could 'defensive medicine' possibly

be more than equal to the total risk measured in premiums, much less 10 to 20 imes the risk, as HHS assumes? This makes no economic sense at all."

The Bush Administration Says: "The Increasingly Unpredictable, Costly, and Slow Litigation System Is Responsible"

"Insurance premiums are largely determined by the expensive litigation system . . . Its application is unpredictable, largely random, and standard-less . . . Although most cases do not actually go to trial, it costs a significant amount of money to defend each claim—an average of $24,669 . . . Awarded on top of compensation for the injured patient's actual economic loss, non-economic damages are said to be compensation for intangible losses, such as pain and suffering, loss of consortium, hedonic (loss of the enjoyment of life) damages, and various other theories that are imaginatively created by lawyers to increase the amount awarded . . . The average award rose 76% from 1996–1999. The median award in 1999 was $800,000, a 6.7% increase over the 1998 figure of $750,000; and between 1999 and 2000, median malpractice awards increased nearly 43%."

The Facts: The medical malpractice litigation process is logical, and awards are explained by income, cost of health care, and injury severity.

- *Government data show that medical malpractice awards have increased at a much slower pace than claimed by Jury Verdict Research.* According to the federal government's National Practitioner Data Bank (NPDB), the median medical malpractice payment by a physician to a patient rose 35 percent from 1997 to 2001, from $100,000 to $135,000. By contrast, data from Jury Verdict Research (JVR), a private research firm, which was cited in the HHS report shows that awards rose 100 percent from 1997 to 2000, from $503,000 to $1 million. The reason for the huge difference, which is explained in more detail below: JVR collects only jury *verdict* information that is reported to it by attorneys, court clerks and stringers. The NPDB is the most comprehensive source of information that exists because it includes both verdicts *and* settlements. Ninety-six percent of all medical malpractice cases are settled, as opposed to decided by a jury, and settlements result in much lower awards than jury verdicts. Jury verdicts are higher than the average settlement because cases involving severe injuries are more likely to go to trial, and the defendant has usually rejected a settlement offer for a much smaller amount. JVR reported that the median final plaintiff demand in 2000 was $562,000, and the median final settlement offer from the doctor was $80,000. Thus, in the twenty percent of trials that doctors lost, a conscious decision was made to risk a much higher jury verdict. The plaintiffs were usually willing to settle for about half of what the jury awarded. According to NPDB's database of all medical malpractice settlements and judgments, the median payment in a settlement in 2000 was $125,000, same as the median for all payments; but the median payment for a judgment was $235,000. This figure is lower than the jury verdict figure because the ultimate payment received by a successful plaintiff reflects remittiturs ordered by judges, and discounts agreed to by plaintiffs in order to avert appeals.

- *Government data show that medical malpractice awards have increased at a slower pace than health insurance premiums.* While NPDB data show that the median medical malpractice payment rose 35 percent from 1997 to 2001 (an average of 8.5 percent a year), the average premium for single health insurance coverage increased 39 percent over that time period (9.5 percent a year). Payments for health care costs, which directly affect health insurance premiums, make up the lion's share of most medical malpractice awards.

- *"Non-economic" damages are not as easy to quantify as lost wages or medical bills, but they compensate real injuries.* So-called "non-economic" damages are awarded for the pain and suffering that accompany any loss of normal functions (e.g. blindness, paralysis, sexual dysfunction, lost bowel and bladder control) and inability to engage in daily activities or to pursue hobbies, such as hunting and fishing. This category also encompasses damages for disfigurement and loss of fertility. The fact that Americans spend a great deal of money to remedy these conditions (e.g. on pain relief medication, reconstructive surgery, etc.) belies any notion that such damages are "non-economic." According to Physician Insurer Association of America (PIAA), the average payment between 1985 and 2001 for a "grave injury," which encompasses paralysis, was only $454,454.

- *No evidence supports the claim that jury verdicts are random "jackpots."* Studies conducted in California, Florida, North Carolina, New York, and Ohio have found that jury verdicts bear a reasonable relationship to the severity of the harm suffered. In total the studies examined more than 3,500 medical malpractice jury verdicts and found a consistent relationship between the severity of the injury and the size of the verdict. Uniformly the authors concluded that their findings did not support the contention that jury verdicts are frequently unpredictable and irrational.

- *The insurance industry's own numbers demonstrate that awards are proportionate to injuries.* PIAA's Data Sharing Report also demonstrates the relationship between the severity of the injury and the size of the settlement or verdict. PIAA, as do most researchers, measures severity of injury according to the National Association of Insurance Commissioners' classifications. The average indemnity paid per file was $49,947 for the least severe category of injury and increased with severity, to $454,454 for grave injuries. All researchers found that the amount of jury verdicts fell off in cases of death, for which the average indemnity was $195,723. This is not surprising, as the costs of medical treatment for a grave injury are likely to be greater and pain and suffering would be experienced over a longer time period than in the case of death.

- *The contingency fee system discourages attorneys from bringing frivolous claims.* Medical malpractice cases are brought on a contingency fee basis, meaning the attorney receives payment only in the event there is a settlement or verdict. If the claim is closed without payment, the attorney does not receive a fee. Since attorneys must earn money to stay in business, it follows that they would not intentionally take on a non-meritorious case.

- *The high cost of preparing a medical malpractice case discourages frivolous claims—and meritorious claims as well.* Medical malpractice cases are very expensive for plaintiffs' attorneys to bring, with out-of-pocket costs for cases settled at or near the time of trial (when most cases are settled) ranging from $15,000 to $25,000. If the case goes to trial, the costs can easily be doubled. These costs do not include the plaintiff's attorney's time, and an attorney pursuing a frivolous case incurs opportunity costs in not pursuing other cases. An attorney incurs expenses beginning with the determination of whether a case has merit. First, the attorney is required to obtain copies of the patient's medical records from all the providers for analysis by a competent medically trained person. If that initial consultation reveals a likelihood of medical negligence, the records must then be submitted to medical specialists, qualified to testify in court, for final review. Typically, the records must be sent to experts outside of the plaintiff's state, as physicians within the state will refuse to testify against local colleagues. As a result, the experts who agree to review records and testify can and do charge substantial fees. Fees from $1,000 per hour to several thousand dollars are not uncommon. Discovery involves taking the sworn testimony of witnesses and experts. Such depositions cost $300 and up, depending upon their length and complexity. If an expert witness is deposed, the plaintiff's attorney is charged for the witness' preparation time and time attending the deposition.

- *Plaintiffs drop 10 times more claims than they pursue.* PIAA reports that between 1985 and 2001 a total of 108,300 claims were "dropped, withdrawn or dismissed." This is 63 percent of the total number of claims (172,474) closed during the study period. It is unclear what portion constitutes involuntarily dismissed cases (dismissed after a motion was filed by the defendant) rather than cases voluntarily dismissed by plaintiffs. According to researchers at the University of Washington School of Medicine, about nine percent of claims files are closed after the defendant wins a contested motion. Based on this figure, Public Citizen estimates that about 54 percent of claims are being abandoned by patients. An attorney may send a statutorily-required notice of intent to claim or file a lawsuit in order to meet the requirements of the statute of limitations but, after collecting medical records and consulting with experts, decide not to pursue the claim. We estimate that the number of cases withdrawn voluntarily by plaintiffs was 92,621, *10 times* the number of cases that were taken to trial and lost during that period (9,293). The percentage of claims pursued by plaintiffs to final rejection by a jury is only *five percent.*

- *The small number of claims pursued to a defense verdict are not frivolous.* Researchers at the American Society of Anesthesiologists arranged for pairs of doctors to review 103 randomly selected medical negligence claims files. The doctors were asked to judge whether the anesthesiologist in question had acted reasonably and prudently. The doctors only agreed on the appropriateness of care in 62 percent of the cases; they disagreed in 38 percent of cases. The researchers concluded, "These observations indicate that neutral experts (the reviews were conducted in a situation that did not involve advocacy or financial compensation) commonly disagree in their assessments when using the accepted standard of reasonable and prudent care." The percentage of all medical malpractice claims that go to trial is only 6.6 percent, according to PIAA, meaning that the parties and their attorneys ultimately reach agreement about liability five times more often than neutral doctors do. If truly frivolous lawsuits were being pursued, the proportion of claims going to trial would exceed the 38 percent of claims on which even doctors will disagree.

- *The costs of defending claims that are ultimately dropped are not unreasonable.* Medical liability insurers have complained about the costs of defending cases that are ultimately dropped. But the professional obligation of lawyers to exercise due diligence is essentially identical to the duty of physicians. The lawyer must rule out the possibility of proving medical negligence before terminating a claim, just as doctors must rule out the possibility of illnesses suggested by their patients' symptoms. The doctor performs his duty by administering tests; the lawyer performs hers by using discovery procedures. Both processes can lead to dead ends. But plaintiffs' lawyers have no financial incentive to abuse the litigation process: they are using their own time and money to pursue discovery activities, and are only paid for work on behalf of clients whose cases are successful.
- *Award amounts correlate to plaintiff's income and the cost of living in the plaintiff's home state.* Median malpractice awards vary from state to state. Much of the variation is explained by two factors—median family income and urbanization. Public Citizen's analysis of NPDB and census data found that for every $1,000 increase in a state's median family income, the median award amount increases by about $1,100. Our analysis also found that awards increase in relation to state population density—logical, since urbanized areas have a higher cost of living than rural areas.

The Bush Administration Says: "Insurance Premiums Are Rising Rapidly"

"The cost of the excesses of the litigation system shows up in the cost of malpractice insurance coverage. Premiums have increased rapidly over the past several years."

The Facts: The spike in medical liability premiums was caused by the insurance cycle, not by an "explosion" of lawsuits or "skyrocketing" jury verdicts.

- *There is no growth in the number of new medical malpractice claims.* According to the National Association of Insurance Commissioners (NAIC), the number of new medical malpractice claims declined by about four percent between 1995 and 2000. There were 90,212 claims filed in 1995; 84,741 in 1996; 85,613 in 1997; 86,211 in 1998; 89,311 in 1999; and 86,480 in 2000.

- *For much of the 1990s, doctors benefited from artificially lower premiums.* According to the International Risk Management Institute (IRMI), one of the leading analysts of commercial insurance issues, "What is happening to the market for medical malpractice insurance in 2001 is a direct result of trends and events present since the mid to late 1990s. Throughout the 1990s, and reaching a peak around 1997 and 1998, insurers were on a quest for market share, that is, they were driven more by the amount of premium they could book rather than the adequacy of premiums to pay losses. In large part this emphasis on market share was driven by a desire to accumulate large amounts of capital with which to turn into investment income." IRMI also noted: "Clearly a business cannot continue operating in that fashion indefinitely."

- *West Virginia Insurance Commissioner blames the market.* According to the Office of the West Virginia Insurance Commission (one of the states in the throes of a medical malpractice "crisis"), "[T]he insurance industry is cyclical and necessarily competitive. We have witnessed these cycles in the Medical Malpractice line in the mid-'70's, the mid-'80's and the present situation. This particular cycle is, perhaps, worse than previous cycles as it was delayed by a booming economy in the '90's and is now experiencing not just a shortfall in rates due to competition, but a subdued economy, lower interest rates and investment yields, the withdrawal of a major medical malpractice writer and a strong hardening of the reinsurance market. Rates will, at some point, reach an acceptable level to insurers and capital will once again flow into the Medical Malpractice market."

- *Medical liability premiums track investment results.* J. Robert Hunter, one of the country's most knowledgeable insurance actuaries and director of insurance for the Consumer Federation of America, recently analyzed the growth in medical liability premiums. He found that premiums charged do not track losses paid, but instead rise and fall in concert with the state of the economy. When the economy is booming and investment returns are high, companies maintain premiums at modest levels; however, when the economy falters and interest rates fall, companies increase premiums in response.

- *The same trends are present in other lines of insurance.* Property/casualty refers to a large group of liability lines of insurance (30 in total) including medical malpractice, homeowners, commercial, and automobile. The property/casualty insurance industry has exhibited cyclical behavior for many years, as far back as the 1920s. These cycles are characterized by periods of rising rates leading to increased profitability. Following a period of solid but not spectacular rates of return, the industry enters a down phase where prices soften, supply of the insurance product becomes plentiful, and, eventually, profitability diminishes, or vanishes completely. In the down phase of the cycle, as results deteriorate, the basic ability of insurance companies to underwrite new business or, for some companies even to renew some existing policies, can be impaired. This is because the capital needed to support the underwriting of risk has been depleted through losses. The current market began to harden in 2001, following an unusually prolonged period of soft market conditions in the property-casualty section in the 1990s. The current hard market is unusual in that many lines of insurance are affected at the same time, including medical malpractice. As a result, premiums are rising for most types of insurance. The increases have taken policyholders by surprise given that they came after several years of relatively flat to decreasing prices.

• *Insurer mismanagement compounded the problems.* Compounding the impact of the cycle has been misleading accounting practices. As the *Wall Street Journal* found in a front page investigative story on June 24, 2002, "[A] price war that began in the early 1990s led insurers to sell malpractice coverage to obstetrician-gynecologists at rates that proved inadequate to cover claims. Some of these carriers had rushed into malpractice coverage because an accounting practice widely used in the industry made the area seem more profitable in the early 1990s than it really was. A decade of short-sighted price slashing led to industry losses of nearly $3 billion last year." Moreover, "In at least one case, aggressive pricing allegedly crossed the line into fraud." According to Donald J. Zuk, chief executive of SCPIE Holdings Inc., a leading malpractice insurer in California, "Regardless of the level of . . . tort reform, the fact remains that if insurance policies are consistently under-priced, the insurer will lose money."

The Bush Administration Says: "Insurers Are Leaving the Market"

"The litigation crisis is affecting patients' ability to get care not only because many doctors find the increased premiums unaffordable but also because liability insurance is increasingly difficult to obtain at any price, particularly in non-reform states. Demonstrating and exacerbating the problem, several major carriers have stopped selling malpractice insurance."

The Facts: At least three of the four insurance companies identified by HHS as leaving the market had serious management problems during the past two years.

• *PHICO had been placed under the supervision of insurance regulators and was later sued by the state's Insurance Department.* The lawsuit alleged that PHICO directors ignored signs of financial trouble at the company and pressured the board to pay dividends at a time when the insurer's surplus "was declining drastically and significant strengthening of loss reserves was required."

• *St. Paul exited other insurance markets as well.* St. Paul Companies reported in December 2001 that it had $85 million in exposure as related to the Enron Corporation and that it held approximately $23 million in Enron Corporation senior unsecured debt. At the same time St. Paul announced it would exit its medical malpractice business, it also announced it would add reserves for claims related to the September 11 terrorist attacks, "exit certain reinsurance lines, exit countries where the company is not likely to achieve competitive scale, and reduce corporate overhead expenses, including staff reductions."

• *MIIX was found by Weiss Ratings to be the hardest hit by the property and casualty insurance industry's overall $6.6 billion decline in investment* *gains during the first half of 2002.* MIIX reported the largest capital losses. Weiss, a leading independent provider of ratings and analyses of financial services companies, downgraded MIIX from D– to E+, E being the lowest score possible. A former MIIX official has alleged conflicts of interest on the company's board that may have affected the situation.

The Bush Administration Says: "States with Realistic Limits on Non-Economic Damages Are Faring Better"

"The insurance crisis is less acute in states that have reformed their litigation systems. States with limits of $250,000 or $350,000 on non-economic damages have average combined highest premium increases of 12–15%, compared to 44% in states without caps on non-economic damages . . ."

The Facts: Neither the HHS report nor anyone else has presented a factual case that caps lower premiums; Public Citizen's analysis found that premiums are higher in states with caps.

- *The HHS report's "comparison" of premiums in ten states with caps to just ten states without caps is pure baloney.* HHS omitted data from other states without damage caps that did not have high premium increases. The Pennsylvania Medical Society . . . released a critique of another premium comparison, concluding that "Multivariate modeling must be used to control for outside influences . . . An issue as important as liability insurance reform deserves no less than a careful scientific approach to assessment of the impact of policy changes." While they did not prepare a multivariate model, Public Citizen did.
- *Public Citizen's analysis finds that, controlling for other factors, premiums are higher in states with caps than in states without caps.* Public Citizen entered U.S. Census, NPDB, and Medical Liability Monitor data into a multiple regression model to determine the effect that damage caps have on awards and on doctors' liability insurance premiums. Our preliminary finding is that a damage cap lowers the median payment made by doctors to plaintiffs by $29,000, in turn lowering a doctor's premium by about $11,000. Nevertheless, controlling for this and the rate of lawsuits against doctors in each state, states with caps still have premiums that are $14,000 higher than in states without caps, a $3,000 net increase. We believe that the cap encourages doctors to take more cases to trial, and the resulting higher defense attorney costs more than offset the lower indemnity payments.

POSTSCRIPT

Is It Time to Reform Medical Malpractice Litigation?

The question of medical malpractice litigation must be placed in context. No one disputes the fact that doctors make mistakes. Physicians are human and are therefore subject to human fallibilities. It should be noted that the large majority of these medical errors never result in legal action. But since the United States does not have in place a nationally mandated reporting system for medical mishaps and near mishaps, the public does not have certain knowledge of just how many medical mistakes are made annually. Doctors and their insurance carriers would have people believe that every medical mistake is litigated and that many other lawsuits are brought to the courts when there are no grounds for them. Lawyers, for their part, argue that they file lawsuits for only a small fraction of the medical mistakes that are made annually in the United States. Indeed, they contend that if it were not for the cases they did bring to light, the public would naively believe that doctors are infallible.

The truth of the matter may lie somewhere in the middle. Outside observers generally assume that about one out of every six "medical misadventures" results in a lawsuit. Of those who do seek legal redress, about half of these malpractice lawsuits are settled out of court or withdrawn before they go to trial. It is those that find their way through the court system and result in large financial settlements that are political lightning rods.

Those who litigate medical malpractice cases contend that their jury and settlement awards have little impact on medical malpractice insurance rates. They contend that the appearance of high insurance premiums can be traced to poor management decisions. When times were good and interest rates were high, these companies engaged in excessive competition, which drove the insurance rates down too far in the most competitive markets. When times were not as good and interest rates were low, insurance companies had no choice but to increase their rates. The increase, of course, was most severe in markets where the rates had been driven to the lowest levels.

This issue has been hotly debated in recent months; consequently, you might look to the press for background reading. The *New York Times* is a good source. The March 16, 2003, issue of the *New York Times Magazine* carried an article concerning four individuals who had foreign objects left in their bodies after surgeries. "The Biggest Mistake of Their Lives" discusses the case of Dan Jennings. If the miseries suffered by John Francis, as described in the introduction to this issue, seem remarkably like those of Jennings, that is because Francis is a fictional character based on Jennings.

Those who would limit malpractice awards have written widely. See, for example, "The Tort Mess," by Michael Freeman, *Forbes* (May 13, 2002). The American Medical Association has many such references, including "Medical Liability Reform Background and Talking Points." This summary, which was updated on May 8, 2002, incorporates many of the points found in the HHS report. To see how the medical community interprets history in this area, see James C. Mohr, "American Medical Malpractice Litigation in Historical Perspective," *JAMA* (April 3, 2000). Finally, to read firsthand how the insurance industry feels, see Doctor's Company chairman Richard E. Anderson's July 17, 2002, testimony before the Subcommittee on Health, Committee on Energy and Commerce, in "Harming Patient Access to Care: The Impact of Excessive Litigation."

For a good summary of President George W. Bush's statement on the medical malpractice issue and a panel discussion, see the January 16, 2003, segment of *The News Hour With Jim Lehrer,* which includes Larry Smarr, president of the Physicians Insurers Association of America; Ken Suggs, secretary to the Association of American Trial Lawyers; Donald Palmisano, president-elect of the American Medical Association; and Joanne Doroshow, executive director of the Center for Justice and Democracy.

Internet References . . .

Board of Governors of the Federal Reserve System

The home page for the Board of Governors of the Federal Reserve System provides a number of useful links to information about monetary policy and the financial industry.

http://www.federalreserve.gov/

Bureau of Economic Analysis

The home page of the Bureau of Economic Analysis of the U.S. Department of Commerce provides access to a wealth of economic information on a national, regional, international, and industry basis.

http://www.bea.gov/

Bureau of Labor Statistics

The home page of the Bureau of Labor Statistics of the U.S. Department of Labor provides links to the most recent reports on prices, employment, unemployment, earnings productivity, and job site injuries.

http://www.bls.gov/

Joint Economic Committee

This site describes the work of the Joint Economic Committee of the U.S. Congress. It includes the research reports of the committee on many topics, including tax reform and government spending, monetary policy, and international economic policy.

http://www.house.gov/jec/

National Bureau of Economic Research

The National Bureau of Economic Research (NBER) is "a private, nonprofit, nonpartisan, research organization dedicated to promoting a greater understanding of how the economy works." Its home page provides a number of useful links; of special importance is the information about the business cycle.

http://www.nber.org/

U.S. Macroeconomic and Regional Data

Hosted by the State University of New York, Oswego, Department of Economics, this site contains the full text of recent *Economic Reports of the President* and links to various global and regional economic indicators.

http://www.oswego.edu/~economic/mac-data.htm

Federal Deposit Insurance Corporation

This site provides links to the FDIC's loan modification guide, a program designed to assist bankers, servicers, and investors.

http://www.fdic.gov/consumers/loans/loanmod/loanmodguide.html

Macroeconomic Issues

*T*he economy incorporates the behavior of different groups, including consumers, businesses, and the government. The actions of very large businesses such as the world's largest retailer and credit card companies affect almost everyone, but it is consumers who ultimately decide where they shop and whether to use credit cards. Government policies in the areas of Social Security, benefits to the unemployed, the minimum wage, and immigration have consequences across the economy. But consumers when they act as voting citizens select the political officials who pass the laws. These interactions are reflected in each of the issues and help underscore the importance of the issues.

- Is Wal-Mart Good for the Economy?
- Should Social Security Be Changed to Include Personal Retirement Accounts?
- Should Unemployment Benefits Be Extended?
- Do American Consumers Need a Credit Card Bill of Rights?
- Should Minimum Wage and Living Wage Laws Be Eliminated?
- Do Unskilled Immigrants Hurt the Economy?

ISSUE 7

Is Wal-Mart Good for the Economy?

YES: Los Angeles County Economic Development Corporation, from "Wal-Mart Supercenters: What's in Store for Southern California?" www.laedc.org/consulting/projects/2004_WalMart-Study.pdf (January 2004)

NO: Democratic Staff of the House Committee on Education and the Workforce, from "Everyday Low Wages: The Hidden Price We All Pay for Wal-Mart," www.mindfully.org/Industry/2004/Wal-Mart-Labor-Record16feb04.htm (February 16, 2004)

ISSUE SUMMARY

YES: The Los Angeles County Economic Development Corporation believes that the introduction of Wal-Mart supercenter stores into the Southern California market will generate significant savings for consumers on their grocery, apparel, and general merchandise spending, and the redirected spending from the savings will create over 35,000 new jobs.

NO: The Democratic Staff of the House Committee on Education and the Workforce believes that Wal-Mart, in its efforts to achieve and maintain low prices, has "come to represent the lowest common denominator in the treatment of working people."

$\mathbf{G}$iven the company's ubiquitous presence across the country, it would come as a great surprise to find an American who did not recognize the name "Wal-Mart" or find someone who had not shopped at a Wal-Mart store. Many people are familiar with the yellow smiley face that appears in Wal-Mart television ads, in its newspapers ads, and on its in-store promotions. While many people might not know of the persons who created other major retailers such as Target, Home Depot, and Kmart, a fair number would be able to identify Sam Walton as Wal-Mart's founder. And, some of these would even be able to tell a short story about the company's history.

Such a short story would begin in 1962; this is the year Sam Walton opened the first Wal-Mart store in Rogers, Arkansas. Interestingly enough, 1962 also marked the first year of operations for Kmart and Target. All three retailers are similar in their devotion to discount retailing. Indeed, Sam Walton began his venture into discount retailing in part because his chain of Arkansas and Kansas variety stores (what used to be called five- and ten-cent stores) had experienced competition from regional discount retailers. It was 1968 when Wal-Mart first ventured outside of Arkansas, establishing outlets in Missouri and Oklahoma.

By 1970 there were 38 Wal-Mart stores with annual sales of $44.2 million and 1,500 employees. By the end of the decade, sales had grown to $1.2 billion with 276 stores in 11 states and 21,000 employees. By its twenty-fifth anniversary in 1987, Wal-Mart had reached sales of $15.9 billion with 1,198 stores, and some 200,000 employees. Today, Wal-Mart stands as a "global colossus" with $256 billion in global revenue, 5,000 stores in 10 countries, and 1.3 million employees. It is said to be the largest private or nongovernment employer in the world.

What explains Wal-Mart's business success? According to the company's founder, "The secret of successful retailing is to give your customers what they want." And what do customers want? Sam Walton thought they wanted everything: "a wide assortment of good quality merchandise; the lowest possible prices; guaranteed satisfaction with what you buy; friendly, knowledgeable service; convenient hours; free parking; a pleasant shopping experience." Based on Wal-Mart's business success, Sam Walton's creation appears to give consumers what they want. And many, based on the growth figures previously cited, consider Wal-Mart to be the ultimate business success story.

But not everyone admires this business success. Rather, there are those who believe that Wal-Mart's business success has been built upon a series of abuses, with most of the abuses related to the company's goal of offering the lowest possible prices. These critics charge that in its drive to achieve its goal of lowest prices, Wal-Mart is driven to be antiunion, to pay low wages, to discriminates against women, to refuse to pay workers for some of their work, and to break child labor laws.

This issue examines the role of Wal-Mart in the economy. The first reading is a segment of an economic impact study prepared by the Los Angeles County Economic Development Corporation (LAEDC). In this study, paid for by Wal-Mart, the nonprofit organization assesses what would happen if Wal-Mart began to open a series of so-called Supercenter stores in Southern California. The report concludes that Wal-Mart's entry into the Southern California market would be of major benefit to consumers and create a significant number of new jobs. The second reading, prepared by the Democratic Staff of the House Committee on Education and the Workforce, summarizes a series of reports prepared by others as well as a series of legal actions taken against Wal-Mart. The staff's conclusion from this summary is that Wal-Mart's business success has only been achieved at a very high social cost.

YES

**Los Angeles County Economic
Development Corporation**

Wal-Mart Supercenters: What's in Store for Southern California?

Executive Summary

Wal-Mart Stores, Inc. is now the largest grocery retailer in the country based on sales. It is preparing to introduce its Supercenters, which combine a large general merchandise store with a full service market, into Southern California. The City of Los Angeles, in particular, with its 3.61 million people, 1.28 million households, and annual food store spending of approximately $5.65 billion, is a very attractive market. Wal-Mart's planned expansion into the local grocery business creates both a challenge to the major grocery store chains in the region, and an opportunity for cities to encourage strategic reinvestment in underserved neighborhoods.

The LAEDC [Los Angeles County Economic Development Corporation] agreed to assess the economic implications of Wal-Mart's entry into the Southern California grocery market because existing studies, which tend to tally only the negative impacts of Wal-Mart's operations, miss half the story. Here we aim to provide a fair and balanced assessment of both the good and not so good impacts of Supercenters in Southern California. Thus, we include not only the potential effects on existing grocery chains and their employees, but also the potential savings to consumers, and the potential job creation outside the grocery industry.

Costs and Savings

Wal-Mart Supercenters have a substantial cost advantage relative to traditional supermarkets, based on careful supply chain and inventory management, volume discounts, and lower labor costs. Much of this can be attributed to Wal-Mart's willingness to invest in technology and business practices which make its operations more efficient. Wal-Mart passes the savings on to consumers, offering lower prices on groceries than traditional grocery market chains. If Wal-Mart Supercenters are introduced in Los Angeles, food prices should fall.

Wal-Mart shoppers would immediately save an estimated average of 15 percent relative to what they would have paid under the current status quo. The savings could be higher, particularly in portions of the City of Los Angeles such as South Los Angeles and the northeast San Fernando Valley, which are underserved by traditional grocery stores. The corner stores where much of the food purchases in these areas take place offer uncompetitive prices relative to existing grocery stores, never mind Supercenters. As Wal-Mart gradually builds market share, major competitors will lower their prices as well, thus bringing additional savings to some consumers who will never set foot in a Wal-Mart store. Smaller stores will adjust by emphasizing specific market niches and specialty products which Wal-Mart does not provide.

The LAEDC conservatively calculated the potential savings to consumers in the City of Los Angeles to be *at least* $668 million, or $524 per household, annually, once Wal-Mart reaches 20 percent market share. The savings could be much higher, though the savings will not materialize overnight. They will increase gradually over many years in step with Wal-Mart's market share. These savings add to a household's discretionary *after tax dollars*—the portion of the income actually available for spending. This "found" money will be redirected to other items, including housing, savings, health, entertainment, and transportation. As households redeploy their savings, their spending will create jobs outside the grocery industry. In the City of Los Angeles, redirected grocery savings will create 6,500 additional jobs. The new jobs will be in a wide variety of occupations, reflecting the diverse spending patterns of Los Angeles households and the breadth of the regional economy.

The LAEDC also looked at the potential impact of Wal-Mart Supercenters on the entire Southern California market. In Los Angeles County, the aggregate annual savings to consumers would be at least $1.78 billion. When the savings are redirected to other purchases, the county-wide job creation will total 17,300 jobs. For consumers in Imperial, Los Angeles, Orange, Riverside, San Bernardino, San Diego and Riverside counties, the combined total annual savings will be at least $3.76 billion. The seven-county Southern California job creation total is 36,400 jobs.

Wal-Mart compensation, while lower than for the best-paid unionized grocery employees, is better than most people realize, particularly in its food business. Wal-Mart benefits include health care, a stakeholders' bonus, which is paid to employees at stores that perform well, profit-sharing, company contributions to 401(k) plans, which are the most common form of defined contribution retirement plan, a 15 percent discount on company stock, and a 10 percent discount on purchases of general merchandise. Wal-Mart's health-care plan requires employees to share the upfront costs (Wal-Mart pays 2/3rd; the associates pay 1/3rd), but in return does not have single incident or lifetime caps on coverage.

Two important factors make Wal-Mart's wages appear lower than they might otherwise. First, Supercenters are a relatively new phenomenon. Most Supercenters have simply not been open long enough to have accumulated many employees with lengthy service records, and thus higher rates of pay. Second, and perhaps most important, Wal-Mart's pay among its front line grocery workers is skewed downwards because it promotes from within. Wal-Mart recruits its management primarily from within the ranks of its own employees. This opens up career opportunities for associates, and crucially for wage comparisons, removes some of the most experienced and best paid Wal-Mart employees from the pool of workers typically being compared. In contrast to unionized grocery stores, where some of the most senior employees are cashiers, at Wal-Mart cashier is an entry level position.

Unionized grocery workers earn $2.50–$3.50 per hour more, on average, than Supercenter employees in Southern California could expect. Some union grocery workers are very well compensated, but the wages of the most highly compensated among them are frequently mistaken for *average* union wages, which are lower. The widely-cited Orange County Business Council (OCBC) study calculated the potential wage loss if all union workers in the Southern California grocery industry were to earn the same wages as Wal-Mart employees. Using more realistic assumptions of Wal-Mart Supercenter employee pay (and hence a narrower wage gap), we find the potential cumulative wage loss in Los Angeles County is $150 million to $258 million annually. For the 7-county Southern California region (including Los Angeles), the range is $307 million to $529 million. If all current unionized grocery employees were to eventually earn the equivalent of Wal-Mart Supercenter employees, the lost spending due to eroded household income could cost Los Angeles County alone 1,500 to 2,500 jobs and the 7-county region 3,000 to 5,100 jobs. Should these losses materialize, they would be offset by region-wide gains of 36,400 jobs, meaning that outside the grocery sector at least seven jobs would be added for every one lost.

Timing

Timing will be critical in determining the potential impact of Supercenters. Experience in other regions suggests that existing stores will have time to adjust. The potential benefits as well as the costs of Wal-Mart entering the Southern California grocery market described in this report assume that Wal-Mart will eventually gain a market share of 20 percent. Yet, gaining share will take a long time.

Wal-Mart will struggle to find suitable locations for its stores in many areas of heavily urbanized, built-out Southern California, including most of the City of Los Angeles. By comparison, in Fort Worth, Texas, it took Wal-Mart six years to achieve a 6.5 percent share in a market where stores can be built quickly. Unlike California, permitting, environmental regulation, and community opposition are not generally a factor in Texas, where growth has nonetheless proceeded at only a modest pace. Wal-Mart appears to be proceeding cautiously in California, with plans to build just 40 Supercenters in the state over the next three to five years. This represents just 4 percent of the 1,000 new Supercenters that will be added nationwide during the same period. Based solely on the state's share of the national population and the potential size of its market, the expected number of new Supercenters in California should be in the range of 100 to 150. If the distribution of existing Supercenters were factored in, the California number would be higher still. Again, by comparison, Texas, which is the nation's second most populous state, already has many Supercenters while California, the most populous state, has none.

The slow roll out of Supercenters in Southern California, compared to other regions, will delay the arrival of benefits for consumers, but it will also give Wal-Mart's competitors more time to adapt. With Southern California's rapidly growing population, Wal-Mart is likely to increase its presence by taking a greater share of overall market growth, rather than by luring existing customers from large supermarket chains. While a scenario in which Wal-Mart captures most of this growth may constitute a challenge for the major supermarket chains, their situation—aside from fierce price competition, which benefits consumers, and increased pressure on their balance sheets—is not likely to be significantly different than it is now.

Conclusion

All indicators suggest that Wal-Mart will gradually enter the grocery market in Southern California. A 20 percent market share may be achievable over time, but not in the near future. Unlike what has occurred in other parts of the country, Supercenters will be rolled out slowly here, delaying the arrival of benefits. Conversely, any negative impacts will also be delayed, and lessened, since competitors will have more time to adapt. Over the long term, Wal-Mart is likely to increase its market share by absorbing a larger share of overall market growth, rather than by attracting existing customers from the large grocery chains.

The real choice facing the City of Los Angeles is whether Wal-Mart will serve residents from within the city's boundaries or from without. If Wal-Mart decides to open Supercenters to serve demand in the region, the stores could conveniently serve customers residing in the City of Los Angeles from within the city, or from neighboring jurisdictions. In the former case, the city government would have the opportunity to influence Wal-Mart's presence. The City of Los Angeles could guide Wal-Mart and other large scale retailers to sites where their presence and spending would be a boon for local redevelopment. If, however, Wal-Mart builds in neighboring jurisdictions, the City of Los Angeles will have no control over the development. Wal-Mart customers in Los Angeles would leave the city to shop, taking their taxable spending (and any resulting local sales tax revenues) with them.

Study Highlights
Savings for Consumers and New Jobs Outside the Grocery Industry

- Supercenter customers will save an average of 15 percent on their groceries.
- Price competition will lead to reduced prices at existing grocery chains, providing customers who shop at stores other than Wal-Mart average savings of 10 percent.
- Increased competition in non-grocery items will lead to price reductions averaging 3 percent at general merchandise and apparel competitors.

- Money that people save on groceries will be redirected to other items, including housing, savings, health, entertainment, and transportation. This new spending will, in turn, create jobs outside the grocery industry.

Savings in the City of Los Angeles

- Consumers in the City of Los Angeles are conservatively estimated to save at least $668 million annually, or $524 per household, per year.
- Redirected grocery savings will create 6,500 additional full-time-equivalent jobs.

Savings in Los Angeles County

- Consumers in Los Angeles County are conservatively estimated to save at least $1.78 billion annually, or $569 per household, per year.
- Redirected grocery savings will create 17,300 new jobs County-wide.

Savings in Southern California

- Consumers in Imperial, Los Angeles, Orange, Riverside, San Bernardino, San Diego, and Ventura Counties are conservatively estimated to save at least $3.76 billion annually, or $589 per household, per year.
- In these seven counties, 36,400 new jobs will be created.

Potential Impacts to Major Grocery Chains

- Major grocery companies have used fear of intense competition to seek wage concessions from unionized employees, most likely by lowering the wages of new hires.
- Future foregone wages of unionized grocery employees in Los Angeles County could equal $150 million to $258 million annually, and could reach $307 to $529 million annually across the entire 7-county Southern California region.
- These foregone wages would reduce overall household spending, potentially costing Los Angeles County 1,500 to 2,500 jobs and the 7-county region (including Los Angeles) 3,000 to 5,100 jobs.
- These losses will be offset by region-wide gains of 36,400 jobs outside the grocery business, or a net gain of at least seven new jobs for every one lost.

Catalyst for Redevelopment

- Wal-Mart can be used as a catalyst for redevelopment, particularly in areas saddled with struggling (or failed) retail centers. In Panorama City, Wal-Mart replaced the Broadway department store, creating new jobs and revitalizing the mall and the surrounding neighborhood. Wal-Mart will open stores in an abandoned K-Mart in Canoga Park and in an abandoned AutoNation site in Harbor Gateway.
- Wal-Mart has demonstrated a willingness to enter communities that other businesses appear uninterested in serving. In Baldwin Hills, Wal-Mart brought jobs and retail opportunities to an underserved

community by opening a store in a former Macy's, which had sat vacant for five years.
- There are many parts of Los Angeles that are underserved by retail. The need is acute in the grocery sector and these communities stand to gain the most if Wal-Mart were to enter the market and offer lower prices.

Sales Tax Leakage

- Jurisdictions without Supercenters will lose taxable sales when their residents shop elsewhere. Supercenters have become an issue because they sell groceries, which are non-taxable. Sixty to seventy percent of the sales at Supercenters, however, are taxable. The appeal of Supercenters, for both Wal-Mart and the consumer, is that they allow shoppers to combine trips and do all of their purchasing in one location. If city residents choose to buy their groceries at Supercenters outside of the city, the City of L.A. will lose out on the local share of any taxable purchases shoppers make on those trips.
- Cities without Supercenters will also lose out on sales tax revenue when their residents combine trips to Wal-Mart with shopping at nearby stores.
- Overall sales taxes will increase to the extent that customers spend their savings generated from lower-priced groceries (which are not taxable) on goods which are taxable.
- The modest increase in overall taxable sales should not obscure the key issue—the distribution of taxable sales (and hence tax revenues) among Souhern California jurisdictions based on where consumers choose to shop.

Everyday Low Wages: The Hidden Price We All Pay for Wal-Mart

Introduction

The retail giant Wal-Mart has become the nation's largest private sector employer with an estimated 1.2 million employees.[1] The company's annual revenues now amount to 2 percent of the U.S. Gross Domestic Product.[2] Wal-Mart's success is attributed to its ability to charge low prices in mega-stores offering everything from toys and furniture to groceries. While charging low prices obviously has some consumer benefits, mounting evidence from across the country indicates that these benefits come at a steep price for American workers, U.S. labor laws, and community living standards.

Wal-Mart is undercutting labor standards at home and abroad, while those federal officials charged with protecting labor standards have been largely indifferent. Public outcry against Wal-Mart's labor practices has been answered by the company with a cosmetic response. Wal-Mart has attempted to offset its labor record with advertising campaigns utilizing employees (who are euphemistically called "associates") to attest to Wal-Mart's employment benefits and support of local communities. Nevertheless—whether the issue is basic organizing rights of workers, or wages, or health benefits, or working conditions, or trade policy—Wal-Mart has come to represent the lowest common denominator in the treatment of working people.

This report reviews Wal-Mart's labor practices across the country and around the world and provides an overview of how working Americans and their allies in Congress are seeking to address the gamut of issues raised by this new standard-bearer of American retail.

Wal-Mart's Labor Practices
Workers' Organizing Rights

The United States recognizes workers' right to organize unions. Government employers generally may not interfere with public sector employees' freedom of association. In the private sector, workers' right to organize is protected by

U.S. House of Representatives, February 16, 2004. http://www.mindfully.org/Industry/2004/wal-mart-labor-record16feb04.htm

the National Labor Relations Act.[3] Internationally, this right is recognized as a core labor standard and a basic human right.[4]

Wal-Mart's record on the right to organize recently achieved international notoriety. On January 14, 2004, the International Confederation of Free Trade Unions (ICFTU), an organization representing 151 million workers in 233 affiliated unions around the world, issued a report on U.S. labor standards.[5] Wal-Mart's rampant violations of workers' rights figured prominently. In the last few years, well over 100 unfair labor practice charges have been lodged against Wal-Mart throughout the country, with 43 charges filed in 2002 alone. Since 1995, the U.S. government has been forced to issue at least 60 complaints against Wal-Mart at the National Labor Relations Board.[6] Wal-Mart's labor law violations range from illegally firing workers who attempt to organize a union to unlawful surveillance, threats, and intimidation of employees who dare to speak out.

With not a single Wal-Mart store in the United States represented by a union, the company takes a pro-active role in maintaining its union-free status. Wal-Mart has issued "A Manager's Toolbox to Remaining Union Free," which provides managers with lists of warning signs that workers might be organizing, including "frequent meetings at associates' homes" and "associates who are never seen together start talking or associating with each other."[7] The "Toolbox" gives managers a hotline to call so that company specialists can respond rapidly and head off any attempt by employees to organize.

When employees have managed to obtain a union election and vote for a union, Wal-Mart has taken sweeping action in response. In 2000, when a small meatcutting department successfully organized a union at a Wal-Mart store in Texas, Wal-Mart responded a week later by announcing the phase-out of its meatcutting departments entirely. Because of deficient labor laws, it took the meatcutters in Texas three years to win their jobs back with an order that Wal-Mart bargain with their union.[8] Rather than comply, Wal-Mart is appealing this decision.[9]

Wal-Mart's aggressive anti-union activity, along with the nation's weak labor laws, have kept the largest private sector employer in the U.S. union-free. Breaking the law that guarantees workers' right to organize has material consequences for both the workers and the company. According to data released by the Bureau of Labor Statistics in January 2004, union workers earn median weekly salaries of $760, compared to non-union workers' median weekly salaries of $599—a difference of over 26 percent.[10] In the supermarket industry, the union difference is even more pronounced, with union members making 30 percent more than non-union workers. Union representation also correlates with higher benefits.[11] For instance, 72 percent of union workers have guaranteed pensions with defined benefits, while only 15 percent of non-union workers enjoy such retirement security.[12] On the health care front, which will be explored in more detail later, 60 percent of union workers have medical care benefits on the job, compared to only 44 percent of non-union workers.[13] For companies like Wal-Mart seeking to maintain low labor costs, these statistics obviously provide an incentive to remain union-free. Unfortunately, U.S. labor laws fail to provide a sufficient disincentive against violating workers' rights.

Low Wages

By keeping unions at bay, Wal-Mart keeps its wages low—even by general industry standards. The average supermarket employee makes $10.35 per hour.[14] Sales clerks at Wal-Mart, on the other hand, made only $8.23 per hour on average, or $13,861 per year, in 2001.[15] Some estimate that average "associate" salaries range from $7.50 to $8.50 per hour.[16] With an average on-the-clock workweek of 32 hours, many workers take home less than $1,000 per month.[17] Even the higher estimate of a $13,861 annual salary fell below the 2001 federal poverty line of $14,630 for a family of three.[18] About one-third of Wal-Mart's employees are part-time, restricting their access to benefits.[19] These low wages, to say the least, complicate employees' ability to obtain essential benefits, such as health care coverage, which will be explored in a later section.

The low pay stands in stark contrast to Wal-Mart's slogan, "Our people make the difference." Now-retired Senior Vice President Don Soderquist has explained: "'Our people make the difference' is not a meaningless slogan—it's a reality at Wal-Mart. We are a group of dedicated, hardworking, ordinary people who have teamed together to accomplish extraordinary things."[20] With 2002 company profits hitting $6.6 billion, Wal-Mart employees do indeed "accomplish extraordinary things."[21] But at poverty level wages, these workers are not sharing in the company's success.

Unequal Pay and Treatment

Title VII of the Civil Rights Act prohibits discrimination in employment based on employees' race, color, religion, sex, or national origin.[22] Additionally, the Equal Pay Act, an amendment to the Fair Labor Standards Act, prohibits unequal pay for equal work on the basis of sex.[23] These basic labor and civil rights laws have become an issue at Wal-Mart.

In 2001, six women sued Wal-Mart in California claiming the company discriminated against women by systematically denying them promotions and paying them less than men. The lawsuit has expanded to potentially the largest class action in U.S. history—on behalf of more than 1 million current and former female employees. While two-thirds of the company's hourly workers are female, women hold only one-third of managerial positions and constitute less than 15 percent of store managers.[24] The suit also claims that women are pushed into "female" departments and are demoted if they complain about unequal treatment. One plaintiff, a single mother of four, started at Wal-Mart in 1990 at a mere $3.85 an hour. Even with her persistent requests for training and promotions, it took her eight years to reach $7.32 an hour and seven years to reach management, while her male counterparts were given raises and promotions much more quickly. For this plaintiff, annual pay increases were as little as 10 cents and never more than 35 cents per hour.[25]

Off-the-Clock Work

While wages are low at Wal-Mart, too often employees are not paid at all. The Fair Labor Standards Act (FLSA), along with state wage and hour laws, requires hourly employees to be paid for all time actually worked at no less than a minimum wage and at time-and-a-half for all hours worked over 40 in a week.[26] These labor laws have posed a particular obstacle for Wal-Mart. As of December 2002, there were thirty-nine class-action lawsuits against the company in thirty states, claiming tens of millions of dollars in back pay for hundreds of thousands of Wal-Mart employees.[27]

In 2001, Wal-Mart forked over $50 million in unpaid wages to 69,000 workers in Colorado. These wages were paid only after the workers filed a class action lawsuit. Wal-Mart had been working the employees off-the-clock. The company also paid $500,000 to 120 workers in Gallup, New Mexico, who filed a lawsuit over unpaid work.[28]

In a Texas class-action certified in 2002 on behalf of 200,000 former and current Wal-Mart employees, statisticians estimated that the company short-changed its workers $150 million over four years—just based on the frequency of employees working through their daily 15 minute breaks.[29]

In Oregon, 400 employees in 27 stores sued the company for unpaid, off-the-clock overtime. In their suit, the workers explained that managers would delete hours from their time records and tell employees to clean the store after they clocked out. In December 2002, a jury found in favor of the workers.[30] One personnel manager claimed that, for six years, she was forced to delete hours from employee time sheets.[31]

In the latest class-action, filed in November 2003, noting evidence of systematic violations of the wage-and-hour law, a judge certified a lawsuit for 65,000 Wal-Mart employees in Minnesota. Reacting to the certification, a Wal-Mart spokesperson told the Minneapolis *Star Tribune:* "We have no reason to believe these isolated situations . . . represent a widespread problem with off-the clock work."[32]

Many observers blame the wage-and-hour problems at Wal-Mart on pressure placed on managers to keep labor costs down. In 2002, operating costs for Wal-Mart were just 16.6 percent of total sales, compared to a 20.7 percent average for the retail industry as a whole.[33] Wal-Mart reportedly awards bonuses to its employees based on earnings. With other operating and inventory costs set by higher level management, store managers must turn to wages to increase profits. While Wal-Mart expects those managers to increase sales each year, it expects the labor costs to be cut by two-tenths of a percentage point each year as well.[34]

Reports from former Wal-Mart managers seem to corroborate this dynamic. Joyce Moody, a former manager in Alabama and Mississippi, told the *New York Times* that Wal-Mart "threatened to write up managers if they didn't bring the payroll in low enough." Depositions in wage and hour lawsuits reveal that company headquarters leaned on management to keep their labor costs at 8 percent of sales or less, and managers in turn leaned on assistant managers to work their employees off-the-clock or simply delete time from employee time sheets.[35]

Child Labor and Work Breaks Violations

The Fair Labor Standards Act and state wage and hour laws also govern child labor and work breaks. These work time regulations have likewise posed a problem at Wal-Mart stores.

In January 2004, the *New York Times* reported on an internal Wal-Mart audit which found "extensive violations of child-labor laws and state regulations requiring time for breaks and meals."[36] One week of time records from 25,000 employees in July 2000 found 1,371 instances of minors working too late, during school hours, or for too many hours in a day. There were 60,767 missed breaks and 15,705 lost meal times.[37]

According to the *New York Times* report: "Verette Richardson, a former Wal-Mart cashier in Kansas City, Mo., said it was sometimes so hard to get a break that some cashiers urinated on themselves. Bella Blaubergs, a diabetic who worked at a Wal-Mart in Washington State, said she sometimes nearly fainted from low blood sugar because managers often would not give breaks."[38]

A store manager in Kentucky told the *New York Times* that, after the audit was issued, he received no word from company executives to try harder to cut down on violations: "There was no follow-up to that audit, there was nothing sent out I was aware of saying, 'We're bad. We screwed up. This is the remedy we're going to follow to correct the situation.'"[39]

Unaffordable or Unavailable Health Care

In 2002, 43 million non-elderly Americans lacked health insurance coverage—an increase of almost 2.5 million from the previous year. Most Americans receive their health insurance coverage through their employers. At the same time, most of the uninsured are working Americans and their families, with low to moderate incomes. Their employers, however, either do not offer health insurance at all or the health insurance offered is simply unaffordable.[40]

Among these uninsured working families are a significant number of Wal-Mart employees, many of whom instead secure their health care from publicly subsidized programs. Fewer than half—between 41 and 46 percent—of Wal-Mart's employees are insured by the company's health care plan, compared nationally to 66 percent of employees at large firms like Wal-Mart who receive health benefits from their employer.[41] In recent years, the company increased obstacles for its workers to access its health care plan.

In 2002, Wal-Mart increased the waiting period for enrollment eligibility from 90 days to 6 months for full-time employees. Part-time employees must wait 2 years before they may enroll in the plan, and they may not purchase coverage for their spouses or children. The definition of part-time was changed from 28 hours or less per week to less than 34 hours per week. At the time, approximately one-third of Wal-Mart's workforce was part-time. By comparison, nationally, the average waiting period for health coverage for employees at large firms like Wal-Mart was 1.3 months.[42]

The Wal-Mart plan itself shifts much of the health care costs onto employees. In 1999, employees paid 36 percent of the costs. In 2001, the employee burden rose to 42 percent. Nationally, large-firm employees pay on average 16 percent of the premium for health insurance. Unionized grocery workers typically pay nothing.[43] Studies show that much of the decline in employer-based health coverage is due to shifts of premium costs from employers to employees.[44]

Moreover, Wal-Mart employees who utilize their health care confront high deductibles and co-payments. A single worker could end up spending around $6,400 out-of-pocket—about 45 percent of her annual full-time salary—before seeing a single benefit from the health plan.[45]

According to an AFL-CIO report issued in October 2003, the employees' low wages and Wal-Mart's cost-shifting render health insurance unaffordable, particularly for those employees with families. Even under the Wal-Mart plan with the highest deductible ($1,000)—and therefore with the lowest employee premium contribution—it would take an $8 per hour employee, working 34 hours per week, almost one-and-a-half months of pre-tax earnings to pay for one year of family coverage.[46]

Wal-Mart's spending on health care for its employees falls well below industry and national employer-spending averages. A Harvard Business School case study on Wal-Mart found that, in 2002, Wal-Mart spent an average of $3,500 per employee. By comparison, the average spending per employee in the wholesale/retailing sector was $4,800. For U.S. employers in general, the average was $5,600 per employee.[47]

In the end, because they cannot afford the company health plan, many Wal-Mart workers must turn to public assistance for health care or forego their health care needs altogether. Effectively, Wal-Mart forces taxpayers to subsidize what should be a company-funded health plan. According to a study by the Institute for Labor and Employment at the University of California-Berkeley, **California taxpayers subsidized $20.5 million worth of medical care for Wal-Mart in that state alone.**[48] In fact, Wal-Mart personnel offices, knowing employees cannot afford the company health plan, actually encourage employees to apply for charitable and public assistance, according to a recent report by the PBS news program *Now With Bill Moyers*.[49]

When a giant like Wal-Mart shifts health insurance costs to employees, its competitors invariably come under pressure to do the same. Currently engaged in the largest ongoing labor dispute in the nation, unionized grocery workers in southern California have refused to accept higher health care costs resulting from cost-shifting on health insurance premiums by their grocery chain employers—cost-shifting, the grocers say, inspired by the threat of Wal-Mart competition. Beginning on October 11, 2003, 70,000 grocery employees of Vons, Pavilions, Ralphs, and Albertsons have either been on strike or locked out. The companies want to dramatically increase workers' share of health costs, claiming that the change is necessary in order to compete with Wal-Mart's incursion in the southern California market. E. Richard Brown, the director of the Center for Health Policy at the University of California, Los Angeles, told the *Sacramento Bee* that, if the grocery chains drastically reduce health benefits, the trends toward cost shifting and elimination of health coverage will accelerate. Following the grocers' lead, more employers would offer fewer benefits, would require their workers to pay more, and may even drop health benefits altogether.[50] Whether the current pressure from Wal-Mart is real or imagined or merely a convenient excuse for the grocers' cost-cutting bargaining position, Wal-Mart has sparked a new race to the bottom among American retail employers. Undeniably, such a race threatens to undermine the employer-based health insurance system.

Low Wages Mean High Costs to Taxpayers

Because Wal-Mart wages are generally not living wages, the company uses tax-payers to subsidize its labor costs. While the California study showed how much taxpayers were subsidizing Wal-Mart on health care alone, the total costs to taxpayers for Wal-Mart's labor policies are much greater.

The Democratic Staff of the Committee on Education and the Workforce estimates that one 200-person Wal-Mart store may result in a cost to federal taxpayers of $420,750 per year—about $2,103 per employee. Specifically, the low wages result in the following additional public costs being passed along to taxpayers:

- $36,000 a year for free and reduced lunches for just 50 qualifying Wal-Mart families.
- $42,000 a year for Section 8 housing assistance, assuming 3 percent of the store employees qualify for such assistance, at $6,700 per family.
- $125,000 a year for federal tax credits and deductions for low-income families, assuming 50 employees are heads of household with a child and 50 are married with two children.
- $100,000 a year for the additional Title I expenses, assuming 50 Wal-Mart families qualify with an average of 2 children.
- $108,000 a year for the additional federal health care costs of moving into state children's health insurance programs (S-CHIP), assuming 30 employees with an average of two children qualify.
- $9,750 a year for the additional costs for low income energy assistance.

Among Wal-Mart employees, some single workers may be able to make ends meet. Others may be forced to take on two or three jobs. Others may have a spouse with a better job. And others simply cannot make ends meet. Because Wal-Mart fails to pay sufficient wages, U.S. taxpayers are forced to pick up the tab. In this sense, Wal-Mart's profits are not made only on the backs of its employees—but on the backs of every U.S. taxpayer.

The ultimate costs are not limited to subsidies for underpaid Wal-Mart workers. When a Wal-Mart comes to town, the new competition has a ripple effect throughout the community. Other stores are forced out of business or forced to cut employees' wages and benefits in order to compete with Wal-Mart. The Los Angeles City Council commissioned a report in 2003 on the effects of allowing Wal-Mart Supercenters into their communities. The report, prepared by consulting firm Rodino and Associates, found that Supercenters drive down wages in the local retail industry, place a strain on public services, and damage small businesses. It recommended that the City Council refuse to allow any Supercenters to be built in Los Angeles without a promise from Wal-Mart to increase wages and benefits for its employees.[51]

The findings of the Rodino report are alarming. The labor impacts of a Wal-Mart Supercenter on low-income communities include:

- "Big box retailers and superstores may negatively impact the labor market in an area by the conversion of higher paying retail jobs to a fewer number of lower paying retail jobs. The difference in overall compensation (wages and benefits) may be as much as $8.00."

- "Lack of health care benefits of many big box and superstore employees can result in a greater public financial burden as workers utilize emergency rooms as a major component of their health care."
- "A study conducted by the San Diego Taxpayers Association (SDCTA), a nonprofit, nonpartisan organization, found that an influx of big-box stores into San Diego would result in an annual decline in wages and benefits between $105 million and $221 million, and an increase of $9 million in public health costs. SDCTA also estimated that the region would lose pensions and retirement benefits valued between $89 million and $170 million per year and that even increased sales and property tax revenues would not cover the extra costs of necessary public services."
- "[The threat of Wal-Mart's incursion into the southern California grocery market] is already triggering a dynamic in which the grocery stores are negotiating with workers for lowered compensation, in an attempt to re-level the 'playing field.'"
- "One study of superstores and their potential impact on grocery industry employees found that the entry of such stores into the Southern California regional grocery business was expected to depress industry wages and benefits at an estimated range from a low of $500 million to a high of almost $1.4 billion annually, potentially affecting 250,000 grocery industry employees . . . [T]he full impact of lost wages and benefits throughout Southern California could approach $2.8 billion per year."[52]

Reports such as these have provided supporting evidence to localities which seek to pass ordinances restricting "big box" or supercenter stores. Such ordinances were recently passed in Alameda and Contra Costa counties in California. Wal-Mart, however, has moved to overturn those ordinances. In Contra Costa, Wal-Mart launched a petition drive to challenge that county's ordinance in a referendum in March 2004. In Alameda, the company has filed a lawsuit to void an ordinance passed by the Board of Supervisors in January 2004.[53]

One of the most cited studies on Wal-Mart's impact on local communities was performed by economist Kenneth Stone at Iowa State University in 1993. Stone looked at the impact of Wal-Mart on small towns in Iowa. He found a 3 percent spike in total retail sales in communities immediately after a Wal-Mart opened. But the longer term effects of Wal-Mart were disastrous for nearby independent businesses. Over the course of the next several years, retailers' sales of men's and boys' apparel dropped 44 percent on average, hardware sales fell by 31 percent, and lawn and garden sales fell by 26 percent. Likewise, a Congressional Research Service report in 1994 explained that Wal-Mart uses a saturation strategy with store development. In other words, it builds stores in nearby connected markets in order to stifle any competition in the targeted area by the size of its presence.[54]

By all accounts, Wal-Mart's development strategy has been working. Currently, Wal-Mart operates around 3,000 total stores and close to 1,400 Supercenters. It is the largest grocer in the U.S., with a 19 percent market share, and the third-largest pharmacy, with a 16 percent market share. According to Retail Forward, a global management consulting and research firm, for every one Supercenter that will open, two supermarkets will close.[55] Since 1992, the supermarket industry has experienced a net loss of 13,500 stores.[56] Over the next five years, Wal-Mart plans to open 1,000 more Supercenters in the U.S.[57] By 2007, Wal-Mart is expected to control 35 percent of food and drug sales in the U.S.[58]

Illegal Use of Undocumented Workers

Among the lowest paid workers in the U.S. economy are undocumented immigrants. As was reported in the fall of 2003, these workers are not foreign to the floors of Wal-Mart stores. On October 23, 2003, federal agents raided 61 Wal-Mart stores in 21 states. When they left, the agents had arrested 250 nightshift janitors who were undocumented workers.[59]

Following the arrests, a grand jury convened to consider charging Wal-Mart executives with labor racketeering crimes for knowingly allowing undocumented workers to work at their stores. The workers themselves were employed by agencies Wal-Mart contracted with for cheap cleaning services. While Wal-Mart executives have tried to lay the blame squarely with the contractors, federal investigators point to wiretapped conversations showing that executives knew the workers were undocumented.[60]

Additionally, some of the janitors have filed a class-action lawsuit against Wal-Mart alleging both racketeering and wage-and-hour violations. According to the janitors, Wal-Mart and its contractors failed to pay them overtime totaling, along with other damages, $200,000. One of the plaintiffs told the *New York Times* that he worked seven days per week for eight months, earning $325 for 60-hour weeks, and he never received overtime.[61] A legal question now being raised is whether these undocumented workers even have the right to sue their employers.[62]

Not surprisingly, this recent raid was not the first time Wal-Mart was caught using undocumented workers. In 1998 and 2001, federal agents arrested 102 undocumented workers at Wal-Marts around the country.[63]

President Bush's newly proposed temporary foreign worker plan would legalize such undocumented workers without granting them an opportunity for citizenship, creating a new class of indentured servants and a safer source of cheap labor for companies like Wal-Mart.

Trading Away Jobs

Since the recession began in March 2001, the United States has lost 2.4 million jobs. In every recession, since the Great Depression, jobs were recovered within the first 31 months after the recession began—until now. The latest recession began 34 months ago and officially ended in November 2001, but the jobs have not been recovered. For American working families, by all accounts, the "jobless recovery" has been of little benefit to them. While GDP growth was strong or solid in the third and fourth quarters of 2003, real wages for workers remained stagnant and even declined.[64]

Indeed, of the jobs that remain, the pay is low. The country has seen a dramatic shift from high-paying jobs to low-paying jobs. For instance, in New Hampshire, which still has not recovered the number of jobs it lost in the recession, new jobs pay 35 percent lower wages than lost jobs. In Delaware, those wages are 43 percent lower; in Colorado, 35 percent lower; in West Virginia, 33 percent lower. In fact, the low-pay shift has hit all but two of the fifty states.[65]

Moreover, these changes in the labor market reveal themselves in a marked decline in living standards for low- and middle-income workers. The real weekly earnings for full-time workers age 25 and older fell for the bottom half of the workforce between the fourth quarters of 2002 and 2003. In particular, workers in the 10th percentile saw their weekly earnings fall 1.2 percent; in the 20th percentile, by 0.5 percent, in the 50th percentile, by 0.1 percent.[66] Conversely, earners in the top percentiles of income experienced growth. The 90th percentile, for instance, saw a 1.1 percent increase in weekly earnings. As the Economic Policy Institute points out: "This pattern of earnings growth suggests that while the economy is expanding, the benefits of growth are flowing to those at the top of the wage scale."[67]

These lower-paying jobs are largely service sector jobs, like retail, replacing traditionally higher-paying and unionized manufacturing jobs. Between January 1998 and August 2003, the nation experienced a net loss of 3 million manufacturing jobs.[68] During the "recovery," 1.3 million manufacturing jobs disappeared.[69] American manufacturers find it increasingly difficult to keep jobs in the U.S., given the availability of cheap labor abroad. In 2003, the U.S. trade deficit hit a record high of $551 billion, increasing 15 percent from 2002 and exceeding 5 percent of GDP.[70]

Wal-Mart plays a curiously illustrative role in this jobs phenomenon— not just in the creation of low-paying jobs and the downward pressure on wages and benefits, but also in the export of existing manufacturing jobs to foreign countries offering cheap labor. Wal-Mart markets itself with a patriotic, small-town, red-white-and-blue advertising motif. But Wal-Mart's trade practices are anything but small-town. Indeed, Wal-Mart conducts international trade in manufactured goods on a scale that can bring down entire nations' economies.

While the red-white-and-blue banners remain, long-gone are the days when Wal-Mart abided by the mottos of "Buy American" and "Bring It Home to the USA." In 1995, Wal-Mart claimed only 6 percent of its merchandise was imported. Today an estimated 50–60 percent of its products come from overseas.[71] In the past five years, Wal-Mart has doubled its imports from China. In 2002, the company bought 14 percent of the $1.9 billion of clothes exported by Bangladesh to the United States. Also in 2002, the company purchased $12 billion in merchandise from China, or 10 percent of China's total U.S.-bound exports, a 20 percent increase from the previous year. In 2003, these Chinese purchases jumped to $15 billion, or almost one-eighth of all Chinese exports to the United States.[72] Today, more than 3,000 supplier factories in China produce for Wal-Mart.[73]

Wal-Mart maintains an extensive global network of 10,000 suppliers.[74] Whether American, Bangladeshi, Chinese, or Honduran, Wal-Mart plays these producers against one another in search of lower and lower prices. American suppliers have been forced to relocate their businesses overseas to maintain

Wal-Mart contracts.[75] Overseas manufacturers are forced to engage in cutthroat competition that further erodes wages and working conditions of what often already are sweatshops. To keep up with the pressure to produce ever cheaper goods, factories force employees to work overtime or work for weeks without a day off. A Bangladeshi factory worker told the *Los Angeles Times* that employees at her factory worked from 8 a.m. to 3 a.m. for 10 and 15 day stretches just to meet Wal-Mart price demands. And still, Wal-Mart's general manager for Bangladesh complained of his country's factories, telling the *Los Angeles Times*, "I think they need to improve. When I entered a factory in China, it seemed they are very fast."[76]

While low-wage jobs displace higher-paid manufacturing jobs in the United States, undercutting living standards at home, living standards abroad are not reaping the benefits one might expect. Reports indicate that Wal-Mart's bargaining power is able to maintain low wages and poor working conditions among its foreign suppliers. The *Washington Post* has explained: "As capital scours the globe for cheaper and more malleable workers, and as poor countries seek multinational companies to provide jobs, lift production, and open export markets, Wal-Mart and China have forged themselves into the ultimate joint venture, their symbiosis influencing the terms of labor and consumption the world over."[77] Thanks to a ban on independent trade unions and a lack of other basic human rights, China offers Wal-Mart a highly-disciplined and cheap workforce. A Chinese labor official who asked to remain anonymous for fear of punishment told the *Washington Post* that "Wal-Mart pressures the factory to cut its price, and the factory responds with longer hours or lower pay. And the workers have no options."[78]

One employee of a Chinese supplier described the difficulties of surviving on $75 per month. She could rarely afford to buy meat, and her family largely subsisted on vegetables. Over four years, she had not received a single salary increase.[79]

Wal-Mart has countered that it insists that its suppliers enforce labor standards and comply with Chinese law. One-hundred Wal-Mart auditors inspect Chinese plants, and the company has suspended contracts with about 400 suppliers, mainly for violating overtime limits. An additional 72 factories were permanently blacklisted in 2003 for violating child labor standards. Still, critics point out that the Wal-Mart does not regularly inspect smaller factories that use middlemen to sell to the company. Nor does it inspect the factories of subcontractors. A Chinese labor organizer explained that the inspections are "ineffective," since Wal-Mart usually notifies the factories in advance. The factories "often prepare by cleaning up, creating fake time sheets and briefing workers on what to say."[80]

The factories themselves complain that, because Wal-Mart demands such low prices, they have slim profit margins—if any. A manager of one Chinese supplier told the *Washington Post*, "In the beginning, we made money . . . But when Wal-Mart started to launch nationwide distribution, they pressured us for a special price below our cost. Now, we're losing money on every box, while Wal-Mart is making more money."[81] Obviously, one way to regain a profit for such suppliers would be to begin cutting back on labor costs.

Finally, as testament to Wal-Mart's stalwart anti-union policy, none of its 31 stores in China are unionized, despite the fact that the Communist Party-controlled official union has told the company that it would not help workers fight for higher pay.[82] Oddly enough, Article 10 of China's Trade Union Law requires that any establishment with 25 or more workers must have a union. Wal-Mart, however, claims that it has received assurances from the central government that it need not allow unions in any of its stores.[83] As one reporter has explained, "The explanation for the apparent contradiction may be that the government's desire for foreign investment and jobs trumps any concern for workers' rights. That wouldn't be surprising in the Chinese environment, where strikes are forbidden and the official labor grouping actively supports the government's efforts to block the rise of independent unions."[84] With China, any company in search of pliant and cheap labor has found a perfect mix of cooperative government officials and workers made submissive through fear.

Disability Discrimination

The Americans with Disabilities Act (ADA) prohibits discrimination against persons with disabilities in employment matters. In particular, an employer may not discriminate against an employee or prospective employee who is otherwise qualified to perform the job if given reasonable accommodations.[85]

In addition to lawsuits over lost wages or unequal pay, Wal-Mart has faced a barrage of lawsuits alleging that the company discriminates against workers with disabilities. In 2001, Wal-Mart paid over $6 million to settle 13 such lawsuits. These cases were brought by the U.S. Equal Employment Opportunity Commission (EEOC) on behalf of disabled persons whom Wal-Mart failed to hire. The settlement also required Wal-Mart to change its procedures in dealing with disabled job applicants and provide more training for its employees on anti-discrimination laws.[86]

Yet, on January 20, 2004, the EEOC filed another lawsuit against the retail giant on behalf of a job applicant who claims he was not hired because he needed a wheelchair. The lawsuit was filed in Kansas City after the EEOC failed to obtain a settlement with Wal-Mart.[87]

Worker Safety

The Occupational Safety and Health Act (OSHA) is designed to protect workers from workplace injuries and illnesses.[88] OSHA is enforced by the Department of Labor's Occupational Safety and Health Administration. Regulations issued by that agency lay out clear rules for such safety matters as the provision of exits for employees.[89]

The latest Wal-Mart scandal to hit the news is its reported lockdown of its nighttime shift in various stores around the country. According to a January 18, 2004, *New York Times* report, the company institutes a "lock-in" policy at some of its Wal-Mart and Sam's Club stores.[90] The stores lock their doors at night so that no one can enter or leave the building, leaving workers inside trapped. Some workers are then threatened that, if they ever use the fire exit to leave the building, they will be fired. Instead, a manager is supposed to have a key that will unlock doors to allow employees to escape. Many workers have found themselves locked in without a manager who has a key, as the *New York Times* story detailed.[91]

The company has claimed that the policy is designed to protect stores and employees from crime. Former store managers, however, have claimed the real reason behind the lockdown is to prevent "shrinkage"—i.e., theft by either employees or outsiders. It is also designed to eliminate unauthorized cigarette breaks or quick trips home.[92]

Locked-in workers have had to wait for hours off-the-clock for a manager to show up to let them go home after they completed their shift. One worker claims to have broken his foot on the job and had to wait four hours for someone to open the door. Another worker alleges she cut her hand with box cutters one night and was forced to wait until morning to go to the hospital, where she received thirteen stitches.[93]

In the history of American worker safety, some of the worst tragedies have involved employees locked in their workplaces in an emergency, including the Triangle Waist Company fire of 1911 in which 146 women died in a fire because the garment factory's doors were locked. As recently as 1991, 25 workers perished in a fire at a chicken processing plant in North Carolina. The plant's owner had locked the doors for fear of employee theft and unauthorized breaks. According to recent reports, ten percent of Wal-Mart's stores are subjected to the nighttime lockdown.[94]

In 2002, in a telling junction of alleged labor law violations, the National Labor Relations Board (NLRB) issued a complaint against a Wal-Mart in Texas regarding health and safety threats made by management against employees. According to the complaint, a company official told workers that, after a worker filed complaints regarding unsafe conditions with the Occupational Safety and Health Administration (OSHA), any fines imposed upon the company would come out of employee bonuses.[95] . . .

Conclusion

Wal-Mart's success has meant downward pressures on wages and benefits, rampant violations of basic workers' rights, and threats to the standard of living in communities across the country. The success of a business need not come at the expense of workers and their families. Such short-sighted profit-making strategies ultimately undermine our economy.

In the past few years, Wal-Mart has been subjected to dozens of class-action suits seeking backpay for hundreds of thousands of shortchanged workers, dozens of unfair labor practice complaints by the U.S. government for violations of workers' right to organize, and other legal actions stemming from the company's employment practices. At the same time, it has managed to keep its wages low and put suppliers on a downward spiral to cut their own wages. To keep up with Wal-Mart's low-cost demands, U.S. manufacturers have found it increasingly difficult to remain in the U.S. Cuts in health care benefits to Wal-Mart employees are pushing other U.S. grocers to do the same.

Wal-Mart's current behavior must not be allowed to set the standard for American labor practices. Standing together, America's working families, including Wal-Mart employees, and their allies in Congress can reverse this race to the bottom in the fast-expanding service industry. The promise that every American can work an honest day's work, receive an honest day's wages, raise a family, own a home, have decent health care, and send their children to college is a promise that is not easily abandoned. It is, in short, the American Dream.

Notes

1. Anthony Bianco and Wendy Zellner, "Is Wal-Mart Too Powerful?" *Business Week* 100 (October 6, 2003).

2. Charles Stein, "Wal-Mart Finds Success, Image Breeds Contempt," *Boston Globe* H1 (November 30, 2003).

3. 29 U.S.C. § 141 *et seq.*

4. International Labor Organization, Convention No. 87, Freedom of Association and Protection of the Right to Organize (1948), and No. 98, Right to Organize and Collective Bargaining (1949).

5. International Confederation of Free Trade Unions (ICFTU), *Internationally Recognised Core Labour Standards in the United States: Report for the WTO General Council Review of the Trade Policies of the United States* (Geneva, January 14–16, 2004).

6. *Id.* at 3–4.

7. Wal-Mart, *A Manager's Toolbox to Remaining Union Free* at 20–21 (no date). Available online at. . . .

8. Pan Demetrakakes, "Is Wal-Mart Wrapped in Union Phobia?" *Food & Packaging* 76 (August 1, 2003).

9. Dan Kasler, "Labor Dispute Has Historical Precedent," *Scripps Howard News Service* (November 3, 2003).

10. Bureau of Labor Statistics, Department of Labor, "Union Members in 2003," Table 1 (January 21, 2004).

11. Stephen Franklin and Delroy Alexander, "Grocery Walkouts Have Broad Reach," *Chicago Tribune* C1 (November 12, 2003).

12. Bureau of Labor Statistics, Department of Labor, "Employee Benefits in Private Industry, 2003," Table 1 (September 17, 2003).

13. *Id.*

14. Charles Williams, "Supermarket Sweepstakes: Traditional Grocery Chains Mull Responses to Wal-Mart's Growing Dominance," *The Post and Courier* (Charleston, SC) 16E (November 10, 2003).

15. *Id.*

16. "Unaffordable Health Care, Low Wages, Sexual Discrimination—the Wal-Mart Way of Life," . . . (January 26, 2004).

17. Doug Dority, "The People's Campaign: Justice@Wal-Mart," *Air Line Pilot* 55 (February 2003).

18. Bianco and Zellner, *supra* note 1.

19. PBS, "Store Wars: When Wal-Mart Comes to Town," . . . (February 2, 2004). This percentage of part-time employees was based on the earlier Wal-Mart definition of part-time as working 28 hours or less per week. In 2002, Wal-Mart changed the definition to less than 34 hours per week, which likely increased the company's number of part-time workers.

20. Wal-Mart.com, "3 Basic Beliefs," . . . (January 26, 2004).

21. Karen Olsson, "Up Against Wal-Mart," *Mother Jones* 54 (March/April 2003).

22. 42 U.S.C. § 2000e *et seq.*

23. 29 U.S.C. § 206.

24. Neil Buckley and Caroline Daniel, "Wal-Mart vs. the Workers: Labour Grievances Are Stacking Up Against the World's Biggest Company," *Financial Times* 11 (November 20, 2003).

25. Sheryl McCarthy, "Wal-Mart—Always Low Wages for Women!" *Newsday* (May 1, 2003).

26. 29 U.S.C. § 201 *et seq.*

27. Associated Press, "Federal Jury Finds Wal-Mart Guilty in Overtime Pay Case," *Chicago Tribune,* Business 3 (December 20, 2003).

28. *Id.*

29. Steven Greenhouse, "Suits Say Wal-Mart Forces Workers to Toil Off the Clock," *New York Times* A1 (June 25, 2002).

30. Associated press, *supra* note 27.

31. Kristian Foden-Vencil, "Multiple Lawsuits Accuse Wal-Mart of Violating Workplace Regulations," *NPR Morning Edition* (January 14, 2004).

32. Gwendolyn Freed and John Reenan, "Wal-Mart Suit Gets Class Status," *Star Tribune* 1D (November 6, 2003).

33. Greenhouse, *supra* note 29.

34. United Food & Commercial Workers (UFCW), "Wal-Mart's War on Workers' Wages and Overtime Pay," . . . (January 26, 2004).

35. Greenhouse, *supra* note 29.

36. Steven Greenhouse, "In-House Audit Says Wal-Mart Violated Labor Laws," *New York Times* 16A (January 13, 2004).

37. *Id.*

38. *Id.*

39. *Id.*

40. Kaiser Family Foundation, *The Uninsured: A Primer—Key Facts About Americans Without Health Insurance,* at 1 (December 2003).

41. AFL-CIO, *Wal-Mart: An Example of Why Workers Remain Uninsured and Underinsured,* at 1 (October 2003).

42. *Id.* at 11.

43. *Id.*

44. John Holahan, "Changes in Employer-Sponsored Health Insurance Coverage," *Snapshots of America's Families III,* Urban Institute (September 17, 2003).

45. AFL-CIO, *supra* note 41, at 16.

46. *Id.* at 12.

47. Panjak Ghemawat, Ken Mark, and Stephen Bradley, "Wal-Mart Stores in 2003," case study, Harvard Business School (revised January 30, 2004).

48. Sylvia Chase, "The True Cost of Shopping at Wal-Mart," *Now with Bill Moyers,* Transcript (December 19, 2003).

49. *Id.*

50. Laura Mecoy, "Health Benefits Fight Heats Up: South State Grocery Strike Spotlights a Contentious Trend in Contract Talks," *Sacramento Bee* A1 (January 19, 2004).

51. Nancy Cleeland, "City Report is Critical of Wal-Mart Supercenters," *Los Angeles Times* C1 (December 6, 2003).

52. Rodino Associates, *Final Report on Research for Big Box Retail/Superstore Ordinance,* prepared for Industrial and Commercial Development Division, Community Development Department, at 18–20 (October 28, 2003).

53. Michelle Maitre, "Wal-Mart is Suing Alameda County: Retail Giant Challenges Law that Bars Supercenters in Unincorporated Areas," *Alameda Times-Star* (Alameda, CA) at More Local News (January 27, 2004).

54. Jessica Hall and Jim Troy, "Wal-Mart Go Home! Wal-Mart's Expansion Juggernaut Stumbles as Towns Turn Thumbs Down and Noses Up," *Warfield's Business Record* 1 (July 22, 1994).

55. Bianco and Zellner, *supra* note 1.

56. Matthew Swibel, "How to Outsmart Wal-Mart," . . . (November 24, 2003).

57. Bianco and Zellner, *supra* note 1.

58. Williams, supra note 14.

59. Steven Greenhouse, "Suit by Wal-Mart Cleaners Asserts Rackets Violation," *New York Times,* 12A (November 11, 2003).

60. Greg Schneider and Dina ElBoghdady, "Wal-Mart Confirms Probe of Hiring," *Washington Post* E1 (November 5, 2003).

61. Greenhouse, *supra* note 59.

62. Sarah Paoletti, "Q: Should illegal aliens be able to sue U.S. employers for labor racketeering?; Yes: Employees who have suffered discrimination or exploitation in the workplace are entitled to sue, regardless of their immigration status," *Insight Magazine* 46 (January 19, 2004).

63. Steven Greenhouse, "Illegally in the U.S., and Never a Day Off at Wal-Mart," *International Herald Tribune* 2 (November 6, 2003).

64. Jobwatch.org, Economic Policy Institute, . . . (January 26, 2004).

65. Economic Policy Institute, "Jobs Shift from Higher-Paying to Lower-Paying Industries," *Economic Snapshots* (January 21, 2004).

66. Economic Policy Institute, "Economic Growth Not Reaching Middle- and Lower Wage Earners," *Economic Snapshots* (January 28, 2004).

67. *Id.*

68. Josh Bivens, Robert Scott, and Christian Weller, "Mending Manufacturing: Reversing poor policy decisions is the only way to end current crisis," *EPI Briefing Paper #44* (September 2003).

69. Economic Policy Institute, "Job Growth Up, Job Quality Down," *Economic Snapshots* (December 17, 2003).

70. Economic Policy Institute, "Souring Trade Deficit Threatens to Destabilize U.S. Financial Markets," *Economic Snapshots* (January 7, 2004).

71. Nancy Cleeland, Evelyn Iritani, and Tyler Marshall, "The Wal-Mart Effect: Scouring the Globe to Give Shoppers an $8.63 Polo Shirt," *Los Angeles Times* A1 (November 24, 2003).

72. Peter S. Goodman and Philip P. Pan, "Chinese Workers Pay for Wal-Mart's Low Prices," *Washington Post* A1 (February 8, 2004).

73. Cleeland, Iritani, and Marshall, *supra* note 71.

74. *Id.*

75. Abigail Goodman and Nancy Cleeland, "The Wal-Mart Effect: An Empire Built on Bargains Remakes the Working World," *L.A. Times* 1 (November 23, 2003); Charles Fishman, "The Wal-Mart You Don't Know," *Fast Company* 68 (December 2003).

76. Cleeland, Iritani, and Marshall, *supra* note 71.

77. Goodman and Pan, *supra* note 72.

78. *Id.*

79. *Id.*

80. *Id.*

81. *Id.*

82. *Id.*

83. Carl Goldstein, "Wal-Mart in China," *The Nation* (November 20, 2003).

84. *Id.*

85. 29 U.S.C. § 706 *et seq.*

86. "Disabled Man Sues Wal-Mart," *Business Journal* (Kansas City) (January 20, 2004).

87. *Id.*

88. 29 U.S.C. § 651 *et seq.*

89. 29 C.F.R. 1910.35 *et seq.*

90. Steven Greenhouse, "Workers Assail Lock-Ins by Wal-Mart," *New York Times* 1 (January 18, 2004).

91. *Id.*

92. *Id.*

93. *Id.*

94. *Id.*

95. Walmartwatch.org, "Wal-Mart's War on Workers: Frontline Report from Texas and California," . . . (May 2, 2002).

POSTSCRIPT

Is Wal-Mart Good for the Economy?

LAEDC believes that the entry of Wal-Mart Supercenter stores into Southern California would lead to lower prices for consumers on their grocery, general merchandise, and apparel purchases. The magnitude of the savings is estimated for the City of Los Angeles, for Los Angeles County, and for Southern California. For the latter, the establishment of Wal-Mart Supercenters would eventually lead to savings amounting to $3.76 billion per year. LAEDC believes that consumers would take these savings and spend them on other things and thereby create new jobs. For the City of Los Angeles, the redirected grocery savings alone would create some 6,500 new jobs.

The Democratic Staff of the House Committee on Education and the Workforce cites a number of deficiencies in Wal-Mart's behavior. It charges that Wal-Mart has violated workers' right to organize, maintained low wages, discriminated against women and the disabled, failed to pay employees for all the hours they worked, violated child labor laws, provided inadequate health care insurance, used undocumented workers, and traded away jobs. When all these deficiencies are considered, the Democratic Staff concludes that the costs of Wal-Mart's low prices are just too high.

Perhaps the best place to start with additional readings on this issue is the complete versions of the LAEDC and the Democratic Staff reports. The former can be found at http://www.google.com/search?q=cache:k2x3GeYdFOgJ: www.mayocommunications.com/2003LAEDCIMAGES/WaMart%2520Supercenters% 2520%2520What's%2520in%2520store%2520for%2520Southern%2520California .pdf+Wal-mart+ecoomic+impact+study&hl=en&ie=UTF-8, while the latter can be found at http://edworkforce.house.gov/demcrats/WALMARTREPORT.pdf. There are a number of additional studies on the effects of Wal-Mart, including "The New Colossus" by Jay Nordlinger in the *National Review* (April 19, 2004); *The Case Against Wal-Mart* by Al Norman in *Raphel Marketing* (2004); "The Case for Wal-Mart" by Karen DeCoster and Brad Edmonds (January 31, 2003), http://www. mises.org/fullstory.aspx?control=1151; "Declaring War on Wal-Mart" by Aaron Bernstein in *Business Week* (February 7, 2005); "Rejuvenating Wal-Mart's Reputation" by Thomas A. Hemphill in *Business Horizons* (January/February 2005); "Just Say No" by Julian E. Barnes and Tim Appenzeller in *U.S. News & World Report* (April 19, 2004); and "Up Against Wal-Mart" by Karen Olsson in *Mother Jones* (March/April 2003).

ISSUE 8

Should Social Security Be Changed to Include Personal Retirement Accounts?

YES: The White House, from "Strengthening Social Security for the 21st Century," http://www.whitehouse.gov/infocus/socialsecurity/200501/strengtheningsocialsecurity.html (February 2005)

NO: Dean Baker, from "Bush's Numbers Racket: Why Social Security Privatization Is a Phony Solution to a Phony Problem," *The American Prospect Online Edition* (February 1, 2005)

ISSUE SUMMARY

YES: The White House identifies a number of problems with the present structure of the Social Security system and proposes personal retirement accounts as a way of resolving these problems, and "dramatically reduce the costs of permanently fixing the system."

NO: Dean Baker, co-director of the Center for Economic and Policy Research, argues that President Bush's plan for personal retirement accounts would not fix Social Security; instead, it would "undermine a system that has provided security for tens of millions of workers, and their families, for seven decades, and which can continue to do so long into the future if it is just left alone."

In retrospect, it is not surprising that an event as catastrophic as the Great Depression of the 1930s would produce fundamental change in the American economy. The reality of the human suffering generated by the collapse of one-third of the nation's banks, an unemployment rate of 25 percent, and a 30 percent decline in the production of goods and services as well as household net worth led to a rush of legislation. The legislation, in general terms, was intended to achieve two objectives: to restore confidence in the economy and to provide greater economic security. Today the institutions and programs created by this legislative avalanche are familiar to almost all Americans, including the Federal Deposit Insurance Corporation, the Securities and Exchange Commission, and Social Security.

Social Security, more formally the Old Age, Survivors, and Disability Insurance Program (OASDI), was signed into law on August 14, 1935, by President Franklin D. Roosevelt. As originally designed, OASDI provided three types of benefits: retirement benefits to the elderly who were no longer working, survivor benefits to the spouses and children of persons who had died, and disability benefits to persons who experienced non-work-related illness or injury. The Medicare portion of Social Security, which provides benefits for hospital, doctor, and medical expenses, was created in 1965 (see Issue 4).

There are many terms used to describe OASDI. It is an entitlement program in the sense that everyone who satisfies the eligibility requirements receives benefits. Eligibility is established by employment and contributions to the system (in the form of payroll taxes) for a minimum period of time. It is also a defined benefits program; that is, the level of benefits is determined by legislation. The opposite of a defined benefits program is a defined contributions program, where benefits are determined by contributions and whatever investment income is generated by those contributions. OASDI is also described as a pay-as-you-go system; this means that payments received by recipients are financed primarily by the contributions of current workers. Still another description of OASDI is that it is an income security program. In this context, the reference is to a whole set of government programs designed to provide minimum levels of income to various persons. Finally, OASDI is described as a social insurance program to distinguish it from private insurance programs. The insurance feature rests on the fact that OASDI protects against certain unforeseen events such as disability or early death. The social feature arises from the fact that contributions and the level of benefits are determined by legislation as well as the fact that the contributions are mandatory (payroll taxes that must be paid). In a private insurance program, the beneficiary and the insurance issuer voluntarily negotiate the level of contributions and the level of benefits.

The Social Security "crisis" refers to the fact that with the currently legislated structure of revenues and benefits, the system will eventually be unable to meet its financial obligations. Presently revenues are greater than out-payments, and the excess is accumulated in a trust fund. Around the year 2019, out-payments will exceed revenues, and drawing down the trust fund will cover the difference. Eventually the trust fund will be exhausted, and revenues will only be sufficient to cover a portion of scheduled benefits. According to the most recent report from the Social Security Trustees, that year is 2042, and at that point revenues will be equal to 73 percent of scheduled benefits.

YES

The White House

Strengthening Social Security for the 21st Century

The Problems Facing Social Security

- **A Social Security System designed for a 1935 world does not fit the needs of the 21st Century.** Social Security was designed in 1935 for a world that is very different from today. In 1935, most women did not work outside the home. Today, about 60% of women work outside the home. In 1935, the average American did not live long enough to collect retirement benefits. Today, life expectancy is 77 years. . . .
- **Social Security will not be changed for those 55 or older (born before 1950).** Today, more than 45 million Americans receive Social Security benefits and millions more are nearing retirement. For these Americans, Social Security benefits are secure and will not change in any way.
- **Social Security is making empty promises to our children and grandchildren.** For our younger workers, Social Security has serious problems that will grow worse over time. Social Security cannot afford to pay promised benefits to future generations because it was designed for a 1935 world in which benefits were much lower, life-spans were shorter, there were more workers per retiree, and fewer retirees were drawing from the system.
- **With each passing year, there are fewer workers paying ever-higher benefits to an ever-larger number of retirees.** Social Security is a pay-as-you-go system, which means taxes on today's workers pay the benefits for today's retirees. A worker's payroll taxes are not saved in an account with his or her name on it for the worker's retirement.
  - **There are fewer workers to support our retirees.** When Social Security was first created, there were 40 workers to support every one retiree, and most workers did not live long enough to collect retirement benefits from the system. Since then, the demographics of our society have changed dramatically. People are living longer and having fewer children. As a result we have seen a dramatic change in the number of workers supporting each retiree's benefits. According to the 2004 Report of the Social Security Trustees (page 47):
    - In 1950, there were 16 workers to support every one beneficiary of Social Security.

February 2005, references omitted. http://www.whitehouse.gov/infocus/socialsecurity/200501/strengtheningsocialsecurity.html.

- Today, there are only 3.3 workers supporting every Social Security beneficiary.
- And, by the time our youngest workers turn 65, there will be only 2 workers supporting each beneficiary.
- **Benefits are scheduled to rise dramatically over the next few decades.** Because benefits are tied to wage growth rather than inflation, benefits are growing faster than the rest of the economy. This benefit formula was established in 1977. As a result, today's 20-year old is promised benefits that are 40% higher, in real terms, than are paid to seniors who retire this year. But the current system does not have the money to pay these promised benefits.
- **The retirement of the Baby Boomers will accelerate the problem.** In just 3 years, the first of the Baby Boom generation will begin to retire, putting added strain on a system that was not designed to meet the needs of the 21st century. By 2031, there will be almost twice as many older Americans as today—from 37 million today to 71 million. . . .
- **Social Security is heading toward bankruptcy.** According to the Social Security Trustees, thirteen years from now, in 2018, Social Security will be paying out more than it takes in and every year afterward will bring a new shortfall, bigger than the year before. And, when today's young workers begin to retire in 2042, the system will be exhausted and bankrupt. . . . If we do not act now to save it, the only solution will be drastically higher taxes, massive new borrowing, or sudden and severe cuts in Social Security benefits or other government programs.
- **As of 2004, the cost of doing nothing to fix our Social Security system had hit an estimated $10.4 trillion, according to the Social Security Trustees.** . . . The longer we wait to take action, the more difficult and expensive the changes will be.
  - $10.4 trillion is almost twice the combined wages and salaries of every working American in 2004.
  - Every year we wait costs an additional $600 billion. . . .
  - Today's 30-year-old worker can expect a 27% benefit cut from the current system when he or she reaches normal retirement age. . . . And, without action, these benefit cuts will only get worse.

Personal Retirement Accounts

- **The President believes personal retirement accounts must be part of a comprehensive solution to strengthen Social Security for the 21st century.**
- **Under the President's plan, personal retirement accounts would start gradually. Yearly contribution limits would be raised over time, eventually permitting all workers to set aside 4 percentage points of their payroll taxes in their accounts.** Annual contributions to personal retirement accounts initially would be capped, at $1,000 per year in 2009. The cap would rise gradually over time, growing $100 per year, plus growth in average wages.

- **Personal retirement accounts offer younger workers the opportunity to build a "nest egg" for retirement that the government cannot take away.**
  - **Personal retirement accounts provide ownership and control.** Personal retirement accounts give younger workers the opportunity to own an asset and watch it grow over time.
  - **Personal retirement accounts could be passed on to children and grandchildren.** The money. in these accounts would be available for retirement expenses. Any unused portion could be passed on to loved ones. Permitting individuals to pass on their personal retirement accounts to loved ones will be particularly beneficial to widows, widowers, and other survivors. According to the non-partisan analysis by the Social Security Administration's Office of Retirement Policy, the ability to inherit personal accounts provides the largest gains to widows and other survivors.
  - **Personal retirement accounts help make Social Security better for younger workers.** A personal retirement account gives a younger worker the chance to save a portion of his or her money in an account and watch it grow over time at a greater rate than anything the current system can deliver. The account will provide money for the worker's retirement in addition to the check he or she receives from Social Security. Personal retirement accounts give younger workers the chance to receive a higher rate of return from sound, long-term investing of a portion of their payroll taxes than they receive under the current system.
- **Personal retirement accounts would be voluntary.** At any time, a worker could "opt in" by making a *one-time* election to put a portion of his or her payroll taxes into a personal retirement account.
  - Workers would have the flexibility to choose from several different low-cost, broad-based investment funds and would have the opportunity to adjust investment allocations periodically, but would not be allowed to move back and forth between personal retirement accounts and the traditional system. If, after workers choose the account, they decide they want only the benefits the current system would give them, they can leave their money invested in government bonds like those the Social Security system invests in now.
  - Those workers who do not elect to create a personal retirement account would continue to draw benefits from the traditional Social Security system, reformed to be permanently sustainable.
- **Personal retirement account options and management would be similar to that of the Federal employee retirement program, known as the Thrift Savings Plan (TSP).** A centralized administrative structure would be created to collect personal retirement account contributions, manage investments, maintain records, and facilitate withdrawals at retirement. The structure would be designed to facilitate low costs, ease of use for new investors, and timely crediting of contributions. This centralized investment structure would help minimize compliance costs for employers.
  - Contributions would be collected and records maintained by a central administrator. Similar to the TSP, private investment managers

would be chosen through a competitive bidding process to manage the pooled account contributions.

- The central administrator would answer questions from account participants and distribute periodic account statements.
- The central administrator would also facilitate withdrawals and the purchase of annuities with account balances.
- Like TSP, we expect participants to have easy access to investment information and to their accounts. Participants could easily check account balances and adjust investment allocations.

- **Personal retirement accounts would be invested in a mix of conservative bonds and stock funds.** Guidelines and restrictions would be put in place to provide sound investment choices and prevent individuals from spending the money in these accounts on the lottery or at the race track. Workers would be permitted to allocate their personal retirement account contributions among a small number of very broadly diversified index funds patterned after the current TSP funds.
  - Like TSP, personal retirement accounts could be invested in a safe government securities fund; an investment-grade corporate bond index fund; a small-cap stock index fund; a large-cap stock index fund; and an international stock index fund.
  - In addition to these TSP-type funds, workers could choose a government bond fund with a guaranteed rate of return above inflation.
  - Workers could also choose a "life cycle portfolio" that would automatically adjust the level of risk of the investments as the worker aged. The life cycle fund would automatically and gradually shift the allocation of investment funds as the individual neared retirement age so that it was weighted more heavily toward secure bonds.

- **Personal retirement accounts would be protected from sudden market swings on the eve of retirement.** To protect near-retirees from sudden market swings on the eve of retirement, personal retirement accounts would be automatically invested in the "life cycle portfolio" when a worker reaches age 47, unless the worker and his or her spouse specifically opted out by signing a waiver form stating they are aware of the risks involved. The waiver form would explain in clear, easily understandable terms the benefits of the life cycle portfolio and the risks of opting out. By shifting investment allocations from high growth funds to secure bonds as the individual nears retirement, the life cycle portfolio would provide greater protections from sudden market swings.

- **Personal retirement accounts would not be eaten up by hidden Wall Street fees.** Personal retirement accounts would be low-cost. The Social Security Administration's actuaries project that the ongoing administrative costs for a TSP-style personal account structure would be roughly 30 basis points or 0.3 percentage points, compared to an average of 125 basis points for investments in stock mutual funds and 88 basis points in bond mutual funds in 2003. . . .
  - The low costs are made possible by the economies of scale of a centralized administrative structure, as well as limiting investment options to a small number of prudent, broadly diversified funds.

- Most of these administrative costs are for recordkeeping which would be done by the government, not investment management done by Wall Street. . . .
- **Personal retirement accounts would not be accessible prior to retirement.** American workers who choose personal retirement accounts would not be allowed to make withdrawals from, take loans from, or borrow against their accounts prior to retirement.
- **Personal retirement accounts would not be emptied out all at once, but rather paid out over time, as an addition to traditional Social Security benefits.** Under a system of personal retirement accounts, procedures would be established to govern how account balances would be withdrawn at retirement. This would involve some combination of annuities to ensure a stream of monthly income over the worker's life expectancy, phased withdrawals indexed to life expectancy, and lump sum withdrawals. Individuals would not be permitted to withdraw funds from their personal retirement accounts as lump sums, if doing so would result in their moving below the poverty line. Account balances in excess of the poverty-protection threshold requirement could be withdrawn as a lump sum for any purpose or left in the account to accumulate interest. Any unused portion of the account could be passed on to loved ones.
- **Personal retirement accounts would be phased in.** To ease the transition to a personal retirement account system, participation would be phased in according to the age of the worker. In the first year of implementation, workers currently between age 40 and 54 (born 1950 through 1965 inclusive) would have the option of establishing personal retirement accounts. In the second year, workers currently between age 26 and 54 (born 1950 through 1978 inclusive) would be given the option and by the end of the third year, all workers born in 1950 or later who want to participate in personal retirement accounts would be able to do so.
- **The President's personal retirement account proposal is fiscally responsible.** The President's proposal is consistent with his overall goal of cutting the deficit in half by 2009. Based on analysis by the Social Security Administration Actuary, the Office of Management and Budget estimates that the President's personal retirement account proposal will require transition financing of $664 billion over the next ten years ($754 billion including interest). This transition financing will not have the same effect on national savings, and thus the economy, as traditional government borrowing. Personal retirement accounts will not reduce the pool of savings available to the markets because every dollar borrowed by the Federal government to fund the transition is fully offset by an increase in savings represented by the accounts themselves. Moreover, the transition financing for personal retirement accounts should be viewed as part of a comprehensive plan to make the Social Security system permanently sustainable. Publicly released analysis by the Social Security Administration has found that several comprehensive proposals including personal accounts would dramatically reduce the costs of permanently fixing the system. . . .
- **Establishing personal retirement accounts does not add to the total costs that Social Security faces.** Personal retirement accounts

effectively pre-fund Social Security benefits already promised to today's workers and do not represent a net increase in Federal obligations. The obligation to pay Social Security benefits is already there. While personal retirement accounts affect the timing of these costs, they do not add to the total amount obligated through Social Security.

Dean Baker

 **NO**

Bush's Numbers Racket: Why Social Security Privatization Is a Phony Solution to a Phony Problem

The word from President Bush and his minions is that Social Security is on its last legs, facing imminent danger of bankruptcy. Fortunately, Bush is prepared to rescue this antiquated program by offering workers the opportunity to invest a portion of their Social Security taxes in private accounts. He would like us to believe that this plan will both get the government out from under a crushing debt burden, in the form of future Social Security obligations, and provide younger workers with a more secure retirement.

Almost every part of this story is untrue. First, Social Security does not face any crisis in the normal meaning of the term. Second, private accounts would not give workers a more secure retirement; they reduce security. And third, the basic logic of the story is faulty; it is impossible to both reduce government spending on Social Security and increase benefits, unless the plan somehow increases growth. And no economist seriously contends that putting Social Security money in the stock market will increase growth.

The Basic Numbers

Starting with the crisis story, the first place to look is the Social Security trustees' projections, the standard basis for analysis of the program. The most recent projections show that the program, with no changes whatsoever, can pay all benefits through the year 2042. Even after 2042, Social Security would always be able to pay a higher benefit (adjusted for inflation) than what current retirees receive, although the payment would only be about 73 percent of scheduled benefits.

The Social Security trustees' projections are based on extremely pessimistic assumptions about the future. (Four of the six trustees are political appointees of President Bush: the treasury, labor, and health and human services secretaries, plus the Social Security commissioner.) For example, the trustees assume that economic growth over the 75-year planning period will be less than half as fast as over the last 75 years. While most of this difference is due to the assumption of slower labor-force growth following the retirement of the baby-boomer generation, the trustees also assume that productivity growth will revert back to the rate of productivity growth during the slow-down years of 1973–95. Even so, the trustees themselves have begun using slightly more realistic assumptions. In 1997, they placed the year that Social Security would begin facing a shortfall at 2029. By 2003, they had revised that projection to 2042. Any system that gains 13 years of health in six years is hardly bankrupt.

The nonpartisan Congressional Budget Office (CBO) did its own analysis of the program last summer. Using only slightly more optimistic assumptions, the CBO found that the program, with no changes at all, could pay all benefits through the year 2052 and more than 80 percent of scheduled benefits in sub-sequent years.

On the face of it, the fact that Social Security may face a shortfall in just under 40 years (according to the trustees' report) or 50 years (according to the CBO) hardly sounds like a crisis. After all, the program faced projected shortfalls in the 1950s, '60s, '70s, and '80s. Each of these shortfalls was dealt with—usually with modest tax increases, and in the case of the '80s shortfall, a phased increase in the retirement age beginning in 2003. In the past, no one seemed to feel the need to begin whining about a looming crisis 40 or 50 years ahead of time.

But the proponents of the crisis story have been largely successful in spreading fear. Part of this success is due to the use of deceptive language in framing the issue. The promoters of the crisis routinely speak of an $11 trillion "unfunded liability" for Social Security. But most of the people who hear the $11 trillion figure or use it (including reporters) probably have no idea what it means.

The $11 trillion is obtained by projecting Social Security taxes and spending for the infinite future. The gap between projected spending and taxes for all time is then summed up (using a 3-percent real-discount rate) to get a projection of $11 trillion of debt.

However, more than two-thirds of this projected debt is due to spending beyond the 75-year planning period for Social Security. This means that the debt is not something that we are imposing on our children or grandchildren. Rather, it is a debt that we are projecting that our great-grandchildren would impose on their grandchildren—assuming pessimistic economic projections.

The basic story is that life expectancies are projected to increase through time. This raises the cost of the program through time. If taxes are never raised and benefits are never reduced, the shortfall would eventually be very large.

But serious people don't worry about designing Social Security for the 22nd century. (The secret here is that we don't actually get to design Social Security for the 22nd century anyhow—the people who are alive in 50, 60, and 70 years will design the program in a way that makes sense to them. They will not care at all about what we thought was a good system in 2005.)

If we just confine ourselves to the already lengthy 75-year planning period, the projected shortfall comes to $3 trillion. This may still sound very large. However, the Social Security trustees calculate that this shortfall is 0.7 percent of national income over the planning period. The CBO projects an even smaller number, just 0.4 percent of income over the next 75 years.

By comparison, the increase in annual defense spending since 2001 has been more than 1 percent of the gross domestic product, twice the size of the Social Security shortfall projected by the CBO. And Bush's tax increases equal about 2 percent of the GDP. In fact, rolling back Bush's tax cuts on the very wealthiest would raise sufficient revenue to cover the shortfall for 75 years.

The Trust-Fund Scare Stories

The promoters of privatization have one other standard trick to promote fear about Social Security's future: They point out that, beginning in 2018, Social Security will be forced to rely on income from the trust fund to pay benefits. But this was deliberate. The 1983 Social Security Commission, chaired by Alan Greenspan, deliberately designed a system that would build up a surplus— taxing more than was necessary to pay benefits—so that the income from this surplus could be used help pay the costs of the baby boomers' retirement. Drawing on the trust fund is no more of a problem for Social Security than it is for any pension fund to use some of its accumulated assets to pay benefits to retirees. Indeed, that is exactly what is supposed to happen.

Some conservatives have even derided the Social Security trust fund as an "accounting fiction." Like most claims to wealth in a modern economy, it exists primarily as an accounting entry (how much gold does Bill Gates have in his basement?), but it is hardly fiction. Under the law, the federal government is obligated to repay the government bonds held by the Social Security trust fund, just as it is obligated to repay other government bonds. While tax revenue will be needed to repay these bonds, it is slated to come from personal and corporate income taxes, both very progressive forms of taxation. By contrast, the Social Security tax is a highly regressive wage tax. The meaning of the trust fund is that workers effectively prepaid their Social Security taxes. Now, the government is obligated to tax the Bill Gates and Pete Petersons of the world to repay this debt.

Funny Numbers on Private Accounts

After telling people that Social Security poses the risk of economic disaster, the privatizers promise that individual accounts would provide everyone with a secure retirement. The basic argument is that high returns in the stock market would allow workers to get more money from their Social Security taxes than what they can get through the current system.

There is a simple and obvious problem with this logic. When they project rates of return in the stock market, the privatizers routinely assume that the returns in the future will be equal to the returns in the past, 6.5 percent to 7 percent above the rate of inflation. But the whole basis for projecting a Social Security shortfall is the assumption that the future will have far slower growth than in the past.

Given the much slower projected rate of profit growth, and the fact that price-to-earnings ratios in the stock market continue to be far higher than the historic average, it will be impossible for stock returns to be as high in the future as they were in the past. Projections of stock returns that are consistent with projections of profit growth and current price-to-earnings ratios are approximately 5 percent above the rate of inflation. Because most projections assume a 50-50 mix of stocks and bonds, the implied return on private accounts, after deducting administrative costs, would be about 3.5 percent. This is not much different than the 3-percent return projected for the government bonds held by the trust fund.

In short, there is no untapped bonanza to be claimed by putting Social Security money in the stock market. This step would add little, if anything, to average returns. It would simply add risk. Individual workers may do worse than the average because they make bad investment choices or they happen to retire during a downturn in the stock market. Going in this direction makes sense if the purpose is to increase fees for the financial industry, but it is not a step toward increasing workers' retirement security. Moreover, with individual accounts, retirees would have to worry about living too long, whereas Social Security is guaranteed for life.

Even with individual accounts, most workers would still see large benefit cuts under the second plan produced by President Bush's Social Security Commission, the one that Bush indicated would be the model for his proposal. An average wage earner who is age 20 at the time the plan is implemented could expect his or her basic Social Security benefit to be cut by $200,000, or more than 30 percent, over the course of his or her retirement. He or she could expect to make back less than $70,000, or about one-third of this cut, through his or her private account.

But it is not just the retirement security of individual workers that would be threatened by privatization. President Bush's plan would also lead to transition costs that could be as high as $200 billion a year (almost 2 percent of the GDP) for more than 30 years. The transition problem stems from the fact that workers would begin placing their money in private accounts immediately, leading to large losses of revenue to the government. However, the commission's plan proposes phasing in cuts to new retirees, beginning five years after the plan takes effect. These cuts would not get large enough to offset the lost revenue (and resulting interest burden) for more than three decades, which would lead to a substantial deficit increase in the intervening years.

In order to avoid the appearance that his plan would lead to record-breaking deficits (measured as a share of the GDP), President Bush wants to take this transition by not counting this borrowing as part of the budget. The argument is that we would pay this money back (with benefit cuts) 40 or 50 years in the future, so the current borrowing should not be viewed as adding to the deficit.

The question of whether the transition borrowing could be taken off the books is a political one, but politics won't determine the impact of this borrowing on the nation's economy. There is little evidence that financial markets look 40 and 50 years into the future (and it's not clear what they would see if they did). But every other country that has privatized its Social Security system has felt the need to offset the immediate loss of tax revenue with some spending cuts and/or tax increases. And none of them started with deficits that are as large as those the United States is currently running.

There were already grounds for believing that the Bush deficits were too large and would lead to a substantial increase in interest rates if not reduced quickly. Adding $200 billion a year to these deficits makes it far more likely that the country would face considerably higher interest rates in the near future.

There is also a good example of what can happen when a country tries the Bush approach to Social Security privatization (even if it didn't go quite as far). In 1994, Argentina partially privatized its social-security system. While there were some cuts included in this package, it cost the government an amount of tax revenue equal to approximately 0.9 percent of the GDP, equivalent to $100 billion a year in the United States. In 2001, Argentina went into bankruptcy and defaulted on its debt. If the social-security revenue had still been coming to the government over the period between 1994 and the default, Argentina would have been running a balanced budget in 2001.

The United States is obviously very different from Argentina, but this example is not encouraging for proponents of privatization. The financial markets were not impressed with the fact that Argentina's social-security payments would be lower 20 years in the future. The markets focused on the deficits the country was running in the present. It is likely that they would also focus on the $600 billion (plus deficits) that would result from President Bush's Social Security plan.

In short, Bush's plan would undermine a system that has provided security for tens of millions of workers, and their families, for seven decades, and which can continue to do so long into the future if it is just left alone. His private accounts would provide far less security, while hugely raising costs in the form of fees to the financial industry. Finally, the cost of transitioning to this new system could throw the country into an economic crisis. It's small wonder that Bush is facing increasing skepticism.

POSTSCRIPT

Should Social Security Be Changed to Include Personal Retirement Accounts?

The White House begins by describing what it believes are the problems facing Social Security. One central problem is that there are "fewer workers paying ever-higher benefits to an ever-larger number of retirees." Consequently, Social Security is facing critical financing problems; it is heading toward "bankruptcy." The White House refers to an estimate from the Social Security Trustees: "As of 2004 the cost of doing nothing to fix our Social Security system had hit an estimated $10.4 trillion." The White House lists the advantages of personal retirement accounts. One advantage is that ownership and control of the account would rest with the individual. Another advantage is that an individual could pass the account on to his or her children and grandchildren. Perhaps most importantly, the White House believes that the creation of these accounts "would dramatically reduce the costs of permanently fixing the system."

Baker begins his analysis by denying the claims that he says the Bush administration makes about Social Security and personal retirement accounts. Baker argues (1) there is no Social Security "crisis," (2) the retirement accounts would not make retirement "more secure," and (3) "it is impossible to both reduce government spending on Social Security and increase benefits, unless the plan somehow increases growth." Baker then turns to the numbers that are used to support the claims of those who believe that there is a Social Security crisis. He finds fault with these numbers on a variety of criteria. For example, he disputes the forecast by the Social Security Trustees that by 2042 the Social Security trust fund will be exhausted; he believes this prediction is based on "extremely pessimistic assumptions about the future." He cites an alternative forecast by the nonpartisan Congressional Budget Office that sets 2052 as the corresponding date. He then proceeds to discuss the Social Security trust fund in more detail; in particular, he disputes the charge that it is an "accounting fiction." In the last part of his analysis, Baker discusses the numbers associated with private accounts. He asserts that these accounts would add little to average returns but would add risk. He concludes that the burdens of moving to the system proposed by the Bush administration "could throw the country into an economic crisis."

The Social Security "crisis" has been a major concern to economists and policymakers for at least the last 10 years. As a consequence, a vast amount of information is available about the "crisis" and personal retirement accounts, and there are several Web sites devoted exclusively to the issue. They include

The Social Security Network, available at http://www.socsec.org/, and the Cato Institute Project on Social Security Choice, available at http://www.socialsecurity.org/. A visit to the Social Security Administration's official Web site at http://www.ssa.gov/ provides access to an array of useful information, including the latest Trustees Report. Another batch of studies regarding Social Security can be found at the research center of the American Association of Retired Persons (AARP) at http://search.aarp.org/cgi-bin/htsearch?config=htdig_research_aarp_org&method=and&restrict=research.aarp.org%2Fecon&words=social+security. Several additional readings on Social Security are available from the Century Foundation at http://www.tcf.org/about.asp. Several specific plans for Social Security reform been developed. For example, see the description of The Ryan-Sununu Social Security reform bill by Peter Ferrara: "Personal Social Security Accounts That Work," Policy Report 185 Institute for Policy Innovation (November 2004). Another plan is offered by Michael Tanner, "The 6.2 Percent Solution: A Plan for Reforming Social Security," Cato Project on Social Security Choice SSP No. 32 (February 17, 2004). A third plan is offered by Peter A. Diamond and Peter R. Orszag in *Saving Social Security: A Balanced Approach* (Brookings Institution Press, 2003).

ISSUE 9

Should Unemployment Benefits Be Extended?

YES: Rebecca Blank, from "Testimony before the Subcommittee on Income Security and Family Support of the House Committee on Ways and Means" (April 10, 2008)

NO: Alex Brill, from "Testimony before the Subcommittee on Income Security and Family Support of the House Committee on Ways and Means" (April 10, 2008)

ISSUE SUMMARY

YES: University of Michigan Professor Rebecca Blank supports an extension of unemployment, arguing that the time to extend the time period for unemployment benefits is in the early stages of an economic slowdown.

NO: American Enterprise Institute Research Fellow Alex Brill argues against a simple extension of the benefit period, in part because it "could likely lead to higher unemployment and slower growth in the United States."

T he Social Security Act of 1935 did more than create the Social Security System; it also created the unemployment compensation program, more formally known as the Federal-State Unemployment Compensation Program. Everyone is familiar with the general outline of the unemployment compensation program: it provides income assistance to unemployed workers and in the process helps stabilize the economy. The details are less well known but are worthy of review.

First, the U.S. Department of Labor oversees the program with each state whereas the District of Columbia, Puerto Rico, and the Virgin Islands administer their own programs. Each of these 53 governmental units has its own method for determining eligibility. Among the major factors included in state eligibility requirements are recent employment and earnings, as well as the reasons for the individual's current state of unemployment. Second, there is a time limit on the receipt of benefits: the basic package is set at 26 weeks. Third, benefits are subject to the federal personal income tax. Fourth, individuals must file a claim in order to receive benefits, and these individuals must refile on a weekly or biweekly basis to continue to receive benefits. In addition, claimants must register for work with the State Employment Service. Thus, unemployed persons may not receive benefits for several reasons: because they did not have an employment history that established eligibility, because they failed to file a claim for benefits, or because they were unemployed for more than 26 weeks.

The U.S. Department of Labor issues an Unemployment Insurance Weekly Claims Report. For example, the Report issued on October 16, 2008, indicated that in the week ending October 11, 2008, initial unemployment benefits claims totaled 447,000. The number of initial claims is frequently used as an indicator of conditions in the labor market as well as the overall macroeconomy: claims above 400,000 indicative of a weak labor market and rising unemployment, and claims below 300,000 a sign of a tightening labor market. The weekly Report also provides information on the magnitude of insured unemployment and the insured unemployment rate. For the week ending October 4, 2008, insured unemployment stood at 3.7 million persons while the insured unemployment rate was 2.8 percent. These numbers are in comparison to the September 2008 unemployment rate of 6.1 percent with 9.5 million unemployed persons. These numbers suggest that more than half of the persons classified as unemployed do not (for some of the reasons indicated above) receive unemployment compensation.

In almost all states, benefits are funded exclusively by taxes on employers. The Federal Unemployment Tax Act establishes the federal tax rate at 6.2 percent of taxable wages with the taxable wage base set at the first $7,000 paid in wages to each employee during a calendar year. But employers who pay the state unemployment tax (each state's unemployment tax rate is determined by that state's law) receive an "offset credit of up to 5.4% regardless of the rate of tax they pay the state." So the maximum federal unemployment tax an employer can pay is $56 per employee.

The issue here concerns the extension of unemployment benefits beyond the basic period of 26 weeks. As macroeconomic conditions began to deteriorate in response to the problems in the housing sector and the ensuing credit crunch, some economists and a number of politicians began to call for an increase in the basic period by 13 weeks. In her Congressional testimony Professor Blank supports such an extension, while in his testimony Research Fellow Brill does not. Even though President Bush subsequently signed legislation that provided an additional 13 weeks of benefits, it is useful to review the arguments that were being presented to Congress before the legislation became law.

YES

Rebecca Blank

Testimony before the Subcommittee on Income Security and Family Support

. . . I plan to make several remarks about the labor market and its current problems and then discuss the implications of these facts for the debate over extended benefits.

The discussion of potential recession has dominated the economic news over the past few months. Yet the unemployment rate – one of our most-utilized measures of labor market weakness – has stayed relatively low. It was at or below 5% for the past two and a half years; the data release last Friday showed that it crept up to 5.1% in March 2008. While a significant increase, this is still lower than in many past recessions.

Some have argued that this relatively low unemployment rate means that it's too early to think about extended benefits. In the past few recessions, extended benefits have not been enacted until unemployment rates were 5.7% or higher. I want to make two primary points in this testimony. First, the current unemployment rate cannot be easily compared to past unemployment rates. If we had a similar population in the labor force today as in earlier periods, our current unemployment rate would be much higher. Second, a variety of other labor force measures suggest that those Americans who lose their jobs are facing serious economic problems.

Changes in the Composition of the Labor Market Have Driven Unemployment Rates Down

There are two primary reasons why unemployment rates in 2008 are not entirely comparable to those from earlier periods.

Most important is the *shifting age distribution of the civilian labor force.* As the baby boom generation has aged, the share of workers in older age groups has steadily grown, while the share in younger age groups has fallen. This has the effect of lowering the overall unemployment rate because older workers tend to have lower unemployment rates. . . .

If you take the age-specific unemployment rates in March 2008 and weight them as if the labor force looked as it did in July 1990, the unemployment rate in 2008 would be 5.5% rather than 5.1%, the same as the actual unemployment rate of 5.5% in July 1990. Similarly, the March 2008 unemployment rate would be 5.3% if age groups are weighted by the March 2001 labor force weights, far above the actual March 2001 unemployment rate of 4.3%.

U.S. House of Representatives, April 10, 2008, excerpts.

In short, the shifting age distribution in the population should change our expectations about what constitutes low versus high unemployment. Because older workers have lower unemployment rates, base unemployment rates have fallen with an aging workforce. Hence, the same unemployment rate in March 2008 signals more problems than it would have in early 1990 or even in early 2001. From the point of view of any worker who compares herself to her age peers, unemployment is worse now than at those earlier moments in time.

There is another effect depressing unemployment rates, and that is *the rising share of younger men in jail or prison.* I suspect most of you saw the report from the Pew Foundation in February noting that 1 out of every 100 adult Americans are now in prison (Pew Center on the States, 2008). Our labor force statistics are based on civilian non-institutionalized persons. Those in prison are not counted. This particularly affects younger men. Of course, the civilian labor force data also excludes those in the Armed Forces, all of whom are employed. This also disproportionately affects younger men.

Rather than working with the civilian non-institutionalized population, I add Armed Forces personnel and those in jails and prisons to the population numbers and add Armed Forces personnel to the employment numbers. I do this calculation for 2006, the latest year for which all these data are available.

It has hard to calculate an adjusted unemployment rate because we are not sure how many men currently in prison would be actively seeking work. For a back-of-the-envelope calculation, I assume that 80% of those in prison would be in the workforce if they were not in prison, and that the unemployment rate among these men would be 25%. (This is only slightly higher than the current 21% unemployment rate among young men ages 16–19.) Under these circumstances, the 2006 male unemployment rate would rise from its reported level of 4.6% to 4.9%.

Of course, most of the men in prison or in the Armed Forces are younger. If I assume that all of these men are between the ages of 16 and 34, I can look at the effect on employment-to-population ratios and on the unemployment rate for that group in the population. Taking account of both the Armed Forces and the large number of men in prisons or jails, the 2006 employment-to-population ratio among men ages 16–34 would fall from 72.3% to 69.5%. Their unemployment rate would rise from its reported 2006 level of 7.2% to an estimated 7.8%.

In short, by expanding the prison population, we have removed more and more young men from our labor market count. This reduces aggregate unemployment rates and raises employment shares, since these are often persons who would have difficulty finding jobs if they were not in prison.

These two shifts – in the age distribution of the population and in the share of men who are part of the civilian labor force – mean that the equivalent unemployment rates are lower now than in the past. If we had a similar population now as in 1990, the unemployment rates in both periods would be very similar. Hence, we can't just compare the level of today's unemployment rate to earlier periods without realizing that equivalent problems are occurring at a lower level of reported joblessness today than in the past.

Finally, if we want to understand why unemployment rates look low right now, there is one other very important comment to make: *Unemployment rates and employment changes are lagging indicators of an economic slowdown.* Unemployment rates are typically low at the point a recession begins. They rise during a recession and often peak after a recession has ended. Hence, unemployment rates are NOT a good indicator of whether an economy has entered a recession. . . . In every recession, unemployment rates are low in the first month, and often peak after the end of a recession. . . .

Because unemployment rises slowly, the political impetus to enact extended benefit legislation often occurs later in a recession, once unemployment rates are higher. . . . In fact, in both the early 1990s and the early 2000s, extended benefits were enacted after the official end of the recession (but at a time when unemployment rates were still rising).

What Other Evidence Do We Have of Problems in the Labor Market?

The unemployment rate is hardly the only measure of labor market health. Let me summarize five other indicators that suggest there are serious problems in today's labor market.

First, recent months have shown a *marked slowdown in employment growth.* From March 2006 through March 2007, employment grew by 1.8%. Over this past year, from March 2007 through March 2008, employment actually declined by 0.1%. . . .

Second, the *declines in employment are widespread in the economy.* In the last month, employment fell or was flat in almost every industry except health care services, food services, and local government. This widespread job loss is particularly worrisome, and I take it as a sign that we are almost surely in recession in this country. We don't have an economy with some weak spots and some areas of ongoing strength. The employment data suggests weakness in almost all sectors.

Third, *wage growth has slowed over the last six months.* . . . This is due to the combination of very slow growth in nominal wages and faster inflation, leading to a decline in real (inflation-adjusted) wages. . . .

Fourth, *the share of the population that is working or looking for work has fallen over the past year.* If we're losing jobs, but unemployment hasn't increased, this means that some people are dropping out of the labor market entirely. This "discouraged worker" effect is often a sign that workers are pessimistic about their chances of finding a new job. The declines in labor force participation are particularly noticeable among high-risk groups of workers, namely, younger workers and those with low skill levels. If unemployment remains low because the number of discouraged workers is rising, that's not a good sign for the labor market.

Fifth, *indicators of labor market slackness are at high levels.* . . . Overall unemployment rates are higher now than at the beginning of the 2001 recession, but slightly lower than at the beginning of the 1990 recession. Long-term unemployment measures the number of workers whose unemployment spell has lasted 27 weeks or longer. Long-term unemployment is currently quite high, with almost 1% of the workforce in long-term unemployment in March 2008.

The standard unemployment rate measures those who actively looked for work. The Bureau of Labor Statistics also computes a measure of those they call "marginally attached," which are those who want a job and have recently looked for a job, but are currently not looking because jobs are so scarce. They also measure those who are working only part-time because of economic reasons, the so-called "involuntary part-time workers." If one expands the labor force to include marginally attached workers, and looks at the share who report themselves as either unemployed, marginally attached, or involuntarily working part-time, this is 9.1% of the labor force in March 2008. . . . In March 2001, the beginning of the last recession, this number was only 7.3%. . . .

. . . As of March 2008, 16.7% of the unemployed had been unemployed for more than a half year. This is substantially higher than in 1990 (at 12.9%) or 2001 (at 11.1%). This suggests that a substantial fraction of those who lost jobs in 2007 are having serious difficulties finding reemployment. . . .

Do Extended Benefits Make Sense in the Current Labor Market?

If you believe the U.S. economy is entering a serious economic slowdown, unemployment rates are likely to increase steadily in the months ahead. Should we enact extended benefits now or, as in past recessions, wait for the unemployment rate to rise further? Even adjusting for population shifts, the unemployment rate is still lower than it was when extended benefits were put in place in past years. This might argue for waiting.

I would recommend an extended benefits bill for two primary reasons. First, the unusually high rates of long-term unemployment in the current economy suggest that a growing share of the unemployed who receive unemployment benefits will exhaust them without finding a job. Extended benefits can particularly assist long-term unemployed workers who are having difficulty finding jobs.

Second, I believe that we waited too long in past recessions. Waiting until after a recession has ended to enact extended benefits makes little sense. We know that unemployment rates are a lagging indicator. Given the serious problems signaled by many economic indicators, there is every reason to believe that labor market problems will rise steadily in the months ahead. We should take proactive measures to protect workers who become unemployed, rather than waiting until the problem has grown much larger.

Let me respond to two concerns often raised with regard to extended benefits. Unemployment Insurance is received by only a minority of the unemployed, and the share receiving UI has been falling in recent years. Only 34% of the unemployed received UI at the end of 2007 (U.S. Department of Labor 2007). For the many unemployed who are not eligible or who do not take unemployment benefits, extended UI benefits will have little effect on their economic situation.

I would note that those who face long-term unemployment are much more likely to be eligible for and to receive UI. In part this is because a higher share of the long-term unemployed are displaced workers, who lose jobs due to plant closures or large-scale layoffs. Virtually all of these workers are eligible for unemployment insurance and many of them receive information encouraging them to apply. A recent study by CBO notes that more than 60% of those in long-term unemployment spells receive UI benefits (CBO 2007). This is the group most likely to benefit from extended benefits.

(Of course, the very low receipt of UI among the unemployed is an important issue, but beyond the scope of this morning's hearing. In the longer run, reform of the entire UI program is necessary if you want more unemployed workers to have access to an economic cushion when they lose their jobs.)

Another concern about extending UI benefits focuses on the unequal distribution of unemployment across the states. Some states have very high unemployment at present, in excess of 6%, particularly some of the upper Midwestern states like Michigan or Ohio. Other states have relatively low unemployment rates, below 3%. If long-term unemployment is concentrated in high unemployment states, it might make sense to limit extended benefits only to states with particularly high unemployment rates.

Unfortunately, long-term unemployment is not particularly concentrated in the high unemployment states. Long-term unemployment data by state is not reported by the BLS, but these numbers can be calculated. [The] data provided by the Economic Policy Institute for the year 2007 . . . groups the states in four groups. The top group is the five states with the highest rates of unemployment. These states contain about 10% of the labor force, but 13% of the unemployed. The share of long-term unemployed in these states is 15%, quite close to their share of overall unemployment. This means that long-term unemployment is not disproportionately concentrated in high-unemployment states. Indeed, if you provided extended unemployment benefits only to these high-unemployment states, 85% of the long-term unemployed would not benefit. . . .

Conclusions

Given all of these facts, now is the time to enact extended unemployment benefits. This will assist the long-term unemployed as they continue to search for work. The unusually high share of long-term unemployed workers at this relatively early stage in the economic slowdown is a warning sign; history suggests these numbers will grow as the recession affects more and more jobs. Waiting for the unemployment rate to rise higher before we act would be a mistake.

References

Congressional Budget Office. 2007. *Long-Term Unemployment.* Washington, D.C.: Congress of the United States. October. . . .

Pew Center on the States. 2008. *One in 100: Behind Bars in America 2008.* Washington, D.C.: Pew Charitable Trusts. February. . . .

U.S. Department of Labor, Employment and Training Administration. *Unemployment Insurance Data Summary.* 3rd Quarter 2007. Washington, D.C.: U.S. Department of Labor. . . .

Alex Brill  **NO**

Testimony before the Subcommittee on Income Security and Family Support

My testimony today will address five topics: first, the current economic outlook from an aggregate, sector and regional perspective; second, the theoretical concepts for optimal unemployment insurance design; third, the importance of labor market flexibility for economic growth and lessons from Europe; fourth, extended unemployment insurance as a tool for economic stimulus; and finally, alternatives to consider to the existing UI system.

Current Economic Outlook

At present, the aggregate growth of the U.S. economy is at a near standstill. Growth in the fourth quarter of 2007 was a paltry 0.6 percent (all GDP growth figures are annualized rate) and indicators for the first quarter of 2008 suggest that growth remained very slow and was possibly negative. An excessive supply of residential housing, inflated home prices, and turmoil in the credit markets are at the center of the current economic weakness. Other sectors and industries could become ensnarled as well. The outlook for the economy for the remainder of 2008 is highly uncertain. Many economists expect an improvement in the second half of the year, though such a timely return back toward trend growth depends on a prompt recovery of credit markets and financial institutions.

While the performance of the *aggregate* U.S. economy is a useful thumbnail for gauging the simple trends of the economy, our economy is an amalgamation of numerous sectors, industries and distinct labor markets. Looking more closely at specific sectors and geographic areas reveals considerable variation in our economic performance. Our economy is clearly faltering in some areas while growth remains relatively robust in other areas.

Consider the fourth quarter of 2007, the most recent period for which we have complete data. In the aggregate, the U.S. economy expanded 0.6 percent but the components of GDP performed very quite differently. The service sector of the economy grew 3.1 percent while the goods-producing sector contracted 1.6 percent. Export growth added 0.8 percentage points to GDP while the decrease in motor vehicle output reduced the overall growth by 0.9 percentage points.[1]

U.S. House of Representatives, April 10, 2008.

GDP growth varies considerably by region as well, though government statistics are not as timely for state output as they are for state employment or industry production. That said, the Far West, Rocky Mountain, and Southwest regions of the U.S. have been growing considerably faster than the Plains, Great Lakes, and New England states. For example, Washington State grew 5.6 percent in 2006 while Illinois grew 3.0 percent.[2]

Similarly, labor markets are performing differently across the country and across industries, with some areas of elevated unemployment and other areas where jobs are still relatively plentiful. For example, employment in the healthcare sector increased nearly 1 million from January 2003 to September 2006 and has since grown by an additional 530,000 jobs. In the construction sector, employment also increased by about 1 million from January 2003 to September 2006 but has since fallen by 400,000 jobs.

By state, the employment situation varies considerably as well. During the twelve months from February 2007 to February 2008, twenty-six states and the District of Columbia saw an increase in their unemployment rate and twenty states saw a decrease in their unemployment rate. In February, the unemployment rate was the highest in Michigan at 7.2 percent and lowest in Wyoming at 2.7 percent. . . .

Forty-three states and the District of Columbia saw employment gains in February 2008. The largest percent increases in employment were in Wyoming, Texas, Utah, Washington, and Colorado. Seven states experienced declines in employment, the largest of which were Rhode Island, Michigan, Florida, Wisconsin, and Nevada.[3] . . .

Proper comparisons between the current labor market data and previous labor market statistics are difficult for a number of reasons. First, there is no obvious benchmark period for comparison. We do not know where we are precisely in the business cycle. Second, the structural and demographic characteristics of the labor market have changed. While some may choose to compare current labor market data to conditions at the onset of the last recession, that date (March 2001) was not known to be a business cycle peak until much later in the year. Indeed, economists still debate if that was the appropriate date for the turning point at all. A more appropriate comparison may be to compare current labor market conditions to conditions when unemployment benefits were first extended.

Second, the labor force has changed considerably over time as it has become older, more educated, and contains more foreign-born workers. All three groups are associated with lower levels of unemployment. And finally, the characteristics of the jobs in our economy have changed and the relative share of jobs that are unionized has declined.

The characteristics of the current unemployment situation can be summarized as follows. The unemployment rate, 5.1 percent in March, is low by historical measure, though shifts in demographics and industry composition have contributed notably to its decline. The unemployment rate increased significantly from February to March. While gross job creation and gross job destruction are both over 2 million a month, net job creation has been negative for three consecutive months. Neither the long-term unemployment rate nor the share of unemployed that are long-term unemployed are high by historical average. Both initial jobless claims and long-term unemployment as a share of total employment have increased over the past year but remains low by historical comparison. . . . Finally, aggregate labor market conditions, even after controlling for shifts in the workers' age, are better than when extended benefits were passed by Congress in February 2002.

Theoretical View on Optimal Unemployment Insurance

The theory of optimal unemployment insurance design suggests a balancing act between two competing forces. On one hand, labor market rigidities (such as minimum wage, union bargaining powers, and employment protections), liquidity constraints for many households (namely the inability for many households to borrow against future earnings), and a tax system that distorts the decision between current consumption and savings (thereby discouraging precautionary savings for unemployment spells) make it appropriate for a program such as unemployment insurance to assist displaced workers so that they have resources to obtain the next best employment opportunity.

On the other hand, too much unemployment insurance (determined by the duration of benefits, the replacement rate of previous wages or both) will lead to an increased duration of unemployment through a decreased incentive to find a job. This will lead to a higher unemployment rate and lower levels of economic output and growth.

Furthermore, the unemployed are a heterogeneous population. Unemployed workers have varying degrees of precautionary savings (including zero) and may or may not have spousal income to rely on during a period of unemployment. As a result, optimal unemployment insurance varies across the unemployed population and therefore a single benefits rule is inherently imperfect.

The optimal duration of unemployment benefits for a given worker is also a function of current labor market conditions that are inherently local in nature and skill specific. Therefore, when conditions deteriorate in a particular labor market, it is reasonable to offer additional benefits since finding a job is likely to take longer. Of course, the current law extended benefit (EB) program is designed to address these concerns by providing additional benefits for states with high and rising unemployment. However, due to a variety of changes to the U.S. economy, population, and labor market, these triggers may be too high to be effective. In general, the triggers for the current law EB program were set when the natural rate of unemployment was considerably higher. Therefore in today's economy, EB is considerably less likely to be triggered during a period of weak labor markets than when it was first implemented.[4]

Therefore, when Congress considers changes to unemployment insurance to provide additional assistance to unemployed workers, it is important to design a targeted program that, to the extent possible, provides additional benefits only to workers where labor markets are slack and only on a temporary basis.

The Stimulus Digression

I would like to emphasize that the benefit of a well-designed UI system is that it promotes labor market efficiencies and long-run economic growth. One commonly emphasized economic perspective of unemployment insurance (UI) is that providing extended benefits is an effective tool for economic stimulus. I disagree and believe that while a well designed system, which compensates for labor market imperfections and rigidities, will boost economic growth in the long-run, providing UI benefits that exceed the optimal level and duration will not provide measurable positive short-term stimulus.

Why do I believe that there are only small short-term effects? First, while providing additional dollars to unemployed workers is likely to result in a relatively large share of those dollars being used to stimulate aggregate demand, there is a potentially offsetting effect as workers may remain out of the workforce longer. As a result, they will not contribute to aggregate supply and not receive as much income as they would if employed. Second, even the most generous proposals for extending unemployment benefits are small relative to the $14 trillion U.S. economy. Furthermore, estimates of the multiplier effect of UI cited by some policy analysts (Chimerine et al., 1999) relate to the effects of the current program, not the marginal effect of an expansion of the program. Finally, Harvard University Professor of Economics Martin Feldstein testified in 2007 that notes, "[w]hile raising unemployment benefits or extending the duration of benefits beyond 26 weeks would help some individuals . . . it would also create undesirable incentives for individuals to delay returning to work. That would lower earnings and total spending."[5] UI policy should be based on labor-market efficiency, not short-run stimulus.

Labor Market Flexibility

Unemployment insurance is a key government policy that affects the degree of labor market flexibility in an economy and labor market flexibility is a key for economic growth. Countries with more generous unemployment insurance tend to have higher levels of unemployment and slower growth. The International Monetary Fund's 2003 *World Economic Outlook* noted that "The persistence of high unemployment in a number of industrial countries . . . is arguably one of the most striking economic policy failures of the last two decades. A wide range of analysts and international organizations . . . have argued that the cause of high unemployment can be found in labor market institutions."[6] The IMF also estimates that if Europe were to adopt labor market institutions and structures similar to the United States that economy could experience additional economic growth of five percent.

While extending unemployment benefits beyond 26 weeks is only one change in labor market protections among the many differences that exist between the U.S. and Europe, it is one that in a full-employment economy would tend to raise unemployment and slow economic growth. . . . [The] U.S. had a lower unemployment rate and a lower long-term unemployment rate lower in 2006 compared to most OECD countries. The U.S. also has smaller public expenditures on labor market programs as a share of GDP, less labor market regulations, and lower income and social security tax burdens for average workers than most OECD countries. Over the last ten years, the U.S. economy has grown faster on a per capita basis than all of Western Europe except Ireland, Spain, and Sweden. Taken together, this data suggests that increasing the generosity of unemployment benefits to be more similar to other developed countries could likely lead to higher unemployment and slower growth in the U.S. . . .

Alternatives to Current Unemployment Insurance Program

I would like to conclude my testimony by noting that alternatives to the current unemployment insurance program could be designed to adequately address the limited liquidity of a large fraction of unemployed and other short-comings in labor markets without creating a discouraging job search. For example, Joseph Stiglitz and Jungyoll Yun (2005)[7] propose combining an unemployment insurance system with the public pension system (Social Security). Martin Feldstein and Daniel Altman (2007)[8] propose unemployment insurance savings accounts (UISAs), where workers would contribute a share of their wages and be allowed to draw from the account should they become unemployed. The UISAs would provide an incentive for workers to find employment promptly. Only those with a negative balance in their account would face the biased incentives which exist in the current system.

Other alternatives are also worthy of consideration, including mandating that employers purchase private insurance to provide unemployment insurance to their workers, or offering reemployment incentives to encourage shorter unemployment spells. Wage insurance is yet another alternative or complementary policy that could assist workers during changes in labor markets. Finally, more incremental reforms could also improve the efficiency of the current system such as reforms to improve the experience rating system – which currently imprecisely relates the employers' history of laying off workers to their unemployment tax.

Conclusion

While the U.S. labor market has deteriorated in the last few months, aggregate conditions are not worse than they were when extended UI benefits were enacted in 2002. More important than national statistics are those related to specific labor markets and industries. Any legislation to provide additional unemployment benefits should be carefully targeted to limit the moral hazard effect. Furthermore, any extension of benefits should be temporary so not to continue when the economy returns to trend growth. Finally, I encourage the Committee to consider fundamental reforms to the UI system as alternative approaches may improve labor market efficiencies, raise employment and strengthen the U.S. economy.

References

1. See "Gross Domestic Product: Fourth Quarter 2007 (Final)," Bureau of Economic Analysis News Release, March 27, 2008, Appendix A. . . .

2. See "Gross Domestic Product (GDP) by State, 2006," Bureau of Economic Analysis (BEA) New Release, June 2, 2002. . . .

3. See "Regional and State Employment and Unemployment: February 2008," Bureau of Labor Statistics News Release, March 28, 2008. . . .

4. The Congressional Budget Office estimates the natural rate of unemployment in the U.S. to be 5.0 percent, a decrease of over 1 percentage point since 1981 when the extended benefits program was last changed. See Brauer, David, "The Natural Rate of Unemployment," Working Paper Series 2007–06 Congressional Budget Office, April 2007.

5. The Senate Finance Committee, "Testimony of Martin Feldstein" January 24, 2007. . . .

6. The IMF, World Economic Oultook: Growth and Institutions, 2003.

7. Stiglitz, Joseph and Yun, Jungyoll "Integration of unemployment insurance with retirement insurance," *Journal of Public Economics,* Vol. 89. December 2005, pp. 2037–2067. . . .

8. Feldstein, Martin S. and Altman, Daniel. "Unemployment Insurance Savings Accounts." in James Poterba, ed., *Tax Policy and the economy.* Vol. 21. Cambridge, MA: MIT, 2007, pp. 35–58.

POSTSCRIPT

Should Unemployment Benefits Be Extended?

University of Michigan Professor Rebecca Blank begins her testimony in support of extending unemployment benefits by arguing that recent unemployment rates through early 2008 may have fallen because of changes in the labor market. Here, she notes the aging of the population lowers the unemployment rate because older workers tend to have lower unemployment rates. Also the share of young men in jail is rising. This affects the unemployment rate in two ways: persons in prisons are not counted as part of the labor force, and, because of their youth, these persons would tend to have higher unemployment rates. She then proceeds to look at five indicators of "serious problems" in the early 2008 labor market: (i) a marked slowdown in employment growth, (ii) the fact that job loss is now spread across the entire country, (iii) wages are growing more slowly, (iv) an increase in the number of discouraged workers, and (v) an overall high level of labor market slackness. With all this in perspective, she then offers two primary reasons for extending unemployment benefits immediately. First, the share of unemployed who will exhaust their benefits will be growing. Second, the pattern revealed in prior recessions is that "we have waited too long" before extending unemployment benefits. She concludes: "Waiting for the unemployment rate to rise higher before we act would be a mistake."

American Enterprise Institute for Public Policy Research fellow Alex Brill divides his testimony into several major parts. First, he reviews the macroeconomy. Here he finds that as of March 2008 the aggregate labor market is actually in better condition than the last time extended unemployment benefits were passed by Congress. For example, between February 2007 and February 2008, the unemployment rate decreased in twenty-six states and the District of Columbia. Second, he reviews elements that factor into the design of optimal unemployment insurance. In this context, he believes that extended benefits should only be part of a targeted program designed to help workers only in slack labor markets and only on a temporary basis. Third, he argues that the extension of benefits is not a very effective countercyclical policy action; that is, it only offers "small short-term benefits." Fourth, he believes that there is empirical evidence that "increasing the generosity of unemployment benefits" in developed countries like the United States "could likely lead to higher unemployment and slower growth." Finally, he proposes that Congress consider alternatives, including "mandating that employers purchase private insurance to provide unemployment insurance to their workers" and the creation of unemployment insurance savings accounts.

Data on employment, unemployment, and the unemployment rate are released on the first Friday of every month and can be accessed through the Bureau of Labor Statistics home page at http://www.bls.gov/. A rather complete description of the unemployment compensation program is provided by the Almanac of Policy Issues at http://www.policyalmanac.org/social_welfare/archive/unemployment_compenstaion.shtml. The weekly unemployment insurance claims report can be accessed at http://www.dol.gov/opa/media/press/eta/ui/current.htm.

The hearings at which Blank and Brill presented their testimony include the testimony of Heidi Shierholz of the Economic Policy Institute and Maurice Emsellem of the National Employment Law Project. Finally, additional material and analysis can be found in the sources cited by Blank and Brill in their testimony.

ISSUE 10

Do American Consumers Need a Credit Card Bill of Rights?

YES: Travis B. Plunkett, from Testimony before the Subcommittee on Financial Institutions and Consumer Credit of the House Committee on Financial Services (April 17, 2008)

NO: John P. Carey, from Testimony before the Subcommittee on Financial Institutions and Consumer Credit of the House Committee on Financial Services (April 17, 2008)

ISSUE SUMMARY

YES: Travis Plunkett, Legislative Director for the Consumer Federation of America, argues that creating a credit cardholder's bill of rights would have a number of beneficial effects, including the elimination of abusive pricing.

NO: John Carey, Chief Administrative Officer of Citi Cards, admits that there is broad dissatisfaction with the credit card industry but asserts that a credit cardholder's bill of rights will create more problems than it will solve.

When a consumer makes a purchase, he or she can "pay" for the item in a variety of ways. There is the old-fashioned way of paying with cash—exchanging Federal Reserve notes and Treasury currency for the item. A second option, also of fairly long standing, involves paying by check. The options then evolve to more recent creations—credit cards, debit cards, and stored-value cards. There is even something called a smart card and electronic checking.

Concentrating on credit cards, the statistics on their use are almost mind-boggling. The U.S. Census Bureau provides the following data for 2005:

- There were 164 million credit cardholders.
- These credit cardholders had about 1.4 billion cards—nearly 9 each.
- They charged approximately $2.1 trillion to their cards.
- The average cardholder has about $5,000 in credit card debt.

Of course, profit-seeking financial institutions issue credit cards, and it appears to be a lucrative business: in 2003 the before-tax-profits of the credit card industry exceeded $30 billion.

These numbers become more impressive when one realizes that the ubiquitous credit card has been around for just a little more than 50 years. The creation of the credit card is usually attributed to Frank X. McNamara. Legend has it that he conceived of a credit card when he had insufficient cash to pay for a "power lunch" at Major's Cabin Grill in New York City. So in 1951 Diners Club credit cards were issued to some 200 customers who were then able to charge their meals at 27 participating New York City restaurants.

Today, people are most familiar with what are called general-purpose credit cards: Visa, MasterCard, Discover, and American Express. Other credit cards carry the name of a particular retailer (for example, the credit cards issued by oil companies, large department stores, and so on). Bank of America usually gets credit (pun intended) for creating the first general-purpose credit card in 1958; back then it was called BankAmericard. In 1965, Bank of America began licensing other banks to issue BankAmericards. In 1977, BankAmericard became Visa. MasterCard, on the other hand, traces its origin to 1967, when four California banks introduced MasterCharge to compete with BankAmericard. MasterCharge became MasterCard in 1979.

Visa and MasterCard credit cards can be obtained from any number of financial institutions. Each issuer can establish whatever terms it wishes; that is, a bank issuing a Visa or MasterCard is free to set its own conditions. These conditions include the APR (annual percentage rate) that applies to unpaid credit card balances, various fees (annual membership fee, cash advance fee, late payment fee, etc.), and incentives (rebates, airline ticket awards, car rental insurance, etc.). Making matters more complex, a single credit card may have multiple APRs: one for purchases, another for cash advances, a third for balance transfers. There may also be a special penalty APR, an introductory APR, and a delayed APR.

A rising chorus of criticism about credit cards has matched the increased availability and use of credit cards. These range from complaints about pricing tricks, to retroactive application of penalty rates, to double-cycle billing. In response to these criticisms legislation was introduced into the 110th Congress to eliminate abuses and improve consumer protections. The selections in this issue are taken from the hearings on this legislation: H.R. 5244, "The Credit Cardholder's Bill of Rights: Providing New Protections for Consumers." Plunkett argues for passage of the legislation while Carey opposes its passage.

YES

Travis B. Plunkett

Testimony before the Subcommittee on Financial Institutions and Consumer Credit

Chairwoman Maloney, Ranking Member Biggert, and members of the Sub-commitee, my name is Travis Plunkett and I am the legislative director of the Consumer Federation of America (CFA).[1] I am testifying today on behalf of CFA and Consumers Union, the publisher of Consumer Reports.[2] I appreciate the opportunity to offer our comments on H.R. 5244, the Credit Cardholders' Bill of Rights and on the effect of some current credit card industry practices on consumers. . . .

A. Consumers Have Shown Far More Caution in Taking on Credit Card Debt Than Issuers Have Used in Marketing and Extending Credit

It is conventional wisdom that consumer demand has fueled the growth of revolving debt to about $950 billion.[3] However, a careful analysis of lending patterns by credit card companies shows that aggressive and even reckless lending by issuers has played a huge role in pushing credit card debt to record levels. Since 1999, creditor marketing and credit extension has increased about twice as fast as credit card debt taken on by consumers,[4] even though the rate of growth in credit card debt in 2007 was the highest it has been since 2000.[5]

The total amount of credit made available by issuers is now about $5 trillion.[6] The average amount of credit available per household is $43,007.[7] Of that amount, only 24 percent has been taken on as debt by consumers. According to figures from VERIBANC Inc., there were about $4 trillion in unused credit lines in the fiscal quarter ending in September 2006. Between December 1999 and December 2007, revolving debt grew by 50 percent, but unused credit card lines made available by creditors grew by 90.4 percent, almost twice as fast.[8]

A similar trend is evident when examining the consumer response to massive increases in marketing by creditors. The most significant form of marketing for creditors remains solicitation by mail. Over half of credit cards held by consumers are the result of mail solicitation.[9]

Issuers increased the number of mailed credit card offerings by six-fold from 1990 to 2005, from just over 1.1 billion to a record 6.06 billion.[10]

U.S. House of Representatives, April 17, 2008, excerpts.

Since then, solicitations have dropped to 5.8 billion in 2006 and 5.2 billion in 2007.[11] Wealthier families receive the highest number of credit card mailings, but low-income families are more likely to open the solicitations they receive.[12] The figures of survey indicate that issuer interest in marketing credit cards has grown much faster than consumer interest in accepting new cards. The consumer response rate to mail solicitations declined seven-fold from 2.1 percent in 1990 to .3 percent in 2005, picking up slightly to .5 percent in 2006 and 2007. This means that for every 250 solicitations consumers receive, they reject more than 249. The tiny response rate demonstrates that the vast majority of consumers are being responsible when offered unsolicited credit.

The huge increase in mail marketing despite a plummeting response rate is yet more evidence that credit cards are highly profitable. In a normal business, declining consumer demand would result in reduced product marketing.

Issuers also spend extremely large sums on many other forms of marketing and advertising, through television, telemarketing, the internet, radio, print and even outdoor billboards. *Nielsen Monitor* reported that credit card companies were among the top advertisers nationally and the fastest growing segment of purchased advertising in 2004, with credit card television advertising growing to $1.7 billion in 2004, a $438 million and 32.4 percent increase over 2003.[13] These figures are before the fourth largest credit card issuer, MBNA, started its first national advertising campaign during the 2005 Super Bowl.[14]

Credit cards also promote and advertise their cards by establishing significant networks of co-branded affinity relationships, which offer credit cards with the logo and affiliation of a sports team, university, association or non-profit. This allows credit card companies to gain access to mailing lists and market the credit card branded with the group's logo directly to the group's membership. Organizations are paid a bounty for each account that is opened as well as revenue from any open balances on the affinity cards. Once a consumer relationship is established with the affinity card, the credit card issuers can market other lending products including student loans, home equity loans or auto loans to their affinity card customers.[15]

B. Issuers Encourage the Least Sophisticated and Riskiest Households to Run Up Unsustainable Levels of Debt

The growth of revolving debt in this country to $950 billion has obviously not affected all Americans equally. The extraordinary expansion of the credit card industry in the 1990s was fueled by the marketing of credit cards to populations that had not had widespread access to mainstream credit, including lower- and moderate-income households, consumers with seriously blemished credit histories, college students, older Americans and minorities.

In a practice widely known as risk-based pricing, creditors charged riskier consumers more to cover potential losses, usually in the form of higher interest rates. To make the assumption of debt more attractive to these households – and to entice them into carrying debt for longer periods – creditors lowered minimum payment balances from around five percent of principal to just over two percent. As a result, an estimated eighty percent of all households now have at least one card.[16] According to the Federal Reserve Board, about 42 percent of cardholding households pay their credit card bill in full every month,[17] which means that the remaining 50 million or so families that carry debt owe an average of about $17,000.[18] . . .

Lower-Income and Minority Households

Close to half of all minority families in the U.S. carry credit card debt.[19] Although lower- and moderate-income households are less likely to have bank credit cards than more affluent families, they are more likely to carry over debt from month-to-month. Sixty-one percent of the lowest income households with a card carry balances, compared to 96 percent of higher income families.[20] Credit card debt also represents a significant portion of lower-income families' income. A 2004 Gallup poll found that families with credit card debt earning under $20,000 a year owed 14.3 percent of their income in credit card debts, those earning between $20,000 and $29,999 owed 13.3 percent and those earning between $30,000 and $39,999 owed 11.0 percent. Compare this to the 2.3% of their income owed by families earning over $100,000.[21] The increase in credit card debt has contributed to alarmingly high overall levels of debt for many of these lower and moderate-income families. More than one-quarter of the lowest income families spent over 40 percent of their income on debt repayment in 2001.[22]

Younger and Older Americans

Starting in the early 1990s, credit card issuers targeted massive marketing efforts at college campuses throughout the country, resulting in a sharp growth of credit card debt among college-age and younger Americans. CFA and Dr. Robert Manning were among the first to document the serious consequences of this trend.[23] Since Dr. Manning's report for CFA in 1999, this issue has been the subject of much public and media scrutiny. And yet, Americans under 35 years of age continue to show more signs of trouble managing credit card debt than any other age group. The amount of credit card debt held by students graduating from college more than doubled to $3,262 between the mid-1990s and 2004.[24] Americans under 35 are less likely to pay off their credit card balances every month than average Americans,[25] are paying more for debt obligations than in the past and are increasingly likely to pay more than 40 percent of their incomes on credit card debt.[26] Not surprisingly, more young Americans are declaring bankruptcy than in the past.[27] Moreover, there is increasing evidence that issuers are now targeting high school students with credit card offers.[28] They are also marketing branded debit cards to adolescents, in part to encourage these young consumers to use similarly branded credit cards when they are older.[29]

. . . Between 1992 and 2001, Americans over age 65 saw their credit card debt nearly double from $2,143 to more than $4,000.[30] The number of seniors filing for bankruptcy more than tripled from 1991 to 2001.[31] Other warning signs are also evident. The proportion of income spent to pay off debts by households headed by individuals 65 to 74 years of age has risen steadily over the past decade[32] while about one in seven senior households paid more than 40 of their income towards their debts in 2001.[33]

Seniors have fewer credit cards than other age groups and are more likely to pay their credit cards in full every month, but a greater proportion of older Americans also have lower incomes.[34] This means that credit card debt has a more severe impact on this age group. For example, credit card debt can threaten older homeowners, who stand to lose their home – and their most significant hedge against poverty – if they use home equity to pay off credit card debt.

The Downsizing of Minimum Payments

As credit card issuers dramatically expanded their marketing and extension of credit in the 1990s, they lowered monthly minimum payment amounts. By reducing the minimum payment, issuers could offer more credit, encourage consumers to take on more debt, and ensure that consumers would take far longer to pay off their debts, thus making them more profitable for the industry.[35] Monthly minimum payment rates were reduced from around 5 percent of principal owed in the 1970s to just over 2 percent by the turn of the century.[36] In 2005, 19 million credit card borrowers make only the minimum payments.[37]

The number of consumers paying just above the minimum rate is even larger. In a representative survey conducted for the Consumer Federation of America by Opinion Research Corporation in November of 2005, 34 percent of those questioned said that they usually pay the minimum rate or somewhat more. More than 40 percent of respondents earning less than $50,000 a year said they paid the minimum rate or somewhat more, while 45 percent of African Americans and 51 percent of Hispanics did so.[38] An examination by the Credit Research Center of 310,000 active credit card accounts over 12 consecutive months in 2000 and 2001 found similar results. Just under one-third of the accounts paid 5 percent or less per month of the total amount due.[39] Moreover, payment habits for many cardholders are not static over time.

Depending on the economic circumstances of the cardholder involved, he or she could shift from fully paying outstanding balances every month to paying at or near the minimum rate.

However, paying only the minimum on credit cards can increase the length of time the debt is carried and significantly add to the interest cost of the credit card loan. Julie Williams, the First Senior Deputy Comptroller and Chief Counsel of the Office of the Comptroller of the Currency (OCC) has noted that reduced minimum payments "dig borrowers into an ever deeper hole, requiring increasingly more difficult measures" for consumers to get out of debt.[40] CFA has concluded that reduced minimum payments were a significant cause of increasing bankruptcies in the last decade.[41]

One way to alert consumers to the consequences of paying off credit card balances at the minimum rate is to offer each consumer a personalized notice on the billing statement about how long it would take to pay off the balance at the minimum rate, and what would be the total costs in interest and principal.[42] Such a personalized disclosure is, unfortunately, not included in the recent bankruptcy law, which requires consumers to call a toll-free number to get information about how long it would take to pay off their balances.[43] . . .

One positive development regarding credit card minimum payments is that regulatory guidance issued by federal banking regulators in January 2003 directed credit card lenders to set minimum payments that "amortize the current balance over a reasonable period of time" and noted that prolonged negative amortization would be subject to bank examiner criticism.[44] Many major credit cards began increasing their minimum payments requirements in 2005, including Bank of America, Citibank, Discover and JP Morgan Chase,[45] in some cases to as high as 4 percent.[46] All issuers were required to fully phase in the changes by the end of 2006.[47]

The Office of the Comptroller of the Currency (OCC) has warned banks that increasing minimum payments may need to be accompanied by a reduction in Annual Percentage Rates (APRs) or eliminating fees to ensure that cardholders can actually reduce their balances and not just tread water with higher minimum bills.[48] Since the increases took effect, consumers with interest rates above 20 percent have had to cope with payments that have roughly doubled.[49]

Targeting Consumers on the Brink of Financial Distress

Nothing illustrates the perverse incentives (and dangers) of the credit card market better than the marketing of cards to consumers with tarnished credit histories, or even worse, to those who are literally on their way to or just coming out of bankruptcy. For example, in the first half of 2007, as home mortgage foreclosures shot up and signs of a serious economic slowdown started to appear, some of the nation's largest credit card issuers increased the number of solicitations they mailed to sub-prime consumers by 41 percent compared to the first half of 2006.[50]

. . . Credit card industry consultant Andrew Kahr estimates that average sub-prime consumers will make two or three late payments a year, from which the industry can generate a separate fee, and that these fees can greatly exceed the interest payments on the small lines of credit themselves.[51]

Sub-prime consumers haven't just encountered high-cost offers of credit, but deceptive marketing practices. In 2000, Providian was required to pay more than $300 million in restitution to its sub-prime cardholders for unfair and deceptive practices.[52] Cross Country Bank, the sub-prime and secured credit card issuer that has been investigated by state and federal regulators for misleading consumers about the terms of its sub-prime credit card accounts and engaging in abusive collection practices, has advertised on late-night and daytime television when more unemployed potential sub-prime customers are more likely to be watching television.[53]

Consumers exiting bankruptcy are often swamped with offers at prime terms – low interest rates and without annual fees.[54] Many bankruptcy attorneys believe these offers are being made because consumers leaving bankruptcy court cannot erase their debts for another six years. Under the new bankruptcy legislation consumers will not be able to wipe away any credit card debts for eight years. Some categories of credit card debt will not be "dischargeable" at all, no matter how long the consumer waits.[55]

C. Cardholders Show Serious Signs of Economic Stress While Issuers Reap Record Profits

As the economy has worsened and home foreclosures have increased to record levels, consumers are increasingly having difficulty paying their credit card bills. Credit card charge-offs, the percentage of the value of credit card loans removed from the books (net of recoveries), or "written off," have been persistently high for most of the last twelve years. During the decade between the end of 1995 and the start of 2006, credit card charge-offs were not below 4 percent in a single quarter.[56] They increased to more than 4 percent in the fourth quarter of 2006 and broke 4 percent again during the later half of 2007. There is a very good chance that charge-offs will keep rising because the number of delinquent credit card payments – an early sign of payment difficulty – are approaching historically high levels. Thirty-day credit card delinquencies are now at their highest point in five years, since the last economic recession ended.[57] The difficulty that many families are having affording their credit card bills may have been exacerbated by the mortgage crisis. As home values have dropped sharply, Americans have been unable to use home equity loans and home refinancing to pay off their credit card debts.[58] Moreover, despite rising credit card delinquencies, there is evidence that some families are staying current on their credit card loans but not their mortgage payments, a shift in behavior from past economic crises.[59]

Despite these losses, the credit card industry continues to be the most profitable in the banking sector, earning a return on assets (ROA) since 1995 that is more than three times greater than that for commercial banks overall.[60] Because of the high mortgage losses that many large banks experienced in 2007, there was more than a five-fold difference between bank and credit card profits.[61] Credit card issuers reaped their highest return on assets ever in 2007, exceeding the record year of 2006. In fact, the credit card industry's return on assets grew every year between 1998 and 2004, and in 2007 was almost 90 percent higher than in 1998.[62]

According to credit card industry consultant Andrew Kahr, the basic profitability of the credit card industry is tied to those who carry revolving debt. Borrowers who pay off their balances in full and on time each month do not earn as much profit for the industry.[63] With revolving debt nearly quadrupling since 1990, credit card companies' profitability should remain strong.

Second, credit card issuers earn a significant piece of their revenues from penalty fees alone. In 2007, issuers collected $18 billion in penalty fees, up from $10.7 billion in 2002.[64] Credit card analysts have consistently predicted that the trend toward "repricing" of products and new and higher fees will continue, especially the use of higher late and over-limit fees, and universal default provisions that trigger higher penalty interest rates.[65]

Bankruptcy legislation enacted by Congress in 2005 could further improve the bottom line for credit card companies. By preventing some consumers from eliminating their credit card debts, various estimates show that credit card companies could recover an additional $3 billion to $40 billion annually from households in bankruptcy.[66]

D. Issuers Have Pursued Abusive Interest Rate and Fee Policies That Have a Harmful Impact on Many Households

There is considerable evidence linking the rise in bankruptcy in recent years to the increase in consumer credit outstanding, and, in particular, to credit card debt. For example, research by Professor Ronald Mann of Columbia University has found that an increase in credit card spending in the U.S. and four other countries has resulting in higher credit card debt, which is strongly associated with an increase in bankruptcy filings.[67] To make matters worse, credit card companies have become far more aggressive in implementing questionable fees and interest rate practices in recent years. The upshot of these practices is that penalty interest rates, high and accumulating fees and interest on fees can push consumers with high debts over the financial brink into bankruptcy.[68] In fact, consumers in debt trouble sometimes owe as much or more in fees and penalty interest charges, as in principal.

High fees and interest rates can often result in negative amortization, where the principal owed on credit card debt continues to rise despite making payments. Negative amortization in effect traps credit card borrowers on a debt treadmill that keeps moving faster. Although they are making regular payments, their debts continue to mount. In 2004, a Cleveland judge ruled against Discover Card's efforts to collect debts from a cardholder whose balance nearly tripled from $1,900 to $5,564 without making additional purchases because of fees and penalties, including $1,158 in over-limit fees alone.[69]

In another case, a bankruptcy court in North Carolina ordered a credit card company to itemize the claims it files in chapter 13 bankruptcy cases.[70] In its findings in support of the Order, the bankruptcy judge listed claims filed in eighteen separate cases broken down between principal and interest and fees. On average, interest and fees consisted of more than half (57 percent) of the total amounts listed in the claims. In one case, the card company filed a claim in the amount of $943.58, of which $199.63 was listed as principal and $743.95 was listed as interest and fees. In another case, a claim of $1,011.97 consisted of $273.33 in principal and $738.64 in interest and fees. It is almost certain that pre-bankruptcy payments in these cases had more than paid off the real charges made by the consumers.[71]

Penalty Fees

Traditionally, penalty fees were designed to deter irresponsible cardholder behavior, but in recent years these fees have become primarily a revenue enhancer for credit card issuers. An analysis by the United States Governmental Accountability Office (GAO) found that, ". . . typical cards today now include higher and more complex fees than they did in the past for making late payments, exceeding credit limits, and processing returned payments."[72] The GAO also identified several new fees that issuers have begun using in recent years, some of which they are not required to disclose to consumers in advance. One example of such a fee is for the payment of bills by telephone, which can range from 5 to 15 dollars.[73]

A substantial number of Americans are paying these fees. Thirty-five percent of the credit card accounts from the six largest issuers that the GAO examined had at least one late fee in 2005,[74] representing about 242 million credit cards.[75] Thirteen percent of all accounts – or about 90 million cards – were assessed over-limit fees in 2005.

Late fees have been steadily rising over the past decade and can easily exceed monthly payments for consumers paying low minimum balances.[76] In 1996, a Supreme Court decision prohibited states from setting limits on the fees credit card companies could charge their cardholders. Prior to this court ruling, credit card late fees were commonly around five to ten dollars, but have risen sharply since the decision.[77] The GAO analysis found that late fees jumped sharply after the court ruling. The GAO examined fee data collected by CardWeb.com and found that late fees jumped by 160 percent from $12.83 in 1995 to $33.64 in 2005. The GAO also found a sharp fee increase from data collected by Consumer Action, which showed a 119 percent increase from $12.53 in 1995 to $27.46 in 2005.[78] Even more striking, the GAO found that late fees paid by borrowers with typical balances were an average of $37 in 2005.[79] This is important to note as credit card issuers are increasingly assessing "tiered" fees based on the borrower's balance.

Credit card issuers used to reject transactions that exceeded a cardholder's credit limit, but it has become common for issuers to accept the transaction and then apply an over-limit fee on cardholders who exceed their credit limits.[80] These fees are often applied by issuers in addition to a higher "penalty" interest rate charge for exceeding the credit limit or carrying a high balance.[81] These monthly fees are charged every month a consumer carries a credit balance higher than their credit limit. According to the GAO report, data collected by Consumer Action shows a 114 percent increase in over-limit fees between 1995 and 2005.[82] Critics of this practice argue that issuers should not assess a penalty fee when they can simply enforce the credit limit if they wish to prevent consumers from exceeding it.

Penalty Interest Rates

The vast majority of credit card issuers also increase interest rates for credit card account holders who pay their bills late, even by a few hours. In 2005, Consumer Action found that 78.7 percent of issuers charged penalty rates for late payments on their cards.[83] For example, representatives for one large issuer told the GAO that they *automatically* increase a customer's interest rate if this person pays late or exceeds the credit limit. The GAO found that all but one of the 28 cards from the six largest issuers they reviewed charged default rates in 2005. The average default rate was 27.3 percent, up from 23.8 percent in 2003.[84] Some consumers with low-rate cards could have their interest rates double overnight for being late on one payment to their credit card.[85] Some issuers also say that they will charge default interest rates for exceeding the credit limit on the card or for returned payments, or that they will increase interest rates for cash advances and balance transfers for violations of card terms.[86]

There is increasing evidence that those who can least afford these higher interest rates – financially vulnerable families – are most likely to be paying them. A study by the research organization Demos found that cardholders that carry debt who earn less than $50,000 a year are more than twice as likely to pay interest rates above 20 percent as the highest income Americans who carry debt. African-American and Latino credit card holders with balances are more likely than whites to pay interest rates higher than 20 percent.[87]

Retroactive Application of Penalty Rates

All issuers also apply penalty interest rates retroactively to prior purchases. This has the effect of increasing the price on purchases already made but not paid off.[88] Some cards even apply penalty rates to debts that were already paid at a lower rate.[89] There is simply no legal or economic justification for assessing a penalty interest rate to an existing balance. . . .

Universal Default

Universal default clauses in credit card contracts allow credit card companies to raise interest rates on debtors who have problems with other creditors or whose credit scores decline. The increases are triggered not just by a late mortgage or credit card payment to other lenders but also to payment disputes with other types of creditors, like utilities or book clubs.[90] A review of credit card disclosures issued in October 2006 by Consumer Action found five major issuers that said they reserved the right to assess universal default interest rates. Since that time, Citigroup and JP Morgan Chase have said that they will not use the practice. On the other hand, representatives for Bank of America and Discover testified before the Senate late last year that they still use consumer credit scores, at least in part, to trigger higher default interest rates.[91]

It is fundamentally unfair to impose a penalty interest rate on a consumer who has not made a late payment or defaulted on an obligation, especially when this rate increase is applied retroactively. Another concern with using credit reports to trigger a penalty rate is the problems with inaccuracies in credit scoring and credit reporting that CFA and other organizations have documented.[92] Moreover, issuers who impose sharp interest rate increases on consumers who are meeting their obligations often fail to provide any rationale – much less a legitimate one – for the increase. In January, Bank of America began increasing interest rates on some cardholders to as high as 28 percent but did not inform consumers [of] the reason for the increase in the notification they mailed.[93] . . .

Indiscriminate, Undisclosed Changes in Rates and Fees

Many credit card companies reserve the right to change the terms of their credit card contract at any time and for any, *or no,* reason. This allows credit card companies to arbitrarily raise interest rates even for cardholders in good standing and with perfect credit histories. Media reports of recent rate hikes by Bank of America demonstrate the unfairness of any-time/any-reason changes: some consumers saw their interest rates triple without explanation.[94] The result of these unfair clauses is that consumers can't depend on the interest rate promised to them.

Pricing Tricks: Double Cycle Billing and Manipulation of Payment Order

The GAO found that two of six major creditors are using a practice called double-cycle billing, which results in illegitimate interest charges on balances that have already been paid on time.[95] Since then, one of these issuers, JP Morgan Chase, has announced that it will no longer use double-cycle billing. With this practice, issuers consider two billing cycles in assessing interest. A consumer who begins with no balance and pays off most but not all of the purchases he or she makes in the first month would still be charged interest for the *entire* amount of the balance in the second month. A fair billing process would only result in an interest charge on the amount of the unpaid balance.

The GAO also determined that for 23 of the 28 large issuer cards they reviewed, cardholder payments were first allocated to the balance assessed at a lower rate of interest.[96] This practice is problematic for the many cardholders who now carry balances at different rates of interest, such as introductory "teaser" rates, cash advance rates, and balance transfer rates. The lower interest rate balances must first be paid off before the issuer will allocate payments to higher rate balances. Allocating payments to lower interest rate balances first unfairly extends the length of time it takes consumers to pay down their balances while increasing the finance charges that issuers earn.

Fewer Consumers Benefit from Lower Interest Rates as Issuers Switch to Fixed Rate Cards

For many years, analysts and observers of the credit card industry have noted a phenomenon called "sticky" interest rates. This typically refers to the fact that creditors are often slow to pass on savings when the cost of funds decline, but quicker to increase rates when cost rise. As a result, the "spread" between the credit card issuers' cost of funds and the interest rates charged to cardholders have tended to benefit the credit card companies, regardless of the direction of the interest rate changes. For example, although interest rates were at historical lows at the turn of the century, issuers did not pass the cost savings completely through to their customers.[97]

Over the past six years, it appears that the distribution of credit cards between variable and fixed rates is related to the interest rate picture. As interest rates increase, issuers tend to switch consumers over to variable rate cards. As interest rates began to increase from historic lows, *CardTrak* reported in November 2004 that more than half (55 percent) of credit card debt was carried on variable interest rate cards, a major change from three years earlier when rates were declining and card issuers were shifting to fixed rate products.[98] As rates rose further in 2007, *CardTrak* reported that 86 percent of credit card balances were carried on cards with variable rates.[99] Now that rates are declining again, issuers are shifting back to fixed rate cards. Thirty-nine percent of credit card offers mailed in October of 2007 included fixed rate offers, compared to 29 percent during the third quarter of the year.[100]

Increases in Credit Card Fees and Interest Rates Significantly Affect Consumer Debt

Penalty fees and interest made up more than three-quarters of credit card issuers' revenues throughout 2002 and 2003. Credit card issuers earned $65.4 billion in interest and $7.7 billion in penalty fees in 2003 or 75.7 percent of the total $96.5 billion in revenue.[101] In 2002, penalty fees and interest made up 76.8 percent of the industry's $97.1 billion in revenues. For the approximately 88 million credit cardholding households, penalty fees and interest on their credit card debt cost an average of $830 in 2003.[102]

E. Americans Are Highly Critical of Many Current Credit Card Practices

Our organizations regularly conduct public opinion surveys regarding consumer attitudes and behavior. We have rarely encountered the kind of broad, nearly universal condemnation that Americans have for many common practices used by credit card issuers regarding interest rates, fees and the extension of credit.

For example, a nationally representative poll of 1,005 adults conducted by the Opinion Research Corporation for the Consumer Federation of America from September 13 to September 16, 2007 found that:

- 82 percent of Americans think it is unfair to offer several credit cards to a student with little income. (62 percent believe it is very unfair.)
- 91 percent of Americans think it is unfair to raise interest rates or fees at any time for any reason. (76 percent believe it is very unfair.)
- 83 percent of Americans think it is unfair to increase the interest rate on one card because of a person's payment history on another card. (62 percent believe it is very unfair.)
- 84 percent of Americans think it is unfair to apply interest rate increases not only to new balances but also to past balances. (61 percent believe it is very unfair.)
- 85 percent of Americans think it is unfair to increase an interest rate to 30 percent for making two late payments. (64 percent believe it is very unfair.)
- 76 percent of Americans think it is very unfair to charge $30 for making a late payment. (51 percent believe it is very unfair.)
- 82 percent of Americans think it is unfair to charge a $30 fee each month if a balance is over the credit limit when a person is no longer using the card. (64 percent believe it is very unfair.)
- 90 percent of Americans think it is unfair to charge $10 for payment by phone. (72 percent believe it is very unfair.)

- 80 percent of Americans think it is unfair to not allow a person to pay off higher-interest rate debt first, such as on a cash advance, but instead applying payments first to lower-rate debt. (54 percent believe it is very unfair.)
- 81 percent of Americans think it is unfair to have only one week between the time a person receives a monthly statement and the time he or she must mail the payment. (54 percent believe that it is very unfair.)
- 93 percent of Americans think it is unfair to charge a late fee even though a person has mailed the payment a week or more in advance of the due date. (79 percent believe that it is very unfair.)
- 71 percent of Americans think it is unfair to require that disputes be settled by mandatory arbitration without being allowed to go to court. (45 percent believe that it is very unfair.)

F. Issuer "Risk-Based" Pricing Often Looks Predatory

Credit card issuers often claim that their interest rate and fee policies are justifiable because they are necessary to compensate for the increased financial risk of lending to borrowers with blemished or limited credit histories. It is true that borrowers who pay their balance every month are receiving a valuable service at no cost in many cases. It is quite possible, in fact, that riskier borrowers who revolve their debt and pay higher interest rates and fees are subsidizing in-part the cost of services that these non-revolvers receive. It is important to note, though, that issuers still receive substantial fee income from merchant "interchange" fees and, in some cases, from annual fees. . . .

The amount of fees and penalty interest rates do not appear to be proportional to the risk or cost incurred by issuers. For many years, issuers have justified "sticky" interest rates that rise faster than they decline by stating that these higher interest rates were necessary to compensate for increased risk. As issuers have increased the number and amount of fees and penalty interest rates they charge, it seems that higher baseline interest rates alone are not sufficient anymore to compensate for risk. There is very little evidence that relatively modest problems, like one or two late payments – significantly increase a consumer's chances of default. It would appear to be impossible to justify charging a consumer with a reasonably good credit history with a late payment fee of $35 and a default interest rate of 29 percent on prior purchases, *in addition to* the finance charge the consumer would already pay on a fairly high interest rate, such as 17 percent. One sign that default rates may not be truly reflective of costs or risk incurred by issuers is that the "fixed amount" that issuers add to the index rate in setting default rates rises when the cost of funds declines. The GAO found that this fixed amount increased from about 19 percent in 2003 to 22 percent in 2005 on the 28 large issuer cards they evaluated.[103]

A rational market would lead lenders to limit their risk by restricting the credit available to consumers with riskier credit records or histories, instead of increasing this risk by leveling higher charges on consumers who may be in significant financial trouble. Allowing higher-risk consumers to continue borrowing at a more expensive, higher rate does not limit consumers' risk of default, it increases it. If the cardholders are indeed higher-risk, lenders would limit their exposure by cutting off new purchases more frequently, preventing balances from increasing and helping to keep the cardholder out of default. However, in many cases, credit card issuers have not cut off credit, frozen credit limits or closed the accounts of cardholders that the issuers deem increased risk. Instead they have allowed borrowers to rack up more credit under more expensive terms,[104] making it more likely that the consumer might suffer serious financial consequences.[105]

If risk-based pricing truly reflects risk, it should decline or at least moderate as risk decreases. For example, as noted above, the amount of credit written off by issuers declined for the first three quarters of 2006, dipping below 4 percent for the first time since the end of 1995. Given that issuers stated so frequently that they adhered to the doctrine of risk-based pricing, it is perfectly appropriate for consumers to ask why they did not see interest rates or fees decline or moderate during that time in response to a more positive credit environment.

The assessment of retroactive interest rates is another sign of abusive rather than genuinely risk-based pricing. As stated above, interest rate increases that apply to past purchases cannot be justified under a true risk-based pricing model. Issuers assess risk based on the best information available on a consumer's credit history. If the risk profile of the consumer declines, the only way issuers could possibly justify a rate increase would be if it were legitimately related to the customer's increased risk, if it did not violate the creditor's agreement to offer credit under certain terms for a specific length of time, and if it were applied prospectively.

Increased expenditures on marketing when consumers reduce their use of credit is also a red flag that pricing in the credit card industry is skewed. As documented above, issuers increased their marketing expenditures significantly through 2005, even as consumers respond less frequently to mail solicitations and showed more caution in taking on new debt. A rational market response to this dynamic would be to pull back on marketing expenditures unless other factors existed that justified this spending, such as windfall profits resulting from abusive pricing.

In response to these "tell-tale" signs of price gouging, it is time for issuers to provide more information to lawmakers and to the public about their real costs to demonstrate that their pricing practices are truly fair.

G. H.R. 5244 Helps Curb Major Credit Card Abuses

The "Credit Cardholders' Bill of Rights Act" helps restore fairness to the credit card marketplace. The bill would require credit card issuers to take a number of steps to treat consumers more fairly, including:

1. Ending Bait and Switch Contract Clauses.
2. Limiting Retroactive Application of Rate Hikes for Consumers in Good Standing.

3. Preventing Credit Card Companies from Gaming Consumer Payments.
4. Prohibiting Unfair and Hidden Interest Rate Charges on Balances Repaid During the Grace Period.
5. Ending Unfair Late Fees for On-Time Payments.

We recommend that the Subcommittee include in H.R. 5244 several additional provisions that would enhance consumer protection not yet addressed by the bill, including: a ban on all universal default rate hikes; a prohibition on retroactive application of *any* rate hike to prior balances; a requirement that the size of penalties charged by issuers be directly related to actual costs incurred; and a requirement that credit card issuers ensure that young consumers have the ability to repay the loans they are offered.

We also recommend that the Subcommittee eliminate a provision in H.R. 5244 allowing issuers to charge over-limit fees for three consecutive months, even if the cardholder only exceeds the credit limit with a single transaction. Instead, H.R. 5244 should prohibit issuers from charging over-limit fees if they choose to allow a cardholder to exceed the credit limit. Similarly, a provision requiring consumers to pay all charges for low-credit-limit, high-fees cards *before* they receive these cards is a well-intentioned effort to ensure that consumers really understand how expensive these cards are. There is a very good chance, however, that unscrupulous lenders will defraud consumers who might pay huge fees before receiving *any* credit. Therefore, we recommend that the Subcommittee either place significant limits on the fees that can be charged on these extremely expensive cards or give consumers meaningful rights to reject these cards before they are activated.

Notes

1. **The Consumer Federation of America** is a nonprofit association of over 280 pro-consumer groups, with a combined membership of 50 million people. CFA was founded in 1968 to advance consumers' interests through advocacy and education.

2. **Consumers Union** is a nonprofit membership organization chartered in 1936 under the laws of the state of New York to provide consumers with information, education and counsel about good, services, health and personal finance, and to initiate and cooperate with individual and group efforts to maintain and enhance the quality of life for consumers. Consumers Union's income is solely derived from the sale of Consumer Reports, its other publications and from noncommercial contributions, grants and fees. In addition to reports on Consumers Union's own product testing, Consumer Reports with more than 5 million paid circulation, regularly carries articles on health, product safety, marketplace economics and legislative, judicial and regulatory actions which affect consumer welfare. Consumers Union's publications carry no advertising and receive no commercial support.

3. As of February 2008, the amount of revolving debt held by Americans was $951.7 billion. Although this figure is often used as a proxy for credit card debt, most experts believe that outstanding credit card debt is slightly lower. First, approximately 5 percent of consumer revolving credit is not

on credit cards. Second, between 4 to 9 percent of the debt does not truly revolve. It is repaid to the credit card issuer before the next billing cycle starts. Taking these two factors into account, outstanding credit card debt is likely to be between $818.5 and $866 billion.

4. VERIBANC, Inc. . . . and Federal Reserve Consumer Credit Outstanding. According to Federal Reserve figures, consumer revolving debt grew by 50 percent from $627.5 billion in December 1999 to $941.4 billion in December 2007. According to VERIBANC, unused lines of credit grew at almost double the rate (90.5 percent) consumers increased their use of credit card lines, increasing from $2.1 trillion in 1999 to just under $4.0 trillion ($3,983,200,614) at the end of 2007.

5. The amount of revolving debt increased by 7.8 percent in 2007, which was the sharpest increase since revolving debt grew by 11.6 percent in 2000. Federal Reserve, Statistical Release, Consumer Credit Outstanding, Table G.19.

6. As of December 2007, the total amount was $4.92 trillion. VERIBANC, Inc. and Federal Reserve Consumer Credit Outstanding, Table G.19.

7. There are 114.4 million households in the U.S., U.S. Census Bureau, "American's Families and Living Arrangements: 2006."

8. VERIBANC, Inc. and Federal Reserve Consumer Credit Outstanding, Table G.19.

9. Vertis Inc. press release, "Financial Direct Mail Readers Interested in Credit Card Offers," January 25, 2005; "Card Marketing 101," *CardTrak,* September 2002.

10. Synovate Mail Monitor, press release, "Mail Monitor Reports Record Six Billion Credit Card Offers Mailed in U.S. during 2005," April 27, 2006.

11. Synovate Mail Monitor, press release, "U.S. Credit Card Mail Volume declined in 4th Quarter 2007 as Troubled Issuers Pull Back," February 2008. The drop in solicitations in 2006 occurred primarily because of the merger between Bank of America and MBNA. Synovate stated that the decline in 2007 occurred because some issuers were "straining from the fall-out due to the mortgage crisis and concern about an uncertain economy." However, some issuers like JP Morgan Chase that have not been as affected by economic problems actually increased their mail marketing in 2007.

12. Kidane, Amdetsion and Sandip Mukerji, Howard University School of Business, "Characteristics of Consumers Targeted and Neglected by Credit Card Companies," *Financial Services Review,* Vol. 13, No. 3, 2004 at 186.

13. Nielsen Monitor, "U.S. Advertising Spending Rose 6.3% in 2004, Nielsen Monitor-Plus Reports," March 1, 2005.

14. Sidel, Robin, "Card Issuer MBNA Lets the Public Take a Peek at Its Hand," *Wall Street Journal,* January 20, 2005 at C1.

15. *Ibid.*

16 Cardweb.com

17. "Recent Changes in U.S. Family Finances: Evidence from the 2001 and 2004 Survey of Consumer Finances," Brian K. Bucks, Arthur B. Kennickell, and Kevin B. Moore, *Federal Reserve Bulletin,* vol. 92 (February 2006), p. 31.

18. CFA calculation based on estimated credit card (as opposed to revolving) debt of $850 billion. If a conservative estimate of 75 percent of 114.4 million

households have credit cards, and only 58 percent of these households carry debt, then the remaining 49.7 million households have an average of $17,103 in debt.

19. Bucks, Brian K., Arthur B. Kennickell and Kevin B. Moore, "Recent Changes in U.S. Family Finances: Evidence from the 2001 and 2004 Survey of Consumer Finances," *Federal Reserve Bulletin*, vol. 92, February 2006, pg. 24.

20. Board of Governors of the Federal Reserve System, "Report to the Congress on Practices of the Consumer Credit Industry in Soliciting and Extending Credit and their Effects on Consumer Debt and Insolvency," submitted to the Congress pursuant to section 1229 of the Bankruptcy Abuse Prevention and Consumer Protection Act of 2005, June 2006 at 9 Table 6.

21. Gallup Poll News Service, "Average American Owes $2,900 in Credit Card Debt," April 16, 2004.

22. Aizcorbe, Kennickell and Moore 2003 at 29, Table 14. In 2001, more than one in four (27.0%) families in the lowest income quintile spent more than 40% of their income on debt payments, compared to less than one in six (16.0%) of families in the second lowest income quintile and one in nine (11.0%) of all families who spent 40% or more of their income on debt payments.

23. Manning, Robert, "Credit Cards on Campus: Costs and Consequences of Student Debt," June 8, 1999. CFA Press Release available at . . .

24. Trigaux, Robert, "Generation Broke: New Grads Bear Heavy Load," *St. Petersburg Times*, November 22, 2004.

25. Draut, Tamara, Director of Demos Economic Opportunity Program, Testimony Before the House Banking Committee Subcommittee on Financial Institutions and Consumer Credit, September 15, 2004, at 8. More than half (55%) of Americans carry revolving balances compared to 71% of borrowers aged 25–34.

26. *Ibid.* at 4–5. In 1992, about one in thirteen (7.9%) Americans aged 25–34 had debt greater than 40% of their income; by 2001, about one in eight (13.3%) had these high debt burdens.

27. Sullivan, Theresa A., Deborah Thorne and Elizabeth Warren, "Young, Old, and In Between: Who Files for Bankruptcy?" *Norton Bankruptcy Law Advisor*, Iss. No. 9A, September 2001.

28. Mayer, Caroline E., "Girls Go From Hello Kitty to Hello Debit Card; Brand's Power Tapped to Reach Youth," *The Washington Post*, October 3, 2004.

29. *See* Ludden, Jennifer, "Credit Card Companies Target Kids," *All Things Considered*, National Public Radio, February 6, 2005.

30. Demos, "Retiring in the Red," January 19, 2004 at 3.

31. Sullivan, Theresa A., Deborah Thorne and Elizabeth Warren, "Young, Old, and In Between: Who Files for Bankruptcy?" *Norton Bankruptcy Law Advisor*, Iss. No. 9A, September 2001, at 5. The number of older Americans declaring bankruptcy during this period rose from 23,890 to 82,207.

32. Aizcorbe, Kennickell and Moore 2003 at 28, Table 14. According to the Federal Reserve Survey of Consumer Finances, the median debt services ratio of households aged 65–74 grew by 54% from 9.8% in 1992 to 15.1% in 2001 and the debt services ratio for households 75 and older grew 169% from 2.6% to 7.0% in 2001.

33. *Ibid.* 13.9% of households aged 65–74 and 14.3% of households aged 75 and over spent more than 40 percent of their income on debt service.

34. Hanway, Steve, Gallup News Organization, "Do Credit Card Habits Improve with Age?" May 18, 2004. Nearly half (48%) of households over 65 years old have incomes below $30,000, compared to 16% of those aged 30–49 and 18% of those aged 50–64.

35. Interview with Andrew Kahr, credit card industry consultant, "The Secret History of the Credit Card," *Frontline,* November 2004.

36. Kim, Jane J., "Minimums Due on Credit Cards are on the Increase," *Wall Street Journal,* March 24, 2005.

37. Der Hovanesian, Mara "Tough Love for Debtors," *Business Week,* April 25, 2005.

38. Opinion Research Corporation, "Consumer Financial Services Survey," November 3–7, 2005.

39. Credit Research Center, McDonough School of Business, Georgetown University.

40. OCC, Remarks by Julie L. Williams, First Senior Deputy Comptroller and Chief Counsel before the Risk Management Association's Retail Risk Management Conference on Regulatory Concerns about Certain Retail Banking Practices, Chicago, June 3, 2003, in "Speeches and Congressional Testimony," *OCC Quarterly Journal,* Vol. 22, No. 3, September 2003 at 107.

41. Consumer Federation of America, "Consumer Restraint Pressures Lenders to Reduce Credit Card Marketing and Credit Extension," January 18, 2000.

42. Proposed in S. 1176 by Senators Akaka, Durbin, Leahy and Schumer.

43. Public Law 109-8.

44. Joint press release of Board of Governors of the Federal Reserve System, Federal Deposit Insurance Corporation, Office of the Comptroller of the Currency and Office of Thrift Supervision, "FFIEC Agencies Issue Guidance on Credit Card Account Management and Loss Allowance Practices," January 8, 2003, see attached "Account Management and Loss Allowance Guidance" at 3.

45. American Financial Services Association, "Credit Card Minimum Payments Going Up," *Spotlight on Financial Services,* April 2005.

46. Warnick, Melody, "Credit Card Minimum Payments Doubling," . . . May 3, 2005. Citibank and Bank of America have announced they are doubling their minimum payment requirements from 2% to 4% of the balance.

47. Day, Kathleen and Caroline E. Mayer, "Credit Card Penalties, Fees Bury Debtors," *Washington Post,* March 6, 2005.

48. Der Hovanesian, Mara "Tough Love for Debtors," *Business Week,* April 25, 2005.

49. "Minimum Payments," *CardTrak,* September 6, 2006.

50. Gavin, Robert, "Credit Card Companies Pursue Subprime Borrowers," *Boston Globe,* September 5, 2007.

51. Interview with Andrew Kahr, credit card industry consultant, "The Secret History of the Credit Card," *Frontline,* November 2004.

52. OCC, Statement of Comptroller of the Currency John D. Hawke J., June 28, 2000.

53. Pacelle, Mitchell, "Pushing Plastic," *Wall Street Journal,* November 5, 2004.

54. Mayer, Caroline E., "Bankrupt and Swamped with Credit Offers," *Washington Post,* April 15, 2005.

55. *Ibid.*

56. Federal Reserve Board, Charge-Off and Delinquency Rates on Loans and Leases at All Commercial Banks, available at . . . accessed January 19, 2007. Most experts attribute lower charge-offs in 2006 to the surge of bankruptcy filings (and corresponding increase in charge-offs) that occurred in the third and fourth quarters of 2005.

57. 30-day credit card delinquencies during the fourth quarter of 2007 were 4.54 percent, the highest since the last quarter of 2002. Federal Reserve Board, Charge-Off and Delinquency Rates on Loans and Leases at 100 Largest Commercial Banks.

58. Westrich, Tim and Weller, Christian E., "House of Cards, Consumers Turn to Credit Cards Amid the Mortgage Crisis, Delaying Inevitable Defaults," Center for American Progress, February 2008.

59. Chu, Kathy, "More Americans Using Credit Cards to Stay Afloat," *USA Today,* February 28, 2008.

60. "Card Profits 04," *CardTrak,* January 24, 2005; "Banner Year," *CardTrak,* February 2004; FDIC, *FDIC Quarterly Banking Profile,* Third Quarter 2006 at 5, Table I-A; FDIC, *FDIC Quarterly Banking Profile,* Fourth Quarter 2000 at 4, Table I-A. Commercial banks average return on assets between 1995 and 2004 was 1.23 percent,less than one third the size of the credit card industry average return on assets of 3.73 percent over the same period, according to R.K. Hammer and Associates.

61. ROA for credit card issuers in 2007 was 4.65%, R.K Hammer and Associates, January 2008. ROA for commercial banks in 2007 was .86%, FDIC, "Banks and Thrifts Earned $105.5 billion in 2007," February 26, 2008.

62. R.K. Hammer and Associates, January 2008. The industry's ROA was 2.5% in 1998, 3.1% in 1999, 3.6% in 2000, 4.0% in 2001, 4.2% in 2002, 4.4% in 2003, 4.5% in 2004, 4.3% in 2005, 4.6% in 2006 and 4.65% in 2007.

63. Interview with Andrew Kahr, credit card industry consultant, "The Secret History of the Credit Card," *Frontline,* November 2004.

64. CardTrak, "Card Costs," . . . Card issuers charged an estimated $30 billion in fees in 2007, about six percent higher than in 2006. More than half, or $18 billion, were penalty fees. Late fees accounted 70 percent of the penalty fees charged. R.K. Hammer and Associates found that $8 billion of the penalty fees were for cash advances. Day, Kathleen and Caroline E. Mayer, "Credit Card Penalties, Fees Bury Debtors," *Washington Post,* March 6, 2005.

65. Card Profits 04," *CardTrak,* January 24, 2005.

66. Heller, Michelle, "Gauging the Bottom-Line Effects of Bankruptcy Bill," *American Banker,* April 15, 2005.

67. Mann, Ronald J., "Credit Cards, Consumer Credit and Bankruptcy," Law and Economics Research Paper No. 44, The University of Texas School of Law, March 2006.

68. Day, Kathleen and Caroline E. Mayer, "Credit Card Penalties, Fees Bury Debtors," *Washington Post,* March 6, 2005.

69. National Consumer Law Center, "Responsible Consumers Driven into Default," February 22, 2005.

70. *In re* Blair, No. 02-1140 (Bankrate. W.D.N.C. filed Feb. 10, 2004)

71. National Consumer Law Center, "Responsible Consumers Driven into Default," February 22, 2005.

72. "Credit Cards: Increased Complexity in Rates and Fees Heightens Need for More Effective Disclosures to Consumers," U.S. Government Accountability Office, September 2006, p. 18.

73. *Ibid,* p. 23.

74. *Ibid,* p. 1.

75. CFA calculation based on 691 million credit cards, as reported in, *Ibid,* p. 9.

76. "The Ugly Issuer," *Credit Card Management,* September 2004.

77. Bergman, Lowell and David Rummel, "Secret History of the Credit Card," *Frontline,* November 2004.

78. "Credit Cards: Increased Complexity in Rates and Fees Heightens Need for More Effective Disclosures to Consumers," U.S. Government Accountability Office, September 2006, p. 18.

79. *Ibid,* p. 20.

80. "The Ugly Issuer," *Credit Card Management,* September 2004.

81. Bergman, Lowell and David Rummel, "Secret History of the Credit Card," *Frontline,* November 2004.

82. "Credit Cards: Increased Complexity in Rates and Fees Heightens Need for More Effective Disclosures to Consumers," U.S. Government Accountability Office, September 2006, p. 20.

83. Consumer Action, 2005 Credit Card Survey, "Card Companies Use Common 'Risk Factors' to Impose Unfair Rate Hikes, Finds CA," *Consumer Action News,* Summer 2005.

84. The GAO did find that some issuers do not assess default rates unless there are multiple violations of card terms. "Credit Cards: Increased Complexity in Rates and Fees Heightens Need for More Effective Disclosures to Consumers," U.S. Government Accountability Office, September 2006, pgs. 24, 25.

85. Bergman, Lowell and David Rummel, "Secret History of the Credit Card," *Frontline,* November 2004.

86. "Credit Cards: Increased Complexity in Rates and Fees Heightens Need for More Effective Disclosures to Consumers," U.S. Government Accountability Office, September 2006, p. 25.

87. Wheary, Jennifer, Draut, Tamara, "Who Pays? The Winners and Losers of Credit Card Deregulation," Demos, August 1, 2007.

88. Draut, Tamara, Director of the Economic Opportunity Program Demos, Testimony Before the House Banking Committee Subcommittee on Financial Institutions and Consumer Credit, September 15, 2004, at 16–17.

89. McGeehan, Patrick, "The Plastic Trap," *New York Times,* November 21, 2004. Discover disclosed to its customers that it had changed the terms

of its interest rates from a low of zero to 19.99% for a single late payment, but it applied that rate increase for late payments from 11 months prior to the disclosure of the changing interest rate terms.

90. Burt, Bill, "Pay One Bill Late, Get Punished by Many," . . . January 20, 2004.

91. Credit Card Practices: Unfair Interest Rate Increases, U.S. Senate Permanent Subcommittee on Investigation, December 4, 2007.

92. Consumer Federation of America and National Credit Reporting Association, "Credit Score Accuracy and Implications for Consumers," December 17, 2002. CFA and NCRA reviewed over 500,000 credit files and found that 29 percent of consumers have credit scores that differ by at least 50 points between the credit bureaus.

93. "A Credit Card You Want to Toss," *Business Week,* February 7, 2008.

94. *Ibid.*

95. "Credit Cards: Increased Complexity in Rates and Fees Heightens Need for More Effective Disclosures to Consumers," U.S. Government Accountability Office, September 2006, p. 27.

96. *Ibid.*

97. "The Ugly Issuer," *Credit Card Management,* September 2004.

98. "5% Prime," *CardTrak,* November 10, 2004.

99. "Rate Gap," *CardTrak,* January 18, 2007.

100. Synovate Mail Monitor, press release, "Synovate Mail Monitor Shows Credit Card Terms Improve, More Fixed Rate Offers," December 2007.

101. Daly, James J., "Smooth Sailing," *Credit Card Management,* May 2004 at 31.

102. CFA calculation from Daly, James J. 2004 and Census Bureau figures.

103. "Credit Cards: Increased Complexity in Rates and Fees Heightens Need for More Effective Disclosures to Consumers," U.S. Government Accountability Office, September 2006, p. 24.

104. Pacelle, Mitchell, "Growing Profit Source for Banks: Fees From Riskiest Card Holders," *Wall Street Journal,* July 6, 2004.

105. As the economy slows, there is evidence that some issuers are raising credit standards and tightening access to credit in ways that do not lead to further financial exposure for their existing cardholders. Others appear to be using old tricks, such as using credit scores to suddenly and sharply raise interest rates on existing balances, that will likely destabilize economically fragile households. A Credit Card You Want to Toss," *Business Week,* February 7, 2008.

John P. Carey

Testimony before the Subcommittee on Financial Institutions and Consumer Credit

Introduction

Good morning Chairwoman Maloney, Ranking Member Biggert, and Members of the Subcommittee. My name is John Carey, and I am the Chief Administrative Officer of Citi Cards. I appreciate the opportunity to appear before you today to discuss our views on H.R. 5244 and its implications for credit card customers and issuers.

Citi Cards is one of the leading providers of credit cards, with roughly 45 million active bank card customer accounts in the United States, served by 33,000 employees in 20 states. This is a complex business—managing literally billions of individual financial transactions for our customers each month—and we strive to get it right. This is a highly competitive business, so we are continually analyzing our business practices and looking for ways to do a better job of meeting our customers' needs.

That's why last year we were one of the first issuers to stop two practices that were the focus of widespread customer concerns: repricing customers during the term of the card based on delinquent behavior with other creditors, often referred to as universal default, and so-called "any time any reason" repricing.

More broadly, we know customers are not satisfied with the status quo across the industry and, frankly, we are not satisfied either. We understand the concerns motivating legislative action. They are real. They are the same concerns that underlie the Federal Reserve Board's (Fed) proposed modification to the regulatory regime that governs credit cards. There is, in fact, a broad consensus—across the credit card industry and among consumers, advocacy groups, and academics—about the need for action. The question for robust discussion is what kind of action.

We have studied H.R. 5244 closely, and we welcome the opportunity to share our views. My testimony today will: (1) examine how the evolution of the credit card industry created the challenges we face today; (2) identify what we think are the best solutions to those challenges; and (3) offer our views about why H.R. 5244 is not the right approach.

U.S. House of Representatives, April 17, 2008.

Evolution of the Credit Card Industry: Roots of Today's Challenges

Background. To understand the roots of today's challenges in the credit card industry, it is important to appreciate how credit cards have evolved over the past half-century: they have transformed from an accommodation by local merchants for a few trusted customers to an integral part of the national economy and the principal form of credit for millions of Americans.

The industry's roots are found in small retail stores where customers charged purchases and paid the merchant back monthly; these arrangements were based on face-to-face relationships and the credit issuer's knowledge of the borrower's financial situation and ability to repay the loan. Even as recently as 25 years ago, credit cards were available only to a relatively small group of high-income individuals who had strong credit histories. But even those reliable customers had little choice and more onerous terms than what is available to most Americans today. Before 1990, nearly all credit cards carried an annual fee, ranging from $20 to $50, and most cards charged fixed interest rates of roughly 20%. Today, the situation is nearly reversed. By 2005, 75% of cards had no annual fee, and 80% of cardholders had interest rates lower than 20%.

Risk-Based Pricing. Before the late 1980s, two factors combined to create a one-size-fits-all credit card market, with fewer cards available and more restrictive terms: first, for lenders, credit card transactions are not secured by a lien on a tangible asset, which makes them a risky form of loan; and second, lenders at that time had no good way to evaluate and calibrate that credit risk for individual customers.

Because credit cards are now so familiar and ubiquitous, it is easy to lose sight of what they are. While most people may not think of it this way, the fact is that every time a person uses a credit card, that consumer is taking out an unsecured loan through a revolving line of credit. Although credit cards are treated interchangeably with cash, checks, or debit cards during a transaction, they operate quite differently. When a customer pays with cash, check, or debit card, she is simply choosing among different methods of transferring *her own funds* to a merchant. But a credit card is more than a method of payment; when a customer uses a credit card, she borrows funds from the issuer of the credit card and directs the issuer to transfer that *borrowed money* to the merchant at the same time.

And because the loan a customer takes out when using a credit card is an unsecured revolving loan, it carries a lot of risk from a lender's perspective. Unlike other common consumer loans, such as car loans and mortgages, which are backed up by tangible security, a credit card loan is secured only by a customer's promise to repay. Moreover, it is an open line of credit, which the customer can access at any time from almost anywhere in the world. Finally, these loans typically are made not through personal interaction, but through the mail, by telephone, or over the Internet, to someone the lender in all likelihood has never met.

The unsecured, open-ended nature of credit card loans means that lenders need to take steps to protect themselves against unanticipated changes in credit risk. Twenty-five years ago, issuers did that by lending only to customers with the strongest credit histories and by imposing across-the-board 20% interest rates and charging annual fees. At that point, credit card companies simply did not have sufficiently developed technology or the analytical tools to permit the pricing of credit card loans based on a customer's risk profile.

In the last 15 years, new technology and more sophisticated risk management analytics and practices have made it possible for issuers to evaluate an individual customer's risk profile more effectively at account opening and throughout the relationship, and to base credit card loan pricing on those evaluations. Thus, while issuers still have to contend with the inherently riskier nature of an unsecured, revolving loan, these technological and analytical advances have given issuers more precise and effective tools to mitigate that risk. This is risk-based pricing, and it has revolutionized the credit card market, with many benefits for consumers.

Benefits to Consumers. Issuers now can set prices and credit limits at the time a credit card application is approved that will better correspond to an individual customer's credit risk profile, and they also can react in "real-time" to changes in risk over the life of a customer's account.

This risk-based pricing is good for consumers in two ways. First, by allocating the cost of risk to individual customers, issuers can reward customers who have solid credit histories with more competitive pricing, while the customer who poses a higher risk appropriately absorbs the cost of that risk himself.

Second, risk-based pricing actually grows the pie, providing more people with access to regulated credit, including consumers who were previously underserved or had no access to unsecured, revolving credit. With the ability to adjust pricing so that it has a nexus to risk, issuers can expand access to credit, giving a broader range of consumers across the economic spectrum the opportunity to establish a credit history, better manage their cash flow, and deal with costs associated with unexpected life events such as job loss or health emergencies. These benefits are particularly important for Americans who may not have been able to build up a cash nest egg and otherwise would have to dip into retirement savings or seek credit from payday lenders or others in the unregulated market.

These improvements derived from risk-based pricing also have led to increased competition in the industry, which, in turn, has created both more choices for consumers and overall lower prices. Issuers offer affinity, co-branded, and special feature credit cards, including cards with rewards programs tied to airlines or retail stores, with special pricing for higher payments, or that provide contributions to an associated 529 college savings plan. In addition, credit card interest rates have declined since mid-1991, largely through greater competition and reduced cost of funds. As a result, in 1991 only 11% of cardholders reported interest rates below 16%, while 71% did so in January 2007. According to the 2006 report by the Government Accountability Office (GAO), the average interest rate on cards declined by almost six percentage points as compared to 1990.[1]

Taking Action: Solving the Challenges

There is widespread agreement on the need for comprehensive changes—beyond individual companies' actions—to improve the credit card marketplace. As the credit card market has evolved and the products have become more numerous and complex, it is all the more important for consumers to have complete, clear, consistently-presented information to make informed choices. Unfortunately, federal disclosure requirements have not kept pace with market innovation. Nor has the industry been able on its own to develop a uniform set of rules that would effectively inform consumers about the credit card products they choose and use every day. This lack of transparency prevents consumers from being able to make fully informed decisions and distorts the marketplace.

Citi's Experience as an Innovator. I can tell you from our own experience that the lack of complete, understandable information about credit card practices undermines the incentive to make consumer-friendly changes. Last year, we led the industry in responding to consumers and policymakers who criticized two practices that, while rational from a purely credit risk-pricing perspective, were viewed as heavy-handed. First, we eliminated the practice—known as universal default—of adjusting our customers' interest rates during the term of their card based on their delinquent behavior with other creditors, even though a customer's credit behavior with another creditor has proven to be predictive of that customer's behavior with us. Some issuers continue to assert that they have eliminated universal default simply because they give customers *notice* before they reprice on the basis of behavior with another issuer. But we mean more than that: we have eliminated not just "automatic" repricing (*i.e.,* without notice) based on such behavior, but *any* repricing.

Second, we also gave up the ability—commonly known as "any time any reason repricing"—to increase rates or fees during the term of the card (typically two years) for reasons such as changes in economic conditions, including our own cost of funds, which obviously affect our business.

We hoped and expected that these two points of differentiation would lead customers to vote with their feet. These changes were widely applauded, both by consumer advocates and by many of you. But we have been disappointed with the results we have seen so far. So, what happened? The problem is that customers cannot recognize the differences between us and our competitors; disclosures across the industry are not providing sufficient, straightforward information that allows a layperson to use a side-by-side comparison to select the best value.

Simple, clear disclosures stimulate innovations that benefit consumers, encourage firms to adopt policies and practices that are distinctive and attractive to consumers, and help to prevent potentially unfair practices by shining a light on them. If properly designed, disclosures provide a clear understanding of credit card policies and practices; help consumers in selecting the card best suited to their needs; help consumers avoid being surprised by unexpected fees; provide sufficient notice of potential changes in practices; and promote greater competition within the industry.

We have invested significant time and effort in making sure our own disclosures communicate effectively. While we are, of course, always looking for ways to improve, our disclosures were the only ones singled out by the GAO in its September 2006 industry-wide report on credit cards as effective and simpler to read. We also have introduced an enhanced *"Facts About Rates and Fees"* table in our cardmember agreements, summarizing all rates and fees in clear, easier to read language; adopted a more consumer-friendly notice to better inform each customer of a change in terms and the right each customer may have to opt out of that change; and enhanced our "responsible lender" disclosures by adding a simple paragraph to the front page of all solicitation letters making clear, among other things, any balance transfer fee, the circumstances under which a customer may lose a promotional rate, and the balances to which the promotional rate does and does not apply.

We recognize, however, that our own efforts, and those of a number of other issuers, are not enough. The industry cannot solve this problem itself because there is no incentive for companies with poor practices to have clear disclosures. In fact, quite the opposite is true. That is why we applaud the Fed's efforts to modernize and improve the disclosure regime for the entire industry for the first time in 30 years.

Regulatory Action by the Fed. When we last appeared before this Subcommittee in June 2007, the Fed had just announced its proposed changes to Regulation (Reg) Z, which implements the Truth in Lending Act (TILA). Our initial reaction was quite positive, and now, having had the opportunity to study the Fed's detailed proposal carefully, we fully support this approach to reform.

The nuanced and extensively reviewed proposal aims to improve the clarity and consistency of disclosures at every important point in the customer's relationship with her bank, and to enhance the customer's understanding of key credit card terms and conditions. The proposal is rooted in the belief, as expressed by Congress in TILA, that economic stability and competition among consumer credit providers are strengthened when consumers make informed judgments about the cost of credit. The Fed would, for example, require a standardized presentation of information in easy-to-read tables that show key rate and fee information, including penalty fees.

In essence, the proposed Reg Z changes seek to move credit card disclosures toward the successful model of food labeling, where consumers can get all the information they need in simple, uniform terms that allow them to readily compare one product to another. Consumers should be able to do the same thing in the world of credit cards, relying on the consistent, easily-understandable presentation of important information in table-form when applying for credit, when opening an account, when receiving their statement, or when the terms of the account change. We also want consumers to have ample opportunity to exercise their leverage and negotiate with the issuer or seek out a new credit card provider if they are not satisfied with a change in terms proposed by their current issuer. And because meaningful disclosure and financial literacy go hand-in-hand, we also support a broader, sustained investment in financial literacy on a national basis, in conjunction with improved disclosures.

While all of these changes certainly would benefit consumers, they also would ensure that financial services providers compete on a level playing field. At Citi, we want consumers to be able to compare us to our competitors on an apples-to-apples basis. In fact, we relish that comparison. We want disclosures that will highlight our best practices and enable us to compete effectively in the marketplace against issuers whose practices may be less consumer-friendly.

We agree that industry-wide change is necessary to address the real challenges in the system, but, in our view, the regulatory changes underway at the Fed offer a better path to reform than H.R. 5244.

H.R. 5244: Not the Right Approach

We understand the impetus for this bill. We have heard the dissatisfaction of consumers and policymakers loud and clear. But we urge Congress to tread cautiously here in order to avoid unintended consequences—particularly at a fragile time for the economy.

Premature. First, passing legislation—which itself would result in months of rulemaking to develop implementing regulations—would slow down the regulatory train, which is already nearing its destination. The Fed's thorough revision of Reg Z—which reflects extensive consumer testing and review—will be finalized before the end of the year. We are confident that, if given the chance to work, the Fed's revamped disclosure requirements will largely address the problems H.R. 5244 is intended to address. Uniform disclosure that enables customer understanding is the best way to address practices that are not consumer friendly; in a fully effective marketplace, consumers will be the judge, and issuers who adopt the best practices will enjoy a competitive advantage. We think that the Fed's approach should be given an opportunity to take effect before Congress makes a determination as to whether legislative action is necessary.

Regulatory Expertise and Flexibility. There are other practical reasons—in addition to timing—to favor the Fed's regulatory approach. As the regulator responsible for addressing consumer concerns with the credit card industry, the Fed has an unparalleled understanding of this complex and evolving business, so it makes sense to take advantage of this expertise in designing solutions to the challenges facing the industry. Regulations are also more flexible than legislation and can be modified more easily than statutes to take into account changes in market conditions or consumer demands.

Unintended Consequences. We have significant concerns that H.R. 5244 would fundamentally alter the credit card business in ways that would dramatically affect consumers and the broader economy. I will highlight a few of our key concerns below, and we would be happy to discuss our concerns in greater detail with the Committee.

First, H.R. 5244 would seriously impair issuers' ability to reflect consumer risk in credit card pricing. At bottom, the bill's restrictions amount to price controls—not because they impose specific numerical caps, but because they limit the amount of risk an issuer can incorporate into the price of the loan. For example, by prohibiting issuers from using credit bureau information to evaluate a customer's risk when her card is up for renewal, the bill (as we understand it) would have the perverse result of forcing the issuer to make a pricing decision based on anything *except* the customer's own risk profile.

The capacity to consider relevant information about risk when making credit available is a fundamental foundation of safe and sound lending practices. Without that ability to differentiate risk, less creditworthy consumers would have fewer means of accessing regulated credit, relatively risk-free consumers would face a higher cost of credit, and banks would have to re-think their lending models. The Congressional Research Service (CRS), for example, reports that legislation that limits the ability of issuers to reprice for risk could lead to increased minimum payments, reduced credit limits, and less access to credit cards.[2]

In short, if this bill is enacted, the financial burdens associated with the higher-risk customers will be spread across all customers, instead of being borne by the higher-risk customers themselves.

Second, the bill effectively bars a lender from charging interest on an outstanding loan. That result would fundamentally alter the credit card economic model. Under current industry practice, a cardholder qualifies for a grace period and can avoid paying interest on her loan when she pays the entire balance on time and in full. This is an extraordinary feature in the world of lending. It is good for issuers because it encourages customers to pay on time, and it is good for customers because it gives them an interest-free loan. In fact, 55% of our customers use it. But because it is so unusual, and so contrary to the basic business model of lending money for interest, this deal has set terms: a cardholder must pay off the *entire* balance by the due date. The bill would completely rewrite the terms of the deal to make the lender give an interest free loan for *any* amount paid by the due date, greatly expanding the grace period concept. If such a provision were enacted into law, card issuers would be forced to change their pricing models, and to consider eliminating the grace period altogether.

Third, by prohibiting any changes to the terms of the card agreement except for reasons that are specifically set out in the agreement at the time the account was opened, H.R. 5244 undermines the push to simplify disclosures, as issuers will be forced to set forth every potential eventuality in the original agreement.

Fourth, by barring issuers from notifying credit reporting agencies about the existence of a new card until it is actually used, this bill will distort customers' credit risk profiles and could adversely affect their credit scores. Moreover, this bill will make it more difficult to prevent fraud and identity theft. Prohibiting this flow of information means that no one will be able to flag unusual and inappropriate patterns of card activity, which are key triggers to stopping fraud and identity theft before it happens.

Conclusion

I believe that this legislation is unnecessary in light of the targeted regulatory efforts underway to address these concerns, and that its unintended consequences would undermine the genuine benefits the risk-based model has brought to consumers and threaten to destabilize the credit markets.

Thank you for the opportunity to discuss these important issues with the Subcommittee.

Notes

1. *Credit Cards: Increased Complexity in Rates and Fees Heightens Need for More Effective Disclosures to Consumers,* GAO at 15, Sept. 2006.
2. Darryl E. Getter, T*he Credit Card Market: Recent Trends, Funding Cost Issues, and Repricing Practices,* CRS REPORT TO CONGRESS at 11, Feb. 27, 2008.

POSTSCRIPT

Do American Consumers Need a Credit Card Bill of Rights?

In making the case for a credit card bill of rights, Consumer Federation of America Legislative Director Travis B. Plunkett makes a number of points. He argues that "aggressive and even reckless lending has played a huge role in pushing credit card debt to record levels." He also argues that since the 1990s credit card issuers in their marketing have targeted those who have "not had widespread access to mainstream credit." With the economic downturn and rising home foreclosures, payments of credit card bills have become increasingly difficult, but the recent bankruptcy legislation may actually benefit credit card companies. Plunkett then reviews a number of interest rate and fee policies adopted by credit card issuers that he believes "have a harmful impact on many households." For these and other reason, he believes a credit card bill of rights would help "restore fairness to the credit card market place."

Credit card company executive John P. Carey begins his testimony opposing a credit card bill of rights by admitting that there is a need for action. He believes the real issue is about the kind of action. He notes that the credit card industry has been moving to a system of risk-based pricing. Consumers benefit from this for two major reasons. First, "by allocating the cost of risk to individual customers, issuers can reward customers who have solid credit histories with more competitive pricing." Second, risk-based pricing provides "more people with access to regulated credit, including consumers who were previously underserved or had no access to unsecured, revolving credit." After reviewing the areas of agreement regarding "comprehensive changes," Carey proceeds to his specific objections to H.R. 5244. Among other things, Carey believes (i) the proposed legislation is premature; (ii) regulation through the Federal Reserve provides greater expertise and flexibility than legislation; (iii) the legislation amounts to price control and restricts the use of risk-based pricing; (iv) the legislation "undermines the push to simplify disclosures"; and (v) the proposed credit card bill of rights would "make it more difficult to prevent fraud and identity theft." Thus, Carey concludes, this legislation is "unnecessary."

General information on credit cards is available from money-zine.com: at http://www.money-zine.com/Financial-Planning/Debt-Consolidation/Credit-Card-Debt-Statistics/ and from the Financial Services Fact Book available at http://www.eiii.org/fiancial2/savings/cbd. General information is also available from the Federal Reserve at http://www.federalreserve.gov/pubs/shop/. The Federal Reserve also makes information available from its survey of banks that issue credit cards; the information includes, among other things, the name of the bank, the types of credit cards it issues, the APRs, and annual fees: http://www.federalreserve.gov/pubs/shop/survey.htm. To find more information regarding Visa and MasterCard, visit their home sites. The hearings at which Plunkett and Carey presented their testimony contain remarks from a number of other individuals, including Senators Levin of Michigan and Wyden of Oregon, Sandra Braunstein of the Federal Reserve, Marty Gruenberg of the Federal Deposit Insurance Corporation, Julie Williams of the Office of the Comptroller of the Currency, John V. Bowman of the Office of Thrift Supervision, Larry Sharnak of the American Express Company, Carlos Minetti of the Discover Financial Services, Linda Sherry of Consumer Action, and Ed Mierzwinski of U.S. Public Interest research Group. They are all available at http://financialservices.house.gov/hearing110/hr041708.shtml.

ISSUE 11

Should Minimum Wage and Living Wage Laws Be Eliminated?

YES: D. W. MacKenzie, from "Mythology of the Minimum Wage," Ludwig von Mises Institute, http://www.mises.org/story/2130 (May 3, 2006)

NO: Jeannette Wicks-Lim, from "Measuring the Full Impact of Minimum and Living Wage Laws," *Dollars & Sense* (May/June 2006)

ISSUE SUMMARY

YES: Economics instructor D. W. MacKenzie believes that eliminating minimum wage laws would "reduce unemployment and improve the efficiency of markets for low productivity labor." He also believes that the "economic case for a living wage is unfounded."

NO: Economist Jeannette Wicks-Lim stresses the ripple effects of minimum and living wage laws; these effects increase the "effectiveness" of minimum and living wage laws as "antipoverty strategies."

Congress passed the Fair Labor Standards Act (FLSA) of 1938 in the midst of the Great Depression. In one bold stroke, it established a minimum wage rate of $.25 an hour, placed controls on the use of child labor, designated 44 hours as the normal workweek, and mandated that time-and-a-half be paid to anyone working longer than the normal workweek. Sixty-eight years later the debates concerning child labor, length of the workweek, and overtime pay have long subsided, but the debate over the minimum wage rages on.

The immediate and continued concern over the minimum wage component of the FLSA should surprise few people. Although $.25 an hour is a paltry sum compared to today's wage rates, in 1938 it was a princely reward for work. It must be remembered that jobs were hard to come by and unemployment rates at times reached as high as 25 percent of the workforce. When work was found, any wage seemed acceptable to those who roamed the streets with no safety net to protect their families. Indeed, consider the fact that $.25 an hour was 40.3 percent of the average manufacturing wage rate for 1938.

Little wonder, then, that the business community in the 1930s was up in arms. Business leaders argued that if wages went up, prices would rise. This would choke off the little demand for goods and services that existed in the marketplace, and the demand for workers would be sure to fall. The end result would be a return to the depths of the depression, where there was little or no hope of employment for the very people who were supposed to benefit from the Fair Labor Standards Act.

Simple supply-and-demand analysis supports this view. As modern-day introductory textbooks in economics invariably show, unemployment occurs when a minimum wage greater than the equilibrium wage is mandated by law. The simplistic analysis, which assumes competitive conditions in both the product and factor markets, is predicated upon the assumptions that as wages are pushed above the equilibrium level, the quantity of labor demanded will fall and the quantity of labor supplied will increase. Wage rigidity prevents the market from clearing. The end result is an excess in the quantity of labor supplied relative to the quantity of labor demanded. The same would be true for the imposition of a living wage above the equilibrium wage.

The question that should be addressed in this debate is whether or not a simple supply-and-demand analysis is capable of adequately predicting what happens in real-world labor markets when a minimum wage or living wage is introduced or an existing minimum/living wage is raised. The significance of this is not based on idle curiosity. The minimum wage has been increased numerous times since its introduction in 1938. The current federal minimum wage of $5.15 was set in 1997. Did this minimum wage increase, and other increases before it, do irreparable harm to those who are least able to defend themselves in the labor market, the marginal workers? That is, if a minimum wage of $5.15 is imposed, what happens to all those marginal workers whose value to the firm is something less than $5.15? Are these workers fired? Do firms simply absorb this cost increase in the form of reduced corporate profits? What happens to productivity?

D. W. MacKenzie argues that eliminating the minimum wage would increase economic efficiency in the labor market for teenagers and ethnic minorities, lowering their unemployment rates. Imposition of living wages would make their unemployment rates rise higher than they are already. Jeannette Wicks-Lim focuses on the ripple effects of minimum wages and living wages, that is, how much would the wages of *other* workers increase as a result of an increase in the minimum wage? The larger the ripple effects, the stronger the case for higher wage minimums to improve the lives of the working poor.

YES

D. W. MacKenzie

Mythology of the Minimum Wage

Once again politicians and pundits are calling for increases in the legal minimum wage. Their reasons are familiar. Market wages are supposedly immoral. People need to earn a "living wage." If the minimum wage went up at least to $7, or better still to near $10 an hour, millions would be lifted out of poverty.[1]

The economic case against minimum wage laws is simple. Employers pay a wage no higher than the value of an additional hour's work. Raising minimum wages forces employers to dismiss low productivity workers. This policy has the largest affect on those with the least education, job experience, and maturity. Consequently, we should expect minimum wage laws to affect teenagers and those with less education. Eliminating minimum wage laws would reduce unemployment and improve the efficiency of markets for low productivity labor.

There are a few economists who have been leading the charge for higher minimum wages. Some of these economists have obvious ideological leanings. Economists connected with the Left-orientated Economic Policy Institute and the Clinton Administration have concocted a rational for minimum wage increases. According to these economists higher wages make employees more content with their jobs, and this leads to higher worker productivity. Thus workers will be worth paying a minimum wage once their employers are forced to pay these wages. Of course, if this were true—if employers could get higher productivity out of less educated and experienced workers by paying higher wages—they would be willing to do this without minimum wage legislation. But the economists who make this case claim to have empirical evidence that proves them right. Economists David Card and Alan Krueger have published studies of the fast food industry [indicating] that small increases in the minimum wage would cause only minor job losses, and might even increase employment slightly in some instances. These studies by Card and Krueger show only that a small increase in minimum wage rates might not cause much of an increase in unemployment. Such studies ignore the fact that the current level of minimum wages are already causing significant unemployment for some workers.

The economic case for minimum wage increases has gained some ground with public and even professional opinion. Even some free market leaning economists, like Steven Landsburg, have conceded that minimum wage increases do

From Mises.org *Daily Articles*, May 3, 2006, by D. W. MacKenzie. Copyright © 2006 by Ludwig von Mises Institute. Reprinted by permission. www.mises.org.

not affect employment significantly.[2] Landsburg notes that critics of minimum wage laws emphasize that they have a disproportionate effect on teens and blacks. But he dismisses these critics because "minimum wages have at most a tiny impact on employment . . . The minimum wage kills very few jobs, and the jobs it kills were lousy jobs anyway. It is almost impossible to maintain the old argument that minimum wages are bad for minimum-wage workers."

Real statistics indicate that the critics of minimum wage laws were right all along. While it is true that minimum wages do not drive the national unemployment rate up to astronomical levels, it does adversely affect teenagers and ethnic minorities. According to the Bureau of Labor Statistics the unemployment rate for everyone over the age of 16 was 5.6% in 2005. Yet unemployment was 17.3% for those aged 16–19 years. For those aged 16–17 unemployment was 19.7%. In the 18–19 age group unemployment was 15.8%. Minimum wage laws do affect ethnic minorities more so than others.[3] The unemployment rate for white teens in the 16–17 age group was 17.3% in 2005. The same figures for Hispanic and black teens were 25% and 40.9% respectively. Of course, these figures decrease for older minorities. Blacks aged 18–19 and 20–24 had 25.7% and 19.9% unemployment in 2005. For Hispanics unemployment was slightly lower—17.8% at age 18–19 and 9.6% at age 20–24.

Landsburg might maintain that most of these lost jobs are lousy jobs that teens will not miss. DeLong thinks that minimum wage laws can help to avert poverty—workers who keep their jobs at the minimum wage gain much, while unemployed workers lose little. Part of the problem with this argument is that it involves arbitrary value judgments. According to mainstream economic theory, we achieve economic efficiency when markets clear because this is how we realize all gains from trade. With teen unemployment in double digits—running as high as 40.9%—it is obvious that some labor markets are not clearing. If labor market imperfections led to such levels of unemployment, economists like DeLong, Card, and Krueger would call for government intervention to correct these "market failures." Yet they find double digit teen unemployment acceptable when it derives from government intervention. Why? Because they want to use such policies to redistribute income.[4]

Mainstream economic theory lacks any basis for judging the effects of income redistribution. According to textbook economics we attain the highest level of economic efficiency when markets clear, when we realize the maximum gains from mutually advantageous trade. Income transfers benefit some at the expense of others. Economists have no scientific methods for comparing gains and losses through income transfers.[5] Once economists depart from discussing efficiency conditions and begin to speak about income redistribution, they become advocates of a political agenda, rather than objective scientists. The jobs lost to minimum wage laws might not seem worthwhile to DeLong or Landsburg, but they obviously are worthwhile to the workers and employers whom these laws affect. Why should the value judgments of a few armchair economists matter more than the interests of would be employees and employers? These jobs may be "lousy jobs," but one could also argue that these jobs are quite important because they are a first step in gaining job experience and learning adult responsibility.

A second problem with the case against minimum wages is that they affect older workers too. As already noted, workers in the 20–24 age group appear to be affected by minimum wage laws. Unemployment rates in the 25–34 age group are higher than for the 35–44 age group. The unemployment rate for blacks and Hispanics aged 25–34 were 11.1% and 5.8% in 2005. Unemployment for whites and Asians in this age group were 4.4% and 3.5%. In the 35–44 age group the unemployment rates for these four ethnicities were 7.2%., 5.1%, 4.4%, and 2.7%. A comparison of black to Asian unemployment is revealing. In the United States, Asians tend to attain higher levels of education than blacks. Thus minimum wage laws are relatively unimportant to Asian Americans. Consequently, Asians are able to attain unemployment as low as the 2–3% range. For Asians aged 16+ the unemployment rate was only 3.3% in 2005. For Asians in the 20–24 age group unemployment was 5.1%. These figures are only a fraction of the unemployment rates experienced by blacks in 2005. There is no reason why white, Hispanic, and black Americans cannot also reach the 2–3% range of unemployment.

Supporters of minimum wage laws do not realize that prior to minimum wage laws the national unemployment rate did fall well below 5%. According to the US Census, national unemployment rates were 3.3% in 1927, 1.8% in 1926, 3.2% in 1925, 2.4% in 1923, 1.4% in 1919 and 1918, 2.8% in 1907, 1.7% in 1906, and 3.7% in 1902.[6] Even today, some states have unemployment rates as low as 3%. Virginia now has an unemployment rate of 3.1%. Wyoming has an unemployment rate of 2.9%. Hawaii has an unemployment rate of 2.6%. National unemployment rates seldom drop below 5% because some categories of workers are stuck with double digit unemployment. Given these figures, it is quite arguable that minimum wage laws keep the national unemployment rate 3 percentage points higher than would otherwise be the case.

Economist Arthur Okun estimated that for every 1% increase in unemployment GDP falls by 2.5–3%. If minimum wage laws are responsible for keeping the national unemployment rate 3 percentage points above where it would otherwise be, then the losses to minimum wage unemployment are substantial. Since Okun's law is an empirical proposition it is certainly not constant. Eliminating minimum wages might not increase GDP as much as this "law" indicates. However, the elimination of minimum wage laws would surely have a positive effect on GDP. In any case, economic theory and available data indicate that minimum wage laws do result in economic inefficiency. The implementation of a "living wage" would only increase these losses. Do proponents of living wages really want to see unemployment rates among ethnic minorities and teens climb even higher?

The economic case for a living wage is unfounded. Current minimum wage rates do create high levels of unemployment among low productivity workers. Higher "living wages" would only make these problems worse. The alleged moral case for a living wage ignores the fact that minimum wage increases adversely affect the very people whom advocates of living wages intend to help. If politicians wish to pursue sound policies, they should consider repealing minimum wage laws, especially where teens are concerned.

Unfortunately, most politicians care more about political expediencies than sound economic policy. This being the case, minimum wages will increase unless public opinion changes significantly.

Notes

1. See Dreier and Candeale *A Moral Minimum Wage,* April 27 2006 and Cauchon *States Say 5.15 too little,* April 27 2006.
2. See *"The Sin of Wages"* by Steven Landsburg and *"The Minimum Wage and the EITC"* by J. Bradford DeLong.
3. This is likely due to the poor quality of many inner city public schools.
4. It is worth noting that Landsburg opposes redistribution via minimum wage laws.
5. This would require interpersonal comparisons of welfare. Robbins (1933) proved that such comparisons are unscientific.
6. US Bureau of the Census *Historical Statistics,* p. 135.

Jeannette Wicks-Lim

 **NO**

Measuring the Full Impact of Minimum and Living Wage Laws

Raising the minimum wage is quickly becoming a key political issue for this fall's midterm elections. In the past, Democratic politicians have shied away from the issue while Republicans have openly opposed a higher minimum wage. But this year is different. Community activists are forcing the issue by campaigning to put state minimum-wage proposals before the voters this fall in Arizona, Colorado, Ohio, and Missouri. No doubt inspired by the 100-plus successful local living-wage campaigns of the past ten years, these activists are also motivated by a federal minimum wage that has stagnated for the past nine years. The $5.15 federal minimum is at its lowest value in purchasing-power terms in more than 50 years; a single parent with two children, working full-time at the current minimum wage, would fall $2,000 below the poverty line.

Given all the political activity on the ground, the Democrats have decided to make the minimum wage a central plank in their party platform. Former presidential candidate John Edwards has teamed up with Sen. Edward Kennedy (D-Mass.) and ACORN, a leading advocacy group for living wage laws, to push for a $7.25 federal minimum. Even some Republicans are supporting minimum wage increases. In fact, a bipartisan legislative coalition unexpectedly passed a state minimum wage hike in Michigan this March.

Minimum-wage and living-wage laws have always caused an uproar in the business community. Employers sound the alarm about the dire consequences of a higher minimum wage both for themselves and for the low-wage workers these laws are intended to benefit: Minimum wage mandates, they claim, will cause small-business owners to close shop and lay off their low-wage workers. A spokesperson for the National Federation of Independent Business (NFIB), commenting on a proposal to raise Pennsylvania's minimum wage in an interview with the Philadelphia Inquirer, put it this way: "That employer may as well be handing out pink slips along with the pay raise."

What lies behind these bleak predictions? Mark Shaffer, owner of Shaffer's Park Supper Club in Crivitz, Wisc., provided one explanation to the Wisconsin State Journal: ". . . increasing the minimum wage would create a chain reaction. Every worker would want a raise to keep pace, forcing up prices and driving away customers." In other words, employers will not only be forced to raise the wages of those workers earning below the new minimum wage, but also

From *Dollars & Sense*, May/June 2006. Reprinted by permission of Dollars & Sense, a progressive economics magazine. www.dollarsandsense.org.

the wages of their co-workers who earn somewhat more. The legally required wage raises are difficult enough for employers to absorb, they claim; these other raises—referred to as ripple effect raises—aggravate the situation. The result? "That ripple effect is going to lay off people."

Ripple effects represent a double-edged sword for minimum-wage and living-wage proponents. Their extent determines how much low-wage workers will benefit from such laws. If the ripple effects are small, then a higher minimum (or living) wage would benefit only a small class of workers, and boosting the minimum wage might be dismissed as an ineffective antipoverty strategy. If the ripple effects are large, then setting higher wage minimums may be seen as a potent policy tool to improve the lives of the working poor. But at the same time, evidence of large ripple effects provides ammunition to employers who claim they cannot afford the costs of a higher wage floor.

So what is the evidence on ripple effects? Do they bloat wage bills and overwhelm employers? Do they expand the number of workers who get raises a little or a lot? It's difficult to say because the research on ripple effects has been thin. But getting a clear picture of the full impact of minimum and living wage laws on workers' wages is critical to evaluating the impact of these laws. New research provides estimates of the scope and magnitude of the ripple effects of both minimum-wage and living-wage laws. This evidence is crucial for analyzing both the full impact of this increasingly visible policy tool and the political struggles surrounding it.

Why Do Employers Give Ripple-Effect Raises?

Marge Thomas, CEO of Goodwill Industries in Maryland, explains in an interview with The Gazette (Md.): "There will be a ripple effect [in response to Maryland's recent minimum wage increase to $6.15], since it wouldn't be fair to pay people now making above the minimum wage at the same level as those making the new minimum wage." That is, without ripple effects, an increase in the wage floor will worsen the relative wage position of workers just above it. If there are no ripple effects, workers earning $6.15 before Maryland's increase would not only see their wages fall to the bottom of the wage scale, but also to the same level as workers who had previously earned inferior wages (i.e., workers who earned between $5.15 and $6.15).

Employers worry that these workers would view such a relative decline in their wages as unfair, damaging their morale—and their productivity. Without ripple effect raises, employers fear, their disgruntled staff will cut back on hard-to-measure aspects of their work such as responding to others cheerfully and taking initiative in assisting customers.

So employers feel compelled to preserve some consistency in their wage scales. Workers earning $6.15 before the minimum increase, for example, may receive a quarter raise, to $6.40, to keep their wages just above the new $6.15 minimum. That employers feel compelled to give non-mandated raises to some of their lowest-paid workers because it is the "fair" thing to do may appear to be a dubious claim. Perhaps so, but employers commonly express anxiety about the costs of minimum-wage and living-wage laws for this very reason.

The Politics of Ripple Effects

Inevitably, then, ripple effects come into play in the political battles around minimum-wage and living-wage laws—but in contradictory ways for both opponents and supporters. Opponents raise the specter of large ripple effects bankrupting small businesses. At the same time, though, they argue that minimum-wage laws are not effective in fighting poverty because they do not cover many workers—and worse, because those who are covered are largely teens or young-adult students just working for spending money. If ripple effects are small, this shores up opponents' assertions that minimum-wage laws have a limited impact on poverty. Evidence of larger ripple effects, on the other hand, would mean that the benefits of minimum-wage laws are larger than previously understood, and that these laws have an even greater potential to reduce poverty among the working poor.

The political implications are complicated further in the context of living-wage laws, which typically call for much higher wage floors than state and federal minimum-wage laws do. The living-wage movement calls for wage floors to be set at rates that provide a "livable income," such as the federal poverty level for a family of four, rather than at the arbitrary—and very low—level current minimum-wage laws set. The difference is dramatic: the living-wage ordinances that have been passed in a number of municipalities typically set a wage floor twice the level of federal and state minimum wages.

So the mandated raises under living-wage laws are already much higher than under even the highest state minimum-wage laws. If living-wage laws have significant ripple effects, opponents have all the more ammunition for their argument that the costs of these laws are unsustainable for employers.

How Big are Ripple Effects?

My answer is a typical economists' response: it depends. In a nutshell, it depends on how high the wage minimum is set. The reason for this is simple. Evidence from the past 20 years of changes to state and federal minimum wages suggests that while there is a ripple effect, it doesn't extend very far beyond the new minimum. So, if the wage minimum is set high, then a large number of workers are legally due raises and, relatively speaking, the number of workers who get ripple-effect raises is small. Conversely, if the wage minimum is set low, then a small number of workers are legally due raises and, relatively speaking, the number of workers who get ripple-effect raises is large.

In the case of minimum-wage laws, the evidence suggests that ripple effects do dramatically expand their impact. Minimum wages are generally set low relative to the wage distribution. Because so many more workers earn wages just above the minimum wage compared to those earning the minimum, even a small ripple effect increases considerably the number of workers who benefit from a rise in the minimum wage. And even though the size of these raises quickly shrinks the higher the worker's wage rate, the much greater number of affected workers translates into a significantly larger increase in the wage bills of employers.

For example, my research shows that the impact of the most recent federal minimum-wage increase, from $4.75 to $5.15 in 1997, extended to workers earning wages around $5.75. Workers earning between the old and new minimums generally received raises to bring their wages in line with the new minimum—an 8% raise for those who started at the old minimum. Workers earning around $5.20 (right above the new minimum of $5.15) received raises of around 2%, bringing their wages up to about $5.30. Finally, those workers earning wages around $5.75 received raises on the order of 1%, bringing their wages up to about $5.80.

This narrow range of small raises translates into a big overall impact. Roughly 4 million workers (those earning between $4.75 and $5.15) received mandated raises in response to the 1997 federal minimum wage increase. Taking into account the typical work schedules of these workers, these raises translated into a $741 million increase to employers' annual wage bills. Now add in ripple effects: Approximately 11 million workers received ripple-effect raises, adding another $1.3 billion to employers' wage bills. In other words, ripple-effect raises almost quadrupled the number of workers who benefited from the minimum-wage increase and almost tripled the over-all costs associated with it.

Dramatic as these ripple effects are, the real impact on employers can only be gauged in relation to their capacity to absorb the higher wage costs. Here, there is evidence that businesses are not overwhelmed by the costs of a higher minimum wage, even including ripple effects. For example, in a study I co-authored with University of Massachusetts economists Robert Pollin and Mark Brenner on the Florida ballot measure to establish a $6.15 state minimum wage (which passed overwhelmingly in 2004), we accounted for ripple-effect costs of roughly this same magnitude. Despite almost tripling the number of affected workers (from almost 300,000 to over 850,000) and more than doubling the costs associated with the new minimum wage (from $155 million to $410 million), the ripple effects, combined with the mandated wage increases, imposed an average cost increase on employers amounting to less than one-half of 1% of their sales revenue. Even for employers in the hotel and restaurant industry, where low-wage workers tend to be concentrated, the average cost increase was less than 1% of their sales revenue. In other words, a 1% increase in prices for hotel rooms or restaurant meals could cover the increased costs associated with both legally mandated raises and ripple-effect raises.

The small fraction of revenue that these raises represent goes a long way toward explaining why economists generally agree that minimum-wage laws are not "job killers," as opponents claim. According to a 1998 survey of economists, a consensus seems to have been reached that there is minimal job loss, if any, associated with minimum-wage increases in the ranges that we've seen.

Just as important, this new research revises our understanding of who benefits from minimum wage laws. Including ripple-effect raises expands the circle of minimum-wage beneficiaries to include more adult workers and fewer teenage or student workers. In fact, accounting for ripple effects decreases the prevalence of teenagers and traditional-age students (age 16 to 24) among workers likely to be affected by a federal minimum-wage increase from four out of ten to three out of ten. In other words, adult workers make up an even larger majority of likely minimum-wage beneficiaries when ripple effects are added to the picture.

The Case of Living-Wage Laws

With living-wage laws, the ripple effect story appears to be quite different, however—primarily because living wage laws set much higher wage minimums.

To understand why living-wage laws might generate far less of a ripple effect than minimum-wage hikes, it is instructive to look at the impact of raising the minimum wage on the retail trade industry. About 15% of retail trade workers earn wages at or very close to the minimum wage, compared to 5% of all workers. As a result, a large fraction of the retail trade industry workforce receives legally mandated raises when the minimum wage is raised, which is just what occurs across a broader group of industries and occupations when a living-wage ordinance is passed.

My research shows that the relative impact of the ripple effect that accompanies a minimum-wage hike is much smaller within retail trade than across all industries. Because a much larger share of workers in retail receive legally required raises when the minimum wage is raised, this reduces the relative number of workers receiving ripple effect raises, and, in turn, the relative size of the costs associated with ripple effects. This analysis suggests that the ripple effects of living wage laws will likewise be smaller than those found with minimum-wage laws.

To be sure, the ripple effect in the retail trade sector may underestimate the ripple effect of living-wage laws for a couple of reasons. First, unlike minimum-wage hikes, living-wage laws may have ripple effects that extend across firms as well as up the wage structure within firms. Employers who do not fall under a living-wage law's mandate but who are competing for workers within the same local labor market as those that do may be compelled to raise their own wages in order to retain their workers. Second, workers just above living-wage levels are typically higher on the job ladder and may have more bargaining power than workers with wages just above minimum-wage levels and, as a result, may be able to demand more significant raises when living-wage laws are enacted.

However, case studies of living-wage ordinances in Los Angeles and San Francisco do suggest that the ripple effect plays a smaller role in the case of living-wage laws than in the case of minimum-wage laws. These studies find that ripple effects add less than half again to the costs of mandated raises—dramatically less than the almost tripling of costs by ripple effects associated with the 1997 federal minimum-wage increase. In other words, the much higher wage floors set by living-wage laws appear to reverse the importance of legally required raises versus ripple-effect raises.

Do the costs associated with living-wage laws—with their higher wage floors—overwhelm employers, even if their ripple effects are small? To date, estimates suggest that within the range of existing living-wage laws, businesses are generally able to absorb the cost increases they face. For example, Pollin and Brenner studied a 2000 proposal to raise the wage floor from $5.75 to $10.75 in Santa Monica, Calif. They estimated that the cost increase faced by a typical business would be small, on the order of 2% of sales revenue, even accounting for both mandated and ripple-effect raises. Their estimates also showed that some hotel and restaurant businesses might face cost increases amounting to up to 10% of their sales revenue—not a negligible sum. However, after examining the local economy, Pollin and Brenner concluded that even these cost increases would not be likely to force these businesses to close their doors. Moreover, higher productivity and lower turnover rates among workers paid a living wage would also reduce the impact of these costs.

Ultimately, the impact of ripple-effect raises appears to depend crucially on the level of the new wage floor. The lower the wage floor, as in the case of minimum-wage laws, the more important the role of ripple-effect raises. The higher the wage floor, as in the case of living-wage laws, the less important the role of ripple-effect raises.

Making the Case

The results of this new research are generally good news for proponents of living- and minimum-wage laws. Ripple effects do not portend dire consequences for employers from minimum and living wage laws; at the same time, ripple-effect raises heighten the effectiveness of these laws as antipoverty strategies.

In the case of minimum-wage laws, because the cost of legally mandated raises relative to employer revenues is small, even ripple effects large enough to triple the cost of a minimum-wage increase do not represent a large burden for employers. Moreover, ripple effects enhance the somewhat anemic minimum-wage laws to make them more effective as policy tools for improving the lot of the working poor. Accounting for ripple effects nearly quadruples the number of beneficiaries of a minimum-wage hike and expands the majority of those beneficiaries who are adults—in many instances, family breadwinners.

However, ripple effects do not appear to overwhelm employers in the case of the more ambitious living-wage laws. The strongest impact from living-wage laws appears to come from legally required raises rather than from ripple-effect raises. This reinforces advocates' claims that paying a living wage is a reasonable, as well as potent, way to fight poverty.

POSTSCRIPT

Should Minimum Wage and Living Wage Laws Be Eliminated?

The impact of the minimum wage can be expressed in many ways. Two important ways of looking at such legislative initiatives are to examine minimum wages over time in real dollars and as a percentage of manufacturing wages. In real terms the 1965–1970 period saw the highest level of the minimum wage. In constant 1982–1984 dollars, the minimum wage for these years was approximately $4.00 an hour, reaching nearly 50 percent of the prevailing manufacturing wage. For the next 20 years, however, the value of the minimum wage in real terms and as a percentage of the manufacturing wage fell. This is especially true for the last nine years, when the minimum wage has not changed in nominal terms.

The renewed interest in the minimum wage can be traced in part to the research findings of David Card and Alan Krueger. They found that moderate increases in the minimum wage have few negative effects on employment patterns and in some cases are associated with increases in employment. Their work was published in professional journals: *Industrial and Labor Relations Review* (October 1992 and April 1994) and the *American Economic Review* (September 1994 and May 1995). They also detailed their findings in a book entitled *Myth and Measurement: The New Economics of the Minimum Wage* (Princeton University Press, 1995).

D. W. MacKenzie claims that studies by Card and Krueger do not recognize that the current level of minimum wages is already causing significant unemployment for some workers. Here, he cites the high unemployment rates for Hispanic and black teens (and even for older age groups). He also suggests that minimum wage laws keep the national unemployment rate 3 percentage points higher than it otherwise would be, and that elimination of minimum wage laws might have a positive effect on GDP.

While MacKenzie dismisses the "moral case" for a living wage, Jeannette Wicks-Lim estimates that the ripple effect associated with the increase in the minimum wage from $4.75 to $5.15 in 1997 quadrupled the number of workers who benefited from the increase. Moreover, there is evidence that businesses are not overwhelmed by the higher wage costs—in one study, legally mandated raises and the ripple effect raises amounted to less than half of 1 percent of business sales revenue. Ripple effects of living wage laws also do not appear to overwhelm employers, making living wages "a reasonable, as well as potent, way to fight poverty."

Two vocal critics of Card and Krueger's research are David Neumark and William Wascher. Their empirical studies are supportive of the traditional neoclassical findings that the minimum wage causes unemployment, particularly among teenagers and young adults. See their work published in *Industrial and Labor Relations Review* (September 1992 and April 1994); NBER Working Paper No. 4617 (1994); *Journal of Business and Economic Statistics* (April 1995); and *American Economic Review Papers and Proceedings* (May 1995). Still considered the best anti-minimum wage statement, however, is George J. Stigler's 1946 essay "The Economics of Minimum Wage Legislation," *American Economic Review.*

ISSUE 12

Do Unskilled Immigrants Hurt the Economy?

YES: Steven Malanga, from "How Unskilled Immigrants Hurt Our Economy," *City Journal* (Summer 2006)

NO: Diana Furchtgott-Roth, from "The Case for Immigration," *The New York Sun* (September 22, 2006)

ISSUE SUMMARY

YES: Columnist Steven Malanga believes the influx of unskilled immigrants into the U.S. economy has imposed large costs on the larger society, including job loss by native workers and lower investment in labor-saving technology. More importantly, he argues that this immigration has increased utilization of the "vast U.S. welfare and social-services apparatus."

NO: Diana Furchtgott-Roth, senior fellow at the Hudson Institute and director of Hudson's Center for Employment Policy, and a former chief economist at the U.S. Department of Labor, observes that annual immigration is "a tiny fraction of our labor force," and immigrant laborers are "complements, rather than substitutes for native born Americans." She also cites a National Academy of Sciences study that concluded that foreign-born households are no more likely to use "welfare" than native-born households.

Between 700,000 and 900,000 legal immigrants enter the United States each year. There were 34 million immigrants (defined as naturalized American citizens, permanent residents, temporary residents, and undocumented immigrants) in the United States in 2003, amounting to 12 percent of the population (*Economic Report of the President,* 2005). Over half are from Latin America, and over a fifth have less than nine years of education. Between 1996 and 2003, foreign-born workers accounted for 58 percent of the net increase in employment and 41 percent of the increase in population growth. Undocumented immigrants are estimated at 10 million (half from Mexico).

In May 2006, President Bush offered a strategy for "comprehensive" immigration reform consisting of securing the U.S. border (signing the Secure

Fence Act into law in October 2006), enforcement of immigration laws, and creating a lawful path for foreign workers to enter on a temporary basis—"a rational middle ground" between amnesty and deportation.

The economic impact of immigrants is a fundamental consideration in the current discourse on immigration in the United States. There are questions about their effect on efficiency and distribution. Debate on issues such as the fiscal (and broader economic) costs and benefits of immigrants, illegal immigration, whether immigrants displace natives, lower natives' wages, and contribute to income inequality, has intensified over the last two decades. The issues are complex and emotionally and politically charged, and empirical evidence is not definitive.

Testimonies to Congress in July 2006 reflect the disagreement on costs and benefits of immigrants today. Some, like Michael Fix (vice president and director of studies, Migration Policy Institute), argue that social welfare use by immigrants is declining since the 1996 welfare reforms, and "fears that welfare systems will be swamped by increased legal immigration and by a legalization program are overstated." Others, like Steven A. Camarota (director of research, Center for Immigration Studies), argue that large-scale immigration of less-educated immigrants creates significant funding problems for social programs, citing the National Research Council's 1997 report showing the net lifetime fiscal burden of an immigrant without a high school diploma ($89,000), with only a high school education ($31,000), and with an education beyond high school (fiscal benefit of $105,000).

The papers by Steven Malanga and Diana Furchtgott-Roth are part of the ongoing debate on the impact of immigrants on the U.S. economy. Malanga argues that today's immigrants are unlike earlier immigrants and that supporters of today's immigration are wrong on many counts and zeroes in on unskilled immigrants, particularly Mexican (legal and illegal) immigrants. Furchtgott-Roth offers a point-for-point rebuttal.

YES

Steven Malanga

How Unskilled Immigrants Hurt Our Economy

The day after Librado Velasquez arrived on Staten Island after a long, surreptitious journey from his Chiapas, Mexico, home, he headed out to a street corner to wait with other illegal immigrants looking for work. Velasquez, who had supported his wife, seven kids, and his in-laws as a *campesino,* or peasant farmer, until a 1998 hurricane devastated his farm, eventually got work, off the books, loading trucks at a small New Jersey factory, which hired illegals for jobs that required few special skills. The arrangement suited both, until a work injury sent Velasquez to the local emergency room, where federal law required that he be treated, though he could not afford to pay for his care. After five operations, he is now permanently disabled and has remained in the United States to pursue compensation claims. . . .

Velasquez's story illustrates some of the fault lines in the nation's current, highly charged, debate on immigration. Since the mid-1960s, America has welcomed nearly 30 million legal immigrants and received perhaps another 15 million illegals, numbers unprecedented in our history. These immigrants have picked our fruit, cleaned our homes, cut our grass, worked in our factories, and washed our cars. But they have also crowded into our hospital emergency rooms, schools, and government-subsidized aid programs, sparking a fierce debate about their contributions to our society and the costs they impose on it.

Advocates of open immigration argue that welcoming the Librado Velasquezes of the world is essential for our American economy: our businesses need workers like him, because we have a shortage of people willing to do low-wage work. Moreover, the free movement of labor in a global economy pays off for the United States, because immigrants bring skills and capital that expand our economy and offset immigration's costs. Like tax cuts, supporters argue, immigration pays for itself.

But the tale of Librado Velasquez helps show why supporters are wrong about today's immigration, as many Americans sense and so much research has demonstrated. America does not have a vast labor shortage that requires waves of low-wage immigrants to alleviate; in fact, unemployment among unskilled workers is high—about 30 percent. Moreover, many of the unskilled, uneducated workers now journeying here labor, like Velasquez, in shrinking industries, where they force out native workers, and many others work in industries where the availability of cheap workers has led businesses to suspend investment in new technologies that would make them less labor-intensive.

Yet while these workers add little to our economy, they come at great cost, because they are not economic abstractions but human beings, with their own culture and ideas—often at odds with our own. Increasing numbers of them arrive with little education and none of the skills necessary to succeed in a modern economy. Many may wind up stuck on our lowest economic rungs, where they will rely on something that immigrants of other generations didn't have: a vast U.S. welfare and social-services apparatus that has enormously amplified the cost of immigration. Just as welfare reform and other policies are helping to shrink America's underclass by weaning people off such social programs, we are importing a new, foreign-born underclass. As famed free-market economist Milton Friedman puts it: "It's just obvious that you can't have free immigration and a welfare state."

Immigration can only pay off again for America if we reshape our policy, organizing it around what's good for the economy by welcoming workers we truly need and excluding those who, because they have so little to offer, are likely to cost us more than they contribute, and who will struggle for years to find their place here.

Hampering today's immigration debate are our misconceptions about the so-called first great migration some 100 years ago, with which today's immigration is often compared. . . . If America could assimilate 24 million mostly desperate immigrants from that great migration—people one unsympathetic economist at the turn of the twentieth century described as "the unlucky, the thriftless, the worthless"—surely, so the story goes, today's much bigger and richer country can absorb the millions of Librado Velasquezes now venturing here.

But that argument distorts the realities of the first great migration. . . . Those waves of immigrants—many of them urban dwellers who crossed a continent and an ocean to get here—helped supercharge the workforce at a time when the country was going through a transformative economic expansion that craved new workers, especially in its cities. A 1998 National Research Council report noted "that the newly arriving immigrant nonagricultural work force . . . was (slightly) more skilled than the resident American labor force": 27 percent of them were skilled laborers, compared with only 17 percent of that era's native-born workforce.

Many of these immigrants quickly found a place in our economy, participating in the workforce at a higher rate even than the native population. Their success at finding work sent many of them quickly up the economic ladder: those who stayed in America for at least 15 years, for instance, were just as likely to own their own business as native-born workers of the same age, one study found. . . .

What the newcomers of the great migration did not find here was a vast social-services and welfare state. They had to rely on their own resources or those of friends, relatives, or private, often ethnic, charities if things did not go well. That's why about 70 percent of those who came were men in their prime. It's also why many of them left when the economy sputtered several times during the period. . . .

Today's immigration has turned out so differently in part because it emerged out of the 1960s civil rights and Great Society mentality. In 1965, a new immigration act eliminated the old system of national quotas, which critics saw as racist because it greatly favored European nations. Lawmakers created a set of broader immigration quotas for each hemisphere, and they added a new visa preference category for family members to join their relatives here. Senate immigration subcommittee chairman Edward Kennedy reassured the country that, "contrary to the charges in some quarters, [the bill] will not inundate America with immigrants," and "it will not cause American workers to lose their jobs."

But, in fact, the law had an immediate, dramatic effect, increasing immigration by 60 percent in its first ten years. Sojourners from poorer countries around the rest of the world arrived in ever-greater numbers, so that whereas half of immigrants in the 1950s had originated from Europe, 75 percent by the 1970s were from Asia and Latin America. And as the influx of immigrants grew, the special-preferences rule for family unification intensified it further, as the pool of eligible family members around the world also increased. Legal immigration to the U.S. soared from 2.5 million in the 1950s to 4.5 million in the 1970s to 7.3 million in the 1980s to about 10 million in the 1990s.

As the floodgates of legal immigration opened, the widening economic gap between the United States and many of its neighbors also pushed illegal immigration to levels that America had never seen. In particular, when Mexico's move to a more centralized, state-run economy in the 1970s produced hyper-inflation, the disparity between its stagnant economy and U.S. prosperity yawned wide. Mexico's per-capita gross domestic product, 37 percent of the United States' in the early 1980s, was only 27 percent of it by the end of the decade—and is now just 25 percent of it. With Mexican farmworkers able to earn seven to ten times as much in the United States as at home, by the 1980s illegals were pouring across our border at the rate of about 225,000 a year, and U.S. sentiment rose for slowing the flow.

But an unusual coalition of business groups, unions, civil rights activists, and church leaders thwarted the call for restrictions with passage of the inaptly named 1986 Immigration Reform and Control Act, which legalized some 2.7 million unauthorized aliens already here, supposedly in exchange for tougher penalties and controls against employers who hired illegals. The law proved no deterrent, however, because supporters, in subsequent legislation and court cases argued on civil rights grounds, weakened the employer sanctions. Meanwhile, more illegals flooded here in the hope of future amnesties from Congress, while the newly legalized sneaked their wives and children into the country rather than have them wait for family-preference visas. The flow of illegals into the country rose to between 300,000 and 500,000 per year in the 1990s, so that a decade after the legislation that had supposedly solved the undocumented alien problem by reclassifying them as legal, the number of illegals living in the United States was back up to about 5 million, while today it's estimated at between 9 million and 13 million.

The flood of immigrants, both legal and illegal, from countries with poor, ill-educated populations, has yielded a mismatch between today's immigrants and the American economy and has left many workers poorly positioned to succeed for the long term. . . . Nearly two-thirds of Mexican immigrants, for instance, are high school dropouts, and most wind up doing either unskilled factory work or small-scale construction projects, or they work in service industries, where they compete for entry-level jobs against one another, against the adult children of other immigrants, and against native-born high school dropouts. Of the 15 industries employing the greatest percentage of foreign-born workers, half are low-wage service industries, including gardening, domestic household work, car washes, shoe repair, and janitorial work. . . .

Although open-borders advocates say that these workers are simply taking jobs Americans don't want, studies show that the immigrants drive down wages of native-born workers and squeeze them out of certain industries. Harvard economists George Borjas and Lawrence Katz, for instance, estimate that low-wage immigration cuts the wages for the average native-born high school dropout by some 8 percent, or more than $1,200 a year. . . .

Consequently, as the waves of immigration continue, the sheer number of those competing for low-skilled service jobs makes economic progress difficult. A study of the impact of immigration on New York City's restaurant business, for instance, found that 60 percent of immigrant workers do not receive regular raises, while 70 percent had never been promoted. . . .

Similarly, immigration is also pushing some native-born workers out of jobs, as Kenyon College economists showed in the California nail-salon workforce. Over a 16-year period starting in the late 1980s, some 35,600 mostly Vietnamese immigrant women flooded into the industry, a mass migration that equaled the total number of jobs in the industry before the immigrants arrived. Though the new workers created a labor surplus that led to lower prices, new services, and somewhat more demand, the economists estimate that as a result, 10,000 native-born workers either left the industry or never bothered entering it.

In many American industries, waves of low-wage workers have also retarded investments that might lead to modernization and efficiency. Farming, which employs a million immigrant laborers in California alone, is the prime case in point. Faced with a labor shortage in the early 1960s, when President Kennedy ended a 22-year-old guest-worker program that allowed 45,000 Mexican farmhands to cross over the border and harvest 2.2 million tons of California tomatoes for processed foods, farmers complained but swiftly automated, adopting a mechanical tomato-picking technology created more than a decade earlier. Today, just 5,000 better-paid workers—one-ninth the original workforce—harvest 12 million tons of tomatoes using the machines.

The savings prompted by low-wage migrants may even be minimal in crops not easily mechanized. Agricultural economists Wallace Huffman and Alan McCunn of Iowa State University have estimated that without illegal workers, the retail cost of fresh produce would increase only about 3 percent in the summer-fall season and less than 2 percent in the winter-spring season, because labor represents only a tiny percent of the retail price of produce and because without migrant workers, America would probably import more foreign fruits and vegetables. . . .

As foreign competition and mechanization shrink manufacturing and farm worker jobs, low-skilled immigrants are likely to wind up farther on the margins of our economy, where many already operate. For example, although only about 12 percent of construction workers are foreign-born, 100,000 to 300,000 illegal immigrants have carved a place for themselves as temporary workers on the fringes of the industry. In urban areas like New York and Los Angeles, these mostly male illegal immigrants gather on street corners, in empty lots, or in Home Depot parking lots to sell their labor by the hour or the day, for $7 to $11 an hour. . . .

Because so much of our legal and illegal immigrant labor is concentrated in such fringe, low-wage employment, its overall impact on our economy is extremely small. A 1997 National Academy of Sciences study estimated that immigration's net benefit to the American economy raises the average income of the native-born by only some $10 billion a year—about $120 per household. And that meager contribution is not the result of immigrants helping to build our essential industries or making us more competitive globally but instead merely delivering our pizzas and cutting our grass. Estimates by pro-immigration forces that foreign workers contribute much more to the economy, boosting annual gross domestic product by hundreds of billions of dollars, generally just tally what immigrants earn here, while ignoring the offsetting effect they have on the wages of native-born workers.

If the benefits of the current generation of migrants are small, the costs are large and growing because of America's vast range of social programs and the wide advocacy network that strives to hook low-earning legal and illegal immigrants into these programs. A 1998 National Academy of Sciences study found that more than 30 percent of California's foreign-born were on Medicaid—including 37 percent of all Hispanic households—compared with 14 percent of native-born households. The foreign-born were more than twice as likely as the native-born to be on welfare, and their children were nearly five times as likely to be in means-tested government lunch programs. Native-born households pay for much of this, the study found, because they earn more and pay higher taxes—and are more likely to comply with tax laws. Recent immigrants, by contrast, have much lower levels of income and tax compliance (another study estimated that only 56 percent of illegals in California have taxes deducted from their earnings, for instance). The study's conclusion: immigrant families cost each native-born household in California an additional $1,200 a year in taxes.

Immigration's bottom line has shifted so sharply that in a high-immigration state like California, native-born residents are paying up to ten times more in state and local taxes than immigrants generate in economic benefits. Moreover, the cost is only likely to grow as the foreign-born population—which has already mushroomed from about 9 percent of the U.S. population when the NAS studies were done in the late 1990s to about 12 percent today—keeps growing. . . . This sharp turnaround since the 1970s, when immigrants were less likely to be using the social programs of the Great Society than the native-born population, says Harvard economist Borjas, suggests that welfare and other social programs are a magnet drawing certain types of immigrants—nonworking women, children, and the elderly—and keeping them here when they run into difficulty.

Not only have the formal and informal networks helping immigrants tap into our social spending grown, but they also get plenty of assistance from advocacy groups financed by tax dollars, working to ensure that immigrants get their share of social spending. Thus, the Newark-based New Jersey Immigration Policy Network receives several hundred thousand government dollars annually to help doctors and hospitals increase immigrant enrollment in Jersey's subsidized health-care programs. Casa Maryland, operating in the greater Washington area, gets funding from nearly 20 federal, state, and local government agencies to run programs that "empower" immigrants to demand benefits and care from government and to "refer clients to government and private social service programs for which they and their families may be eligible." . . .

Almost certainly, immigrants' participation in our social welfare programs will increase over time, because so many are destined to struggle in our workforce. Despite our cherished view of immigrants as rapidly climbing the economic ladder, more and more of the new arrivals and their children face a lifetime of economic disadvantage, because they arrive here with low levels of education and with few work skills—shortcomings not easily overcome. Mexican immigrants, who are up to six times more likely to be high school dropouts than native-born Americans, not only earn substantially less than the native-born median, but the wage gap persists for decades after they've arrived. A study of the 2000 census data, for instance, shows that the cohort of Mexican immigrants between 25 and 34 who entered the United States in the late 1970s were earning 40 to 50 percent less than similarly aged native-born Americans in 1980, but 20 years later they had fallen even further behind their native-born counterparts. Today's Mexican immigrants between 25 and 34 have an even larger wage gap relative to the native-born population. Adjusting for other socioeconomic factors, Harvard's Borjas and Katz estimate that virtually this entire wage gap is attributable to low levels of education. . . .

One reason some ethnic groups make up so little ground concerns the transmission of what economists call "ethnic capital," or what we might call the influence of culture. More than previous generations, immigrants today tend to live concentrated in ethnic enclaves, and their children find their role models among their own group. Thus the children of today's Mexican immigrants are likely to live in a neighborhood where about 60 percent of men dropped out of high school and now do low-wage work, and where less than half of the population speak English fluently, which might explain why high school dropout rates among Americans of Mexican ancestry are two and a half times higher than dropout rates for all other native-born Americans, and why first-generation Mexican Americans do not move up the economic ladder nearly as quickly as the children of other immigrant groups.

In sharp contrast is the cultural capital transmitted by Asian immigrants to children growing up in predominantly Asian-American neighborhoods. More than 75 percent of Chinese immigrants and 98 percent of South Asian immigrants to the U.S. speak English fluently, while a mid-1990s study of immigrant households in California found that 37 percent of Asian immigrants were college graduates, compared with only 3.4 percent of Mexican immigrants. Thus, even an Asian-American child whose parents are high school dropouts is more likely to grow up in an environment that encourages him to stay in school and learn to speak English well, attributes that will serve him well in the job market. Not surprisingly, several studies have shown that Asian immigrants and their children earn substantially more than Mexican immigrants and their children.

Given these realities, several of the major immigration reforms now under consideration simply don't make economic sense—especially the guest-worker program favored by President Bush and the U.S. Senate. Careful economic research tells us that there is no significant shortfall of workers in essential American industries, desperately needing supplement from a massive guest-worker program. Those few industries now relying on cheap labor must focus more quickly on mechanization where possible. Meanwhile, the cost of paying legal workers already here a bit more to entice them to do such low-wage work as is needed will have a minimal impact on our economy.

The potential woes of a guest-worker program, moreover, far overshadow any economic benefit, given what we know about the long, troubled history of temporary-worker programs in developed countries. They have never stemmed illegal immigration, and the guest workers inevitably become permanent residents, competing with the native-born and forcing down wages. Our last guest-worker program with Mexico, begun during World War II to boost wartime manpower, grew larger in the postwar era, because employers who liked the cheap labor lobbied hard to keep it. By the mid-1950s, the number of guest workers reached seven times the annual limit during the war itself, while illegal immigration doubled, as the availability of cheap labor prompted employers to search for ever more of it rather than invest in mechanization or other productivity gains.

The economic and cultural consequences of guest-worker programs have been devastating in Europe, and we risk similar problems. When post–World War II Germany permitted its manufacturers to import workers from Turkey to man the assembly lines, industry's investment in productivity declined relative to such countries as Japan, which lacked ready access to cheap labor. When Germany finally ended the guest-worker program once it became economically unviable, most of the guest workers stayed on, having attained permanent-resident status. Since then, the descendants of these workers have been chronically underemployed and now have a crime rate double that of German youth. . . .

"Importing labor is far more complicated than importing other factors of production, such as commodities," write University of California at Davis prof Philip Martin, an expert on guest-worker programs, and Michael Teitelbaum, a former member of the U.S. Commission on Immigration Reform. "Migration involves human beings, with their own beliefs, politics, cultures, languages, loves, hates, histories, and families."

If low-wage immigration doesn't pay off for the United States, legalizing illegals already here makes as little sense as importing new rounds of guest workers. The Senate and President Bush, however, aim to start two-thirds of the 11 million undocumented aliens already in the country on a path to legalization, on the grounds that only thus can America assimilate them, and only through assimilation can they hope for economic success in the United States. But such arguments ignore the already poor economic performance of increasingly large segments of the *legal* immigrant population in the United States. Merely granting illegal aliens legal status won't suddenly catapult them up our mobility ladder, because it won't give them the skills and education to compete. . . .

If we do not legalize them, what can we do with 11 million illegals? Ship them back home? Their presence here is a fait accompli, the argument goes, and only legalization can bring them above ground, where they can assimilate. But that argument assumes that we have only two choices: to decriminalize or deport. But what happened after the first great migration suggests a third way: to end the economic incentives that keep them here. We could prompt a great remigration home if, first off, state and local governments in jurisdictions like New York and California would stop using their vast resources to aid illegal immigrants. Second, the federal government can take the tougher approach that it failed to take after the 1986 act. It can require employers to verify Social Security numbers and immigration status before hiring, so that we bar illegals from many jobs. It can deport those caught here. And it can refuse to give those who remain the same benefits as U.S. citizens. Such tough measures do work: as a recent Center for Immigration Studies report points out, when the federal government began deporting illegal Muslims after 9/11, many more illegals who knew they were likely to face more scrutiny voluntarily returned home.

If America is ever to make immigration work for our economy again, it must reject policies shaped by advocacy groups trying to turn immigration into the next civil rights cause or by a tiny minority of businesses seeking cheap labor subsidized by the taxpayers. Instead, we must look to other developed nations that have focused on luring workers who have skills that are in demand and who have the best chance of assimilating. Australia, for instance, gives preferences to workers grouped into four skilled categories: managers, professionals, associates of professionals, and skilled laborers. Using a straightforward "points calculator" to determine who gets in, Australia favors immigrants between the ages of 18 and 45 who speak English, have a post–high school degree or training in a trade, and have at least six months' work experience as everything from laboratory technicians to architects and surveyors to information-technology workers. Such an immigration policy goes far beyond America's employment-based immigration categories, like the H1-B visas, which account for about 10 percent of our legal immigration and essentially serve the needs of a few Silicon Valley industries.

Immigration reform must also tackle our family-preference visa program, which today accounts for two-thirds of all legal immigration and has helped create a 40-year waiting list. Lawmakers should narrow the family-preference visa program down to spouses and minor children of U.S. citizens and should exclude adult siblings and parents.

America benefits even today from many of its immigrants, from the Asian entrepreneurs who have helped revive inner-city Los Angeles business districts to Haitians and Jamaicans who have stabilized neighborhoods in Queens and Brooklyn to Indian programmers who have spurred so much innovation in places like Silicon Valley and Boston's Route 128. But increasingly over the last 25 years, such immigration has become the exception. It needs once again to become the rule.

Diana Furchtgott-Roth  **NO**

The Case for Immigration

It was raining in Washington last week, and vendors selling $5 and $10 umbrellas appeared on the streets. They had Hispanic accents, and were undoubtedly some of the unskilled immigrants that Steven Malanga referred to in his recent City Journal article, "How Unskilled Immigrants Hurt Our Economy."

I already had an umbrella. But the many purchasers of the umbrellas did not seem to notice that the economy was being hurt. Rather, they were glad of the opportunity to stay dry before their important meetings.

The City Journal article is worth a look because it reflects an attitude becoming more common these days in the debate. The article speaks approvingly of immigrants from Portugal, Asia, China, India, Haiti, and Jamaica. But it also makes it clear that we have too many Mexicans, a "flood of immigrants" who cause high unemployment rates among the unskilled. They work in shrinking industries, drive down wages of native-born Americans, cost millions in welfare, and retard America's technology.

These are serious charges indeed. Similar charges, that immigrants have caused native-born Americans to quit the labor market, have been made by Steven Camarota of the Center for Immigration Studies. But are they true?

Annual immigration is a tiny fraction of our labor force. The Pew Hispanic Center Report shows that annual immigration from all countries as a percent of the labor force has been declining since its recent peak in 1999.

Annual immigration in 1999 equaled 1% of the labor force—by 2005 it had declined to 0.8%. Hispanics, including undocumented workers, peaked in 2000 as a percent of the labor force at 0.5%, and by 2004 accounted for only 0.4% (0.3% for Mexicans) of the labor force.

Looking at unskilled workers, Hispanic immigration as a percent of the American unskilled labor force (defined as those without a high school diploma) peaked in 2000 at 6%, and was 5% in 2004 (4% for Mexicans). Five percent is not "floods of immigrants."

Mr. Malanga writes that America does not have a vast labor shortage because "unemployment among unskilled workers is high—about 30%." It isn't. In 2005, according to Bureau of Labor Statistics data, the unemployment rate for adults without a high school diploma was 7.6%. Last month it stood at 6.9%.

Data from a recent study by senior economist Pia Orrenius of the Dallas Federal Reserve Bank show that foreign-born Americans are more likely to work than native-born Americans. Leaving their countries by choice, they are naturally more risk-taking and entrepreneurial.

In 2005 the unemployment rate for native-born Americans was 5.2%, but for foreign-born it was more than half a percentage point lower, at 4.6%. For unskilled workers, although the total unemployment rate was 7.6%, the native-born rate was 9.1% and the foreign-born was much lower, at 5.7%.

According to Mr. Malanga, unskilled immigrants "work in shrinking industries where they force out native workers." However, data show otherwise. Low-skilled immigrants are disproportionately represented in the expanding service and construction sectors, with occupations such as janitors, gardeners, tailors, plasterers, and stucco masons. Manufacturing, the declining sector, employs few immigrants.

One myth repeated often is that immigrants depress wages of native-born Americans. As Professor Giovanni Peri of the University of California at Davis describes in a new National Bureau of Economic Analysis paper last month, immigrants are complements, rather than substitutes, for native-born workers. As such, they are not competing with native-born workers, but providing our economy with different skills.

Education levels of working immigrants form a U-shaped curve, with unusually high representation among adult low- and high-skilled. In contrast, the skills of native-born Americans form a bell-shaped curve, with many B.A.s and high school diplomas but relatively few adult high school drop-outs or Ph.D.s

Low-skill immigrants come to be janitors and housekeepers, jobs native-born Americans typically don't want, but they aren't found as crossing guards and funeral service workers, low-skill jobs preferred by Americans. Similarly, high-skilled immigrants also take jobs Americans don't want. They are research scientists, dentists, and computer hardware and software engineers, but not lawyers, judges, or education administrators.

Because immigrants are complements to native-born workers, rather than substitutes, they help reduce economic bottlenecks, resulting in income gains. Mr. Peri's new study shows that immigrants raised the wages of the 90% of native-born Americans with at least a high school degree by 1% to 3% between 1990 and 2004. Those without a high school diploma lost about 1%, an amount that could be compensated from the gains of the others.

If immigrants affect any wages, it's those of prior immigrants, who compete for the same jobs. But we don't see immigrants protesting in the streets to keep others out, as we see homeowners in scenic locations demonstrating against additional development. Rather, some of the biggest proponents of greater immigration are the established immigrants themselves, who see America's boundless opportunities as outweighing negative wage effects.

Mr. Malanga cites a 1998 National Academy of Sciences study to say, "The foreign-born were more than twice as likely as the native-born to be on welfare." Yet this study contains estimates from 1995, more than a decade ago, and mentions programs such as Aid to Families with Dependent Children that no longer exist. Even so, the NAS study says that foreign-born households "are not more likely to use AFDC, SSI, or housing benefits."

The NAS study concludes that, since the foreign-born have more children, the "difference in education benefits accounts for nearly all of the relative deficit . . . at the local government level." Mr. Malanga, writing about how unskilled immigrants hurt the economy, would likely be in favor of these immigrants trying to educate their children, especially since these children will be contributing to his Social Security benefits.

Mr. Malanga suggests that the availability of low-wage immigrants retards investments in American technology. He cites agriculture as an example where machines to pick produce could be invented if labor were not available. Or, Mr. Malanga says, we could import produce from abroad at little additional cost.

Although consumers don't care where their food comes from, farmers certainly do. Farms provide income to farmers as well as to other native-born Americans employed in the industry as well as in trucking and distribution, just as immigrants in the construction industry have helped fuel the boom that sent employment of native-born construction workers to record levels. It makes little sense to send a whole economic sector to other countries just to avoid employing immigrants.

If unskilled immigrants don't hurt our economy, do they hurt our culture? City Journal editor Myron Magnet writes that Hispanics have "a group culture that devalues education and assimilation." Similar concerns about assimilation were made about Jews, Italians, Irish, Germans, Poles, and even Norwegians when they first came to America. All eventually assimilated.

Moreover, for those who are concerned with Spanish-speaking enclaves, a September 2006 paper by a professor at Princeton, Douglas Massey, shows that within two generations Mexican immigrants in California stop speaking Spanish at home, and within three generations they cease to know the language altogether. He concludes, "Like taxes and biological death, linguistic death seems to be a sure thing in the United States, even for Mexicans living in Los Angeles, a city with one of the largest Spanish-speaking urban populations in the world."

Legalizing the status of the illegal immigrants in America by providing a guest-worker program with a path to citizenship would produce additional gains to our economy. This is not the same as temporary worker programs in Germany, which did not have a path to citizenship, and so resulted in a disenfranchised class of workers.

With legal status, workers could move from the informal to the formal sector, and would pay more taxes. It would be easier to keep track of illegal financial transactions, reducing the potential for helping terrorists.

For over 200 years, American intellectual thought has included a small but influential literature advocating reduced immigration. The literature has spawned political parties such as the Know-Nothing Party in the mid-19th century and periodically led to the enactment of anti-immigrant laws. Immigrants, so the story goes, are bad for our economy and for our culture.

The greatness of America is not merely that we stand for freedom and economic prosperity for ourselves, but that we have consistently overcome arguments that would deny these same benefits to others.

POSTSCRIPT

Do Unskilled Immigrants Hurt the Economy?

Steven Malanga contrasts today's immigrants unfavorably with immigrants who came a hundred years ago. Today's flood of legal and illegal immigrants are less educated, unskilled, and from poorer countries. Two-thirds of Mexican immigrants are high school dropouts doing unskilled factory work, small-scale construction, or work in entry-level jobs in service industries for low wages. They compete for these jobs with other immigrants and with native-born high school dropouts. Malanga selectively cites from diverse studies on the effects of the unskilled workers on the economy to show that (i) "immigrants drive down the wages of native-born workers and squeeze them out of certain industries"; (ii) the "waves of low-wage workers have also retarded investments that might lead to modernization"; (iii) without illegal workers, the retail cost of farm produce would be "only" 2 to 3 percent higher because labor is a "tiny percent of the retail price," and because the United States would probably import more fruit and vegetables; and (iv) the overall impact of legal and illegal immigration on the U.S. economy is to raise "the average income of the native-born by only some $10 billion a year." Malanga then turns to the costs associated with the current generation of migrants, which he claims are large and growing. Again he draws from several studies, including one that concludes immigrant families cost each native-born household in California an additional $1,200 a year in taxes. He believes that a guest-worker program doesn't make economic sense since "economic research tells us that there is no significant shortfall of workers in essential American industries." He also notes that unemployment among unskilled workers is about 30 percent. Further, legalizing the illegal immigrants "won't suddenly catapult them up our mobility ladder because it won't give them the skills and education to compete."

Diana Furchtgott-Roth begins by refuting Malanga's "flood of immigrants" charge: Annual immigration declined from 1 percent (1999) to 0.8 percent (2005) of the labor force and undocumented workers accounted for only 0.4 percent of the labor force (0.3 percent for Mexicans) based on the Pew Hispanic Center Report. Next, she disputes Malanga's figure of 30 percent unemployment among the unskilled by referring to the government's unemployment rate of 7.6 percent for adults without a high school diploma in 2005. Third, Furchtgott-Roth cites a recent study showing that foreign-born Americans are more likely to work than native-born Americans. Fourth, unskilled workers are employed in *expanding,* not shrinking, industries where they force out native workers. Fifth, Furchtgott-Roth dispels the myth that immigrants depress wages of natives, refering to a 2006 study showing immigrants are complements, providing our economy with different skills. Sixth, low-skilled immigrants take jobs that natives do not want and do not take low-skill jobs that natives prefer. Sixth, Furchtgott-Roth questions the relevancy of Malanga's citation of a study showing the foreign-born were twice as likely to be on welfare as it uses decade-old data and some programs mentioned in the study no longer exist. Seventh, she defends the use of immigrant labor on farms (rather than importing food) because they provide income and employment to truckers and distributors as well as to farmers. Eighth, Furchtgott-Roth notes that concerns that Mexicans may not assimilate are not well-founded: All other groups eventually assimilated. She concludes her analysis by endorsing the guest-worker program.

There is a large and growing body of literature on the economic impact of immigration. Recent papers include testimonies before the House Committee on Ways and Means on July 26, 2006 by Michael Fix, vice president and director of studies, Migration Policy Institute, available at http://waysandmeans .house.gov/hearings.asp?formmode=view&id=5175, and by Steven A. Camarota, director of research, Center for Immigration Studies, available at http://www.cis .org/articles/2006/sactestimony072606.html. "Immigration Nation" by Tamar Jacoby in *Foreign Affairs,* November/December 2006, considers the need for unskilled and skilled immigrants. It is available at http://www.foreignaffairs.org. Her other papers on the subject are available at http://www.manhattan-institute.org/html/jacoby .htm. *The Economic Consequences of Migration* by Julian L. Simon (Cambridge, MA: Basil Blackwell, 1989) is an early study with a favorable view of immigration. For a more critical early view, see *Friends or Strangers: The Impact of Immigrants on the U.S. Economy* by George J. Borjas (New York: Basic Books, 1990). The reader should also refer to the studies cited in both the Malanga and Furchtgott-Roth arguments.

Internet References . . .

European Central Bank (ECB)

The home page for the ECB provides a number of useful links that provide information regarding ECB's monetary policy, the structure of the ECB, and economic conditions in the European Union countries.

http://www.ecb.int/home/html/index.en.html

European Union: Delegation of the European Commission to the U.S.A.

This site provides access to information regarding EU membership and its basic organization and structure, to lists of EU publications, and to overviews of EU law and policy.

http://www.eurunion.org

Geography IQ

This site provides, among other things, rankings of countries on a variety of characteristics ranging from the number of radios to the growth rates of gross domestic product.

http://www.geographyiq.com/index.htm

International Monetary Fund

The home page of the International Monetary fund provides links to information about its purposes and activities, its news releases, and its publications, including the most recent *World Economic Outlook.*

http://www.imf.org

International Trade Administration (ITA)

The U.S. Department of Commerce's ITA is dedicated to helping U.S. businesses compete in the global marketplace. This site offers assistance through many Web links under such headings as Trade Statistics, Tariffs and Taxes, Market Research, and Export Documentation. It also provides information regarding recent actions taken to promote trade.

http://www.ita.doc.gov

Social Science Information Gateway (SOSIG)

The SOSIG catalogs 17 subjects and lists more URL addresses from European and developing countries than many U.S. sources do.

http://sosig.esrc.bris.ac.uk

The World Bank

The home page of the World Bank offers links to a vast array of information regarding developing countries. Of special interest is the link to *World Development* Indicators.

http://www.worldbank.org

The World Around Us

*T*he issues explored in this unit are more diverse than those of Units 1 and 2. Two of the issues deal with international trade; two deal with the collapse of the housing bubble and the ensuing credit crisis; one addresses federal government deficits and debt; one spotlights U.S. dependence on foreign oil; another explores the effectiveness of a recent and ongoing attempt to improve public education; and the remaining issue examines the distribution of income in the United States.

- Is a Fair Trade Policy Superior to a Free Trade Policy?
- Is Loan Mitigation the Answer to the Housing Foreclosure Problem?
- Will Biofuels Like Ethanol Reduce U.S. Dependence on Foreign Oil?
- Are Spending Cuts the Right Way to Balance the Federal Government's Budget?
- Has the North American Free Trade Agreement Benefited the Economies of Canada, Mexico, and the United States?
- Do the Testing and Accountability Elements of the No Child Left Behind Act Prevent a Proper Cost-Benefit Evaluation?
- Is the Inequality in U.S. Income Distribution Surging?
- Is the Treasury's $700 Billion Bailout the Solution to the Credit Crisis?

ISSUE 13

Is a Fair Trade Policy Superior to a Free Trade Policy?

YES: Joseph E. Stiglitz, from "Fair Trade," *The National Interest* (May/June 2008)

NO: Gary Hufbauer, from "Free Trade," *The National Interest* (May/ June 2008)

ISSUE SUMMARY

YES: Former chief economist of the World Bank, Joseph E. Stiglitz, argues that trade liberalization can make everyone worse off when markets are not perfect. Furthermore, "free trade" agreements protect special interests in the advanced industrial countries. Stiglitz maintains that the United States should move toward fairer trade and should manage trade liberalization better so that the rich and the poor in all countries share the benefits of trade.

NO: Gary Hufbauer, senior fellow at the Peterson Institute for International Economics, claims that free trade, when properly implemented with market reforms, "can lift the lives of hundreds of millions of people." Free trade "pays off" for the United States and "is not some sort of 'gift' to foreign countries." He is critical of political rhetoric in the United States on halting or opting out of trade agreements, including NAFTA.

The large majority of economists accept the economic logic that supports international trade. David Ricardo argued nearly 200 years ago that if there are differences in "opportunity costs" of producing goods and services, trade will occur between countries and that, more important, the countries that engage in trade will all benefit.

If markets work the way they are expected to work, free trade increases the size or the extent of a purely domestic market and, therefore, increases the advantages of specialization. Market participants should be able to buy and consume a greater variety of inexpensive goods and services after the establishment of free trade than they could before free trade.

There are two sets of winners and two sets of losers in the game of free trade. The most obvious winners are the consumers of the less expensive imported goods. These consumers are able to buy the low-priced color television sets, automobiles, or steel that is made abroad. Another set of winners is the producers of the exported goods. All the factors in the export industry, as well as those in industries that supply the export industry, experience an increase in market demand. Therefore, their income increases. In the United States, agriculture is one such export industry. As new foreign markets are opened, farmers' incomes increase, as do the incomes of those who supply the farmers with fertilizer, farm equipment, gasoline, and other basic inputs.

On the other side of this coin are the losers. The obvious losers are those who own the factors of production that are employed in the import-competing industries. These factors include the land, labor, and capital that are devoted to the production of such U.S.-made items as color TV sets, automobiles, and steel. The less expensive foreign imports displace the demand for these products. The consumers of exported goods are also the losers. For example, as U.S. farmers sell more of their products abroad, less of this output is available domestically. As a result, the domestic prices of these farm products and other export goods and services rise.

The bottom line is that there is nothing really "free" in a market system. Competition – whether it is domestic or foreign – creates winners and losers. Historically, we have sympathized with the losers when they suffer at the hands of foreign competitors. However, we have not let our sympathies seriously curtail free trade.

Both of the following selections also look at the winners and losers from free trade. In the first selection, Stiglitz maintains that in reality markets are imperfect and trade agreements are "managed" for special interests and not really "free." As a result, trade liberalization has made people in developed and developing countries worse off. He argues that fairer trade and "better-managed trade liberalization" will produce more winners and fewer losers in all countries. Gary Hufbauer echoes the bottom line that there is no free lunch, but he holds that free trade is benefiting the United States as well as foreign countries. He acknowledges that popular opinion in the United States appears to have swung against free trade but asserts that Democratic rhetoric on NAFTA should change from "opt out" to "upgrade."

YES

Joseph E. Stiglitz

Fair Trade

It has become commonplace for politicians of both political parties to trot out rhetoric about how we need free-but-fair trade. Expanding markets through trade liberalization, it is urged, is a win-win situation. How is it, then, that in spite of assertions that *everyone* benefits from trade, there is so much opposition, in both developed and developing countries? Is it that populists have so misled ordinary citizens that, though they are really better-off, they have come to believe they are doing worse?

Or is it because trade liberalization has, in fact, made many people worse off, in developed and developing countries alike? Not only can low-skilled American workers lose their jobs or be paid less, those in developing countries suffer, too. They end up having to take the short end of the stick time and time again in trade agreements because they have little leverage over the big boys. And the links between trade liberalization and growth are far weaker than liberalization advocates claim.

A closer look at both data and standard economic theory provides further insight into the strength of the opposition to trade liberalization. In most countries around the world, there is growing inequality. In the United States, not only is there a steady uptick in poverty, but median household income has been falling for at least eight years. There are many factors contributing to these changes: technology, weakening of social mores, labor unions and, lest we forget, trade liberalization. More than sixty years ago, prominent economists Paul Samuelson and Wolfgang Stolper explained that trade liberalization in high-income countries would lower wages of unskilled workers. The economists showed that even a movement toward free trade brought wages of unskilled workers around the world closer together, meaning, for example, that America's unskilled workers' pay would fall toward that of India and China. Although their model stems from the mid-twentieth century, some of its assumptions hold even more true today. In particular, globalization has greatly reduced disparities in knowledge and technology between the developed and developing world. Lower-paid workers in the developing world now often have the tools, and increasingly, even the education, to perform the same tasks as their counterparts in developed countries. American workers simply get paid more to do the same task. Quite obviously, this can hurt even the higher-paid skilled American worker.

More generally, *standard* economic theory does not say that everyone will be better-off as a result of trade liberalization, only that the winners *could* compensate the losers. They could take a portion of their gains, give it to the losers and *everyone* could be better-off. But, of course, the winners, which in much of America are the very well-off, haven't compensated the losers; indeed, some have been arguing that to compete in the new world of globalization requires cutbacks in government spending, including programs for the poor. The losers then lose doubly.

These results of traditional economic theory are based on assumptions like perfect information, perfect-risk markets, perfect competition and no innovation. But, of course, we do not live in such a perfect world. Modern economic theory has shown that in the imperfect world in which we live, trade liberalization can actually make *everyone* worse off. For instance, trade liberalization may expose individuals and firms to more risk. In the absence of adequate insurance markets, firms respond by shifting production away from high-return risky activities to safer, but lower-return areas, thereby lowering national income.

Careful studies have found, at best, weak links between trade liberalization and growth. Many studies do show that countries that have increased their levels of trade—China is a good example—have grown faster. But these countries did not liberalize in their earlier stages of development. They promoted exports and restricted imports. And this export promotion worked.

A standard argument for reducing tariffs is that it allows resources, especially labor, to move from lower-productivity sectors into higher-productivity ones. But all too often, it results in moving workers from low-productivity employment into zero-productivity unemployment. For example, workers in Jamaica's dairy industry cannot compete with America's highly subsidized milk exports, so when Jamaica liberalized, opening up its markets to these subsidized imports, its dairies were put out of business. But the dairy workers didn't automatically get reemployed elsewhere. Rather, they simply added to the already-high unemployment rolls. In many countries, where there is high unemployment, there is no need to "release" resources to expand exports. There are a variety of impediments to expanding exports—including internal barriers to trade (such as the absence of infrastructure, which highlights the need for aid-for-trade) and, on an even-more-basic level, the absence of capital. Ironically, under today's rules, trade liberalization may again make matters worse. That is because countries are being forced to open up their markets to foreign banks, which are more interested in lending to multinationals and national monopolies than to local small- and medium-sized businesses, the sources of job creation.

Waxing Politic

The case for trade liberalization is far weaker than most economists will admit. Those who are more honest fall back on political arguments: it is not that trade liberalization is such a good thing; it is that protectionism is such a bad thing. Inevitably, it is argued, special interests prevail. But in fact, most successful economies have evolved with at least some protection of new industries at critical stages of their development. In recent work, my colleague from Columbia University, Bruce Greenwald, and I have built on that idea by developing an "infant-economy argument" that looks at how using protection as countries grow can encourage the industrial sector—the sector most amenable to learning and technological progress. The benefits of that support then diffuse throughout the economy. Such policies do not require governments to "pick winners," to identify which particular industries are well suited to the country. These policies are based on a recognition that markets do not always work well, particularly when there are externalities, where actions in one part of the economy affect another. That there are huge spillovers from successful innovation is incontrovertible.

Politicians, of course, are not constrained by economics and economic logic. Even if we see in our model that safeguarding nascent sectors is the best way to support economic growth, trade advocates claim, for instance, that trade creates jobs. But exports create jobs; imports destroy them. If one justified trade liberalization on the basis of job creation, one would have to support export expansion but simultaneously advocate import restrictions—these days, typically through nontariff barriers called dumping and countervailing duties. This is the curious position taken by many politicians who *say* they favor free trade. George W. Bush, for instance, while bandying about terms such as free trade and free markets, imposed steel tariffs at a prohibitive level even against desperately poor and tiny Moldova. This in spite of the fact that Moldova was struggling to make the transition from communism to a market economy. American steel producers could not compete and demanded these kinds of tariffs—they couldn't compete, not because of unfair competition from abroad, but rather because of failed management at home. In this case, eventually the World Trade Organization (WTO) ruled against the United States, and this time, the United States complied.

The important point missed by these politicians—and the economists who serve them ill by using such arguments—is that trade is not about job creation. Maintaining the economy at full employment is the responsibility of monetary and fiscal policies. When they fail—as they have now done once again—unemployment increases, *whatever the trade regime*. In reality, trade is about standards of living. And that raises an important question: whose standards of living, exactly?

Double Standards

In developing countries, there is another set of arguments against the kind of trade liberalization we have today. The so-called free-trade agreements being pushed by the Bush administration are, of course, not free-trade agreements at all. If they were, they would be a few pages long—with each party agreeing to eliminate its tariffs, nontariff barriers and subsidies. In fact, they go on for hundreds of pages. They are *managed*-trade agreements—typically managed for the special interests in the advanced industrial countries (especially those that make large campaign contributions, like the drug industry). The United States keeps its agricultural subsidies, and developing countries are not allowed to impose countervailing duties. And the agreements typically go well beyond trade, including investment agreements and intellectual-property provisions.

These investment agreements do far more than just protect against expropriation. In a perfect show of how all of this is supporting the developed countries while hurting the developing, they may even give American firms operating overseas protections that American firms operating domestically do not have—such as against loss of profits from new regulations. They represent a step backward in creating a rule of law: disputes are adjudicated in processes that fall far short of the standards that we expect of others, let alone of ourselves. Even worse, the ambiguous provisions can put countries in crisis in an impossible bind. They have given rise to large lawsuits, forcing developing countries to pay out hundreds of millions of dollars. In a particularly egregious example, Indonesia was forced to pay compensation for profits lost when it abrogated an almost-surely corrupt contract that then-President Suharto signed. Even though the abrogation of the agreement took place when Indonesia was falling into crisis and receiving support from the International Monetary Fund, the country was still held responsible for repayment of *anticipated* profits, which were unconscionably large because of the very corruption that many believe contributed to the country's problems in the first place.

In addition, beyond the terms of the investment agreements, the intellectual-property provisions, too, are onerous on developing countries. In fact, the intellectual-property-rights regime that is being foisted on developing countries is not only bad for developing countries; it is not good for American science and not good for global science. What separates developed from less-developed countries is not only a gap in resources but a gap in knowledge. The intellectual-property provisions reduce access to knowledge, making it more difficult to close the knowledge gap. And even beyond their impact on development, the provisions make it more difficult for developing countries to gain access to lifesaving medicines by making it harder for them to obtain generic drugs, which sell for a fraction of the price of the brand-name ones. The poor simply cannot afford brand-name prices. And because they cannot afford these prices, thousands will needlessly die. At the same time, while the drug companies demand these high prices, they spend little on the diseases that afflict the poor. This is hardly surprising: the drug companies focus on profits; one of the problems of being poor is that you have no money—including no money to buy drugs. Meanwhile, the drug companies have been reluctant to compensate the developing countries adequately for the genetic material that they obtain from them that often provides the basis of new drugs; and the intellectual-property regimes almost never provide any protection for developing countries' traditional knowledge, giving rise to worries about biopiracy. The United States, for instance, granted patents for basmati rice (which had been consumed in India for generations), for the healing properties of turmeric and for many uses of neem oil. Had India recognized and enforced these patents, it would have meant, for instance, that every time an Indian had eaten his traditional staple basmati rice, or used turmeric for healing an ailment, he would have had to send a check to the United States in payment of royalties.

Recent bilateral trade agreements are, of course, even worse in many respects than the earlier multilateral ones: how could one expect a developing country to have much bargaining power when negotiating with the United States? As several trade negotiators have told me bluntly, the United States demands, and they either take it or leave it. The United States says, if we make a concession for you, we would have to make it for everyone. In addition, not only does the array of bilateral and regional agreements undermine the multilateral trading system, but it also weakens market economics, as countries must look not for the cheapest inputs, but for the cheapest inputs satisfying the rules of origin. A Mexican apparel firm might be able to produce shirts more cheaply using Chinese buttons, but if he turns to the lowest-cost provider, his shirt will no longer be considered sufficiently "Mexican" to warrant duty-free access to the United States. Thus, the bilateral trade agreements actually impede global trade.

In both the multilateral and bilateral agreements, there has been more of a focus on liberalization and protection of capital than of labor; the asymmetry alters the bargaining power of labor versus capital because firms threaten that if the workers don't accept wage cuts, they will move elsewhere, contributing to the growing inequality around the world.

The cards are stacked against the developing countries in other ways as well. The WTO was a step in the right direction, creating an international rule of law in trade; even an unfair rule of law may be better than no rule of law at all, where the big countries can use their economic muscle without constraints. But the legal process is expensive, and this puts poor countries at a disadvantage. And even when they win, there is little assurance of compliance. Antigua won a big case against the United States, but has no effective way of enforcing its victory. The WTO has ruled that American cotton subsidies are illegal, yet the United States continues to provide them—twenty-five thousand rich American farmers benefit at the expense of millions of very poor people in the developing world. It is America's and Europe's refusal to do anything about their agricultural subsidies, more than anything else, that has stalled the so-called Doha Development Round.

But even in its conception, the Doha Development Round was a development round in name only; it was an attempt by the developed countries to put old wine into new bottles while hoping the developing countries wouldn't notice. But they did. A true development round—a trade regime that would promote development—would look markedly different.[1] It would, for instance, allow freer movement of labor—the global gains from labor-market liberalization are in fact much greater than from the liberalization of capital. It would eliminate agricultural subsidies. It would reduce the nontariff barriers, which have taken on increasing importance as tariff barriers have come down. What the trade ministers from the advanced industrial countries are trying to sell as a development round looks nothing like what a true development round would look like.

Trade Agreements and America's National Interest

The gap between American free-trade rhetoric and the unfair managed-trade reality is easily exploited by the critics of markets and of America. It provides an all-too-easy target. In some countries, America's trade agreements have helped promote democracy: citizens have been so aroused by America's unfair bilateral trade agreements that they have activated civil society, uniting disparate groups to work in unison to protest against the United States. The reason we wanted a trade agreement with Morocco was not because of the importance of our trade relations but because we wanted to build better relations with a moderate Arab country. Yet, by the time the U.S. trade representative put forth his largely nonnegotiable demands, the country had seen its largest street protests in years. If building goodwill was the intent of this and other trade agreements, the effect has been, at least in many cases, just the opposite.

None of this is inevitable. We could easily manage trade liberalization in a way in which there are more winners and fewer losers. But it is not automatic, and it is not easy. We have to devise better ways of safeguarding the losers—we need social protections, not protectionism. To take but one example: America is one of the few advanced industrial countries where there is reliance on employment-related health insurance, and it has, at the same time, a poor unemployment-insurance system. A worker who loses his job, whether as a result of foreign competition or technological change, loses his health insurance; and the paltry sums he gets in unemployment insurance make private purchase unaffordable for most. It is understandable why Americans are worried about losing their jobs as the economy slips into recession. But with most Americans today worse off than they were eight years ago, this recession is beginning even before fully recovering from the last; Americans are seeing their life savings being wiped away by the ever-declining price of housing (their one and only asset). It provides these Americans little comfort to know that someone making more than $100,000 a year, who has just gotten big tax breaks in 2001 and again in 2003, may be better-off as a result of trade liberalization. Vague promises that in the long run they, too, will be better-off provide little comfort—as Keynes quipped, "in the long run we are all dead." The median American male in his thirties has a lower income today than his counterpart thirty years ago. Trade may not have been the only reason for the decline, or even the most important, one, but it has been part of the story. Individuals can't do anything about technology; they can do something about trade. If there are benefits from trade and the winners want to sustain support for trade liberalization, they must be willing to share more of the gains with the losers.

If more developing countries are to benefit more from trade liberalization, we need a fairer trade regime; and if more people are to benefit from trade liberalization, we need to manage trade liberalization better. The United States should move toward a more comprehensive agenda for fairer trade and better-managed trade liberalization.[2] This agenda will ensure that the fruits of trade are shared by both the poor and the rich, in both the developing and developed countries. Without it, we should not be surprised about the backlash we are seeing, both in the United States and abroad.

Notes

1. In my book with Andrew Charlton. *Fair Trade for All* (Cambridge: Oxford University Press, 2005), we describe in more detail what this regime would look like.
2. I explain this agenda further in my book *Making Globalization Work* (New York: W. W. Norton, 2006).

Gary Hufbauer  **NO**

Free Trade

Free trade can benefit everyone—the developed and developing world. In large part because of open markets, the global economy is experiencing its greatest half century. In fact, free trade has increased American household income by lowering costs of products, increasing wages and making more-efficient American companies. And even though open markets may come with costs, the gains of globalization exceed them five times over. So, this means when there are burdens to be borne at home, Congress can well afford to help spread the benefits as workers transition. And if done right, free trade benefits the developing world, too, helping bring states out of poverty, allowing them to bargain on equal terms with far-larger countries and potentially stemming state failure.

Yet, the Democrats have splattered their primaries with nonsense about a "time-out" from trade agreements and "opting out" of the North American Free Trade Agreement (NAFTA). As president, neither Senator Hillary Clinton (D-NY) nor Senator Barack Obama (D-IL) could indulge such foolishness. The purpose of their catchy phrases, as everyone knows, is to snare convention delegates, not make policy. But enthusiastic supporters will call their candidate to account if he or she reaches the Oval Office.

Throughout the history of the world trading system—which is to say since the end of the Second World War—the twin objectives of U.S. commercial policy have been to foster economic prosperity and promote U.S. political alliances. These objectives will not vanish when a new president enters the White House in January 2009.

"Opting out" of NAFTA is the sort of ludicrous suggestion that can only surface on the campaign trail. Trade between the United States and its NAFTA partners represented almost 30 percent of total U.S. trade with the world in 2007. U.S. exports to Canada and Mexico totaled $378 billion in 2007, and some of this trade would be jeopardized—to the consternation of American farmers, industrialists and their congressmen. The United States needs the cooperation of Canada and Mexico on multiple fronts, from energy supplies to missile defense. Retreating from NAFTA would not only imperil relations with close neighbors, it would severely diminish U.S. credibility around the world.

⚜

Trade is almost miraculous in its effects. Even before NAFTA, the General Agreement on Tariffs and Trade (GATT—now the World Trade Organization,

WTO) was born in Havana in 1947, part of a grand design to ensure European economic recovery. The GATT's role was to slash the protectionist thicket that sprang from the Depression and political divisions in the 1930s. During its first year, the GATT sponsored negotiations among twenty-three countries that led to forty-five thousand tariff concessions, covering 20 percent of world trade. Since then, seven successive "rounds" have reduced barriers on a progressively wider scope of commerce, now including more than 150 countries and reaching 90 percent of trade in the global marketplace. The payoff from GATT far exceeds the wildest expectations of those delegates meeting at Havana over a half century ago. World trade has expanded twenty-seven times between 1950 and 2005 (adjusted for inflation), and the world economy has enjoyed the best fifty years in recorded history.

Opposition to free trade is shortsighted—forgivable perhaps for an unemployed machinist in Ohio, but hardly the stuff of presidential policy. Free trade boosts growth and provides meaningful employment. A serious danger in the decades ahead is cascading violence in regions of low development, countries often characterized by political instability and feeble growth. Collectively, they are home to billions of people. Some of them, like Mexico and Colombia, are fighting drug lords and insurgents. Others, like Pakistan and Afghanistan, are fighting al-Qaeda. These are precisely the countries that will benefit the most from open trade and investment policies. Yet many of these countries have either marginalized themselves by erecting one barrier after another to world commerce or have been marginalized not only by the restrictive practices of the United States, Europe and Japan, but also by their own peers in the developing world.

Thus, for example, Tunisia maintains an import-weighted average tariff wall of 20 percent, which, among other harmful effects, slashes trade with its neighbors in the Middle East and North Africa as well as the rest of the world. In a perfect stroke of trade-policy inequity, the United States collects about the same tariff duties annually (approximately $400 million) from impoverished Cambodia as from wealthy Britain, even though Britain exports more than twenty times as much as Cambodia to American shores each year ($57 billion versus $2.5 billion). An outstanding example of the power of open markets is South Korea, a country that has handsomely prospered. In contrast, North Korea, which has followed a path of isolation, remains mired in poverty.

A country that accedes to the WTO, such as Ukraine is now doing, must first undertake a series of legislative and structural reforms to bring its trade regime up to par with the practice of other WTO members. This process gives the newly admitted states the basis for a stronger economy, thanks to the spillover effects to commercial law, property rights and many other areas. Over past decades, many developing countries have prospered from these disciplines. Once in, the country can join negotiations with other members and bring trade complaints to the WTO's dispute-settlement body. The new inductee becomes a full-fledged member of the WTO "club," with all the attendant rights and privileges. Thus, tiny Antigua won an important case against the mighty United States, and midsized Peru was victorious over the European Union.

Put simply, the World Trade Organization engages countries of all economic sizes and political shapes in a cooperative setting designed to liberalize commerce to their mutual advantage. It is hard to imagine President Obama or President Clinton paying serious attention to naysayers such as Senator Sherrod Brown (D-OH) or Lou Dobbs, who would have the United States turn its back on the most successful piece of economic architecture since 1945.

❦

Furthermore, Democratic and Republican presidents alike have often pushed the free-trade agenda to buttress their foreign-policy objectives. Foreign policy was a core reason why President Harry Truman supported the GATT in the late 1940s in the face of opposition from leading Republicans, notably Senator Robert Taft (R-OH and intellectual godfather of the aforementioned Senator Sherrod Brown). Truman wanted to banish the specter of American isolationism in the Great Depression and forge an enduring transatlantic alliance. More recently, trade agreements have changed the political tenor with partners as varied as our immediate neighbors to the north and south, and China, our potential peer to the east.

Foreign-policy logic has thus informed many of the U.S. trade-policy choices that find expression in free-trade agreements (FTAs), beginning with Israel (1958), then Canada (1989) and Mexico (1994), and more recently Jordan (2000), Chile (2004), Australia (2004), Bahrain (2004), Morocco (2004) and Peru (2007). In each of these cases, the goal was to strengthen political relations as well as boost two-way trade and investment. Likewise, the two FTAs now awaiting congressional ratification with South Korea and Colombia are motivated by hopes of cementing alliances—in Asia where U.S.-Korea military ties are gradually supplanted by economic alliances and in South America where the overarching U.S. priorities are to root out terrorism and drug trafficking and establish a bulwark against Venezuela's Hugo Chávez. But FTAs are not just foreign-policy tools; FTA partners now buy more than 42 percent of total U.S. exports.

Our memories of the vital role played by trade diplomacy during the cold war are now fading. Even as we expand our global commerce, and even when rising exports are offsetting economic weakness at home, public support has slipped—both for the WTO and for other parts of the free-trade agenda. Polls suggest that U.S. popular opinion has swung into opposition; NAFTA and China have become metaphors for all that is supposedly wrong with globalization. But, no other tools of foreign policy—from traditional diplomacy to military operations—have the same change-making potential as trade. When properly implemented, in association with market reforms, free trade can lift the lives of hundreds of millions of people.

❦

Still, economists teach that there is no such thing as a free lunch, and this is just as true of free trade as anything else. Dismantling trade barriers almost always entails adjustment costs as workers and firms change their jobs and products. This applies to the United States just like other countries. Moreover, gains are spread widely across the American population while costs are concentrated on older workers in less-dynamic industries (think clothing and auto parts)—a severe political handicap. But serious analysis shows that gains exceed costs by *at least* five to one. In fact, U.S. gains from globalization are so large that Congress could easily afford to quintuple the size of our meager trade-adjustment programs (now under $1 billion a year), in order to cover far-more impacted workers in manufacturing and service industries with much-better transition assistance.

The important point is that free trade is not some sort of "gift" to foreign countries; it pays off for the United States as well, to the tune of $10,000 annually for each American household. U.S. firms and consumers alike benefit from low prices. U.S. companies and their employees gain new access to markets abroad. More efficient U.S. firms thrive and expand, and in this way, trade creates new and higher-paying jobs for American workers.

In the heated Ohio primary, one of the presidential candidates tossed out bogus numbers about "jobs lost" on account of NAFTA (supposedly a million) and trade agreements in general (supposedly millions). The image evoked by these sound bites—huge annual permanent job losses with no offsetting job gains—has no foundation in economics and can best be attributed to poetic license.

⋘◉⋙

The challenge awaiting the next president, in contrast to the current presidential contestants, is to move forward, not backward. NAFTA will be fifteen years old in January 2009, and improvements based on experience would be a tonic for North American relations. Labor provisions could be given sharper teeth; and the North American partners could pioneer sensible measures to address climate change, energy needs and security concerns. If Senator Obama or Senator Clinton should reach the White House, the NAFTA sound bite should be transformed by political alchemy from "opt out" to "upgrade."

Apart from NAFTA, the next president will be faced with multiple challenges outlined by U.S. Trade Representative Susan Schwab. The most important items on the agenda will be a successful conclusion of the Doha Development Round; the ratification of pending free-trade agreements with, namely, South Korea and Panama; and engaging U.S. partners on issues ranging from currency values to climate change. Some features of life in the White House seldom change, and one of them is the essential role of trade policy in international diplomacy.

POSTSCRIPT

Is a Fair Trade Policy Superior to a Free Trade Policy?

Although economists are ardent supporters of free trade, they must grapple with the reality that the world that Ricardo modeled in 1807 is starkly different from the world we know in this new millennium. The concern that Ricardo could ignore is the ability of capital and technology to cross national boundaries almost at will. This mobility suggests that comparative advantages can radically change in a relatively short period of time. This is a far cry from Ricardo's world, in which comparative advantages were stable and predictable. The trade stability seen in Ricardo's world is rarely found in the modern world. Examples abound of comparative advantages won or lost as dollars and technology chase one another around the globe. Alan Blinder points out that advances in computerized telecommunications technology (such as the Internet), and the entry of countries (principally India and China) into the global economy especially in this decade, have also increased the types of services that are tradable today; he argues that many more services are likely to become tradable in the future.

The bottom line is clear. Comparative advantage does lead to economic efficiency, but, as with any market adjustment, there can be serious dislocations as less efficient producers must make way for more efficient producers. While Hufbauer holds to the conventional view that free trade "can lift the lives of hundreds of millions of people," Stiglitz is skeptical. Both Hufbauer and Stiglitz recognize the decline in public support for free trade. Neither favors protectionism. While Stiglitz endorses more social protection to safeguard the losers (e.g., more health and unemployment insurance for Americans), Hufbauer supports "much-better transition assistance" for displaced workers.

The free trade–fair trade debate has been around for a number of decades. From the perspective of developing countries the term "fair trade" often signifies a degree of protection as, for example, in Stiglitz's "infant-economy argument." In developed countries, the notion of fairness is reflected in calls for better environmental and labor standards in developing countries. Hufbauer calls for "sharper teeth" to labor provisions under NAFTA closing remarks.

Stiglitz explains his views in his books *Making Globalization Work* (W.W. Norton, 2006) and (with Andrew Charlton) *Fair Trade for All* (Oxford University Press, 2005).

For an account of the change in American public support for free trade, read Nina Easton's "America Sours on Free Trade," *Fortune,* available at http://money.cnn.com/2008/01/18/news/economy/worldgoaway.fortune/index.htm (January 25, 2008), and "Election Update: Fair Trade Gets an Upgrade," *Public Citizen,* available at http://www.citizen.org/documents/ElectionReportFINAL.pdf (December 8, 2008).

If you are interested in Alan Blinder's views on the nature and consequences of offshoring, see "Offshoring: The Next Industrial Revolution?" *Foreign Affairs,* March/April 2006, available at http://www.foreignaffairs.org/20060301faessay85209/alan-s-blinder/offshoring-the-next-industrial-revolution.html, and "How Many U.S. Jobs Might Be Offshorable," available at http://www.princeton.edu/~blinder/papers/07ceps142.pdf (March 2007).

For a defense of free trade and a rejoinder to Blinder, see Jagdish Bhagwati's article "Don't Cry for Free Trade," available at http://www.cfr.org/publication/14526/dont_cry_for_free_trade.html (October 15, 2007), and J. Bradford De Long's "Free Trade and Fair Trade," available at http://delong.typepad.com/sdj/2008/03/free-trade-and.html (March 7, 2008). To place the free trade argument in its historic context, read John C. Nye's essay "The Myth of Free-Trade Britain," The Library of Economics and Liberty, available at http://www.econlib.org/library/Columns/y2003/Nyefreetrade.html.

ISSUE 14

Is Loan Mitigation the Answer to the Housing Foreclosure Problem?

YES: David G. Kittle, from "A Review of Mortgage Servicing Practices and Foreclosure Mitigation," Statement before the House of Representatives Committee on Financial Services (July 25, 2008)

NO: Julia Gordon, from "A Review of Mortgage Servicing Practices and Foreclosure Mitigation," Testimony before the House of Representatives Committee on Financial Services (July 25, 2008)

ISSUE SUMMARY

YES: Mortgage Bankers Association official David Kittle, after reviewing the cost of foreclosure and loan mitigation options, presents data to back his assertion that loan mitigation is working.

NO: Center for Responsible Lending policy Counsel Julia Gordon stresses both the direct costs and the spillover costs of foreclosures and believes that voluntary loan modifications "have done little to stem the overwhelming tide of foreclosures."

$\mathbf{T}$he American dream, or at least a large part of the American dream, is to own one's own home. The purchase of a home for all but a very few involves borrowing the money, going into debt, and acquiring a mortgage. In applying for a home mortgage loan, most prospective homeowners will get either a prime loan or a subprime loan. The former is a loan made to borrowers with good credit histories, good repayment prospects, and above-minimum down payments. A subprime mortgage loan is one made to a borrower with a poor credit history and/or with a high debt-to-income ratio (the borrower's outstanding debt is high relative to his or her income) or a high loan-to-value ratio (the amount borrowed with the mortgage is close to the value of the home being purchased). Of course, a subprime borrower has to pay a higher interest rate to compensate the lender for the higher risk he or she accepts in making a subprime loan.

Both types of mortgage loans can be made with a fixed interest rate or a variable interest rate. For the former the interest rate that the borrower pays and the lender receives stays constant over the life of the loan, while with the latter, frequently referred to as an adjustable rate mortgage (ARM), the interest rate rises and falls (resets) over time as market interest rates rise and fall. During the housing boom, in the first half of the decade, an increasing proportion of mortgage loans consisted of subprime ARMs. So by early 2008, according to a Federal Reserve report (*A Snapshot of Mortgage Conditions with an Emphasis on Subprime Mortgage Performance,* available at http://federalreserveonline.org/pdf/MF_Knowledge_Snapshot-082708.pdf), the subprime mortgage market, whether measured by the number of loans or the value of loans, accounted for about 12 percent of the total residential mortgage markets. More specifically, the subprime portion had a value of $1.2 trillion while the total residential mortgage market was estimated at $10.1 trillion, with subprime ARMs constituting more than half of the subprime component. The total number of mortgage loans was estimated at 54.7 million, with 6.7 million subprime loans and 3.2 million subprime ARMs.

But the booming housing market of the early part of the decade came to an abrupt halt—the housing bubble burst. As interest rates increased and housing prices began to fall, borrowers had problems meeting their mortgage obligations. This was especially true for those borrowers who had used subprime ARMs to finance their home purchases. The Federal Reserve estimated that as of March 31, 2008, more than 721,000 subprime loans were in foreclosure, including 543,000 subprime ARMs. Foreclosure involves a legal process in which a lender seeks recovery of the borrower's collateral (in the case of a residential mortgage the collateral is the home being purchased by the borrower). A lender will take this action when the borrower is no longer able to meet the obligations of the mortgage agreement. Foreclosure normally means that the current market value of the property is less than the outstanding balance of the mortgage loan; otherwise the borrower would sell the property, pay off the loan, and still have something left over.

Foreclosures obviously create problems for borrowers and lenders, but the damage can and has spread to other property owners, other lending organizations, other borrowers, and local governments. With the rising tide of foreclosures, public and private action was taken. Loan mitigation is a private effort to avoid foreclosure and can take a variety of forms, including loan modification. The issue examined here is whether or not loan mitigation is working effectively in solving the problems created by the rising tide of foreclosures and the collapse of the housing market. Kittle believes loan mitigation is working while Gordon argues that it is not.

YES

David G. Kittle

A Review of Mortgage Servicing Practices and Foreclosure Mitigation

Chairman Frank, Ranking Member Bachus, Members of the Committee, I am David G. Kittle, CMB, President and Chief Executive Officer of Principle Wholesale Lending, Inc. in Louisville, Kentucky and Chairman-Elect of the Mortgage Bankers Association (MBA).[1] I appreciate the opportunity to appear before you to discuss the progress of the mortgage industry in working out troubled loans.

MBA's members strive to keep borrowers in their homes and avoid fore-closures whenever possible. Such goals serve the interests not only of borrowers, but also of our members and of the communities in which they do business. We understand the urgency of borrowers seeking the industry's assistance and our members continue to step up their foreclosure prevention programs.

Avoiding Foreclosures

None of us wants a family to lose its home, and MBA members are devoting significant time and resources to finding ways to help borrowers keep their homes. The tools used to avoid foreclosure and retain a borrower's home include forbearance and repayment plans, loan modifications, refinances and partial and advance claims. Mortgage loan servicers use short sales and deeds in lieu of foreclosure to avoid foreclosure when the borrower does not want to or cannot retain the home.

It makes good economic sense for mortgage servicers to help borrowers who are in trouble. The recent increase in mortgage delinquencies and fore-closures has brought significant attention to the costs of foreclosure to home-owners, communities and mortgage industry participants. While the impact of foreclosure upon homeowners and communities is clear to everyone, statements by some advocates and government officials indicate that confusion still exists about the impact of foreclosures upon industry participants particularly lenders, servicers and investors.

Mortgage lenders and servicers do not profit from foreclosures. In reality, every party to a foreclosure loses – the borrower, the immediate community, the servicer, mortgage insurer and investor. It is important to understand that

U.S. House of Representatives, July 25, 2008, excerpts.

profitability for the mortgage industry rests in keeping a loan current and, as such, the interests of the borrower and lender are mostly aligned.

As a recent Congressional Research Service paper notes, for lenders and investors, foreclosure is a lengthy and extremely costly process and, generally, a losing financial proposition.[2] While losses can vary significantly, several independent studies have found the losses to be quite significant: over $50,000 per foreclosed home[3] or as much as 30 to 60 percent of the outstanding loan balance.[4]

Risk of Loss

When a lender holds a loan in portfolio, it retains the credit risk on the loan and takes a direct loss if the loan goes to foreclosure sale. When a loan has been securitized, the investors in the mortgage securities hold the credit risk and take a direct loss to principal if the loan goes to foreclosure sale. The servicer, if different from the noteholder, also bears certain costs if the loan goes to foreclosure – most notably the loss of its servicing asset.

Once the borrower has obtained a mortgage and the originator has closed the mortgage, the main objective for the mortgage servicer is to keep the loan current. If a loan is terminated through foreclosure, the servicer does not continue to receive the servicing fee (the primary source of a mortgage company's income). The standard servicing fee for a fixed-rated Fannie Mae or Freddie Mac loan is ¼ of 1 percent of the principal balance, or $250 per annum for a typical $100,000 loan. Subprime loans generally carry a higher servicing fee because of the increased delinquency risk and costs. Minimum servicing on subprime loans is ½ of 1 percent of the principal balance. Servicers of MBS, otherwise, do not retain the principal and interest (P&I) payment the borrower makes as those amounts are passed on to the ultimate investor.

In addition to losing the servicing income for the asset, servicers must pay out-of-pocket costs when the loan is delinquent. The servicer must:

- Advance interest and principal to the investors (despite not receiving payments from the borrower);
- Advance taxes and insurance payments;
- Pay for foreclosure attorneys fees, court costs and other fees;
- Pay for bankruptcy attorneys and court costs, if applicable;
- Pay for property inspections and property preservation work (mowing the grass, boarding, rekeying, winterizing, etc.), as applicable;
- Pay for other costs including appraisals, title searches, publications, and other direct costs; and
- Pay for increased staff, contractors and other costs, such as technology costs.

To make principal, interest, tax and insurance advances, mortgage companies have to borrow the funds or use their own capital. These borrowing costs can reach into the millions of dollars per company, as many lenders experienced after Hurricane Katrina and are experiencing today.

State law dictates the foreclosure process and timeline. As a result, foreclosure costs vary significantly from state to state. In certain states, foreclosure requires court action. In these "judicial foreclosure" states, foreclosure takes longer and, consequently, is more costly. Even without a judicial foreclosure, the process is lengthy. The national average time between the first missed payment and the foreclosure sale is approximately one year.[5] After that, it may take additional time to gain possession of the property, clear the title and prepare and sell the real estate owned (REO) property.

If the loan goes to foreclosure sale, the servicer is generally not reimbursed for all its out-of-pocket, direct and indirect costs. For example, the Federal Housing Administration (FHA) only reimburses two-thirds of certain out-of-pocket expenses incurred by the servicer (e.g. foreclosure attorney fees) and sets maximums for foreclosure and bankruptcy costs and property preservation costs that often do not cover the actual expenses. In private label securities, pooling and servicing agreements (PSAs) often establish maximum payments for out-of-pocket costs incurred by the servicers. Moreover, in private label securities, servicers have higher unreimbursed carrying costs because the servicer does not receive reimbursement until it sells the REO property.

Conversely, if the loan is brought current through loss mitigation, out-of-pocket expenses generally are reimbursed through the workout plan or are separately collected by the servicer. Carrying costs are also usually reduced. Curing the delinquency allows the servicer to salvage its valuable servicing asset. Reinstatement, therefore, is far more desirable from an economic standpoint for servicers than foreclosure.

Additional Investor/Noteholder Expenses

Investors and portfolio lenders have added incentives to avoid foreclosure. They incur additional cost and losses as owners of the note or repossessed property. Post foreclosure costs alone can account for over 40 percent of foreclosure-related gross losses.[6] The main expenses during this phase of the process are:

- *Costs of Restoring the Property* – Often homes of borrowers in financial distress fall into disrepair, requiring repairs and capital improvements to sell the property;
- *Property Maintenance* – REO properties must continue to be maintained (grass mowed, property winterized, etc.) and secured (boarded up and rekeyed to avoid break-ins, etc.) and removed of safety code violations (drain and cover pools, etc); and
- *Real Estate Commissions and Closing Costs* – Lenders typically use real estate agents, just as individuals do, to sell properties and must pay the real estate broker commissions.

The last step that creates a major expense for investors and portfolio lenders is the loss on the unpaid principal balance that occurs upon the sale of the REO property. While exceptions occur (mostly in appreciating markets), holders of REO properties do not sell them at a gain. REO properties generally do not attract top dollar, and once sale proceeds are netted against the various costs incurred during the delinquency period and foreclosure process, the investor and lender usually end up with losses.[7] These losses make up approximately 20 percent of the total costs of foreclosure. The current softness of the housing market could push this rate even higher. While private mortgage and government insurance and guarantees may offset some of these losses, coverage can be limited. Moreover, not all noteholders are protected by mortgage insurance. Subprime mortgages generally do not carry mortgage insurance.

Loss Mitigation

Mortgage companies and investors have recognized the impact of foreclosures on their bottom lines and over the last ten years have developed innovative techniques to help borrowers resume payments. These options have proven successful for the homeowner, the servicer and investor.

If a homeowner misses a payment and becomes delinquent, the mortgage servicer will attempt multiple contacts with the homeowner in order to help that borrower work out the delinquency. Servicers have several foreclosure prevention options that can get a borrower back on his or her feet, including those outlined below.

Forbearance Plan: Forbearance is a temporary agreement, which allows the homeowner to make partial or no payments for a period. The forbearance agreement is followed by a further evaluation of the loan and the homeowner's circumstance to identify if there are any permanent workout options such as a repayment plan or modification.

Repayment Plan: A repayment plan is a verbal or written agreement where a delinquent homeowner resumes making regular monthly payments in addition to a portion of the past due payments to reinstate the loan to "current" status.

Loan Modifications: Loan modifications are the next level of loss mitigation options. A loan modification is a change in the underlying loan document. It might extend the term of the loan, change the interest rate, change repayment terms or make other alterations. Often features are combined to include rate reductions and term extensions. . . .

Partial and Advance Claims: Servicers are also using partial or advance claims on government and conventional products (i.e., Fannie Mae's Home-Saver Advanced program). In a partial or advance claim, a junior lien is created in the amount of the arrearage. The loan proceeds from the newly created junior lien are used to pay the arrearage on the first mortgage, thus bringing the borrower current. . . .

Refinances: Servicers also use refinances to assist borrowers who are current, but are at risk of defaulting on the loans in the future or borrowers who are in the early stages of delinquency. FHASecure is one example of a program targeted at borrowers with adjustable rate mortgages who are unable to make payments due to an increase in rate.[8] . . .

Short Sales and Deeds in Lieu of Foreclosure: Not all borrowers want to or can stay in their homes. Some have decided to stop making mortgage payments because to do so no longer suits their economic interests.[9] Others face divorce or relocations for which the current home is no longer viable.

Borrowers who cannot maintain their home for whatever reason may still avoid foreclosure through a short sale or deed in lieu of foreclosure. In both cases, the borrower is usually relieved of the debt despite selling the house for less than the debt or delivering an asset that is worth less than the debt.

All of these loss mitigation options benefit the borrower in varying ways and servicers strive to help as many borrowers as is prudently possible.

Loss Mitigation Is Working

Our servicing members have worked aggressively to make the available tools as efficient as possible. The industry formed the HOPE NOW Alliance in an effort to approach foreclosure prevention in a coordinated fashion and to enhance communication efforts about loss mitigation opportunities with borrowers.

Servicers' actions are clearly working. HOPE NOW estimates that more than 1.7 million homeowners have avoided foreclosure because of industry efforts since July of 2007. In May 2008 alone, servicers provided approximately 170,000 at risk borrowers with repayment and modification plans. Early indications show that servicers are maintaining this pace for June.[10] Of the workout plans offered in May, approximately 100,000 were repayment plans and 70,000 were loan modifications.

Workouts are clearly outpacing foreclosures. In the first quarter of 2008, the number of repayment plans and modifications alone equaled 482,996 as compared with 198,172 foreclosure sales in the same timeframe. Servicers are also engaged in partial or advance claims, delinquent refinances, short sales and deeds in lieu of foreclosure that are not captured currently in the survey. We believe the industry has demonstrated its willingness and commitment to help borrowers avoid foreclosure.

Let me repeat this: despite assertions to the contrary, the numbers are clear. In the first three months of this year, 482,996 families received workouts, more than twice the number of people who experienced foreclosure sales: 198,172. The industry is engaged in an historic effort to assist people in trouble, despite an unending stream of criticism that somehow our efforts are inadequate.

Obviously, the sooner a borrower in trouble can get a workout plan, the greater the chance the borrower has to avoid foreclosure and the less impact there is on the surrounding community. However, servicers cannot forgo due diligence for speed. As some have suggested, granting every borrower a loan modification simply because the borrower requests one is unwise and contrary to the servicer's contractual responsibility to investors or duty to shareholders. As prudent businesses, servicers must review the specific circumstances of the request and tailor the response to the borrower's unique circumstances. Failure to do so would also harm the borrower, as each borrower's financial situation is different, which calls for different solutions.

Lenders continue to explore ways to improve execution and responsiveness. We recognize that we can do better, and we are working to improve even more. Servicers are increasing staff, sending special mailings, making phone calls, developing Web sites, going door-to-door and using other creative means to reach out to distressed homeowners. As a normal course, servicers send numerous letters to delinquent homeowners notifying them about loss mitigation. Additionally, HOPE NOW launched an additional nationwide campaign to reach at-risk homeowners. So far, HOPE NOW members have sent approximately 1.3 million special letters. About 18 to 20 percent of homeowners receiving the HOPE NOW-coordinated letters have contacted their servicer, a 6- to 9-fold increase over the standard 2–3 percent response rate servicers have historically received.

Industry Action

Servicers have also advanced or promoted several other beneficial programs:

HOPE Hotline: The industry, through the HOPE NOW Alliance, continues to promote the Homeownership Preservation Foundation's HOPE Hotline (888-995-HOPE) which is available 24 hours a day, 7 days a weeks, and 365 days a year. There is no cost to homeowners for using the HOPE Hotline. . . . The HOPE Hotline currently has approximately 450 HUD-approved housing counselors available to assist and advise borrowers on mortgages and other debts. However, borrowers must take action. The longer the borrower waits to seek help, the less likely he or she will qualify for loss mitigation.

Streamlined Modifications: Lenders and servicers of HOPE NOW worked with the American Securitization Forum (ASF) to create a framework to more readily modify certain at-risk subprime loans securitized in the secondary market.[11] The focus of the effort has been to identify categories of borrowers with subprime hybrid adjustable rate mortgages (ARM) who can be streamlined into refinancings or modifications. . . .

Foreclosure Prevention Workshops: Members are working with government agencies, federal and state legislative offices and consumer groups to host foreclosure prevention workshops, where borrowers can meet servicers face-to-face to discuss and execute workout options. . . . In the past four months, HOPE NOW alone has connected almost 6,000 homeowners with their lender and/or a HUD-certified housing counselor at workshops in 14 different cities in California, Georgia, Illinois, Pennsylvania, Ohio, Nevada, Texas, Wisconsin, Tennessee, Florida and Indiana.

Use of Third Parties: In addition to the successful use of housing counselors, servicers are also piloting the use of other third parties, such as foreclosure attorneys, to discuss foreclosure prevention alternatives with borrowers. . . . Servicers are also employing third parties to make personal contacts with borrowers at their homes to execute loss mitigation packages.

Innovations with Counselors: The industry, through HOPE NOW and the technology provider Computer Sciences Corporation, have crafted a Web-based tool which housing counselors can use to capture critical borrower information needed to complete a workout by the servicer. . . . The software can generate a workout recommendation that is based on a particular servicer's or investor's rules and the specific borrower information.

Servicer Best Practices: Servicers working through the HOPE NOW Alliance issued guidelines last month that provide greater clarity and uniformity to the workout process. . . .

Web Sites: Servicers have also created Web sites that allow borrowers at any time of the day to learn about the loss mitigation process, educate themselves on the requirements, and download or print the financial forms and other documents necessary to initiate the workout process. . . .

Servicer Challenges

The Committee has inquired whether impediments exist that inhibit increased execution of workouts. We would like to take this opportunity to explore some of the more common reasons modifications and other workout strategies fail or are slow to complete.

Investment Properties: The options for helping borrowers who purchased homes as investments are limited. During the housing boom of the last several years, there were many speculators and investors looking to profit from price appreciation. The strength of our economy relies on the willingness of people to take risks, but risk means one does not always get his or her rewards. During this time, a majority of these properties were purchased to try to capitalize on appreciating home values or to use rents as a source of investment income, or some combination of both. With the downturn in the housing market, a number of these investors are walking away from their properties and defaulting on their loans. In the third quarter of 2007, 18 percent of foreclosure actions started were on non-owner occupied properties. Foreclosure starts for the same period for non-owner occupied properties in Arizona, Florida, Nevada and Ohio were at 22 percent.[12] . . .

Junior Liens: Many borrowers have second and third liens. If the first lienholder seeks to modify the mortgage by adding the arrearage to the balance of the loan – which is common practice to bring the loan current – or seeks to extend the maturity date, the first lienholder must get the junior lienholders to resubordinate their interests to the first lienholder. Failure to get that subordination would jeopardize the first lienholder's priority position and would likely violate the trust and pooling and servicing agreements. . . .

The June HOPE NOW Servicing Guidelines identify these limitations, but also indicate that junior lienholders who are not restricted by servicing agreements to the contrary will resubordinate their interest when:

- a refinancing does not increase the first lien principal amount by more than reasonable closing costs and arrearages and no cash is extracted by the homeowner; and
- A loan modification that lowers or maintains the monthly payment of the first lien via term extension, rate reduction and/or principal write down and no cash is extracted by the homeowner.

Recidivism: Recidivists or serial defaulters are costly to servicers and can create a barrier to repeat offers of loss mitigation. While the industry will consider revising previous modifications or repayment plans based upon true hardship, requests for multiple modifications with no intentions of honoring the terms will – and should – be rejected. Workouts are not free of charge for the servicer. Servicers and investors often incur costs associated with delinquency and foreclosure initiation and those costs mount the longer the delinquency remains outstanding. Servicers also use up valuable resources and incur costs to perform loss mitigation. Borrowers who redefault repeatedly drive up these costs making loss mitigation not viable or financially sound.

One way the industry is attempting to reduce the recidivism problem is to engage in "stipulated payment to modification plans." These "stip to mods" require the borrower to make timely payments according to the proposed revised terms of the mortgage for three or four months. . . .

Contractual Requirements: Despite many efforts to relieve some of the legal barriers to executing modifications, servicers are under a contractual duty to follow the requirements of their pooling and servicing agreement and to maximize the recovery to the trust. As we have explored in the past, many PSAs permit workouts that are "consistent with industry practice." This poses a challenge to define common industry practice, especially when new approaches such as streamline modifications are undertaken. Others, albeit a minority, prohibit modifications altogether or limit the length of repayment plans. Yet others have conflicting provisions, for example, permitting servicers to follow standard industry practices for delinquent borrowers, but prohibiting changes to the interest rate in other sections of the document. These legal issues are difficult to manage and servicers are reluctant to err against the investor for fear of liability.

While we are certain these limitations or conflicts would be resolved if investors could get together and agree, many MBS are widely held and getting the necessary number of investors together to change the PSA terms has proven impossible. Servicers are not remaining idle, however. Servicers are advancing new concepts by creating industry standards through coordinated approaches led by industry groups and seeking approval of actions by the American Securitization Forum, the SEC and IRS. The industry is working as a whole to obtain favorable results for homeowners while not violating their contracts. . . .

Security Requirements: In some cases, a modification cannot be executed until the borrower is delinquent. For example, Ginnie Mae does not permit a loan to be modified and remain in the security. To modify a loan, it must be repurchased from the pool. Servicers, however, are prohibited from repurchasing a loan from the pool until the borrower is 90 days delinquent. This policy has merit to curb run-off at the security level. Unfortunately, in today's environment, it also inhibits the servicer's ability to execute modifications when a borrower is current – but default is imminent – or when the borrower is delinquent by a month or two.

Failure to Respond: While the rate of borrower response has improved dramatically since last year, still far too many borrowers are unresponsive or fail to follow through on workout offers. Some borrowers will request loss mitigation assistance, but when asked to provide necessary documentation, such as income verification or letters describing their financial hardship, the borrowers do not respond. Servicers have also seen borrowers get approved for a modification, but then fail to sign and return a modification agreement that executes the deal. Despite follow up efforts, no action is taken and the servicer is forced to consider the request abandoned. We do not know for certain why these situations are happening. We presume several things. In some cases, the borrower cannot demonstrate a financial hardship. We also believe that the borrower may get overwhelmed with notices and collection calls from other creditors and, therefore, stops opening mail and taking calls. We also believe that some borrowers become suspicious of signing an agreement despite communicating with the servicer. We are sure there are many other reasons. Unfortunately, they are all speculation since servicers are unable to reach these borrowers.

Changing Behavior: Servicers are finding in many cases that borrowers' expenses exceed their income. While income may be sufficient to afford the home and reasonable household expenses, other spending habits and debts incurred by the borrower are draining surplus funds. To retain the home, borrowers must change their spending habits and address their other debts. Servicers are willing to provide assistance by modifying terms of the loan to clear the delinquency and provide more affordable terms. However, borrowers may still also have to negotiate with unsecured creditors to reduce credit card balances in order to continue to afford the home. Servicers are not forcing borrowers to bring down these balances before executing a workout. Servicers will give the borrower the benefit of the doubt and will execute a plan, stop the foreclosure if applicable, and trust that the borrower will take action to reduce their expenses and other debts. . . .

Secondary Marketing Risk: Servicers of FHA and VA loans are subject to secondary marketing risk when modifying loans. As stated previously, in order to modify an FHA or VA loan, the servicer must repurchase the loan from the pool. The servicer generally borrows funds from a bank to make the repurchase at the unpaid principal balance. The repurchase obligation creates risk for the servicer. Servicers who repurchase mortgages out of Ginnie Mae securities incur interest rate risk associated with these modifications. Interest rate risk is the risk that the new modified rate offered to the borrower will be below the prevailing market interest rate (par) and the servicer will incur a principal loss for delivering a less valuable asset. Historically the interest rate risk has been far less than the loss from foreclosure. Servicers do not incur redelivery risk with most private label securities because modified loans do not have to be repurchased from pools to be modified.

Conclusion

Servicers want to assist borrowers who are having difficulty paying their mortgages. Not only do servicers want to preserve the client relationship, but servicers and investors have an economic incentive to avoid foreclosure. As a result, servicers are performing a growing number of workouts, including modifications, as evidenced by the HOPE NOW data. Servicers have increased staff, have funded new technology, are sponsoring homeownership workshops and are funding advertising to educate borrowers about foreclosure prevention options. They are paying for housing counseling sessions so that they remain free to homeowners and are working with regulators and others to resolve legal impediments to performing loss mitigation. Servicers are using third parties in innovative ways, even going door-to-door to reach borrowers, and are paying incentives to staff and third parties for successful workouts. All these efforts demonstrate the industry's dedication to avoiding foreclosure and helping delinquent borrowers get back on their feet. The industry is working to keep pace with changes. We are not standing idle, but seeking new and financial responsible ways to increase workouts.

The incentives of the mortgage servicer are generally in line with the borrower who is in trouble. We are doing our part. Thank you for the opportunity to share our thoughts with the Committee.

Notes

1. The Mortgage Bankers Association (MBA) is the national association representing the real estate finance industry, an industry that employs more than 370,000 people in virtually every community in the country. Headquartered in Washington, D.C., the association works to ensure the continued strength of the nation's residential and commercial real estate markets; to expand homeownership and extend access to affordable housing to all Americans. MBA promotes fair and ethical lending practices and fosters professional excellence among real estate finance employees through a wide range of educational programs and a variety of publications. Its membership of over 2,400 companies includes all elements of real estate finance: mortgage companies, mortgage brokers, commercial banks, thrifts, Wall Street conduits, life insurance companies and others in the mortgage lending field. For additional information, visit MBA's Web site. . . .

2. See Darryl E. Getter, "Understanding Mortgage Foreclosure: Recent Events, the Process, and Costs," CRS Report for Congress (November 5, 2007), p. 9, 11.

3. See Desiree Hatcher, "Foreclosure Alternatives: A Case for Preserving Homeownership," Profitwise News and Views (a publication of the Federal Reserve Bank of Chicago) (February 2006), p. 2 (citing a GMAC-RFC estimate); Craig Focardi, "Servicing Default Management: An Overview of the Process and Underlying Technology," TowerGroup Research Note, No. 033-13C (November 15, 2002). See also Congressional Budget Office (CBO), "Policy Options for the Housing and Financial Markets," (April 2008), p. 17.

4. Karen M. Pence, "Foreclosing on Opportunity: State Laws and Mortgage Credit," Board of Governors of the Federal Reserve System (May 13, 2003), p. 1. See also CBO, p. 17; Community Affairs Department, Office of the Comptroller of the Currency (OCC), "Foreclosure Prevention: Improving Contact with Borrowers," Community Developments (June 2007), p. 3.

5. Amy Crews Cutts and William A. Merrill, "Interventions in Mortgage Default: Policies and Practices to Prevent Home Loss and Lower Costs," Freddie Mac Working Paper #08-01 (March 2008), p. 30 and Table 6.

6. Cutts and Merrill, p. 32.

7. CBO, p. 17; Getter, p. 9; Cutts and Merrill, p. 33.

8. Mortgagee Letter 2008–13 (May 7, 2008)

9. See, for example, Said, Carolyn: "More in Foreclosure Choose to Walk Away," San Francisco *Chronicle:* March 16, 2008. . . .

10. "Mortgage Loss Mitigation Statistics" HOPE NOW issued July 2008. . . .

11. "Streamlined Foreclosure and Loss Avoidance Framework for Securitized Subprime Adjustable Rate Mortgage Loans," American Securitization Forum, December 6, 2007 and updated July 8, 2008. . . .

12. Jay Brinkmann, Ph.D., "An Examination of Mortgage Foreclosures, Modifications, Repayment Plans, and Other Loss Mitigation Activities in the Third Quarter of 2007," Mortgage Bankers Association (January 2008).

Julia Gordon  **NO**

A Review of Mortgage Servicing Practices and Foreclosure Mitigation

T he U.S. economy faces significant challenges today, as 20,000 foreclosures take place every single week.[1] It is not an overstatement to say that the way we choose to deal with these issues today has implications for nearly every American. The negative spillover effects from these foreclosures are substantial: a single foreclosure causes neighborhood property values to drop, collectively adding up to billions of dollars of losses. Empty homes lead to higher crime rates. Lost property tax revenue hurts cities and counties that are already strapped. Millions of Americans who depend on a robust housing market are losing jobs and income. As foreclosures accelerate during the next two years, these economic effects will be felt even more strongly.

In announcing the Federal Reserve Board's new rules governing mortgage origination, Federal Reserve Board Chairman Ben Bernanke acknowledged that unfair and deceptive practices by lenders have played a major role in the current housing crisis. According to Bernanke, too many loans were "inappropriate or misled the borrower."[2] As a result, the Federal Reserve will now require all lenders to verify a consumer's ability to afford a mortgage before selling it, and will prohibit a variety of abusive and dangerous practices.

While it is too late to stop the housing crisis that has been caused by reckless lending, it is not too late to minimize the massive damage ahead. Skillful loan servicing can convert distressed mortgages into stable loans that generate revenue for investors, build ownership for families, and contribute to stronger and more stable communities. Ineffective or abusive loan servicing, on the other hand, can produce the opposite results. That is why national policies governing loan servicing ultimately will have enormous implications – not only for people facing foreclosure, but for the future prosperity of our country.

In short, abusive and inappropriate loans were mass-marketed for years, and now, to prevent further damage to the economy, these bad loans must be mass-repaired. The most effective way to repair distressed loans is through loan "modifications" that alter the loan's terms in a way that allows homeowners to continue paying their debt and building equity. Unfortunately, as I will discuss in more detail, today even the best-intentioned loan servicers face major obstacles to making loan modifications, and others lack the incentive or motivation to fix mortgages so that people can stay in their homes.

U.S. House of Representatives, July 25, 2008, excerpts.

To put it bluntly, it is far harder to obtain an affordable loan modification for an unsustainable loan than it was to take out the loan in the first place. As a result, voluntary efforts aimed at increasing loan modifications have done little to stem the overwhelming tide of foreclosures that are dragging down our economy. . . .

I. We Face a Severe Foreclosure Crisis That Will Grow Even Worse Without Significant Government Action

Just one year ago, some in the mortgage industry claimed that the number of coming foreclosures would be too small to have a significant impact on the overall economy.[3] No one makes that claim today. As foreclosures reach an all-time high and are projected to grow higher,[4] the "worst case is not a recession but a housing depression."[5] Projections by Fitch Ratings indicate that 43 percent of recent subprime loans will be lost to foreclosure,[6] and at least two million American families are expected to lose their homes to foreclosures initiated over the next two years.[7] What's more, industry projections forecast that by 2012, 1 in 8 mortgages – that's all mortgages, not just subprime mortgages – will fail.[8] Robert Schiller recently noted that the meltdown and resulting crisis has erased any gains in the homeownership rate made since 2001, and the rate stands to fall further yet.[9]

The negative effects of foreclosures are not confined to the families who lose their homes. Forty million of their neighbors – those who are paying their mortgages on time – will see their property values decline as a result by over $350 billion.[10] Other ripple effects include a reduced tax base, increased crime, further downward pressure on housing prices, and loss of jobs in the industry. According to the IMF, direct economic losses stemming from this crisis will likely top $500 billion, and consequential costs will total close to a trillion dollars.[11]

Sadly, many of the families losing their homes to foreclosure today might not have found themselves in this position if they had been given the type of loan that they actually qualified for. Last December, the *Wall Street Journal* found that of the subprime loans originated in 2006 that were packaged into securities and sold to investors, 61 percent "went to people with credit scores high enough to often qualify for conventional [i.e., prime] loans with far better terms."[12] Even those borrowers who did not qualify for prime loans could have received sustainable, thirty-year, fixed-rate loans for – at most – 50 to 80 basis points above the "teaser rate" on the unsustainable exploding ARM loans they were given.[13]

Wall Street's appetite for risky loans incentivized mortgage brokers and lenders to aggressively market these highly risky ARM loans instead of the sustainable loans for which borrowers qualified. As former Federal Reserve Chair Alan Greenspan told Newsweek:

> The big demand was not so much on the part of the borrowers as it was on the part of the suppliers who were giving loans which really

most people couldn't afford. We created something which was unsustainable. And it eventually broke. If it weren't for securitization, the subprime loan market would have been very significantly less than it is in size.[14]

Market participants readily admit that they were motivated by the increased profits offered by Wall Street in return for risky loans. After filing for bankruptcy, the CEO of one mortgage lender explained it this way to the New York Times, "The market is paying me to do a no-income-verification loan more than it is paying me to do the full documentation loans," he said. "What would you do?"[15] Even the chief economist of the Mortgage Bankers Association, when asked why lenders made so many loans that they knew were unsustainable, replied, "Because investors continued to buy the loans."[16]

Currently, 30 percent of families holding recent subprime mortgages owe more on their mortgage than their home is worth.[17] These families are at an increased risk of foreclosure because their negative equity (being "underwater") precludes the homeowner from selling, refinancing or getting a home equity loan or using any other mechanism for weathering short-term financial difficulty.[18] Regulators like the Chair of the Federal Reserve Board and other economists are increasingly cautioning that loan balances must be reduced to avoid unnecessary foreclosures that will further damage the economy.[19] Unnecessary foreclosures are those that could be avoided with an economically rational, sustainable loan modification that yields the creditor or investor pool at least as much as would be recovered in foreclosure.

II. Voluntary Loan Modifications Have Proven Insufficient to Prevent the Foreclosure Crisis From Continuing to Escalate

To date, Congress and the regulatory agencies have responded to this crisis largely by encouraging voluntary efforts by servicers to reduce the number of foreclosures. Yet despite the loss mitigation encouragement by HOPE NOW, the federal banking agencies, and state agencies, voluntary efforts by lenders, servicers and investors have failed to stem the tide of foreclosures. Seriously delinquent loans are at a record high for both prime and subprime loans.[20] The number of families in danger of losing their homes continues to be near record highs: in May, an estimated 1,977,000 loans were 60 days or more delinquent or had entered foreclosure, the second highest number since the program began reporting data last July. This is an astonishing 43 percent increase since July of last year.[21]

There is an emerging consensus that half-measures in the private sector are not working. FDIC Chairman Sheila Bair recently said that the current economic situation calls for a stronger government response, since voluntary loan modifications are not sufficient.[22] The necessity of government action also is gaining recognition among Wall Street leaders. In April, a senior economic advisor at UBS Investment Bank stated that, "when markets fail, lenders and borrowers need some sort of regulatory and legislative framework within which to manage problems, rather than be forced to act in the chaos of the moment."[23] Moreover, as former Federal Reserve Board Vice Chairman Alan Blinder recently noted, the fact that most of the mortgages at issue have been securitized and sold to investors across the globe "bolsters the case for government intervention rather than undermining it. After all, how do you renegotiate terms of a mortgage when the borrower and the lender don't even know each other's names?"[24]

While the HOPE NOW initiative claims to be making significant progress, its most recent data report reveals that the current crisis in the housing market dwarfs the servicing industry's response. According to their most recent report, almost four times as many families lost their home or are in the process of losing their home as received loan modifications from servicers.[25] The State Foreclosure Prevention Working Group, made up of state Attorneys General and Banking Commissioners, found that seven out of ten seriously delinquent borrowers are *still* not on track for any loss mitigation outcome that could lead to preventing a foreclosure.[26]

There are a number of reasons for this lack of loss mitigation activity. One reason is that the way servicers are compensated by lenders creates a bias for moving forward with foreclosure rather than engaging in foreclosure prevention. As reported in *Inside B&C Lending*, "Servicers are generally dis-incented to do loan modifications because they don't get paid for them but they do get paid for foreclosures." In fact, "it costs servicers between $750 and $1,000 to complete a loan modification."[27] Even when a loan modification would better serve investors and homeowners, some loan servicers have an economic incentive to proceed as quickly as possible to foreclosure.

But even those servicers who want to engage in effective loss mitigation face significant obstacles. One such obstacle is the fear of investor lawsuits, because modifying loans typically affects various tranches of securities differently. Another obstacle is the existence of junior liens on many homes. When there is a second mortgage, the holder of the first mortgage has no incentive to provide modifications that would free up borrower resources to make payments on the second mortgage. At the same time, the holder of the second mortgage has no incentive to support an effective modification, which would likely cause it to face a 100 percent loss; rather, the holder of the second is better off waiting to see if a homeowner can make a few payments before foreclosure. A third to a half of the homes purchased in 2006 with subprime mortgages have second mortgages as well.[28]

It is also important to note the gap between rhetoric and reality about how easy it is to get a loan modification.[29] Servicers coming before Congress often excuse the paucity of loan modifications by claiming that their efforts to modify loans are stymied by homeowners' refusal to respond to servicers' calls and letters. While this no doubt happens in some cases, the bigger problem by far is the reverse. We repeatedly hear from homeowners and housing counselors that the numerous homeowners who actively reach out to their servicers face the same problem: despite repeated calls to the servicer and many hours of effort, they cannot get anyone on the phone with the authority or ability to help. Many professional housing counselors are demoralized by the servicers' practice of incessantly bouncing the caller around from one "on hold" line to another, such that desperate homeowners never reach a live person or one with decision-making authority.

III. When Modifications and Other Workouts Are Made, They Are Frequently Temporary or Unsustainable, Leading to Re-Default and Placing Homeowners in an Even Worse Economic Position Than When They Started

More than a year ago, leading lenders and servicers publicly and unanimously endorsed a set of principles announced at the Homeownership Preservation Summit hosted by Senate Banking Committee Chairman Christopher Dodd, which called upon servicers to modify loans to "ensure that the loan is sustainable for the life of the loan, rather than, for example, deferring the reset period."[30]

Unfortunately, many of the modifications now being made have not adhered to this pledge. To date, neither HOPE NOW nor the Mortgage Bankers Association has been willing to disclose what proportion of the loan modifications entail reductions of principal or long-term reductions of interest rates, what proportion simply entail the capitalization of arrearages or short-term adjustments, and what proportion require the payment of fines and fees as a precondition to getting any modification at all. However, it is clear that most loan modifications or workouts have not fundamentally changed the unsustainable terms of the mortgage by reducing the principal or lowering the interest rate, but instead just add fees and interest to the loan balance and amortize them into the loan, add them to the end of the loan term, or provide a temporary forbearance.

Reduction in interest rates is a key way to provide relief for homeowners whose interest rates jumped significantly – far above market rates – as a result of rate resets. Modification of principal is particularly important for the approximately 30 percent of recent subprime loans whose owners now owe more than the house is worth by reducing principal. In calling for more loan modifications that reduce principal, Chairman Bernanke recently noted that such loan modifications involving have been "quite rare."[31] The State Foreclosure Prevention Working Group agrees.[32]

Unsurprisingly, given the minimal relief these "modifications" frequently provide, a report just released by Moody's has found a high number of re-defaults among the modified loans. Of the servicing companies surveyed by Moody's (accounting for roughly 50 percent of the total U.S. subprime servicing market), fully 42 percent of the loans modified in the first half of 2007 were at least 90 days delinquent as of March 31, 2008. The vice chair of Washington Mutual, who helps run HOPE NOW, admits that many of the homeowners who have sought their assistance "will not receive long-term relief and could ultimately face higher total costs."[33]

Another obstacle to sustainable modifications is the common servicer practice of charging exorbitant fines and "junk" fees. The reasonableness of most default fees is highly doubtful, with many of the "costs" unjustifiable and vastly exceeding the prevailing market rates in a community. Indeed, the fact that mortgage servicers systematically charge unreasonable fees is well-documented by courts.[34] A recent analysis of over 1,700 foreclosures across the country showed that questionable fees were added to borrowers' bills in almost half the loans.[35] Servicers often require that these fees be paid in full before the homeowner receives a loan modification or workout, thereby depleting whatever limited funds the financially strapped homeowner can scrape together and leaving no cushion for short-term cash-flow needs, which results in a much higher possibility of re-default.

Compounding the problem, servicers frequently misapply monthly mortgage payments first to the fees, rather than to the principal and interest owed. In this way, a homeowner who is timely repaying interest and principal nevertheless falls further behind on the mortgage and accumulates still more fees, continuing a vicious cycle.

IV. In Many Cases, Voluntary Loan Modifications or Workouts Are Further Disadvantaging Homeowners in Trouble Because the Servicer Forces Homeowners to Waive All Their Rights, Even Those Unrelated to the Workout

As a precondition to modifications and workout, lenders have been requiring shockingly broad waivers that strip homeowners of fundamental legal rights. These waivers threaten almost all of the borrowers' legal defenses to a fore-closure if the modification is unsustainable. Thus, if the modification fails, the lender can argue the borrower waived all of his federal (such as Truth in Lending or HOEPA) and state law defenses to foreclosure. The waivers also could be read to prevent claims questioning the reasonableness of fees charged.

Indeed, some releases go so far as to waive future claims that have not arisen, including seeking a free pass for future violations of such important federal laws as the Fair Credit Reporting Act, the Fair Housing Act, and Fair Debt Collection Practices Act, and some even ask homeowners to waive rights that are deemed unwaivable under state law. For example, here is one such waiver required by Countrywide:

> In consideration for Countrywide entering into this Agreement, you agree to release and discharge Countrywide, and all of its investors, employees, and related companies, from any and all claims you have or may have against them concerning the Loan. Although California law (specifically Section 1542 of the California Civil Code) provides that "[a] general release does not extend to claims which the creditor does not know or suspect to exist in his favor at the time of executing the release, which if known by him must have materially affected his

settlement with the debtor," you agree to waive that provision, or any similar provision under other state or federal laws, so that this release shall include all and any claim whatsoever of every nature concerning the Loan, regardless of whether you know about or suspect such claims including, but not limited to, claims arising under the Mortgage Disclosure Act, Electronic Fund Transfer Act, Truth in Lending Act, Real Estate Settlement Procedures Act, Fair Credit Reporting Act, Fair Housing Act, and Fair Debt Collection Practices Act. This release shall remain effective even if this Agreement terminates for any reason.[36]

Other institutions include similar clauses in their loan modification agreements.[37] One Option One agreement even forces the homeowner to "admit" that "the Arrearage is the Borrowers' full responsibility and was produced solely by the actions or inactions of the Borrowers."[38]

Given that these waivers are typically signed when a family's only other choice is to lose their home, and given that they are required not just for life-of-the-loan modifications but even for temporary forbearances, we believe they risk compounding the foreclosure crisis. A homeowner should not be coerced into giving up potential defenses if a foreclosure ultimately takes place. As noted below, H.R. 5679 would prohibit these waivers. However, in the absence of legislative action, we strongly recommend that servicers stop requiring such waivers as a condition of modification and that HOPE NOW require its participating servicers to refrain from requiring such waivers. The servicers also should publicly state they will not seek to enforce the waiver clauses in the modifications they have made to date.

V. H.R. 5679, the Foreclosure Prevention and Sound Mortgage Servicing Act of 2008 Will Help Prevent Foreclosures, Improve Servicing Practices, and Enhance Data Collection

Earlier this year, Representative Maxine Waters introduced H.R. 5679, the Foreclosure Prevention and Sound Mortgage Servicing Act of 2008. This bill requires loan servicers to engage in loss mitigation efforts prior to foreclosure, although it does not mandate any particular outcome or result.

Legislation establishing minimal servicing standards is needed because loan servicing is not an industry subject to typical economic incentives. As Tara Twomey of the National Consumer Law Center notes, homeowners "cannot choose the servicer that handles their loan and cannot change servicers if they are dissatisfied."[39] Instead, servicers are driven by the desire to maximize their own profits and to maximize returns to the investors who now stand in the shoes of the original lender.[40]

By requiring loan servicers to engage in loss mitigation prior to foreclosure, this legislation will assist homeowners, lenders, investors, and communities. The bill prioritizes continued homeownership as the highest goal of servicers. It requires that homeowners be able to reach a live person with decision-making authority, and it prohibits the coercive waivers described in Section IV above.

Perhaps most important, the legislation requires that any agreement reached through loss mitigation be affordable by the homeowner. We think careful consideration of the borrower's income as well as any expenses, including debt and residual income left over for other living expenses, is critical in determining the affordability of any solution intended to keep homeowners in their home. . . .

VI. H.R. 6076, the Home Retention and Economic Stabilization Act, Will Provide a Necessary Timeout for Overburdened Servicers and Homeowners with Unsustainable Loans

Given the extensive nature of the foreclosure crisis and the fact that servicers have been unable to reduce foreclosures sufficiently, more time is needed to develop and implement strategies to keep homeowners in their homes. H.R. 6076, the Home Retention and Economic Stabilization Act, is a temporary deferment plan that provides a much-needed "timeout" that will enable lenders and servicers to increase their capacities to meet current need, for credit markets to stabilize, and for legislative solutions, such as the FHA refinancing program under consideration in Congress, to take effect. . . .

VII. Court-Supervised Loan Modifications Are a Necessary Complement to Any Voluntary Efforts

Even if all of the legislation and other suggestions described above are enacted, a significant proportion of troubled homeowners will ultimately face foreclosure because the loan servicer cannot modify the loan due to a conflict between multiple lienholders or other constraints. In those cases, the failure to modify will be to the clear detriment of investors as a whole. It is critical, as a last alternative to foreclosure, to permit a bankruptcy court to adjust the mortgage if the borrower can afford a market rate loan that will be preferable to foreclosure for the creditor or investor pool and the homeowner alike.

Currently, bankruptcy courts can modify any type of loan, including mortgages on yachts and vacation homes, with the exception of one type: primary residences. Removing this exclusion would help homeowners (not speculators) who are committed to staying in their homes, without bailing out investors and without costing taxpayers a dime. The Emergency Home Ownership and Mortgage Equity Protection Act (H.R. 3609) provides a narrow, time-limited mechanism for enabling court-supervised loan modifications to break the deadlock that is forcing families who can afford a market rate loan into foreclosure.[41] The bill has been marked up in both Chambers, and is an important part of any effective solution to the foreclosure crisis.

We believe that the court-supervised loan modifications bill is a necessary complement to the Foreclosure Prevention and Sound Mortgage Servicing Act because it provides an important backstop for families who cannot get a sustainable loan modification due to junior liens or for whatever other reason. Moreover, as loans get modified through the bankruptcy process, these modifications will effectively create a "template" for modification that will ease the process of loss mitigation for servicers, as all parties involved will have a better idea of how the courts would handle a particular situation.[42] . . .

Conclusion

The foreclosure crisis is far from over. Already we have seen the tremendous costs imposed by this crisis. Yet it is not too late to take action to prevent many more foreclosures and a much higher cost. By moving homeowners from abusive loans into sustainable ones, we can keep families in their homes, ensure a continued stream of income to investors, and prevent the neighborhood and societal costs of mass foreclosures. . . .

Notes

1. *See Moody's Economy.com: Hearing before House Subcommittee on Commercial and Administrative Law* (January 28, 2008), (written testimony of Mark Zandi) . . . *See also* Center for Responsible Lending, *Subprime Spillover*, (Rev. Jan. 18, 2008) . . . [hereinafter Subprime Spillover].

2. Statement of Chairman Ben S. Bernanke, Federal Reserve Board, commenting on new FRB regulatory amendments on mortgage lending (July 14, 2008) at . . .

3. *See, e.g.*, Statement of John M. Robbins, CMB, Chairman, Mortgage Bankers Association at the National Press Club's Newsmakers Lunch – Washington, DC (May 22, 2007) (Speaking of predicted foreclosures, Mr. Robbins stated: "As we can clearly see, this is not a macro-economic event. No seismic financial occurrence is about to overwhelm the U.S. economy."); Julia A. Seymour, *Subprime Reporting, Networks blame lenders, not borrowers for foreclosure 'epidemic,'* Business & Media Institute, Mar. 28, 2007 ("[T]here are experts who say the subprime 'meltdown' is not the catastrophe reporters and legislators are making it out to be. 'We don't believe it will spill over into the prime market or the U.S. economy,' said [Laura] Armstrong [Vice President, Public Affairs] of the Mortgage Bankers Association.").

4. Renae Merle, *Home Foreclosures Hit Record High*, Washington Post, March 6, 2008.

5. David M. Herszenhorn and Vikas Bajaj, *Tricky Task of Offering Aid to Homeowners*, The New York Times, Apr. 6, 2008 (quoting Susan M. Wachter, a real estate finance professor at the Wharton School of the University of Pennsylvania. According to Professor Wachter, "In the market that we have in front of us, prices decline and supply increases, driving prices down further.").

6. Fitch Ratings estimates total losses of 25.8 percent of original balance in Q4 2006 loans placed in MBS they rated, and that loss severity will be at 60 percent, which means that 43 percent of the loans are projected to be lost

to foreclosure (25.8/60); lack of home price appreciation said to increase defaults. Glenn Costello, Update on U.S. RMBS: Performance, Expectations, Criteria, Fitch Ratings, at 17-18 (not dated, distributed week of February 25, 2008). According to Michael Bykhovsky, president of Applied Analytics, an estimated 40 percent of outstanding subprime mortgage loans could go into default over the next three years; the dire outlook due to declining home values (press briefing at the Mortgage Bankers Association's National Mortgage Servicing Conference, February 27, 2008).

7. *See Moody's Economy.com Hearing before House Subcommittee on Commercial and Administrative Law* (January 28, 2008) (written testimony of Mark Zandi) . . .

8. Rod Dubitsky et al., *Foreclosure Trends – A Sobering Reality*, Credit Suisse, Fixed Income Research, Apr. 28, 2008.

9. Robert J. Schiller, *The Scars of Losing a Home*, New York Times, May 18, 2008 (noting that the homeownership rate has fallen from 69.1 percent in 2005 to 67.8 percent in the first quarter of 2008, nearly the 67.5 percent rate at the beginning of 2001).

10. See Center for Responsible Lending, *The Impact of Court-Supervised Modifications on Subprime Foreclosures*, (Feb. 25, 2008) . . . for CRL's methodology for computing spillover, *see Subprime Spillover, supra* note 1 (Rev. Jan. 18, 2008) . . .

11. Christopher Swann, *IMF Says Financial Losses May Swell to $945 Billion*, April 8, 2008 . . .

12. Rick Brooks and Ruth Simon, Subprime Debacle Traps Even Very Credit-Worthy As Housing Boomed, Industry Pushed Loans to a Broader Market, The Wall Street Journal at A1 (Dec. 3, 2007).

13. Letter from CFAL to Ben S. Bernanke, Sheila C. Bair, John C. Dugan, John M. Reich, JoAnn Johnson, and Neil Milner (January 25, 2007) at 3.

14. Jon Meacham and Daniel Gross, *The Oracle Reveals All*, NEWSWEEK, Sept. 24, 2007, at 32, 33.

15. Vikas Bajaj and Christine Haughney, *Tremors At the Door – More People with Weak Credit Are Defaulting on Mortgages*, The New York Times, Jan. 26, 2007, at C1, C4.

16. Les Christie, *Subprime Loans Defaulting Even Before Resets*, CNNMoney.com, February 20, 2008 . . .

17. Edmund Andrews, *Relief for Homeowners Is Given to a Relative Few*, New York Times, March 4, 2008 (loans originated in 2005 and 2006).

18. Kristopher Gerardi, Adam Hale Shapiro & Paul S. Willen, *Subprime Outcomes: Risky Mortgages, Homeownership Experiences, and Foreclosures*, 3-4 (Federal Reserve Bank of Boston, Working Paper No 07-15, Dec. 3, 2007) (this otherwise good article misses the fact that certain loans themselves can create the cash flow shortfall that causes underwater loans to fail, when they are structured with initial low payments that are scheduled to rise, such as subprime 2/28 hybrid ARMs, and that certain loan terms have been statistically demonstrated to increase foreclosures, such as prepayment penalties).

19. Federal Reserve Chairman Ben Bernanke recently said, "When the mortgage is 'underwater,' a reduction in [loan] principal may increase the

expected payoff by reducing the risk of default and foreclosure." "Preventable foreclosures" could be reduced, he said, by enabling loan servicers to "accept a principal writedown by an amount at least sufficient to allow the borrower to refinance into a new loan from another source." This would "remove the downside risk to investors of additional writedowns or a re-default." See Chair Ben S. Bernanke, "Reducing Preventable Mortgage Foreclosures" (March 4, 2008) . . . ; see also, Edmund L. Andrews, Fed Chief Urges Breaks for Some Home Borrowers, The New York Times, Mar. 4, 2008; John Brinsley, Bernanke Call for Mortgage Forgiveness Puts Pressure on Paulson, Bloomberg.com, Mar. 5, 2008; Phil Izzo, Housing Market Has Further to Fall, The Wall Street Journal, Mar. 13, 2008 ("Last week, Federal Reserve Chairman Ben Bernanke suggested that lenders could aid struggling homeowners by reducing their principal—the sum of money they borrowed—to lessen the likelihood of foreclosure. Some 71 percent of respondents [i.e., economists surveyed by the NYT] agreed with the suggestion.").

20. Press Release, Center for Responsible Lending, Statement on HOPE NOW, (July 2, 2008) . . .

21. *Id.*

22. FDIC Chairwoman Sheila Bair (stating "We've got a real problem. And I do think we need to have more activist approaches. And I think it will be something we need to be honest with the American public about. We do need more intervention. It probably will cost some money."), Real Time Economics, The Wall St. Journal (April 7, 2008) . . .

23. George Magnus, *Large-scale action is needed to tackle the credit crisis*, Financial Times, Apr. 8, 2008.

24. Alan S. Blinder, *From the New Deal, a Way Out of a Mess*, The New York Times, Feb. 24, 2008.

25. Furthermore, the data provided by HOPE NOW understates the number of loans in foreclosure, as it only includes those homes that entered foreclosure and those that completed foreclosure during the month, not the total number currently in the foreclosure process. In fact, 1.1 million families were in foreclosure at the end of March.

26. Conference of State Bank Supervisors, *Analysis of Subprime Servicing Performance, Data Report No. 2*, (April 2008), at 1 . . . [hereinafter *Analysis of Subprime Servicing*].

27. Center for Responsible Lending, *Inside Mortgage Finance Reprints, Subprime Debt Outstanding Falls, Servicers Pushed on Loan Mods* (Nov. 16, 2007) . . . (quoting Karen Weaver, a managing director and global head of securitization research at Deutsche Bank Securities).

28. Credit Suisse Report, *Mortgage Liquidity du Jour: Underestimated No More* (March 12, 2007) at 5.

29. *See generally*, Gretchen Morgenson, *Silence of the Lender: Is Anyone Listening?* New York Times, July 13, 2008.

30. Homeownership Preservation Summit Statement of Principles (May 2, 2007) . . . (The Principles were announced by Senator Dodd, and endorsed by the Mortgage Bankers Association, CitiGroup, Chase, Litton, HSBC, Countrywide, Wells, AFSA, Option One, Freddie Mac, and Fannie Mae).

31. Statement of Federal Reserve Chairman Ben Bernanke on March 4, 2008, reprinted by Bloomberg.com and . . . ("Bernanke statement").

32. *Analysis of Subprime Servicing, supra* note 26, at 9 (the majority of servicers are not reporting significant levels of modifications that reduce principal alone, although principal reductions may be combined with other modifications and therefore may not evidenced in our reporting).

33. David Cho and Renae Merle, *Merits of New Mortgage Aid Are Debate – Critics Say Treasury Plan Won't Bring Long-Term Relief,* The Washington Post, Mar. 4, 2008 (citing remarks of Bill Longbrake, senior policy adviser for the Financial Services Roundtable and vice chair of Washington Mutual).

34. Court have repeatedly found servicers' inspection fees, broker price opinions, forced place insurance, and legal fees either unreasonable or unjustifiable. See e.g., *In re Stewart,* 2008 WL 2676961, No. 07-11113 (Bankr. E.D. La. July 9, 2008) (Wells Fargo charging unnecessary inspection fees, unnecessary broker price opinions, and requiring excessively priced forced-place insurance); *In re Payne,* 387 B.R. 614, 628 (Bankr. D. Kan. 2008) (Everhome charging unjustified inspection fees, late fees, and foreclosure costs); *In re Jones,* 366 B.R. 584, 597-98 (Bankr. E.D. La. 2007) (Wells Fargo charging unreasonable inspection fees, unreasonable attorney's fees).

35. Gretchen Morgenson & Jonathan D. Glater, *Foreclosure Machine Thrives on Woes,* The New York Times, Mar. 30, 2008 (citing Katherine Porter, Misbehavior and Mistake in Bankruptcy Mortgage Claims, University of Iowa College of Law Legal Studies Research Paper Series, *Misbehavior and Mistake in Bankruptcy Mortgage Claims,* (Nov. 7, 2007) . . .

36. Countrywide, Repayment Plan Agreement (February 5, 2007) (on file with Center for Responsible Lending).

37. *Id*; Countrywide, Loan Modification Agreement (June 17, 2008); Homecomings Financial, Foreclosure Repayment Agreement, July 18, 2007; Ocwen Loan Servicing LLC, Forbearance Agreement (May 16, 2008); Ocwen Loan Servicing LLC, Proposed Modification Agreement (June 26, 2008); Option One Mortgage Corporate, Forbearance Agreement (August 24, 2007); NovaStar, Repayment Plan Agreement, (January 2008) (on file with Center for Responsible Lending).
    Ocwen: By executing this modification, you forever irrevocably waive and relinquish any claims, action or causes of action, statute of limitation or other defense, counterclaims or setoffs of any kind which exist as of the date of this modification, whether known or unknown, which you may now or hereafter assert in connection with the making, closing, administration, collection or the enforcement by Ocwen of the loan documents, this modification or any other related agreements.
    By executing this modification, you irrevocably waive all right to a trial by jury in any action, proceeding or counterclaim arising out of or relating to this modification and any related agreement or documents or transactions contemplated in this modification. Ocwen Loan Servicing LLC, Proposed Modification Agreement, June 26, 2008 (on file with Center for Responsible Lending). Customer expressly relinquishes and waives any rights, claims, and defenses Customer may have under any of the Code of Civil Procedure Sections or under the Loan with regard to any whole or partial payment, whether current, pass or future. Homecomings Financial,

Foreclosure Repayment Agreement, July 18, 2007 (on file with Center for Responsible Lending).

38. Option One Mortgage Corporate, Forbearance Agreement (August 24, 2007). (on file with Center for Responsible Lending).

39. *Hearing before the U.S. House of Representatives Subcommittee on Housing and Community Opportunity*, 8 (April 16, 2007) (testimony of Tara Twomey, National Consumer Law Center).

40. *Id.* at 7 (Cutting costs is one reason for heavy reliance on often frustrating voicemail and touch tone menu options, as well as for the lack of adequate staff to handle requests for negotiation or information).

41. CRL Issue Brief, *Solution to Housing Crisis Requires Adjusting Loans to Fair Market Value through Court-Supervised Modifications*, (Apr. 1, 2008), . . .

42. *Straightening Out the Mortgage Mess: How Can WE Protect Homeownership and Provide Relief to Consumers in Financial Distress: Hearing before the House Judiciary Committee, Subcommittee on Commercial and Administrative Law* 5 (Oct. 30, 2007) (Testimony of Richard Levin, Partner, Cravath, Swaine & Moore LLP, on behalf of the National Bankruptcy Conference) . . .

POSTSCRIPT

Is Loan Mitigation the Answer to the Housing Foreclosure Problem?

Mortgage Bankers Association official David G. Kittle begins his testimony by explaining why everyone, including lenders, loses with a home mortgage foreclosure. He refers to studies that put the losses of a foreclosure at as much as $50,000 per foreclosure or as much as 30 to 60 percent of the outstanding loan balances. He then reviews the "innovative techniques" mortgage companies have developed to prevent foreclosures. These include (i) forbearance plans, (ii) repayment plans, (iii) loan modifications, (iv) partial and advance claims, (v) refinances, and (vi) short sales and deeds in lieu of foreclosure. He also reviews what he calls "other beneficial programs." These include (i) HOPE Hotline, (ii) streamlined modifications, (iii) foreclosure prevention workshops, (iv) use of third parties, (v) innovations with counselors, (vi) servicer best practices, and (vii) Web sites. While he admits that problems remain, he believes that the programs he has described "have proven successful for the homeowner, the servicer and the investor."

Center for Responsible Lending policy counsel Julia Gordon begins her testimony by asserting that government action is required to arrest the spiraling foreclosure problem. She cites one study that estimates the direct economic losses from foreclosures at more than $500 billion and "consequential costs" at close to a trillion dollars. She then proceeds to explain why voluntary loan modifications are inadequate. One reason involves servicer incentives; that is, organizations that service mortgages are paid for foreclosures but not for modifications. In addition the modifications that are arranged are typically either temporary or unsustainable. Because of these problems, Gordon endorses H.R 6076, the Home Retention and Economic Stabilization Act. This proposed government action would require loan servicers to engage in loss mitigation prior to foreclosure. Moreover, the legislation would require that "any agreement reached through loss mitigation be affordable to the homeowner."

Federal Reserve Chairman Ben S. Bernanke surveys the issue in a recent speech "Housing, Mortgage Markets, and Foreclosures" available at http://www .federalreserve.gov/newsevents/speech/bernanke20081204a.htm. Additional material on loan mitigation and the housing foreclosure problem can be found in a number of places. First, there is the complete hearings held by the House Committee on Financial Services on July 25, 2008. Besides Kittle and Gordon, six other individuals offered their views on the issue. These individuals included, among others, representatives from the American Bankers Association, Bank of America, Wells Fargo Home Mortgage, the HOPE NOW Alliance, and the National Council of La Raza. These hearings can be found at http://www.house .gov/apps/list/hearing/financialsvcs_dem/hr072508.shtml. The House Committee on

Financial Services held additional hearings on the issue on September 17, 2008 and on November 12, 2008. The September 17th hearings included, among others, the testimony of the chair of the Federal Deposit Insurance Corporation Sheila Bair, as well as representatives of the Federal Reserve, the U.S. Department of the Treasury, The U.S. Department of Housing and Urban Affairs, and several mortgage lending institutions. They can be found at http://www.house.gov/apps/list/hearing/financialsvcs_dem/hr091708.shtml. The November 12th hearings focused on privative sector cooperation and included representatives from the Managed Funds Association, the American Securitization Forum, Bank of America, and JPMorgan Chase. These hearings can be found at http://www.house.gov/apps/list/hearing/financialsvcs_dem/hr111208.shtml.

ISSUE 15

Will Biofuels Like Ethanol Reduce U.S. Dependence on Foreign Oil?

YES: Bob Dinneen, from "Should Congress Reassess the Renewable Fuel Standard in the Energy and Independence Security Act? (Pro)," *Congressional Digest* (June 2008)

NO: Charles T. Drevna, from "Should Congress Reassess the Renewable Fuel Standard in the Energy and Independence Security Act? (Con)," *Congressional Digest* (June 2008)

ISSUE SUMMARY

YES: Bob Dinneen, president and chief executive officer of the Renewable Fuels Association, states that America's ethanol producers are providing significant economic, environmental, and energy security benefits today. Expansion of the domestic biofuels industry will reduce America's dependence on imported oil.

NO: Charles T. Drevna, president of the National Petrochemical and Refiners Association (NPRA), argues that the biofuels mandate has increased food prices and contributed to food shortages around the world and stressed the ethanol transportation infrastructure.

The term "biofuels" usually refers to ethanol and biodiesel. Biofuels are liquid fuels made from biomass, that is, organic nonfossil material of biological origin, and are largely used for transportation. Ethanol can be made from agricultural crops such as corn, barley, and sugarcane. Most biodiesel in the United States is currently produced from soybean oil (and recently also from waste animal fats or recycled grease from restaurants). The commercial viability of cellulosic ethanol, considered an "advanced" biofuel (made from woody biomass such as bark or switchgrass, which is a native prairie grass), has not yet been demonstrated. One ethanol producer claims there are significant advantages to integrating cellulosic ethanol plants with corn ethanol plants. It selected corn cobs as the first feedstock for production of cellulosic ethanol.

The use of ethanol increased after the Energy Policy Act of 2005 set the Renewable Fuels Standard mandating that transportation fuels sold in the

United States contain a minimum volume of renewable fuels, the level of which will increase each year until 2022. In December 2007, the Energy Independence and Security Act (EISA) of 2007 increased the mandatory level to a total of 36 billion gallons by 2022, including 16 billion gallons of cellulosic biofuels.

According to the Energy Information Administration (EIA), today a little more than half of the gasoline sold in the United States has some amount of ethanol blended into it. As for magnitudes, the EIA states that in 2007 the United States consumed 6.8 billion gallons of ethanol and 491 million gallons of biodiesel, compared to 139 billion gallons and 39 billion gallons of motor gasoline and diesel. It predicts ethanol usage will increase to 24 billion gallons in 2030 (about 16 percent of total gasoline consumption by volume) and expects 36 percent of corn production to be used for ethanol (up from 31 percent likely in 2008).

On May 6, 2008, the Subcommittee on Energy and Air Quality of the House Energy and Commerce Committee held hearings to discuss issues, implementation, and opportunities of the newly enacted Renewable Fuels Standard (RFS). Those testifying included (in addition to firms involved in ethanol and cellulosic ethanol production and project development), for example, representatives of the National Corn Growers Association, the Grocery Manufacturer's Association, OXFAM America, the EPA, and the Natural Resources Defense Council (NRDC). As might be expected, they either welcomed the policy for reducing both America's dependence on foreign oil and global warming by lowering carbon dioxide emissions, and promoting prosperity of domestic (and foreign) farmers, or vilified it for its contribution to higher food prices worldwide with little impact on energy imports, and arguably negative effects on the environment. In taking sides, both groups presented data from a number of sources to support their position and also offered data contradicting the other view. Bob Dinneen and Charles T. Drevna are two who take opposite sides. Their views are presented in the following selections. In his testimony, Bob Dinneen of the Renewable Fuels Association claims the ethanol industry is revitalizing rural America, is benefiting the economy and the environment, and will displace imported crude oil. Charles T. Drevna, president of the National Petrochemical and Refiners Association, contends that the RFS has negative impacts on energy markets, consumers, and the American economy.

In addition to the mandates, the government also supports the ethanol (and renewable fuels) industry through tax and other incentives. A division of the Emergency Economic Stabilization Act of 2008, for example, contains energy production incentives, including renewable energy incentives and carbon mitigation and coal provisions, and transportation and domestic fuel security provisions such as inclusion of cellulosic biofuel in bonus depreciation for biomass ethanol plant property and credits for biodiesel and renewable diesel.

YES

Bob Dinneen

Should Congress Reassess the Renewable Fuel Standard in the Energy and Independence Security Act? (Pro)

The RFS [renewable fuel standard] was first established by the Energy Policy Act of 2005. The passage of this bill was an important step towards this country's energy independence, as well as providing economic and environmental benefits. By expanding the RFS, the Energy Independence and Security Act of 2007 ("2007 Energy Act") capitalizes on the substantial benefits that renewable fuels offer to reduce foreign oil dependence and greenhouse gas emissions and to provide meaningful economic opportunity across this country.

Today's ethanol industry consists of 147 ethanol plants nationwide that have the capacity to turn more than 2 billion bushels of grain into 8.5 billion gallons of high-octane, clean-burning motor fuel, and more than 14 million metric tons of livestock and poultry feed.

There are currently 55 ethanol plants under construction and six plants undergoing expansions. It is a dynamic and growing industry that is revitalizing rural America, reducing emissions in our Nation's cities, and lowering our dependence on imported petroleum. America's domestic ethanol producers are providing significant economic, environmental, and energy security benefits today.

In an overall environment of slowing economic growth, the U.S. ethanol industry stands out in sharp contrast. The increase in economic activity resulting from ongoing production and construction of new ethanol capacity supported the creation of 238,541 jobs in all sectors of the economy during 2007. These include more than 46,000 additional jobs in America's manufacturing sector—American jobs making ethanol from grain produced by American farmers.

Ethanol is also helping to stem the tide of global warming, today. The use of low-carbon fuels like ethanol is reducing greenhouse gas emissions from the more than 200 million cars on American roads. The 9 billion gallons of ethanol we will produce in 2008 will reduce greenhouse gas emissions by more than 14 million tons, or the equivalent of taking 2.5 million vehicles off the road. These benefits will only increase as new technologies, new feedstocks, and new markets for renewable fuels are created.

From *Congressional Digest*, June 2008. Published by Pro & Con® Publishers, a division of Congressional Digest Corporation.

Promoting Investment in Cleaner Alternatives to Fossil Fuels

The RFS provides meaningful incentives for investment in the production and infrastructure for biofuels in the United States to reduce this country's use of fossil fuels. By expanding the RFS, requiring that 36 billion gallons of renewable fuel be used annually by 2022, the 2007 Energy Act represents a significant moment in history when America chose a new energy policy path. The path includes reducing this country's dependence on fossil fuels in favor of renewable fuels that are better for the environment. An analysis conducted for the RFA using the U.S. Department of Energy's (DOE) existing GREET [Greenhouse gases, Regulated Emissions, and Energy use in Transportation] model shows that increasing the use of ethanol and other renewable fuels to 36 billion gallons annually by 2022 could reduce greenhouse gas emissions by some 176 million metric tons, equal to removing the annual emissions of more than 27 million cars from the road.

Although some critics recently attempted to discount the benefits regarding greenhouse gas emission reduction that can be achieved through increased use of renewable fuels, the support for these claims is based on a questionable analysis of alleged international land use changes. Michael Wang with the Argonne National Laboratory and Zia Haq with the DOE, among others, have explained some of the many problems with this analysis, noting that they had found no indication that U.S. corn ethanol production has so far caused indirect land use changes in other countries.

While more work needs to be done to understand the varying factors that may play a role in international land use changes, "conclusions regarding the GHG [greenhouse gas] emissions effects of biofuels based on speculative, limited land use change modeling may misguide biofuel policy development." Moreover, ethanol production has significant benefits over fossil fuel use.

Domestic agricultural and ethanol production continues to develop very effective conservation measures that ensure that biofuels are being produced in the most efficient and sustainable way. The ethanol industry itself is moving toward cleaner energy use and is reducing its water consumption. The expanded RFS and the 2007 Energy Act include additional measures to promote conservation and provide protections for the environment.

In particular, the RFS will greatly enhance the climate change benefits attributable to today's renewable fuels industry by encouraging more sustainable technologies and reducing the carbon footprint of future energy production. The expanded program requires that 21 billion gallons out of the 36 billion gallons come from advanced biofuels. Advanced biofuels, such as cellulosic ethanol, must have more than 50 percent reduction in lifecycle greenhouse gas emissions over gasoline. As such, Congress has provided the necessary assurance for ethanol producers and investors that a market for their product will exist. As a result, the commercialization of these important next-generation technologies will develop far sooner than conventional wisdom suggests.

Promoting the U.S. Economy and Energy Independence

Expansion of the domestic biofuels industry will provide significant economic benefits in terms of a larger and more robust economy, increased income, new job creation in all sectors of the economy, and enhanced tax revenues at both the Federal and State levels. Increased biofuels production and use stimulated by the expanded RFS will also enhance America's energy security by displacing imported crude oil. Specifically, expansion of the U.S. biofuels industry will:

- Add more than $1.7 trillion (2008 dollars) to the U.S. economy between 2008 and 2022.
- Generate an additional $366 billion (2008 dollars) of household income for all Americans over the next 15 years.
- Support the creation of as many as 987,000 new jobs in all sectors of the economy by 2022.
- Generate $353 billion (2008 dollars) in new Federal tax receipts.
- Improve America's energy security by displacing 11.2 billion barrels of crude oil over the next 15 years and reduce the outflow of dollars to foreign oil producers by $1.1 trillion (2008 dollars).

Benefits to the Consumer

With the ever-increasing price of oil, ethanol is helping to give consumers some relief. Using ethanol in the U.S. transportation fuel market helps lower gasoline prices by expanding gasoline supplies and reducing the need for importing expensive, high-octane, petroleum-based gasoline components or more crude oil from unstable parts of the world.

Recently, ethanol has received harsh criticism for allegedly driving up the price of corn and contributing to a rise in food prices. However, the evidence does not support that conclusion. A host of reasons play a role in driving food prices higher, including, for example, record oil prices, soaring global demand for commodities from oil to grains, poor weather conditions, a collapsing dollar, and restrictive agricultural policies around the world.

In fact, energy prices are a large component of the retail food dollar. The U.S. Department of Agriculture's Economic Research Service estimates direct energy and transportation costs account for 7.5 percent of the overall average retail food dollar. "This suggests that for every 10 percent increase in energy costs, the retail food prices could increase by 0.75 percent if fully passed on to consumers." In fact, oil prices have twice the impact on rising consumer food prices than does the price of corn.

Ethanol production also provides highly valuable feed coproducts, keeping food production costs down. A modern dry-mill ethanol refinery produces approximately 2.8 gallons of ethanol and 17 points of distillers grains from one bushel of corn. The distillers grains are a protein-rich animal feed that can be supplemented by low-cost bulk foods like alfalfa, keeping the farmer's costs down.

Critics of the ethanol industry have also failed to recognize the advances that the agricultural and ethanol industries have made to meet demand in the most efficient and environmentally sensitive manner. Technological advances have enabled farmers to boost agricultural productivity to meet demands, including rising global demands with continuing increases in population around the world.

Need for Greater Investment in Renewable Fuel Infrastructure

As the demand for fuel ethanol grows, the infrastructure available to transport, store, and blend ethanol into gasoline has expanded as well. The U.S. ethanol industry has been working to expand a "virtual pipeline" through aggressive use of the rail system, barge, and truck traffic. As a result, we can move products quickly to those areas where it is needed. Many ethanol plants have the capability to load unit trains of ethanol for shipment to ethanol terminals in key markets.

Unit trains are quickly becoming the norm, not the exception, which was not the case just a few years ago. Railroad companies are working with our industry to develop infrastructure to meet future demand for ethanol. We are also working closely with terminal operators and refiners to identify ethanol storage facilities and install blending equipment. We will continue to grow the necessary infrastructure to make sure that in any market we need to ship ethanol, there is rail access at gasoline terminals, and that those terminals are able to take unit trains.

There are more than 230 million cars on American roads today that are capable of running on 10 percent ethanol-blended fuel, while 6 million vehicles are flexible fuel vehicles that are capable of using up to 85 percent ethanol (E85). America's automakers and the ethanol industry continue to work to develop the infrastructure and provide the vehicle fleet necessary to grow the E85 market.

Conclusion

The RFS is a testament to what we can do when we work together toward a shared vision of the future. By increasingly relying on domestically produced renewable fuels, including next-generation technologies such as cellulosic ethanol, we can begin the hard work necessary to mitigate the impact of global climate change, reduce our dependence on foreign oil, and leave a more stable and sustainable future for generations that follow.

Charles T. Drevna  **NO**

Should Congress Reassess the Renewable Fuel Standard in the Energy and Independence Security Act? (Con)

I am grateful for the opportunity to share our views on the significant, and unfortunately negative, impacts that the recently enacted renewable fuel standard increase is having on energy markets, consumers, and the American economy.

There is little doubt that alternative fuels will continue to be a significant component of our Nation's transportation fuel mix. However, as we have stated on many occasions, including last year before this Committee, NPRA opposes the mandated use of alternative fuels and supports the sensible and workable integration of alternative fuels into the marketplace based on market principles.

Energy policy based on mandates is not a recipe for success. There is no free market if every gallon of biofuels—including those that do not exist—is mandated. Mandates distort markets and result in stifled competition and innovation. Last year, 6.49 billion gallons of ethanol were produced domestically and 0.43 billion gallons of ethanol were imported. Biodiesel consumption was about 0.3 billion gallons. Therefore, total renewable fuels for transportation purposes in the United States in 2007 was about 7.2 billion gallons.

Ethanol is currently used in about two-thirds of U.S. gasoline supplies. And despite the misperceptions, our industry supports the use of renewables. In fact, we are currently the largest consumers of ethanol and will continue to rely on ethanol as a vital gasoline blend stock. However, we believe that allowing the market to operate is the best way to address consumer needs at reasonable prices.

Before Congress passed the Energy Independence and Security Act of 2007 (H.R. 6) and sent it to the President for his signature, the facts about ethanol mandates and the unintended consequences for both American consumers and the environment were fully disclosed. Unfortunately, these warnings were ignored.

From *Congressional Digest,* June 2008. Published by Pro & Con® Publishers, a division of Congressional Digest Corporation.

Recent studies and reports have confirmed that biofuels mandates have led to price increases for food. Grocers, restaurant owners, and cattlemen have noted how biofuels mandates have dramatically increased the price of corn, making feed for livestock and cattle more expensive. This situation translates directly into higher food prices for American consumers. A FarmEcon.com study noted:

> The ethanol subsidy program is now increasing the cost of food production through side effects on major crop prices and plantings. The cost increases are already starting to show up in the prices of meat, poultry, dairy, bread, cereals, and many other products made from grains and soybeans.

On April 25, USDA [U.S. Department of Agriculture] reported weekly average corn prices ranging from $5.29 to $5.59 per bushel, compared to $3.22 to $4.41 per bushel 12 months ago for Iowa, Nebraska, and South Dakota; this is a substantial one-year increase for these States, about 60 percent.

A June 2007 GAO [Government Accountability Office] report highlighted the higher costs associated with biofuels. Among several findings, the report noted:

> According to NREL (National Renewable Energy Laboratory), the overall cost of transporting ethanol from production plants to fueling stations is estimated to range from 13 cents per gallon to 18 cents per gallon, depending on the distance traveled and the mode of transportation. In contrast, the overall cost of transporting petroleum fuels from refineries to fueling stations is estimated on a nationwide basis to be about 3 to 5 cents per gallon.

The dramatic increase in the biofuels mandate under the new law continues to increase the strain on our already congested transportation infrastructure that could very likely drive the costs of shipping ethanol up even further. In addition to these costs being passed on to consumers, strained transportation avenues could create fuel supply problems.

The costs and strains of these transportation challenges are only some of the problems associated with dramatically increased mandates of renewable fuels. Ethanol-powered vehicles also have lower fuel efficiency (due to ethanol's lower energy content compared to regular gasoline), as well as limited availability and infrastructure. According to the Department of Energy's Office of Energy Efficiency and Renewable Energy, flex fuel vehicles (FFVs)—cars that can run on either gasoline or a mixture of 85 percent ethanol and 15 percent gasoline (known as E85)—get "about 20–30 percent fewer miles per gallon when fueled with E85." Given this situation, AAA [American Automobile Association] releases an "E85 MPG/BTU Adjusted Price" in its daily fuel gauge report. It has not been uncommon for this report to show an E85 adjusted price that exceeds the price of a gallon of gasoline by as much as 80 cents.

The limited number of FFVs is also a problem if significantly larger volumes of renewable fuels are to be forced into the market. The only vehicles that can operate on fuel blended with more than 10 percent ethanol (known as "E-10") are flex fuel vehicles. The Alliance of Automobile Manufacturers' website . . . notes there are currently 11 million alternative fuel vehicles on American roads—a small fraction of the 240 million plus vehicles Americans are driving today. The National Ethanol Vehicle Coalition estimates that about 6 million of these are FFVs.

In addition, over the next several years, automakers have indicated that while they intend to produce more FFVs, they will still be producing gasoline-only vehicles at a rate of about seven or eight to one in relation to FFV production. The new ethanol mandate will most likely require fuel blends in excess of E-10, possibly as early as 2010. However, in addition to existing legacy fleets (e.g., cars that have been purchased up to this point in time that run only on gasoline and won't be retired for several years), there will be a new class of vehicles that may be unable to operate on required fuel blends. This is particularly important given the fact that engine and fuel pump makers will not provide warranties for fuel-related equipment malfunctions if blends greater than E-10 are used with those products. I will address this in greater detail later in my testimony.

While many point to cellulosic ethanol as a potential solution to problems, that particular fuel poses its own set of challenges. Cellulosic ethanol technology is still very costly and is not commercially available—let alone produced at levels adequate to meet the new mandates in the new energy law. Early last year, the Energy Information Administration noted:

> Capital costs for a first-of-a-kind cellulosic ethanol plant with a capacity of 50 million gallons per year are estimated by one leading producer to be $375 million (2005 dollars), as compared with $67 million for a corn-based plant of similar size, and investment risk is high for a large-scale cellulosic ethanol production facility.

The report noted that given those costs, no cellulosic plant had been built or was in operation at that time (February 2007). At that same time last year, the Department of Energy announced it was allocating $385 million to help fund six cellulosic ethanol plants that would produce about 130 million gallons annually, but it is highly unlikely those plants will be producing at full capacity in time to meet the new law's 2010 mandate of 100 million gallons, and it will not produce enough for the 250 million gallon target for 2011.

The Energy Policy Act of 2005 included a cellulosic ethanol mandate of 250 million gallons starting in 2013. The Food and Agriculture Policy Research Institute (FAPRI), however, projects only about 213 million gallons of cellulosic may be produced in that year. This adds little support to the argument that a mandate will drive the technology and economics of producing a certain product.

As previously mentioned, the new energy law mandates 100 million gallons of cellulosic in 2010—only a year and a half from now. FAPRI's estimate on cellulosic production for that year is only 27 million gallons—27 percent of what is required in the law. That's a lot of ground to make up in a short time frame. Failure to meet these figures will prevent refiners from complying with the law's targeted volumes, leading not only to cost increases from unavoidable and onerous financial penalties, but potentially creating significant supply shortages.

The new energy law calls for a Renewable Fuels Standard [RFS] with not one but four different mandates that will equal 36 billion gallons by 2022. It requires that 9 billion gallons of renewable fuel be blended into the transportation fuel supply *this year* (a large increase from a total of 7.2 billion gallons in 2007), ratcheting up to 36 billion gallons in 2022. In addition, it contains three other subset mandates: an "advanced biofuel" requirement of 600 million gallons in 2009, scaling up to 21 billion gallons in 2022; a specific cellulosic biofuel mandate of 100 million gallons in 2010, ratcheting up to 16 billion gallons in 2022; and a biodiesel mandate of 500 million gallons in 2009, moving up to 1 billion gallons in 2012.

We understand that this is the law of the land and you have the commitment of the domestic refining industry that we will do our very best to comply. However, this mandate will have significant detrimental effects to our country and its consumers that extend beyond what could be accomplished through any sort of legislative change short of repeal.

There are serious questions about whether or not to continue a mandate for increasing amounts of corn ethanol and biodiesel in the midst of a global food crisis. The *Miami Herald* printed an editorial:

> Given the current global food crisis, decisions by the United States, Europe, and other countries to convert corn and other food crops into fuel are beginning to look like good intentions gone awry. The biofuels push is beginning to have harmful unintended consequences, contributing to shortages of basic foods in Haiti, Egypt, Italy, and countries in Africa and Southeastern Asia. The European Union is reconsidering its goal of using biofuels in 10 percent of its transportation fuels—and the U.S. Congress should do the same. . . . It can reverse its mandate to use food crops for fuel.

On April 25, Texas Governor [Rick] Perry [R] requested a waiver from EPA [Environmental Protection Agency] for a portion of the RFS. Governor Perry's "request is for a waiver of 50 percent of the mandate for the production of ethanol derived from grain." He cites "the unintended consequences of harming segments of our agricultural industry and contributing to higher food prices."

The governor of Connecticut has now likewise called for a waiver of the RFS. EPA is required by section 1501(a) of the Energy Policy Act of 2005 to approve or disapprove, after public notice and opportunity for comment, the State petition within 90 days after receipt. Rather than debating whether there is a large or small correlation between the current global food crisis and the renewable fuels mandate in the U.S., Congress should act quickly to repeal the renewable fuel mandate.

Conclusion

Congress should suspend the tariff on imported ethanol in order to maximize the supply of renewable fuels. The present enthusiasm for renewable fuels has resulted in several States and even municipalities adopting local mandates. Local mandates will impose additional strain on the ethanol distribution system and increase costs for shipping and storage. The existing Federal renewable fuels standard mandate, with its credit-trading provisions, contains a degree of freedom that allows the distribution system to operate at a low-cost optimum by avoiding infrastructure bottlenecks (such as lack of storage or rail capacity).

Mandating biodiesel usage in specific areas forces a distribution pattern that is less flexible, and therefore has less capability to minimize costs. Further, these mandates create boutique markets requiring special fuel formulations and transportation logistics, thereby balkanizing the national fuel market. If Congress wishes to allow for as diverse a supply of alternative fuels as possible, and to promote as much flexibility in the system as possible, State and local biofuels mandates should be preempted.

The new RFS creates several problems in the fuels marketplace—many of which may be insurmountable. Backlash from potential negative impacts of this law could ultimately end up threatening the availability of alternative fuels in the marketplace.

POSTSCRIPT

Will Biofuels Like Ethanol Reduce U.S. Dependence on Foreign Oil?

$\mathbf{A}$ccording to the Energy Information Administration (EIA), the United States produces 10 percent of the world's petroleum and consumes 24 percent at the rate of 20.7 million barrels per day. In 2007, the United States imported about 58 percent of the petroleum it consumed. About half of U.S. oil imports are from the Western Hemisphere; five countries (Canada, Saudi Arabia, Mexico, Venezuela, and Nigeria) account for 71 percent of U.S. net imports of crude oil. Estimates of our dependence on foreign oil (net imports as a percentage of consumption) range from 56 percent to over 70 percent. The measure of U.S. dependence used by EIA rose from 46.4 percent in the 1990s to 60.3 percent in 2005 and fell to 56.4 percent in the first half of 2008 – 1.2 percent below the level of import dependence during the same period of 2007 – as a result of reduced U.S. oil consumption and higher exports. EIA projects U.S. petroleum import dependence will fall from nearly 60 percent in 2006 to 54 percent by 2030. Its Web site http://tonto.eia.doe.gov/ask/faq.asp contains a variety of data, including measures of oil import dependence, world reserves, and U.S. imports, exports, production, and consumption of oil.

The extent to which biofuels like ethanol are the answer to our dependence on foreign oil is the subject of much debate as the articles in this selection demonstrate. For one thing, all biofuels are not created equal. For another, agreement on the environmental impact of biofuels is far from unanimous. Moreover, the role of biofuels in the global food crisis has generated an outcry: see for example, the United Nations, World Bank, and IMF Web sites.

Testimony on "The Renewable Fuels Standard: Issues, Implementation, and Opportunities," before the Subcommittee on Energy and Air Quality, available at http://energycommerce.house.gov/index.php?option=com_content&task=view&id=198&Itemid=95 (May 6, 2008), illustrates the difference in views of 10 witnesses (including Dinneen and Drevna) on the impact of biofuels.

Economists C. Ford Runge and Benjamin Senauer chronicle the ascendance of corn-based ethanol and its effects in the United States in "How Biofuels Could Starve the Poor," available at http://www.foreignaffairs.org/20070501faessay86305/c-ford-runge-benjamin-senauer/how-biofuels-could-starve-the-poor.html (*Foreign Affairs*, May/June 2007). According to them, "Thinking of ethanol as a green alternative to fossil fuels reinforces the chimera of energy independence and of decoupling the interests of the United States from an increasingly troubled Middle East." Former Senator Tom Daschle critiques this paper in "Myth versus Reality," claiming that "converting the starch from a portion of the U.S. corn crop into biofuels is an efficient way to reduce the United States' dangerous dependence on imported oil." "Food for Fuel?" available at http://www.foreignaffairs .org/20070901faresponse86512/tom-daschle-c-ford-runge-benjamin-senauer/food-for-fuel.html (*Foreign Affairs*, September 2007), contains Daschle's views and Runge and Senauer's rejoinder.

Of interest is Mark Jacobson's "Review of Solutions to Global Warming, Air Pollution, and Energy Security" (*Environmental Science*, 2009), which finds that cellulosic- and corn-E85 may worsen climate and air pollution problems.

The Department of Energy's "Biofuels Are Helping Your Pocketbook and Our Environment," available at http://www1.eere.energy.gov/cleancities/toolbox/pdfs/ biofuels_impact.pdf, succinctly affirms the benefits of biofuels, including reducing U.S. dependence on foreign oil. On the other hand, "Biofuels: the Basics – Ethanol, Biodiesel and the 'Carbohydrate' Economy," available at http://www .eartheasy.com/article_biofuels.htm, concludes that "Biofuels will never be a 'silver bullet' solution. The energy problems we face are so large and complex that multiple strategies will be needed."

ISSUE 16

Are Spending Cuts the Right Way to Balance the Federal Government's Budget?

YES: Chris Edwards, from "Statement," Senate Committee on Finance, Subcommittee on Long-Term Growth and Debt Reduction (September 28, 2006)

NO: Charlie Stenholm, from "Testimony," Senate Committee on Finance, Subcommittee on Long-Term Growth and Debt Reduction (September 28, 2006)

ISSUE SUMMARY

YES: Chris Edwards, director of tax policy studies at the Cato Institute, believes that federal government overspending is the cause of its current fiscal problems. Higher taxes are not the solution because they "would result in greater tax avoidance, slower growth, less reported income, and thus less than expected tax revenue, perhaps prompting policymakers to jack up tax rates even higher."

NO: Former congressman Charlie Stenholm argues that in addressing deficit and debt problems, everything should be on the table. He stresses that addressing long-term fiscal challenges will require "some combination of stronger economic growth, restraining health care costs, scaling back benefit promises of entitlement programs, increasing the eligibility age for Social Security and Medicare, increasing revenues, and other tough choices."

$\mathbf{T}$he Full Employment and Balanced Growth Act of 1978 lists a number of economic goals for the federal government. Besides the familiar objectives of full employment, price stability, and increased real income, the act specifically mentions the goal of a balanced federal budget. This means that the government is to collect in taxes an amount equal to its expenditures. Despite this legislative call to action, the federal government has, with few exceptions, failed to balance its budget, and recent deficits have been large. For example, between 1940 and 1975 there were only two instances when the deficit was in excess of $50 billion. For the years 1980 through 1990, the federal government deficit averaged about $140 billion. Budget deficits continued until fiscal year 1998: Budget surpluses were recorded in that fiscal year and in each of the next three fiscal years. But the budget then returned to deficit and the estimates are for deficits of $423 billion and $354 billion for fiscal years 2006 and 2007 (*Economic Report of the President, 2006*).

When the federal government runs a deficit, it sells treasury bills, notes, and bonds. In this respect, the government is just like a business firm that sells securities to raise funds. The total of outstanding government securities is called the public or national debt. Thus, when the federal government runs a deficit, the public debt increases by the amount of the deficit. Thus, the public debt at any point in time is a summary of all prior deficits (offset by the retirement of securities if the government chooses to repurchase its securities when it has a budget surplus). By December 2006 the gross federal debt was approximately $8.6 trillion.

But why do deficits arise? One possibility is that the government spends more than it collects in revenues because it does not exercise fiscal restraint: It may be easy for politicians to spend money, but it is difficult for them to increase taxes to fund additional spending. The budget position of the government is also influenced by the state of the economy. The deficit is likely to increase if the economy enters a recession. A downturn in economic activity will decrease tax revenues (lower incomes mean less tax revenue) and will increase government spending (more expenditures for programs such as unemployment compensation). Because a deficit can arise for different reasons, it is important to understand exactly what forces create a deficit.

Another major question about deficits concerns their economic consequences. Some people perceive the deficits as harmful. With a deficit, the government borrows funds that otherwise would be have been available to business firms that might have built new factories or purchased new machinery with the borrowed funds. This is referred to as *crowding out,* since government borrowing to finance deficits presumably reduces the funds available for private investment. The reduction in investment slows the growth of productivity, and this means that the ability of the economy to produce goods and services is also reduced.

Both of the selected views agree that budget deficits must be slashed and the public debt kept from rising, but they disagree on how to achieve this. Chris Edwards, who views the problem primarily as one of overspending, recommends controlling spending, particularly on social programs, and tighter budget rules. Charlie Stenholm agrees that tighter rules are necessary; but he also believes that some tax cuts that are about to expire should be allowed to expire because this will increase government revenues.

America's Public Debt: How Do We Keep It from Rising?

Mr. Chairman and members of the committee, thank you for inviting me to testify today on the topic of controlling growth in the federal public debt. Federal debt continues to rise as spending growth keeps running ahead of the increased tax revenues the government is enjoying as a result of the strong economy. I will discuss some of the relationships between federal debt, spending, and taxation in light of recent budget developments.

Background: The Cost of Federal Spending

To support its large budget, the federal government will extract $2.4 trillion in taxes and about $300 billion in borrowed funds from families, businesses, and investors in fiscal 2006. That extraction transfers resources from the more productive private sector to the generally less productive government sector of the economy. Many studies have shown that, all else equal, the larger the government's share of the economy, the slower economic growth will be.[1] That is true regardless of whether higher spending is financed by increased taxes or higher deficits, which can be considered deferred taxes on future generations.

It is clear that a larger federal budget results in slower growth when you consider that a big share of spending is aimed at "social" goals, not at spurring growth. Indeed, 50 percent of the federal budget goes to transfers, which are typically justified on "fairness" grounds, not economic grounds.[2] For example, the largest federal program, Social Security, has a negative impact on growth the way it is currently structured. People may support the current Social Security system for non-economic reasons, but economists believe that its pay-as-you-go structure reduces national savings and economic growth.

An additional problem is that extracting the current and future taxes needed to support federal spending is a complex and economically damaging process. As a result, substantially more than one dollar of private activities are displaced for every added dollar of spending. Those added costs are called "deadweight losses," which are inefficiencies created by distortions to working, investment, and entrepreneurship. Those distortions reduce the nation's standard of living.

The Congressional Budget Office found that "typical estimates of the economic [deadweight] cost of a dollar of tax revenue range from 20 cents to 60 cents over and above the revenue raised."[3] Studies by Harvard's Martin

U.S. Senate, September 28, 2006.

Feldstein have found that deadweight losses are even larger. He noted that "the deadweight burden caused by incremental taxation . . . may exceed one dollar per dollar of revenue raised, making the cost of incremental governmental spending more than two dollars for each dollar of government spending."[4]

What this means is that the large increases in federal spending of recent years will create a substantial toll on the economy because current or future taxes will be higher than otherwise to fund the expansion. There is no free lunch on the spending side of the federal budget, but we can minimize the damage of raising federal funds by continuing to reform the most distortionary aspects of the income tax system.

Deficits and Tax Cuts

Policymakers opposed to recent tax cuts have argued that tax cuts that are "financed by deficits" don't do much good for the economy. It is true that recent tax cuts have not benefited the economy as much as they would have if they had been matched by spending cuts.[5] To the extent that recent tax cuts have added to federal deficits, a burden is imposed on future taxpayers (assuming that federal spending is not affected).[6]

However, there is a crucial point to consider with regard to the debate over recent tax cuts and budget deficits—***not all tax cuts are created equal.*** "Supply-side" tax cuts that reduce distortions in the tax code will spur economic growth and will not create as large a revenue loss as static calculations suggest. Any added debt from such tax cuts can be compared against the larger gross domestic product that will be generated. Supply-side tax cuts that represent long-term reforms of the federal fiscal system should be implemented regardless of the current budget balance. By contrast, further "social policy" tax cuts that do not simplify the tax code or make it more efficient should be avoided, or at least not considered unless they are matched by equal spending cuts.

Numerous studies have found that supply-side tax cuts on capital income are particularly beneficial to the economy. A 2005 Joint Committee on Taxation study presented the results of a macroeconomic simulation of hypothetical personal and corporate income tax cuts.[7] They found that a corporate tax rate cut (matched by spending cuts) boosted U.S. output twice as much in the long run as an individual rate cut of the same dollar magnitude. The JCT also found that there are much larger positive growth effects when tax cuts are offset by spending cuts to prevent the deficit from increasing.

Federal tax legislation since 2001 has been a mix of supply-side and social policy cuts. About 55 percent of recent tax cuts have been supply-side tax cuts, including the reductions in individual rates, the dividend and capital gains tax cuts, small business expensing, and the liberalization of savings accounts.[8] The other 45 percent of recent tax cuts have been social policy tax cuts, including the new 10 percent income tax bracket, the expansion of the child tax credit, and various education tax benefits.

The economic impact of social policy tax cuts, if combined with higher deficits, is mixed at best because those cuts generally do not reduce the deadweight losses of the tax system. By contrast, supply-side tax cuts boost long-term economic growth.[9] The dividend and capital gains tax cuts of 2003, for example, have helped to reduce long-recognized distortions caused by the double taxation of corporate equity. The markets have responded strongly to the dividend and capital gains cuts, indicating that the prior high rates were creating substantial distortions.

Spending Increases, Not Tax Cuts, Are the Problem

Have tax cuts or spending increases caused today's large budget deficits? Federal outlays have increased from $1.9 trillion in fiscal 2001 to $2.7 trillion by fiscal 2006, an increase of $800 billion. By contrast, the tax cuts enacted in 2001 and 2003 have reduced federal revenues by roughly $200 billion this year.[10] Thus, recent spending increases are four times more important in explaining the current budget deficit than are recent tax cuts.[11]

Another way to think about recent tax cuts is that they have helped reverse the large tax increases of 1990 and 1993. CBO data shows that those tax increases increased federal revenues by a combined 1.1 percent of GDP over the first five years after each was enacted. The 2001 and 2003 tax cuts reduced revenues by a similar magnitude of 1.2 percent of GDP over the first five years after each was enacted.[12]

Regardless of whether or not one supports recent tax cuts, it is clear that there are gigantic long-term fiscal problems on the spending side of the budget. The Government Accountability Office has projected a long-range business-as-usual scenario for the budget.[13] The projections assume that entitlement programs are not reformed, and that other programs and taxes stay at the same size as today relative to GDP. Under that scenario, federal spending would grow from 20 percent of GDP today to a staggering 45 percent of GDP by 2040. Such a European-sized government would bring with it slow growth, lower wages, a lack of opportunities, and many other pathologies.

Unfortunately, the long-term fiscal situation could be even worse than that. The GAO's "static" estimates ignore the economic death spiral that would occur if taxes were raised in an attempt to fund higher spending. Higher taxes would result in greater tax avoidance, slower growth, less reported income, and thus less than expected tax revenue, perhaps prompting policymakers to jack up tax rates even higher.

Consider Social Security and Medicare Part A, which are funded by the federal payroll tax. On a static basis, the cost of these two programs as a share of taxable wages is projected to rise from 14 percent in 2005 to 25 percent in 2040.[14] But as tax rates rise, the tax base will shrink. To get the money it would need to pay for rising benefits, and taking into account this dynamic effect, the government would have to hike the payroll tax rate to about 30 percent by 2040.[15] That would be a crushing blow to working Americans, who would have to pay this tax in addition to all the other federal and state taxes they pay.

Note that on top of these federal costs, state and local governments are also imposing large and unfunded obligations on future generations. State and local governments have rapidly rising levels of bond debt, and they have unfunded costs for their workers' pension and health plans that could total more than $2 trillion.[16]

Reform Options

These figures suggest a bleak fiscal future awaiting young Americans and taxpayers without major reforms. There are many actions that should be taken right away to reduce deficits and unfunded obligations.

- Social Security should be cut by indexing future initial benefits to the growth in prices rather than wages.
- Medicare deductibles and premiums should be increased. Those changes could be phased-in over time, but it is important to get the needed cuts signed into law to reduce the exposure of taxpayers.
- Medicaid should be block-granted and the federal contribution to the program restrained or cut. This was the successful strategy behind the 1996 welfare reform.
- Federalism should be revived and federal aid to the states cut sharply. Aid to the states does not make any economic sense. It has been a bastion of "pork" spending, and it has created massive bureaucracies at all three levels of government. With the coming entitlement crunch, the federal government simply cannot afford to be Santa Claus to the states any longer.

Of course, such cuts are politically difficult for Congress to make. That is why new budgeting structures are needed to get a handle on rising spending and deficits. Considering that federal outlays have increased 45 percent in the last five years and the government has run deficits in 33 of the last 37 years, it is obvious that current budget rules are not working very well.

That is why budget reform proposals, such Senator Gregg's "Stop Over Spending Act of 2006" (S. 3521) are important.[17] The Act contains new rules to control deficits, restrain entitlement spending, cap discretionary spending, limit "emergency" spending, and create a commission to eliminate waste in federal programs.

Some people argue that such new budget restrictions are not needed because Congress has the power to restrain spending anytime it wants. But political scientists have long recognized that the self-interested actions of individual policymakers often lead to overall legislative outcomes that undermine the general welfare. Indeed, frequent statements by many policymakers make it clear that their top priority is to target spending to interests in their states, not to legislate in the national interest. If left to their own devices, many members become activists for narrow causes, while broader concerns such as the size of the federal debt are ignored.

New and improved federal budget rules are needed to channel the energies of members into reforms that are in the interests of average citizens and taxpayers. Without tight budget rules, Capitol Hill descends into an "every man for himself" spending stampede—a budget anarchy that creates unsustainable budget expansion and soaring deficits. That is why there have been numerous, and often bipartisan, efforts to create new budget procedures, such the 1974 Budget Act, the 1985 Gramm-Rudman-Hollings Act, and the 1990 Budget Enforcement Act.

Consider also that the 50 states generally have much tighter budget rules than does the federal government.[18] Virtually all the states have statutory or constitutional requirements to balance their budgets. Governors in 42 states have line-item veto authority. Most state constitutions include limitations on government debt. More than half the states have some form of overall tax and expenditure limitation (TEL).[19] Also, the states are fiscally constrained by the need to prevent their bond ratings from falling.

Capping Total Federal Spending

Senator Gregg's proposals are a good starting point for discussing budget reforms, but Congress should also consider a more comprehensive budget control idea. That is to impose a statutory cap on the annual growth in total federal outlays, including discretionary and entitlement spending.[20] Deficits are a byproduct of the overspending problem, and such a cap would target that core problem directly. The basic principle of a budget growth cap is that the government should live within constraints, as average families do, and not consume an increasing share of the nation's output.

Prior budget control efforts have imposed caps on discretionary spending, but not entitlement spending. Yet the rapid growth in entitlement spending may cause a major budget crisis, and thus should be included under any cap. There has been interest in capping entitlements in the past. In 1992, the bipartisan Strengthening of America Commission, headed by Sens. Sam Nunn (D-GA) and Pete Domenici (R-NM), proposed capping all non-Social Security entitlement spending at the growth rate of inflation plus the number of beneficiaries in programs.[21] The Entitlement Control Act of 1994 (H.R. 4593) introduced by Rep. Charles Stenholm (D-TX) would have capped the growth in all entitlement programs to inflation plus one percent plus the number of beneficiaries. Both of those proposals included procedures for sequestering entitlement spending with broad cuts if the caps were breached.

A simple way to structure a cap is to limit annual spending growth to the growth in an economic indicator such as personal income. Another possible cap is the sum of population growth plus inflation. In that case, if population grew at 1 percent and inflation was 3 percent, then federal spending could grow at most by 4 percent. That is the limit used in Colorado's successful "TABOR" budget law. Whichever indicator is used should be smoothed by averaging it over about five years.

An interesting alternative would be to simply cap total federal spending growth at a fixed percentage, such as four percent. That would make it easy for Congress to plan ahead in budgeting, and would prevent efforts to change caps by fudging estimates of economic indicators. Another interesting advantage of a fixed percentage cap is that it would provide an incentive for Congress to support a low inflation policy by the Federal Reserve Board.

With a spending cap in place, Congress would pass annual budget resolutions making sure that discretionary and entitlement spending was projected to fit under the cap for upcoming years. Reconciliation instructions could be included to reduce entitlement spending to fit under the cap for the current budget year and to reduce out-year spending to fit under projected future caps.

The Office of Management and Budget would provide regular updates regarding whether spending is likely to breach the annual cap, and Congress could take corrective actions as needed. If a session ended and the OMB determined that outlays were still above the cap, the president would be required to cut, or sequester, spending across the board by the amount needed. The GRH and the BEA included sequester mechanisms that covered only portions of the defense, nondefense, and entitlement budgets, but a sequester on the overall budget would be a better approach.

A shortcoming of a statutory spending cap and other budget rules is that Congress would always have the option of rewriting the law if it didn't want to comply. But a cap on overall spending would be a very simple and high-profile symbol of restraint for supporters in Congress and the public to rally around and defend. An overall cap on spending growth of, say, four percent is easy to understand, and watchdog groups would keep the public informed about any cheating by policymakers. Over time, public awareness and budgetary tradition would aid in the enforcement of a cap.

Conclusion

Federal policymakers need a change in mindset and tougher budget rules to ward off large tax hikes and rising debt as entitlement costs soar in future years. Policymakers need to scour the budget for programs and agencies to cut.[22] A cap on total federal spending should be part of the solution to get the budget under control. Clearly, current budget rules have not worked very well, and we should experiment with new rules to try and get a grip on the overspending problem.

Thank you for holding these important hearings. I look forward to working with the committee on its agenda for federal budget reform.

Notes

1. See James Gwartney and Robert Lawson, "Economic Freedom of the World: 2004 Annual Report," Fraser Institute, 2004, and see James Gwartney and Robert Lawson, "Economic Freedom of the World: 2005 Annual Report," Fraser Institute, 2005. For a summary of academic studies, see Daniel J. Mitchell, "The Impact of Government Spending on Economic Growth," Heritage Foundation, March 15, 2005. To state this relationship more precisely, if the government increases its share of the economy beyond a certain modest level of about 15 percent, then growth begins to suffer.

2. Transfers are 50 percent of total program outlays (outlays excluding interest). See Chris Edwards "How to Spend $2.8 Trillion," Cato Institute Tax & Budget Bulletin no. 39, August 2006.

3. Congressional Budget Office, "Budget Options," February 2001, p. 381. For a general discussion, see Chris Edwards, "Economic Benefits of Personal Income Tax Rate Reductions," U.S. Congress, Joint Economic Committee, April 2001. See also William Niskanen, "The Economic Burden of Taxation," presented at a conference at the Federal Reserve Bank of Dallas, Texas, October 22–23, 2003.

4. Martin Feldstein, "How Big Should Government Be?" *National Tax Journal*, Volume 50, no. 2, June 1997, pp. 197–213.

5. Tax cuts matched by spending cuts produce much stronger growth effects in the long run. See the various simulations in Joint Committee on Taxation, "Macroeconomic Analysis of Various Proposals to Provide $500 Billion in Tax Relief," JCX-4-05, March 1, 2005.

6. If higher deficits create a "starve the beast" effect resulting in lower spending, then tax cuts now will not lead to equally large tax increases later.

7. Joint Committee on Taxation, "Macroeconomic Analysis of Various Proposals to Provide $500 Billion in Tax Relief," JCX-4-05, March 1, 2005.

8. Based on the dollar values of extending the cuts between 2012 and 2016. See Office of Management and Budget, *Midsession Review Fiscal Year 2007*, July 11, 2006, Table S-6. The estate tax is not included.

9. For example, see Joint Committee on Taxation, "Macroeconomic Analysis of Various Proposals to Provide $500 Billion in Tax Relief," JCX-4-05, March 1, 2005.

10. Based on CBO's estimate of the revenue loss from EGTRRA and JGTRRA in fiscal 2012 as a share of GDP, then applied to GDP in fiscal 2006. I have not included the alternative minimum tax.

11. Note that this estimate of federal revenue losses is on a static basis. The actual loss is likely to be smaller because of the positive economic effects of the cuts.

12. Chris Edwards, "Social Policy, Supply-Side, and Fundamental Reform: Republican Tax Policy, 1994 to 2004," *Tax Notes*, November 1, 2004, p. 691.

13. Government Accountability Office, "21st Century Challenges: Reexamining the Base of the Federal Government," GAO-05-325SP, February 2005, Figure 2, p. 8.

14. *The 2005 Annual Report of the Board of Trustees of the Federal Old-Age and Survivors Insurance and the Federal Disability Insurance Trust Funds* (Washington: Government Printing Office, April 5, 2005), p. 166. These are the intermediate assumptions.

15. Estimate based on Martin Feldstein, "Prefunding Medicare," National Bureau of Economic Research, Working Paper no. 6917, January 1999, p. 4.

16. Chris Edwards and Jagadeesh Gokhale, "Unfunded State and Local Health Costs: $1.4 Trillion," Cato Institute Tax & Budget Bulletin, September 2006.

17. U.S. Senate, Committee on the Budget, "The Stop Over Spending Act of 2006," Senate Report 109–283, July 14, 2006.

18. For background on state budget processes, see National Association of State Budget Officers, "Budget Processes in the States," January 2002.

19. Michael New, "Limiting Government through Direct Democracy," Cato Institute Policy Analysis no. 420, December 13, 2001.

20. For background, see Chris Edwards, "Capping Federal Spending," Cato Institute Tax & Budget Bulletin no. 32, March 2006. Also see Brian Riedl, "Restrain Runaway Spending with a Federal Taxpayers' Bill of Rights," Heritage Foundation, August 27, 2004.

21. The commission was sponsored by the Center for Strategic and International Studies.

22. For detailed discussion of federal programs that should be cut, see Chris Edwards, *Downsizing the Federal Government* (Washington: Cato Institute, 2005).

 **NO**

America's Public Debt: How Do We Keep It from Rising?

Mr. Chairman, Senator Kerry and Members of the Committee. I am Charlie Stenholm, former Member of Congress from the 17th District of Texas and currently a Senior Policy Affairs Affairs Advisor at Olsson, Frank and Weeda. I am also a member of the Board of Directors of the Committee for a Responsible Federal Budget and the Concord Coalition. This testimony is my own and does not represent any position or conclusion of any of these organizations.

In my twenty-six years in Congress, I worked with many members on both sides of the aisle, including several members of this committee, fighting to leave a better future for our children and grandchildren. We spent many years working extremely hard and casting many tough votes to eliminate the deficit and put us in a position to begin paying down the debt. It has been extremely frustrating to see the fruits of that labor squandered by the "deficit's don't matter" mentality that took hold in recent years. I am hopeful that this hearing and similar discussions about the dangers of continued deficits and the need to take action are a sign that the tide is shifting back to the bipartisan balanced budget consensus we had in the 1990s.

I have been asked to share my thoughts about how to deal with our nation's rising public debt. My testimony can be summarized in three recommendations based on West Texas Tractor Seat Common Sense:

- First, acknowledge that we face a problem. Policymakers need to take to heart the message of The Concord Coalition's Fiscal Wake Up Tour that Bob Bixby described—our nation is on a fiscally unsustainable course and difficult choices must be confronted.
- Second, stop digging the hole deeper through debt financed tax cuts or spending programs.
- Third, begin a bipartisan process in which both parties put everything on the table and honestly negotiate the tradeoffs. . . .

꿈◉ఞ

Deficits Do Matter

Some defenders of our current economic and fiscal policies have argued that deficits don't matter. The reality is that deficits do matter, both for our economic security today as well as the future we leave for our children and grandchildren.

U.S. Senate, September 28, 2006.

The United States has been able to sustain large budget deficits without an increase in domestic interest rates because the increased demand for borrowing has been offset by an increased inflow of capital from global markets. Our increased reliance on foreign capital to finance our deficits places our economic security at the mercy of global bankers and foreign governments. If foreign investors stop buying US bonds we would face higher inflation and higher interest rates, putting our economy at risk of a large scale recession.

Large deficits financed by borrowing from foreign investors are also a major factor contributing to the trade deficits which are exporting jobs overseas. We need to keep the value of the dollar high in order to attract the foreign capital we need to finance our debt. If the value of the dollar declines, US bonds will be less valuable to foreign investors. But the strong dollar we need to help Treasury finance our budget deficits hurts our businesses by making US exports more expensive.

Our current borrow and spend policies are worse than the tax and spend policies of the past, because they will leave a crushing debt tax burden for future generations who don't have any say in what we are doing and don't benefit from the tax cuts and spending programs for current generations. Our grandchildren will face ever higher tax burdens simply to cover increasing interest payments instead of addressing other needs such as keeping our military the strongest in the world, protecting our domestic security, providing health care, strengthening Social Security and Medicare, and investing in our education system.

A German philosopher named Dietrich Bonhoeffer once said that the ultimate test of a moral society is the kind of world that it leaves to its children. We cannot leave it to our grandchildren to shoulder the enormous burden of our debt. Our grandchildren do not have a vote. That is why it is so easy for us to say here today we can fight two wars, we can fund homeland security, we can fight the war on terrorism, we can rebuild the Gulf Coast and we can keep cutting taxes, because we are going to send the bill to our grandchildren. . . .

The First Step Toward Getting Out of the Deficit Hole: Quit Digging

My philosophy on budget issues has always begun with some simple West Texas Tractor Seat Common Sense—When you find yourself in a hole, the first rule is to quit digging. Unfortunately, the legislative agenda is filled with items that would dig the hole deeper through tax cuts and increased spending. The most notable example was the so-called trifecta bill which combined a temporary extension of business tax breaks, a permanent reduction in the estate tax and a new mandatory spending program for mine reclamation along with an increase in the minimum wage. . . .

Dealing with our budget deficit must begin with reinstatement of budget enforcement rules to take away the shovels from Congress and the administration by restricting the ability of Congress and the President to enact legislation that would increase the deficit. The pay as you go budget enforcement rules and discretionary spending limits, which Congress and the President enacted in 1990 and extended in 1997 with bipartisan support, were an important part of getting a handle on the deficits in the early 1990s and getting the budget back into balance.

Reinstating paygo rules and discretionary spending limits would not balance the budget by themselves, but would represent an important first step in bringing discipline to the budget process by prohibiting policy changes that would further enlarge the deficit. They have been tested, and they worked. They didn't always work perfectly, but there is no question that they significantly improved the responsibility and accountability of the budget process.

The principle of paygo—if we want to reduce our revenues or increase our spending, we need to say how we would pay for it within our budget—is something all families understand. If we want to reduce our revenues, we need to say what spending we will do without. If we want to increase spending, we need to say where we will come up with the revenues for the new spending or what other spending we will do without.

The concept of applying PAYGO rules to all legislation—spending and revenues—has received support from both sides of the aisle since it was originally enacted. "Two-sided" PAYGO was originally enacted in the bipartisan budget agreement of 1990 and extended in the bipartisan balanced budget agreement of 1997. Furthermore, it was included in the budget passed by the Republican Congress in 1995. Applying pay-as-you-go rules to tax cuts does not prevent Congress from passing more tax cuts. All it requires is that Congress must identify another source of revenue or spending reduction if it wants to enact or extend a tax cut.

Those who want to extend expiring tax cuts or make the tax cuts permanent should be willing to put forward the spending cuts or other offsets necessary to pay for them. Similarly, those who want to spend more in certain areas need to be willing to say where they would cut or how they would raise revenues to pay for their proposals.

I would say with all due respect to my Republican friends that if you are sincere in what say about controlling spending, you should not have a problem with reinstating pay as you go for taxes as well as spending because it would force Congress to actually cut spending to accompany tax cuts instead of just promising to cut spending in the future. The problem is that the actions of the majority in Congress haven't matched the rhetoric. Congress and the administration have cut taxes without cutting spending, and have charged the difference to our children and grandchildren by increasing the deficit.

The pay-as-you-go principle is not simply a matter of bookkeeping, but a key element of sound economic policymaking. A recent report issued by the Treasury Department providing a dynamic analysis of proposals to permanently extend the 2001 and 2003 tax cuts illustrate the importance of offsetting the revenue loss from tax cuts. Although the report cited economic models which found that certain tax cuts can result in higher savings and increasing capital stock the report noted that "when lower taxes on capital income are financed initially by issuing government debt, private investment is crowded out by an increase in government borrowing," limiting the economic benefit from the tax cuts. The report went on to say that in some instances the benefits from tax relief that increases the deficit are more than offset by the financing of government debt.

No reputable analyst believes that cutting taxes will result in higher revenues than would have occurred without the tax cut. While some tax cuts may result in economic growth that produces some revenue feedback, there is no credible analysis that claims those potential benefits would offset the revenue loss. Analyses from the Congressional Budget Office, the Joint Committee on Taxation, the Federal Reserve Board, and the President's own Council of Economic Advisors have all concluded that the tax cuts enacted over the last four years will have little or no impact on long term economic growth and cause deficits to be larger than they otherwise would have been.

Put Everything on the Table

A serious discussion about balancing the budget will require both parties to make sacrifices. All areas of the budget must be on the table and the burden of deficit reduction should be distributed fairly across the budget. I have always said that those of us in agriculture are willing to accept our fair share of reductions if all other areas of the budget are asked to sacrifice as well, but we aren't willing to shoulder an undue burden of cuts so that other areas of the budget can avoid budget discipline. I believe that this view is shared by advocates of other areas of the budget as well.

The Promise to Our Children and Grandchildren being circulated by For Our Grandchildren, a bipartisan Social Security education organization which has retained me as a spokesman, embodies this approach. The promise asks candidates to seek an honest, bipartisan debate about Social Security and find responsible solutions to meet these challenges that the system will face in the years ahead. It doesn't commit candidates to any specific policy proposals. Rather, it calls on policymakers to put all options on the table to develop a solution which honestly addresses the pressure that the unfunded obligations that the current system will place on taxpayers and other budgetary priorities in a way that is fair to all generations, protects current retirees and strengthens the safety net for the most vulnerable. If all candidates from both parties conduct themselves in this spirit in the debate over Social Security and our other fiscal challenges it will be much easier to reach bipartisan agreement on responsible solutions.

The renewed public focus on the need to address the long-term problems facing entitlement programs has been encouraging. However, rhetoric about the need to make tough choices with regard to entitlement programs is undercut when it is not matched by a willingness to make similarly tough choices on the revenue side of the ledger. It is fiscally irresponsible and politically unrealistic to call for reforms of entitlement programs in the name of fiscal discipline while simultaneously advocating tax cuts that will make the short term deficit and long term fiscal imbalance worse. It is neither fiscally responsible nor politically viable to make cutbacks in some areas of the budget in the name of deficit reduction while exempting other areas of the budget from budget discipline. That is particularly true when deficit reduction efforts focus on the most vulnerable in society, while benefits for those in a better position to accept sacrifices are left untouched. It will take everyone pulling to get the wagon out of the ditch; we won't be able to get it out if some people are riding.

One specific proposal that would provide a substantial source of savings in a way that spreads the burden of deficit reduction broadly is utilizing a more accurate measure for indexing government programs as well as tax brackets and other provisions in the tax code. There is broad agreement among economists that the Consumer Price Index currently used for indexation of government programs overstates inflation. The Bureau of Labor Statistics has begun to publish a new "Chained Consumer Price Index" to provide a more accurate measure of inflation. Using the Chained CPI for indexation of government programs represents sound policy that reflects years of work by economists and other technical experts. Just as importantly, this proposal would achieve substantial budgetary savings—approximately $50 billion over the next five years—in a way which would spread the burden of deficit reduction fairly across the entire span of government.

Increasing the Debt Limit

This Committee has been called on to raise the debt limit four times in the last five years to finance our deficit problem, and probably will need to be asked to do so again next year. While raising the debt limit is something that Congress must do, increasing the debt limit should be accompanied by a full and open debate about the fiscal policies that have made the increase necessary and a discussion about what should be done to stem the tide of red ink. In addition, I believe that any long-term increase in the debt limit should be accompanied by a plan to restore fiscal discipline. I would propose that when Treasury indicates that it is nearing the debt limit Congress approve a short term increase in the debt limit to avert the imminent crisis and provide for a longer increase in the debt limit contingent upon Congress taking action to reinstate paygo rules and other budget enforcement mechanisms.

Addressing Long-Term Fiscal Problems

Although our near term budget deficits are cause for concern in their own right, what makes them particularly worrisome is the looming financial pressures we will face when the baby boom generation begins to retire in 2008. We need to bring more attention to the long-term liabilities facing our nation as part of the budget process.

I had hoped that last year would be the year that Congress and the President would take action to address the financial challenges facing Social Security, but neither party seemed interested in a serious discussion about the tough choices that will be necessary. These challenges will continue to get worse and become harder to address the longer we wait.

According to projections by the Government Accountability Office (GAO), the combination of allowing the growth of entitlement programs to continue unchecked and making tax cuts permanent while keeping discretionary spending constant as a percentage of GDP will result in a deficit of 10 percent of GDP by 2024. By 2030, the costs of Social Security, Medicare, Medicaid and interest on the debt would consume nearly 22 percent of GDP and the debt to GDP ratio would be 150%.

While the higher revenues from allowing the tax cuts to expire would fall far short of closing this long-term fiscal imbalance, it makes no sense to make the gap worse by locking in permanently lower revenues *before* restraining the growth of entitlement spending. Unless Congress enacts major reforms slowing the growth of entitlement spending, revenues will need to increase well above current levels to meet these obligations and keep up with the growth in spending associated with the baby boomers' retirement and health care costs. Congress should defer action on any tax cuts or entitlement spending increases with long term costs—including extension of the tax cuts which expire in 2010 or expansion of Medicare prescription drug benefit—until Congress has addressed the existing long-term fiscal challenges.

There is no magic bullet that will solve our long term fiscal challenges by itself. While stronger economic growth will help meet the burden of an aging population, higher economic growth alone will not be enough. GAO has estimated that we would need double-digit real economic growth for many decades to grow our way out of the fiscal problems. Slowing the rapid growth of health care spending will need to be part of the solution, but a substantial gap would remain even if we were somehow able to eliminate all excess health care cost growth. Proposals that have been put forward to raise revenues to finance the growing costs of entitlement programs should be considered, but it is unrealistic to expect that it is politically feasible or economically desirable to raise taxes enough to close the gap. Although I personally believe that individual accounts can be an important component of a comprehensive reform plan by providing a higher returns on worker contributions and a more reliable method of pre-funding benefit promises than government trust funds, they do not provide a painless solution to the financial challenges facing Social Security as some have claimed.

A serious solution to our long term fiscal challenges will likely require some combination of stronger economic growth, restraining the growth of health care costs, scaling back benefit promises of entitlement programs, increasing the eligibility age for Social Security and Medicare, increasing revenues, and other tough choices. There is plenty of room for debate over the exact mix of options that should be included in a plan, but policymakers need to begin by acknowledging that the solution will require tough choices and difficult tradeoffs.

Fiscal Commission

The experience of last year in which neither party in Congress was willing to take action on the financial challenges facing Social Security convinced me that we need to establish a bipartisan commission to objectively review the fiscal challenges facing our nation and make recommendations to Congress and the President about how to put the nation back on a fiscally sustainable course.

Senator George Voinovich and Congressman Frank Wolf have introduced legislation, the Securing America's Future Economy (SAFE) Act which would establish such a commission. The commission would solicit input from the public and develop proposals to address four key concerns:

1. The unsustainable gap between projected spending and revenue,
2. The need to increase national savings,
3. The implications of foreign ownership of U.S. government debt, and
4. The lack of emphasis on long-term planning in the budget process.

Congress and the president would be required to act on the proposal developed by the Commission under a fast track procedure. . . .

There is justifiably cynicism in Washington about proposals to establish a commission to study an issue. There are bookshelves filled with dust-covered reports from commissions that went nowhere. A commission isn't a silver bullet that will solve our problems. It will still take action by Members of Congress and the administration to make the tough choices. But a commission that reflects the principles I have outlined could provide the leadership necessary to get the process started in a constructive fashion, especially if the President follows through on his pledge to address the issue in a bipartisan manner and continues to make addressing the long-term challenges facing entitlement programs a priority.

Conclusion

Reaching consensus on a balanced package that will prevent the publicly held debt from growing to unsustainable levels will require all of us to accept sacrifices. As long as everyone advocates balancing the budget by cutting someone else's priorities, talk about deficit reduction will remain just that. As a farmer, I choose to be an optimist and believe that all sides will be willing to put aside their individual political interests to find a solution that is in the best interests of our nation and our children's future.

POSTSCRIPT

Are Spending Cuts the Right Way to Balance the Federal Government's Budget?

Chris Edwards defends supply-side tax cuts because they reduce distortions and increase economic efficiency by increasing the incentive to work, save, and invest. For example, corporate tax rate cuts benefit the economy, and there is evidence that if they are matched by spending cuts, there are large positive growth effects. He argues that an increase in federal spending on "social goals" causes slower economic growth. Higher taxes would result in more tax avoidance and slower growth, and would not solve the deficit problem. He recommends cutting Social Security by indexing future initial benefits to the inflation rate instead of wages, making changes to Medicare (increasing premiums and deductibles) and Medicaid (which should be block-granted), and cutting federal aid to states. New budgeting restrictions are needed to overcome the political difficulty of making the cuts. These include a cap on discretionary and entitlement spending. For example, annual spending growth could be limited to the growth in personal income or some other economic indicator such as the rates of growth of population and inflation combined, or even to a fixed percentage.

Charlie Stenholm condemns current "borrow-and-spend policies" as worse than past tax-and-spend policies because they impose a large burden on future generations. He recommends pay-as-you-go rules and limits on discretionary spending as an important first step towards fiscal discipline. He maintains there is no credible analysis showing that potential benefits of tax cuts would offset revenue losses. Extension of tax cuts must be deferred as must entitlement spending increases, at least until Congress addresses the long-term fiscal challenges.

Data on deficits and debt can be found in the yearly *Economic Report of the President.* Even more detail can be found in *Budget of the United States Government: Citizen's Guide to the Federal Budget* (Congressional Budget Office). Additional testimony was presented at the Senate subcommittee hearings from which the Edwards and Stenholm statements are taken: See the statement by Robert L. Bixby on behalf of The Concord Coalition and "Long-Term Growth, Government Debt, and Family Incomes" by Joseph A. Peckman of the Brookings Institution. The Concord Coalition is a nonpartisan organization concerned with prudent fiscal policies. Useful material can be found at their Web site http://www.concordcoalition.org/. Another nonpartisan organization that focuses on the budget is the Center on Budget and Policy Priorities, and their Web site is http://www.cbpp.org/.

ISSUE 17

Has the North American Free Trade Agreement Benefited the Economies of Canada, Mexico, and the United States?

YES: John M. Melle, from "Statement," Senate Subcommittee on International Trade of the Committee on Finance of the United States Senate (September 11, 2006)

NO: Sandra Polaski, from "The Employment Consequences of NAFTA," Senate Subcommittee on International Trade of the Committee on Finance of the United States Senate (September 11, 2006)

ISSUE SUMMARY

YES: Deputy Assistant U.S. Trade Representative John M. Melle outlines the benefits of NAFTA and concludes that the three NAFTA countries "have not only become better customers for each other but better neighbors, more committed partners, and effective colleagues in a wide range of trade-related international organizations."

NO: Sandra Polaski, director of the Trade, Equity and Development Project, argues that NAFTA has produced negative effects in all three countries, including contributing to wage inequality in the United States. But the largest negative effects have been felt by the rural poor in Mexico: They "have borne the brunt of the adjustment to NAFTA and been forced to adapt without adequate government support."

The North American Free Trade Agreement (NAFTA) was signed into law in the fall of 1993. The passage of NAFTA was no simple matter. Although the basic agreement was negotiated by the Republican George H.W. Bush administration during the late 1980s and early 1990s, the Democratic Bill Clinton administration faced the challenge of convincing Congress and the American people that NAFTA would work to the benefit of the United States as well as Mexico and Canada. In meeting this challenge, President Clinton did not hesitate to use a bit of drama to press the case for NAFTA. He arranged for all former, then-living U.S. presidents (Bush, Ronald Reagan, Jimmy Carter, Gerald Ford, and Richard Nixon) to gather together and speak out in support of NAFTA. The public debate probably reached its zenith with a face-to-face confrontation between H. Ross Perot, a successful businessman who ran for president and was perhaps the most visible and outspoken opponent of NAFTA, and then-vice president Al Gore on the *Larry King Live* television show. The vote on NAFTA in the House of Representatives reflected the sharpness of the debate; it passed by only a slim margin.

In pressing the case for NAFTA, proponents in the United States raised two major arguments. The first argument was economic: NAFTA would produce real economic benefits. These benefits were purported to include increased employment in the United States and increased productivity. Note that these arguments are based on the economic notions of specialization and comparative advantage. The second argument was political: NAFTA would support the political and economic reforms being made in Mexico and promote further progress in these two domains. These reforms had made Mexico a "better" neighbor—that is, Mexico had taken steps to become more like the United States—and NAFTA would support greater economic freedom and increased political freedom as well as greater economic stability and increased political stability.

In opposing NAFTA, critics in the United States countered both of these arguments, focusing mostly on U.S.–Mexican relations. They argued that freer trade between the United States and Mexico would mean a loss of jobs in the United States—Perot's reference to a "giant sucking sound" was the transfer of work and jobs from the United States to Mexico. They also argued that NAFTA did not do enough to protect the environment or to improve working conditions in Mexico. They felt that the notion of passing NAFTA as a reward to the Mexican government was premature; the government had not done enough to improve economic and political conditions in Mexico.

Implementation of NAFTA began in 1994, and evaluation was undertaken at the point of its 10-year anniversary, and again at its 12-year anniversary when almost all of its implementation periods were completed—the few remaining tariffs were planned to be eliminated on January 1, 2008. In assessing the impact of NAFTA, there are any number of different perspectives that can be employed. Should the focus be economic, political, or both? Should the evaluation concentrate on the benefits and costs to the United States, to Mexico, to Canada, or to all three countries? How much of the history that follows NAFTA can be attributed to NAFTA, and how much can be attributed to other factors? When is the appropriate time for an evaluation? In short, evaluation is no easy task.

But evaluation of NAFTA is important not only for its own sake. President George W. Bush supported an expansion of NAFTA to 34 countries in North, Central, and South America. This expansion is called the Free Trade Agreement of the Americas (FTAA). Clearly, whether or not a person is willing to support FTAA depends in part on whether that person believes that NAFTA has helped or hurt the three countries. John M. Melle believes that NAFTA has benefited all three countries. Sandra Polaski claims that NAFTA has hurt all three countries, especially Mexico's rural poor.

YES

John M. Melle

Statement

Mr. Chairman, Members of the Committee:

Thank you for the opportunity to appear before the Committee today. I am pleased to represent the Office of the United States Trade Representative and provide an overview of our trade and investment relationship with our NAFTA partners, Canada and Mexico.

The North American Free Trade Agreement (NAFTA) has defined our commercial relationship with Canada and Mexico since its entry into force on January 1, 1994. The NAFTA is a comprehensive trade agreement, covering trade in goods, services and investment, as well as government procurement, intellectual property rights, standards, and dispute settlement. Twelve years after implementation of the NAFTA began, essentially all of the agreement's transitional implementation periods are now complete with the exception of a handful of tariffs that fall to zero on January 1, 2008.

In evaluating the impact of the NAFTA on both the United States and its partners, the appropriate place to start is with trade and investment flows.

- For goods, our total trade (imports plus exports) with Canada and Mexico has more than doubled from pre-NAFTA levels. Growth in trade with our NAFTA partners exceeds growth with the world as a whole. Mexico has passed Japan to become our second largest trading partner and export market, trailing only Canada.
- There has also been a qualitative transformation in goods trade; in the 1980s, 80 percent of Mexico's exports were oil and raw materials. Today, value-added manufactured goods account for 90 percent of Mexico's exports, an indicator that Mexico has joined the United States and Canada as part of a continent-wide market of producers and consumers.
- Much of the recent concern about NAFTA is with agriculture. In fact, growth in agricultural trade has paralleled growth in total trade since 1994. U.S. agricultural exports to Canada and Mexico have grown by 98 percent since 1994, nearly matching the 101 percent total growth in U.S. total exports to those countries over the same period. Canada and Mexico are our top two agricultural export markets.
- Many of the most impressive export successes for the United States are also agricultural. Mexico is our largest market for a wide range of products—beef, dairy, swine, rice, turkey, apples, soymeal, sorghum, and dry beans among them. Our share of Mexico's imports is above

U.S. Senate, September 11, 2006.

90 percent, due in part to the preferential access we have under the NAFTA for five of these seven products. In 2005, Mexico was also our second largest market for corn, port, poultry meats, soybeans, wheat, and pears.

- NAFTA has solidified Canada's position as our largest trading partner. More trade crosses the Ambassador Bridge between Detroit and Windsor than moves between Spain and France.[1]
- U.S. exports of services to Canada and Mexico have grown by 75 percent since 1993. In 2004, the last year for which we have complete data, the United States exported $47.7 billion in private commercial services to our NAFTA partners, and maintained a trade surplus of $14.2 billion.

As a result of the NAFTA and the earlier bilateral free trade agreement, the phase-out of tariffs between the United States and Canada was completed on January 1, 1998, except for tariff-rate quotas which Canada maintains on certain supply-managed agricultural products. Nearly all of the NAFTA tariff cuts with Mexico have been implemented, except for the handful of remaining items whose tariffs will be eliminated in 2008. Since 1994, the average U.S. duty on Mexican goods has fallen to about 0.1 percent in 2005. Mexico's duties on U.S. goods are even smaller—0.003%.

By establishing a framework to promote a secure and predictable environment, investment in each of the NAFTA countries has grown. The NAFTA partners are investing more in each others' economies, and the rest of the world is also investing more in our economies.

- This change is especially important for Mexico. Since 1994, annual Foreign Direct Investment (FDI) inflows have averaged $14 billion, compared to less than $3 billion in the 1980s. Mexico's outward FDI flows have increased fourteen-fold since 1990, and it is now one of the largest developing country overseas investors.
- The United States accounts for approximately two-thirds of total foreign direct investment in Canada. U.S. investment is concentrated in the manufacturing, finance, and mining sectors.
- Investment growth in Canada and Mexico has not come at U.S. expense. Even excluding housing, U.S. business investment has risen by 104% since 1993, compared to a 37% rise between 1981 and 1993.

How much the NAFTA affected the changing trends in goods and services trade and investment cannot be measured precisely. This is especially true when looking at broader measures of economic performance since the NAFTA entered into force. However, there are a wide range of economic indicators that have grown more rapidly since the NAFTA was implemented.

- For the United States, job creation, industrial production, real compensation for manufacturing workers, business productivity and investment have all increased by higher rates in the period since 1993 compared with prior years.

- U.S. employment rose from 112.2 million in December 1993 to 134.4 million in December 2005, an increase of 22.2 million jobs, or nearly 20 percent. The average unemployment rate was 5.1 percent in the period 1994–2005, compared to 7.1 percent during the period 1982–1993.
- U.S. industrial production—78 percent of which is manufacturing—rose by 49 percent between 1993 and 2005, exceeding the 28 percent increase achieved between 1981 and 1993.
- Growth in real compensation for manufacturing workers improved dramatically. Average real compensation grew at an average annual rate of 2.3 percent from 1993 to 2005, compared to just 0.4 percent annually between 1987 (earliest data available) and 1993.
- U.S. business sector productivity rose by 2.6 percent year between 1993 and 2005, or by a total of 36.2 percent over the full period. Between 1981 and 1993 the annual rate of productivity growth was 1.8 percent, or 24.3 percent over the full 12 year period.
- Mexico has seen consistent GDP growth—40 percent since 1993—and annual real wage growth since 1995. This has been accompanied by much lower interest rates and rapid development of consumer finance services, such as home mortgages that have created a boom in consumer lending and home purchases.
- Real GDP in Canada grew from C$773.5 (1997 Canadian dollars) in 1993 to C$1,157.7 in 2005, an increase of nearly 50 percent. Real Canadian GDP per capita surged by 33 percent over the same period. Canadian unemployment fell from 11.2 percent in 1993 to 6.7 percent last year.[2]

NAFTA's Ability to Respond to Changes

The NAFTA remains a vibrant agreement, one that has been able to respond to changes in production methods and sourcing arrangements. For example, the NAFTA establishes schedules for the elimination of tariffs, but the agreement also allows the Parties to accelerate the elimination of tariffs. Since the entry into force in 1994, the NAFTA partners have accelerated the elimination of tariffs four times, in 1997, 1998, 2000 and 2001. The total value of trilateral trade covered by these four rounds of tariff cuts is approximately $28 billion.

Over time, manufacturers often change the way they design and build products. They choose new suppliers, change the materials used in the production of a good, or improve their products by using new parts. Since 2002, the NAFTA partners have worked to update the NAFTA rules of origin, the regulations that specify which goods are eligible for preferential treatment under the agreement. These changes have allowed U.S. companies to export their products duty-free to our NAFTA partners, saving thousands, sometimes millions of dollars in duties. The NAFTA partners have implemented three sets of changes to the rules of origin, in 2002, 2004 and 2006. The total value of trade covered by these changes exceeds $39 billion. We are working to implement a fourth set of changes in 2007.

Recent Successes

In 2006, the United States has resolved a number of our thorniest trade issues with Canada and Mexico.

- In January, the United States and Mexico signed a bilateral agreement on trade in tequila, which will ensure that U.S. bottlers can continue to import tequila in bulk form. The agreement imposes no obligations on the United States beyond current practice.
- In March, the United States and Mexico signed an agreement to promote bilateral trade in cement. The agreement will allow for additional supply of cement at a time of strong domestic demand following the devastation of Hurricanes Katrina and Rita. The agreement also ends all NAFTA and WTO litigation on cement from Mexico, which had stretched back 16 years.
- In July, the United States and Canada reached final agreement on softwood lumber, a dispute that has dogged trade relations for 20 years.
- In August, the United States and Mexico reached an agreement on trade in sweeteners, which puts the two countries on a glide path towards full implementation of the NAFTA sugar provisions in 2008. Mexico agreed to remove its beverage tax and duties on drinks sweetened with high fructose corn syrup and other non-sugar sweeteners, and the United States agreed to an increase in the amount of duty-free sugar that Mexico is allowed to export to the United States. Mexico is providing duty-free access for an equivalent volume of high fructose corn syrup (HFCS).

Current Challenges

To address the challenges the NAFTA framework faces today and in the future, there are three circumstances to consider.

The first is implementation of the remaining NAFTA commitments by January 1, 2008.

As I mentioned earlier, all tariff cuts between the United States and Canada have already been implemented, and the remaining tariffs between the United States and Mexico will be eliminated on January 1, 2008. While less than one percent of our NAFTA trade with Mexico remains subject to duties, final removal of these duties has raised concerns in some sectors. As the three NAFTA trade ministers made clear at their annual oversight meetings in Mexico this past March, they are committed to full implementation of the NAFTA and will not consider any reduction to our NAFTA obligations.

A second set of challenges must take into account the changes in global trade since the NAFTA entered into force. Simply put, each of the NAFTA partners have been reducing trade barriers with other countries, meaning the margins of preference provided by the NAFTA are shrinking.

- In 1993, for example, the average United States duty on imports from all countries in was 3.2 percent. By 2005, it had fallen to 1.4 percent.

Mexico still has a larger margin of preferential access today than it did before NAFTA implementation began, but it has begun to fall.

- The United States also faces more competition in the Mexican and Canadian markets: Mexico has free trade agreements with 42 other countries today, compared with one (Chile) in 1994. Canada has concluded three additional FTAs since 1994, and is currently engaged in negotiations with the Republic of Korea.
- And, of course, all three countries face the challenge of increased competition with economies such as China and India.

A third set of challenges is how to best address today's security concerns while not creating trade barriers. This is the fundamental challenge of the Security and Prosperity Partnership of North America, a trilateral initiative launched in March 2005. The SPP seeks to enhance the security, prosperity, and quality of life for the citizens of all three countries while respecting the sovereignty and unique cultural and legal heritage of each country. The SPP builds on and complements the NAFTA, and we can use both processes to advance common strategic North American goals. For example, under both the NAFTA and the SPP, USTR is soliciting proposals from U.S. industries to liberalize and simplify NAFTA Rules of Origin, making it easier to use the benefits of the duty-free access that the NAFTA provides.

To conclude, with the NAFTA firmly in place, the United States and its NAFTA partners have not only become better customers for each other but better neighbors, more committed partners, and effective colleagues in a wide range of trade-related international organizations.

I am pleased to answer any questions you may have.

Notes

1. Derived from GAO report 02-595R, page 1 and the CIA World Factbook.
2. See "Economic Indicators," on the website of the Department of Foreign Affairs and International Trade. . . .

Sandra Polaski  **NO**

The Employment Consequences of NAFTA

Conclusion: Learning from the NAFTA Experience

At twelve years, the long-term effects of NAFTA on employment, wages, and incomes in the countries of North America cannot be judged definitively. However, short- and medium-term impacts can now be assessed on the basis of substantial, accumulating data, as presented above. That assessment also provides some potentially useful guidance for measures that might improve the employment and distributive outcomes of future trade agreements.

Employment

The most salient result of the NAFTA experience and the one most at odds with predictions of political advocates is that the trade agreement has produced disappointingly small net gains in employment in the countries of North America. In Mexico, employment destruction in domestic manufacturing and agriculture has all but swamped job creation in export manufacturing. In the United States, NAFTA has had either a neutral or very small net positive effect on employment. Meanwhile, in Canada, CUFTA led first to a significant net decrease in jobs in traded sectors, followed by a slow recovery of employment to pre-CUFTA levels after ten years, then a continued increase in subsequent years. The political and rhetorical claims for trade as an engine of net job growth are not borne out by experience, at least in the medium term.

Such claims have always been at odds with the predictions of trade theory. In theory, if an economy is at full employment before opening to trade, the shifting of resources into different productive activities based on comparative advantage will not result in a net gain or loss of jobs, but rather in a different mix of industries and employment. The gains from trade in a full-employment economy would be seen in rising wages and incomes, according to basic trade theory. The United States and, arguably, Canada have been at full employment during most of the NAFTA period. Thus, the lack of any significant job growth due to NAFTA in Canada and the United States is not at odds with the predictions of economic theory, although it certainly contradicts the claims of NAFTA boosters. What is surprising, even from the perspective of economic theory, is the weak job creation in Mexico, which is far from full employment.

U.S. Senate, September 11, 2006.

As noted earlier, it is impossible to determine with certainty the precise share of agricultural job losses and manufacturing job gains in Mexico that resulted directly from NAFTA. However, the trade pact has been the single most important factor in Mexico's changing pattern of trade, and the overall growth of jobs in all traded sectors since 1993 has been very weak. It is thus evident that NAFTA has not been a robust job creator for the low-wage, labor-abundant trading partner.

In developing economies with surplus labor, such as Mexico, the NAFTA experience demonstrates that trade pacts cannot be counted on to produce much, if any, net employment growth in the absence of other targeted policies. Policies to maximize employment gains from trade would include measures to promote domestic supplier and support industries and terms in the trade agreement that reward rather than discourage the use of domestic inputs in the production of exported goods.

The experience of Mexico also suggests that a developing country with a high proportion of its labor force in low-productivity agriculture should negotiate very long transition periods for the phase-out of tariffs on basic crops. The negative situation currently faced by Mexico also demonstrates that a developing country must use that transition time aggressively to prepare the rural population for the wrenching adjustment it will face. Policies should be adopted to shift farmers to competitive crops, to develop alternative sources of employment in rural areas, and to invest heavily in education to prepare the population for more modern occupations. Another important factor for Mexico was that some of its most important basic crops, such as maize, were exposed to competition from subsidized U.S. crops that are sold at artificially low prices, sometimes below the cost of production. Further, U.S. policy on agricultural subsidies changed significantly in ways that were not foreseen during the NAFTA negotiations, most notably in the passage of the farm bill in 2002 that increased subsidies. Successful competition will be impossible for the developing country under those circumstances.

The transition times negotiated by Mexico were too short, and the government did not adopt sufficiently vigorous rural adjustment policies to help subsistence farmers adapt to the new trade conditions. In trade negotiations with developing countries with significant employment in subsistence agriculture, the US and its partners should carefully consider the sequencing of liberalization, to allow the absorption of rural workers into other sectors that expand due to liberalized access to foreign markets, before basic crops are liberalized. Developing countries will also need special safeguard mechanisms to protect the incomes of their rural households during the long transitional period.

The experience of Mexico also suggests that the government relied too heavily on export-led growth, adopting policies that repressed wages in order to pursue global competitiveness. These wage policies had the effect of depressing domestic demand in Mexico, which made the economy even more dependent on export sectors for job creation, in a vicious circle. A more balanced strategy of stimulating domestic demand through wage increases (commensurate with productivity gains) and support to rural households would likely produce better overall employment results.

Productivity

The one employment area where a clear positive impact has been seen during the NAFTA period is the growth of productivity in all three North American countries. At least in Mexico and Canada, which cut tariffs deeply and were exposed to competition from their giant neighbor, NAFTA likely played a significant role in the observed productivity growth. In Canada, increased productivity may have contributed to a medium-term revival and perhaps even long-term survival of the manufacturing sector.

However, the strong productivity growth in the United States and somewhat weaker growth in Mexico and Canada may have had the unwelcome side effect of reducing the pace of job creation in the three countries, as workers produced more and fewer new jobs were created.

Throughout North America, there has been a decoupling of productivity growth from wage growth over the last decade.

Wages

During the NAFTA period, productivity growth in Mexico has not translated into wage growth, as it did in earlier periods. Mexican wages are also diverging from, rather than converging toward, U.S. wages, as trade theory would suggest.

Because the net impact of NAFTA on U.S. employment is small, the impact on overall wages is also likely to be small. But a widening gap between the wages of skilled and unskilled workers is partly attributable to trade, and NAFTA probably accounts for a small portion of the observed growth in wage disparity within the United States.

Overall real wages in Canada were only slightly higher in 2002 than when CUFTA took effect in 1989, but manufacturing earnings had fared somewhat better. This suggests that NAFTA and CUFTA did not have a negative impact on wages, since earnings in non-traded sectors increased more slowly than in manufacturing. As in the case of Mexico, productivity increases in Canada significantly outstripped wage increases.

In all three countries, the evolution of wages and household incomes since NAFTA took effect has been toward greater inequality, with most gains going to the upper 20 percent of households and higher-skilled workers. While this trend is clearly compounded of many factors, more open trade appears to be one element—along with continental and global competition over the location of production—that restrains wage growth.

Whether productivity gains lead to higher wages also depends on the nature and quality of the institutions that determine the distribution of productivity gains within a society between the return to workers as higher wages and the return to investors as higher profits. Institutions that govern the ability of workers to organize unions and bargain collectively over wages are important determinants of distribution, as are government mechanisms such as minimum wage policies. If productivity gains are to be shared with workers in the form of rising wages, the institutions and public policies that affect wage outcomes will need to be strengthened. Weak laws and institutions related to freedom of association and collective bargaining should be addressed in conjunction with trade liberalization. Minimum wage policies need to be reconsidered; dispute resolution mechanisms, such as arbitration, could also be strengthened.

Income Distribution

Income inequality has been on the rise in Mexico since NAFTA took effect, reversing a brief downward trend in the early 1990s. Compared to the period before NAFTA, the top 10 percent of households have increased their share of national income, while the other 90 percent have lost income share or seen no change. Regional inequality within Mexico has also increased, reversing a long-term trend toward convergence in regional incomes.

In a trend that predates NAFTA, income inequality in the United States has been increasing for most of the last two decades. The growing wage gap between high-skilled and low-skilled workers is one of the causes, and to the extent that trade is a factor in the wage gap, it is also implicated in growing inequality.

Incomes in Canada are relatively more equal than in either Mexico or the United States, but inequality has been on a marked upward trend since CUFTA's entry into force in 1989. Because manufacturing wages have performed better than wages in most other sectors, it seems clear that trade-induced wage changes are not the cause of the observed increase in inequality. Rather, a reduction in transfer payments from government, which play an important role in the incomes of the bottom 40 percent of households, accounts for most of the change. The weakening of the Canadian social safety net, which generates these transfer payments, was a concern of CUFTA opponents, but there is currently no clear evidence to support a causal relationship.

If the gains from trade are to be shared widely throughout a country, the institutional mechanisms that govern how costs and benefits of economic change are distributed may need to be strengthened. Government measures that affect income distribution, such as tax and transfer mechanisms, should be reviewed and fortified to deal with the impact of trade opening.

The experience of each of the NAFTA countries confirms the prediction of trade theory that there will always be winners and losers from trade. The number of losers may equal or even surpass the number of winners, especially in the short-to-medium term. In Canada, it took a decade for manufacturing employment to recover from the initial displacements caused by CUFTA. In Mexico, rural farmers are still struggling to adapt to NAFTA-induced changes. The short-to-medium term adjustment costs faced by the losers from trade can be severe, and the losers are often those segments of society least able to cope with adjustment, due to low skills, low savings, and low mobility. It must also be recognized that there may be permanent losers from trade, due to limitations of education, skills, geographic isolation, and other factors.

Because the impacts of trade are uneven, governments should establish mechanisms that help offset the losses suffered by those in declining sectors.

Trade adjustment assistance should provide income support to workers and small farmers during transitional periods, as well as funds for training for new occupations. Such policies are highly desirable complements to trade pacts. The existing trade adjustment assistance program in the United States and the broader social safety net in Canada serve these ends, although both countries' plans have critical gaps that should be addressed. In Mexico, budget constraints and policy choices have precluded the establishment of even the most basic unemployment insurance and social safety net. The harsh impact of agricultural trade liberalization on subsistence farmers there has not been offset by appropriate government policies. Developing countries negotiating with wealthier trading partners will likely need financial assistance from those countries, as part of the trade package, for transitional adjustment programs.

POSTSCRIPT

Has the North American Free Trade Agreement Benefited the Economies of Canada, Mexico, and the United States?

To evaluate the impact of NAFTA on the three partners, Melle points to the larger growth of the United States' trade with Canada and Mexico (compared with U.S. trade with the world), which are now the United States' second and third largest trading partners; to the changing composition of Mexico's exports, 90 percent of which are now manufactured goods (oil and raw materials comprised 80 percent of Mexican exports in 1980); to the near doubling of U.S. agricultural exports to Canada and Mexico since NAFTA's implementation; to the surplus on U.S. trade in services with its NAFTA partners; and to the fall in average U.S. tariffs on Mexican goods (to about 0.5 percent in 2005) and Mexico's tariffs on American goods (0.003 percent). He also notes the more rapid growth in many of the United States' economic indicators since NAFTA's implementation. In Mexico, there has been consistent GDP growth and annual real wage growth since 1995. In Canada there has been a 33 percent increase in real GDP per capita and a drop in unemployment from 11.2 percent in 1993 to 6.7 percent in 2005. In addition, the NAFTA partners have accelerated the elimination of tariffs four times and have been flexible in updating and regulations.

Sandra Polaski is critical of NAFTA's achievements. NAFTA has had at best a very small effect on employment in all three countries. Job creation in Mexico's export manufacturing sector is outweighed by job destruction in its domestic manufacturing sector and in agriculture. Moreover, Mexico's most basic crops were exposed to competition from subsidized U.S. crops sold at artificially low prices. Further, income inequality in Mexico has risen since NAFTA was implemented, and so has regional inequality (reversing its long-term trend). Also, Mexican wages are diverging from U.S. wages, and "NAFTA probably accounts for a small portion of the observed growth in wage disparity within the United States."

There is a large amount of literature relating to NAFTA. Robert Scott, "NAFTA's Hidden Costs: Trade Agreement Results in Job Losses, Growing Inequality, and Wage Suppression for the United States," ERP Briefing Paper (April 2001), and Daniel T. Griswold, "NAFTA at 10: An Economic and Foreign Policy Success," Free Trade Bulletin (December 2003), offer additional analyses of NAFTA's costs. For a more political critique of NAFTA, see *The Selling of "Free Trade": NAFTA, Washington, and the Subversion of American Democracy* by John

R. MacArthur (Hill & Wang, 2000). Besides controversy on the macro effects of NAFTA, there is significant debate on various elements within the NAFTA agreement. One good example is NAFTA's Chapter 11, the so-called investor-to-state protections: see William T. Warren, "NAFTA and State Sovereignty: A Pandora's Box of Property Rights," *Spectrum: The Journal of State Government* (Spring 2002), and "Update on NAFTA Chapter 11 Claim re Methanex," GreenYes Archives, http://greeneyes.grrn./2002/11/msg00069.html>http://greenyes .grrn.org/2002/11/msg00069.html (March 2003). For more about FTAA, see the section entitled "Trade Promotion Authority" in Chapter 6 of the *Economic Report of the President, 2003*.

ISSUE 18

Do the Testing and Accountability Elements of the No Child Left Behind Act Prevent a Proper Cost-Benefit Evaluation?

YES: George Miller, from "Should Congress Make Fundamental Changes in the No Child Left Behind Act? (Pro)," *Congressional Digest* (May 2008)

NO: Raymond Simon, from "Should Congress Make Fundamental Changes in the No Child Left Behind Act? (Con)," *Congressional Digest* (May 2008)

ISSUE SUMMARY

YES: Chairman of the Education and Labor Committee of the United States House of Representatives, California Democrat George Miller states that schools and students are not making enough progress and significant changes must be made to the law so that its goals may be achieved. "America needs and must have an educational law that insists on accountability with high expectations and high-quality assessments; that closes the achievement gap; and helps all children to learn."

NO: Deputy Secretary, U.S. Department of Education, Raymond Simon states that NCLB is working for students. Simon believes that there is consensus for a limited number of changes. He claims that NCLB's insistence on scientifically based research and the gathering and using of reliable data has been one of its major successes.

T he passage of the Elementary and Secondary Education Act (ESEA) in 1965 imparted an important federal component to spending on education that is mostly financed by state and local taxes. Americans are concerned about public education for a variety of reasons. One reason is that public spending absorbs a significant amount of tax dollars. But Americans are also concerned because the results of all the spending are less than impressive. This dissatisfaction goes back to at least 1983, when the National Commission on Excellence in Education released its report, entitled *A Nation at Risk*. This report identified a variety of problems in public education. In spite of a number of "reforms" that have been put in place since then, the dissatisfaction with public education continued into the twenty-first century. For example, the U.S. Department of Education reported that in 2003, "Even after four years of public schooling, most students perform below proficiency in both reading and mathematics." And for the year 2000, the Department reported: "Upon graduation from high school, few students have acquired the math and science skills necessary to compete in the knowledge-based economy."

In his presidential campaign in 2000, candidate George W. Bush emphasized educational reform. He signed the No Child Left Behind Act (NCLBA) into law on January 8, 2002. NCLBA was a bipartisan effort; it passed the House by a 381–41 margin and the Senate with an 87–10 vote. A leading Democrat, Senator Ted Kennedy (D-MA), was a chief sponsor of the legislation in the Senate.

As to its broad objectives, former Secretary Rod Paige states that NCLBA "ensures accountability and flexibility as well as increased federal support for education," and that it "continues the legacy of the *Brown v. Board* decision by creating an education system that is more inclusive, responsive, and fair." Turning to more specific provisions, NCLBA mandates that every state set standards for grade-level achievement and develop a system to see if students are reaching those standards. NCLBA rededicates the country to the goal of having a "highly qualified teacher" in every classroom, where "highly qualified" means the teacher holds a bachelor's degree, holds a certification or licensure to teach in the state of his or her employment, and has proven knowledge of the subjects he or she teaches.

The NCLBA has generated a good deal of controversy beginning just a few years after its passage. Six years later as the law came up for reauthorization, there are those like Deputy Secretary, U.S. Department of Education, Raymond Simon who believe the legislation is generating positive results and that only a few changes might be in order. At the same time, there is a significant vocal opposition, represented by George Miller, Chairman of the Education and Labor Committee of the U.S. House of Representatives, one of the original co-authors of the NCLBA, who believes that the law brought some positive changes but "We didn't get it all right when we enacted the law," and "there are no votes in the U.S. House of Representatives for continuing the No Child Left Behind Act without making serious changes to it." He identifies six key elements, of which assessment and accountability are a major component: "The heart of No Child Left Behind is accountability."

An epilogue is in order about budgetary provisions and the fate of the reauthorization of NCLBA. As to the first, the 2009 budget provides only $125 million above 2008 for NCLB, "a cumulative shortfall of $85.6 billion."

As to the reauthorization: the Educator Roundtable November Bulletin reported that it failed, since a compromise that would satisfy all the critics of NCLB could not be reached. The law continues until it is repealed.

In April 2008, the Department of Education proposed new regulations for Title I of the ESEA covering state assessment and accountability systems. George Miller denounced these as "a series of piecemeal changes to a law that really needs a comprehensive overhaul."

YES

George Miller

Should Congress Make Fundamental Changes in the No Child Left Behind Act? (Pro)

Over 40 years ago, President John F. Kennedy had a vision of sending a man to the moon and bringing him home again. That vision fueled a massive investment by this Nation in all levels of education—an investment that drove nearly four decades of discovery, innovation, and economic growth, allowing America to have the world's strongest economy and lead the community of nations for generations.

Sadly, this investment fell off over the years. With the report *A Nation at Risk,* America woke up and saw an education system that no longer served all its children and was failing our future.

America had an education system that was operating under a policy of acceptable losses. Where only about half of all minority children could read proficiently. Where black and Hispanic 17-year-olds were being taught math to the same level as white 13-year-olds. Where 40,000 teachers in California were without the credentials necessary to teach in the schools.

Nearly four decades after President Kennedy's decision, America realized that its education system was threatening the country's world leadership. Six years ago we decided to do something bold about it.

We made a decision as a Nation to raise our expectations of what America's schools and schoolchildren could achieve. We made a decision to insist upon high standards. We said that it was not good enough for a majority of the children in a school district to be learning and performing at grade level if their success was allowed to mask the fact that many other children were falling behind.

We asked the States to set higher standards for their schools and students, because we believed that every single child—if given access to a highly quali-fied teacher and a good curriculum in a decent school—could achieve educa-tional success.

We made performance at our schools transparent, and we made schools accountable for their performance.

Today, five and a half years after its enactment, the No Child Left Behind Act has brought some positive changes.

From *Congressional Digest*, May 2008. Published by Pro & Con® Publishers, a division of Congressional Digest Corporation.

A recent Center on Education Policy study of all 50 States found gains in students' reading and math proficiency and the narrowing of the achievement gap among groups of students since the implementation of No Child Left Behind.

There are more qualified teachers in the classroom today, because we made it a priority. The law is shining a bright light on the achievement gaps among different groups of students in the United States and among the States. Now—for the first time—we know exactly which students, and which groups of students, are not learning and performing at grade level. This information makes it impossible for us to ignore those students who are not succeeding.

And finally, the law has provoked an energetic national debate about our Nation's system of public education and the need for the next generation of investment in our schools, students, principals, and teachers. That is a good thing.

Let me be clear, though: Schools and students are not making enough progress. Not for a country as great as ours. We didn't get it all right when we enacted the law.

Throughout our schools and communities, the American people have a very strong sense that the No Child Left Behind Act is not fair. That it is not flexible. And that it is not funded. And they are not wrong.

The question is what we are going to do next. America needs and must have an education law that insists on accountability with high expectations, high standards, and high-quality assessments; that closes the achievement gap; and that helps all children to learn. And America needs and must have an education law that treats schools and children fairly, that provides educators and administrators with the flexibility they need to meet high standards, and that delivers to schools the resources they need to improve and succeed. We can and we must meet these objectives in this next stage of education reform in the United States.

We would be wrong to waver when it comes to the existing goals and standards of the No Child Left Behind law. We would also be wrong if we failed to respond to the serious concerns with the law raised by people who sincerely care about America's educational future.

I can tell you that there are no votes in the U.S. House of Representatives for continuing the No Child Left Behind Act without making serious changes to it. It is my intention as chairman of the Education and Labor Committee to pass a bill in September, both in committee and on the floor of the House.

We want a bill that is fair and flexible—that maintains the integrity of the law through accountability while responding to the legitimate concerns that have been raised.

I have always said that I am proud to be one of the original coauthors of the No Child Left Behind Act. But what I really want is to be the proud coauthor of a law that works.

To that end, for the last five years I have traveled this country listening to teachers, administrators, students, parents, governors, and many others about how the law can be improved. I have listened carefully, as have my colleagues. We have heard an emerging consensus about needed changes.

The process by which this bill is being developed is open, transparent, and bipartisan. It reflects the input of Members of Congress from both parties and across the ideological spectrum, many or whom testified before and submitted suggestions to our committee.

It reflects testimony delivered in nearly two dozen congressional hearings begun last year by then-Chairman [Rep. Buck] McKeon [CA-R]. Congressman McKeon and I have been working together on this reauthorization for many months. He has been very helpful to this process.

And it reflects our review of recommendations from more than 100 education, civil rights, and business organizations. Congressman Dale Kildee [MI-D], the subcommittee [on Early Childhood, Elementary and Secondary Education] chair, and I have met with many of these organizations.

My vision for this next bill is to take America's education policy in a new direction by doing six key things:

- Provide much-needed fairness and flexibility.
- Encourage a rich and challenging learning environment and promote best practices and innovation taking place in schools throughout the country.
- Support teachers and principals.
- Continue to hold schools accountable for students' progress.
- Join the effort to improve America's high schools.
- Invest in our schools.

First, the legislation will provide much-needed fairness and flexibility. We hear concerns that schools don't get credit they deserve when their students make real progress over time. The legislation I will introduce will contain a growth model that gives credit to States and schools for the progress that their students make over time.

This builds on a pilot effort started by [U.S. Education] Secretary [Margaret] Spellings. The Secretary deserves great credit for her leadership on this important issue.

These growth models will give us fairer, better, and more accurate information. The information will be timely and helpful to teachers and principals in developing strategies for improvement and in targeting resources. In addition, many Americans do not believe that the success of our students or our schools can be measured by one test administered on one day. I agree with them. This is not fair.

We hear concerns that the law has forced schools to focus on math and reading instruction at the expense of history, art, social studies, music, and physical education. This is not required under the Act—nor should it be—but we must help ensure that all students in all schools have access to a broad, rich curriculum.

Our legislation will continue to place strong emphasis on reading and math skills. But it will allow States to use more than their reading and math test results to determine how well schools and students are doing. We will allow the use of additional valid and reliable measures to assess student learning and school performance more fairly, comprehensively, and accurately. One such measure for high schools must be graduation rates.

The legislation will also drive improvements in the quality and appropriateness of the tests used for accountability. This is especially important for English language learners and students with disabilities who should be given tests that are fair and appropriate, just as they should continue to be included in our accountability system.

In exchange for increased resources, States will be allowed to develop better tests that more accurately measure what all students have learned. These tests will be more useful to teachers and will drive richer classroom instruction.

Second, the legislation will encourage a rich and challenging learning environment, and it will promote best practices and innovation taking place in schools throughout the country. In so many meetings I have had in my district and elsewhere, employers say that our high school graduates are not ready for the workplace. Colleges say that our high school graduates are not ready for the college classroom. This is unacceptable.

In my bill, we will ask employers and colleges to come together as stakeholders with the States to jointly develop more rigorous standards that meet the demands of both.

Many States have already started this process. We seek to build on and complement the leadership of our Nation's governors and provide them with incentives to continue. This requires that assessments be fully aligned with these new State standards and include multiple measures of success.

These measures can no longer reflect just basic skills and memorization. Rather, they must reflect critical thinking skills and the ability to apply knowledge to new and challenging contexts. These are the skills that today's students will need to meet the complex demands of the American economy and society in a globalized world.

Schools must no longer prepare our students to be autonomous problem solvers. The workplace they enter tomorrow will increasingly require them to work in teams, collaborating across companies, communities, and continents. These skills cannot be developed solely by simple multiple choice exams.

For too long we have settled for standards and assessments that do not measure up to the high goals we have for our kids or the skills they must achieve. But let none of us for a moment believe that our students will be able to participate in this interactive and participatory culture and workplace if they cannot read, write, and understand math.

Therefore, the bill will say that if States take this step and commit to the students of their States that they will prepare them for the universities and jobs of the future, then we will provide them with incentives and assistance to do so.

Third, the legislation will support teachers and principals. Even with all of these changes, we will not meet our national goal of closing the achievement gap until and unless we close the teacher quality gap. No factor matters more to children's educational success than the quality of their teachers and principals. All children deserve their fair share of teacher talent and expertise.

We must do more to ensure that poor and minority students are taught by teachers with expertise in the subjects they are teaching.

I have heard from so many teachers who feel they are no longer viewed as critical partners in an educational system but merely an instrument to satisfy a minimum attainment goal. As a Nation, we are not offering teachers the respect and support they deserve today, and as a result we are facing a very real teacher shortage crisis. Particularly in urban and rural communities, in subjects like math, science, foreign language, and for children with disabilities and children learning English, we must hire, train, and retain excellent teachers.

For these reasons, the legislation I will introduce will provide for performance pay for principals and teachers based on fair and proven models, teacher mentoring, teacher career ladders, and improved working conditions. It will also provide incentives consistent with the Teach Act that I introduced two years ago that will help bring top teacher talent into the classrooms that need this the most.

Fourth, the legislation will continue to hold schools accountable for students' progress. The heart of No Child Left Behind is accountability. Our bill will continue to hold schools accountable for all students, including minority and low-income students, students learning English, and those with disabilities. All of these students deserve an improved accountability system. Under current law, schools whose students have not made adequate achievement gains are all treated the same—with the same interventions and sanctions taking place over the same period of time. We need to distinguish among different schools and the challenges facing them, as well as their needs for addressing those challenges.

Schools with specific problems in specific areas should be allowed to use instructional interventions that are appropriate to their needs. High-priority schools, meanwhile, must receive more intensive support and assistance.

I am pleased that the House Appropriations Committee has already committed significant new funding for this purpose next year.

Fifth, the legislation will join the effort to improve America's high schools.

I believe this is part of the solution to addressing our unacceptably high dropout rate. Over 30 percent of all high school students do not receive a diploma. America is better than that. We can no longer give up on these students by allowing them to give up on school.

The bill will include comprehensive steps to turn around low-performing middle and high schools. It will include uniform standards for measuring graduation rates that are fair, accurate, and reliable, and will do more to keep students in school. I tip my hat to the governors for their leadership in this area, and look forward to working with them as we benefit from and build on their reforms.

We must also remember that there are remarkable examples of schools in difficult environments where students are soaring and the achievement gap is closing. We must celebrate and reward these successes. Our bill will help sustain them, build on them, and bring them to scale.

Sixth, and finally, this legislation will invest in our schools. This new direction for education in America is premised on the growing consensus that there is a need for greater and sustained investments in American education.

In the new Congress, the Democratic Leadership has begun this new era of investment—first with the continuing resolution funding, then the appropriations bill, the Innovation and Competitiveness Agenda, and the College Cost Reduction Act.

I expect this legislation to follow suit.

Much has been made of the unusual political coalition that developed the No Child Left Behind Act and the important role that President [George W.] Bush played. Now the discussion has shifted to No Child Left Behind as the most important domestic legacy for this President.

I would only say this: President Bush's legacy will not be established if he vetoes the education funding in the Labor-Health and Human Services-Education Appropriations bill. The legacy of a great American education system for our children and our country cannot be built on the cheap. America deserves better.

I want to close today by talking about why it's so important that we get this right.

Our public education system plays many critical roles in our society. So much of who we are and where we are going is a product of this system combined with our families and our communities.

Social and economic opportunity begins in the classroom. Discovery and innovation begin in the classroom. Economic growth and economic disparity begin in the classroom.

That is why it is essential to have a high-quality and engaged education system to carry out the continuous quest of redeeming America's promise of equality for all people to fully participate in a thriving democratic system.

With this new direction for education in America, I believe we will have a new opportunity to succeed. So many leaders from the education community, the business community, and the civil rights community have already contributed so much understanding and rigor to this reauthorization process.

I am as excited and hopeful today as I have been at any time in the more than 30 years that I have served in Congress about the prospects for finally realizing the vision of excellent educational opportunities for all children in America.

Should Congress Make Fundamental Changes in the No Child Left Behind Act? (Con)

A reading of the U.S. Constitution finds no mention of the Federal Government's role in the education of its citizens, thereby relegating that responsibility primarily to individual States. Although constitutionally absent, events in our country's history have nonetheless established a clear national interest in an educated citizenry, with Federal law so reflecting that.

Most pertinent to today's topic are events dating back to 1965 with the passage of the Federal Elementary and Secondary Education Act (ESEA), beginning for the Nation a new era of responsibility for our country's poorest school children. ESEA was designed to level the playing field between the rich and poor by focusing Federal money on high-poverty areas. The law has been in existence continually since that time, undergoing periodic renewal (what we call reauthorization) roughly every seven years. No Child Left Behind represents its latest reauthorization.

I began my teaching internship just a few weeks after the signing of that historic law. At that time, learning standards were almost exclusively teacher-based. My standards were not necessarily those of the teacher in the adjacent room teaching the same subject. As long as I covered the textbook or major portion thereof, and did it in a way that kids were learning, no one really cared.

Federal financial support, although limited, was welcomed and offered opportunity for new programs beyond what State and local funding provided. Schools met the accountability requirements of the law primarily by documenting that the money was spent on allowable products and services, such as equipment or professional development. State education departments and local school districts were the principal drivers of school reform.

By the late 1980s, even longtime supporters of the law were becoming concerned about the lack of evidence that the Federal funds were making a substantial difference in the education of poor and minority children. It was then that the Federal interest began to shift to standards and accountability for academic achievement.

The 1994 reauthorization, known as the Improving America's Schools Act, required States to develop more rigorous standards, establish tests to

From *Congressional Digest*, May 2008. Published by Pro & Con® Publishers, a division of Congressional Digest Corporation.

measure against those standards, and disaggregate the testing data to identify which population subgroups were being underserved. Because the 1994 version lacked accountability mechanisms for rigorous enforcement, by the time of NCLB in 2001, only 11 of our 50 States were in compliance.

NCLB, signed by President George W. Bush with overwhelming bipartisan support in the Congress, expanded the law's requirements even further, establishing meaningful achievement and compliance provisions. Both the President and Congress made it very clear that this time they really did mean it——children must be able to read and do math at or above grade level. No more excuses.

Today, learning standards are State-based, with annual State-developed and -administered tests in reading and math required in each of the grades three through eight and once in high school. The goal is that every child performs at or above grade level in those subjects by 2014.

Accountability is measured at the school level, with each State setting the improvement trajectory for its schools, taking them from their current level of performance to 100 percent by 2014. In order to accomplish this, every child is expected to have a highly qualified teacher every year.

Schools report annually to parents and the public on how well they are doing. Those that fail to meet their annual improvement goals have additional sums of money targeted to interventions that will help their students get better, including tutoring and, in some cases, allowing children to transfer to another school that is meeting its targets. Schools that chronically underperform are subject to more extreme interventions, including replacing staff, being taken over by other public or private entities, or eventual closure.

Federal aid has been substantially increased under NCLB and now stands at an all-time high, but still accounts for only about 9 percent of the average school district's financial support. In exchange for this money, a State voluntarily agrees to be held accountable for the law's provisions, submitting a plan that sets out the manner in which it will fulfill these requirements. This includes proof that its standards are indeed aligned with its testing and that highly qualified teachers are being distributed equally among the classrooms of poor children and their more affluent counterparts.

Each year, each State is told how much it will receive in Federal funds, and each year the State is free to decline those funds and thus avoid any obligation to implement its plan. No State has yet refused the money. The Federal Government, although a minority funding partner in a voluntary endeavor, is now driving much of the country's school reform efforts.

Some question whether the mission of NCLB, getting every child to grade level or above in reading and math by 2014, is doable. The fact is, it is already being done in a growing number of schools around the country, schools where today all or most of students are meeting that standard. These are what I call the "2014 is today" schools.

What distinguishes these successful schools from those similarly situated in terms of demographics and other measures, but that are not making progress or are among the chronic underperforming schools?

First and foremost, successful schools know what to do—and what to do centers around a really good teacher. Specifically, these schools believe that their students can achieve to high standards. These standards, and the expected behavior to reach them, are clearly communicated to the students and their parents. Highly qualified, effective teachers use data to guide instruction daily and they work with an outstanding school-level administrator who has knowledge and authority to effect change, reward innovation, and enforce high expectations.

One of the immediate challenges for educators and policymakers is to provide information to all schools about what really works and what doesn't. Then, we must have the wisdom and courage to stop what doesn't work and concentrate exclusively on what does.

Does anybody know what this is? It's a slide rule, a calculating device that has its origins dating back to the seventeenth century. I don't mind telling you I had a time getting this through airport security; some of the younger screeners were convinced it was some sort of weapon, but just couldn't prove it.

Slide rules came in various sizes and were made of various materials, including fiberglass, wood, plastic, and metal. The one I am most proud of, and which was given to me in 1963 by my brother as a high school graduation present, is made of fiberglass and has numerous advanced features that are not on the plastic version I hold in my hand. Unsure of whether or not this would be allowed on the plane, I just couldn't risk bringing the better one.

The accuracy of the instrument varied, depending on the material of construction, giving different answers depending on the temperature, relative humidity, and nervousness of the operator. A slight twitch at any point in the process could skew the final answer significantly. The operator had to be good at estimating the answer; for instance, multiplying 572 times 1,320 required the same settings as multiplying 5.72 by 13,200.

No mathematician, scientist, or engineer dared do his or her work without the slide rule. You especially looked cool when you could wear one on your belt in a leather carrying case. The slide rule remained the machine of choice for computation even into the computer age. The first calculators were called "electronic slide rules," just like the first cars were called "horseless carriages." In 1951, IBM bragged that it took 150 slide rules to match the power of one of its new computers.

American engineering achievements that owe their existence to this device include the Empire State Building, Hoover Dam, Golden Gate Bridge, Boeing 707 airliner, and the Saturn 5 rocket used by the Apollo and Skylab programs.

This instrument, that carried the world from the Renaissance to the moon, was rendered obsolete overnight. It was replaced with the microprocessor, represented here by an electronic calculator. These devices are millions of times faster and infinitely more accurate. They are the machine of choice for computation for today's generation.

It took a wizard to use the slide rule, and only after weeks of training and persistent use. Anyone can use a calculator with only a few minutes of training—but you can't look cool carrying it on your belt.

I use this analogy between the slide rule and calculator to illustrate where I believe the United States as a nation finds itself in discussing our system of education and the reforms necessary to make it work better for students.

One of the major successes of NCLB has been in its insistence on scientifically based research and the gathering and use of reliable data—data that can tell the truth, whether or not we want to hear it. There exists in too many of our schools what President Bush has called the "soft bigotry of low expectations" for certain subgroups of students, including those in special education, those whose first language is not English, and our poor and minority children.

Only half of African-American and Hispanic students graduate from high school on time. Ninety percent of the fastest-growing jobs require postsecondary education or training, yet 60 percent of Americans have no postsecondary credentials at all. Only 10 percent of Latinos earn bachelor's degrees by age 29.

Among countries participating in the Organization for Economic Cooperation and Development, the United States ranks first in the percent of the population 55 to 64 years old who have completed both high school and college. When you look at those same statistics among 25 to 34 year olds, we rank tenth in each category. These and other similar statistics illustrate that a large number of our students lack the skills to succeed in the global knowledge economy. If we choose to ignore this reality, too many of our citizens run the risk, as history has documented for the slide rule, of being rendered obsolete overnight.

These young people are being released with slide rule skills to compete in job markets that demand the ability to work not only with multifunctional calculators, but also with advanced computer systems.

Our very best schools are extraordinary, but there is a diversity of quality in far too many, where expectations for students haven't been set high enough. In other words, contentment with the status quo equates to losing ground. When business as usual fails our students, informed innovators need to step forward and give the status quo the heave ho.

On a positive note, it is apparent that No Child Left Behind, in partnership with State and local school reform efforts, is working for students. In addition to annual State testing, the law requires that all States participate every two years in reading and math portions of the National Assessment of Educational Progress (NAEP) at grades four and eight. NAEP, known as our Nation's report card, is the only true national exam given.

Results from the 2007 administration show that at fourth grade, reading and math scores are higher than ever, with math gains between 2003 and 2007 equivalent to adding an extra half-year of instruction. Math scores at eighth grade are higher than ever. The biggest gains in both grades and both subjects came from our Hispanic and African-American students, among those traditionally left behind by our education system.

Similar results have been shown on the State-administered tests. Highly qualified teachers are now found in over 90 percent of our classrooms, which is an all-time high.

To ensure that the goals of NCLB continue to be met for all students, the President has proposed a series of modifications for the Act's current reauthorization. These refinements are meant to foster and honor further innovation, where such new thinking will increase the opportunities for teachers to teach and students to learn. He wants to make sure that the law works better for States, schools, and the children they serve, while not sacrificing its core principles of accountability, high standards, enhanced choices for parents, and sound, proven methods of instruction.

We have learned a lot over the past six years—what works well and what needs to be changed. We have heard from students, teachers, parents, administrators, and policymakers from all levels of school governance, the business community, and advocacy groups. Consensus has generally formed around a limited number of changes, some of which Secretary of Education Margaret Spellings has already addressed through her limited authority provided in the law to waive certain aspects of its provisions.

The Secretary has already made allowances for a limited group of special education students and for those children whose first language is not English. We have worked with States and local districts to make it easier for them to offer more tutoring options for children who fall behind.

We believe the law needs to be changed to accommodate the use of what is known as a growth model, where schools can get credit for improving the performance of the same students over time as they move from grade to grade. When NCLB began, few States had the data capacity to calculate such individual academic progress. The Secretary has already permitted nine States to use this method and recently announced its future availability to all others eligible.

We need to increase the flexibility and capacity for States and school districts to help them turn around struggling schools by going from the current pass–fail system to a more nuanced approach that makes distinctions between those chronic underperformers and those schools that are missing their targets in just one or two areas. This involves both intervening early when signs of trouble develop and being more innovative and aggressive at the other extreme when chronic underperforming schools just don't seem to be able to get it right.

We need to make sure our children graduate prepared for the jobs of the twenty-first century by increasing accountability and access to a more rigorous curriculum in our high schools. States should be required to develop course-level academic standards for English and mathematics that prepare those students to succeed in college and the global workplace, administer assessments aligned to these standards, and publicly report how well the students are doing. Consistent graduation rate calculations should be used, so that we know for sure how many of our students actually finish twelfth grade.

We need to reward our best and most effective teachers by paying them more for helping students achieve to high standards and for working in our most challenging schools. Talented and qualified professionals from math, science, and technology fields outside of education should be encouraged to teach middle and high school courses, especially in low-income areas.

I believe the days are numbered for the traditional system of starting work in an organization or company and then moving up through the ranks to eventually assume leadership or ownership at middle-age or older. We must get these young people ready to lead immediately. They will not all have the luxury of learning on the job or learning, for the first time, what we should have taught them before graduation. In many instances, they will be creating the jobs in which they work.

Let's look ahead to the day that whatever ground some students have lost in the arena of global competitiveness is fully recovered. That day should be viewed not as the end of our efforts, but the beginning. If we become overly satisfied with achieving the goals I just mentioned, if we become content with the fact that we indeed are producing microprocessors rather than slide rules, then we run the risk of becoming complacent. Complacency very likely could lead to the following scene unfolding.

It is the year 2040. One of my grandchildren, Alex now six or Ana now three, is giving an RSA lecture on the relevance of education. At some point he or she will hold this instrument up for view—"Does anybody know what this is? It is a microprocessor-based electronic calculator. It was the machine of choice for computation in the late twentieth and early twenty-first centuries when my granddad was still working. It became obsolete overnight."

POSTSCRIPT

Do the Testing and Accountability Elements of the No Child Left Behind Act Prevent a Proper Cost-Benefit Evaluation?

Economic efficiency requires both productive efficiency (full employment of resources and use of least-cost technology) and allocative efficiency (production of the "right" quantities of goods and services). Competitive markets and the price mechanism operate to yield economic efficiency. But so-called externalities distort the proper functioning of markets and the price mechanism. This is the case with education, where benefits are not confined simply to the individual consumer of education but spill over to society. This means relying on the market to determine the production of education will result in too little education. In the case of this market failure, the government can choose to subsidize producers or consumers of education or might itself produce education—i.e., provide public education—to correct for the under-allocation of resources that would otherwise occur. Achieving the "right" quantity of education (and, in general, of goods and services) calls for production to be increased if benefits, including social benefits, exceed costs, including social costs. Proper measurement of benefits and costs is therefore imperative to achieving allocative efficiency. This is the economic issue underlying the arguments of Miller and Simon in the context of the NCLBA. Miller believes that better testing and accountability are needed to increase the benefits of NCLBA—i.e., to increase student achievement, raise high school graduation rates, and so forth. His view that government investment in education be increased substantially appears to be implicitly based on a belief that better testing and accountability will indicate that the properly measured benefits of NCLBA far exceed its costs. He sees the need for considerable change "that maintains the integrity of the law through accountability." Simon claims that some limited changes are needed in measuring benefits, but maintains that the "meaningful achievement and compliance provisions" established by NCLBA are working.

NCLBA set a deadline of 2014 for public schools to ensure that all students are proficient in reading and math and allows each State to determine what "proficiency" means. The Act focused on improving quality and accountability in exchange for increased resources. In this context, relevant and appropriate measures of testing and accountability will direct resources to schools, students, and teachers who most need them, helping to achieve the Act's objectives. The NCLBA's accountability strategy rests on four premises: clear targets for academic outcomes will provide indicators of improvement; identifying low-performing schools will focus assistance where it is most needed; information about student performance will enable informed decisions; and targeted assistance will stimulate school improvement: see *State and Local Implementation of the No Child Left Behind Act, Volume III—Accountability Under NCLB: Interim Report*, Washington, D.C., 2007 of the U.S. Department of Education, Office of Planning, Evaluation and Policy Development, Policy and Program Studies Service, 2007, available at www.ed.gov/about/offices/list/opepd/ppss/reports.html#title. See also *No Child Left Behind Act—Improvements Needed in Education's Process for Tracking States' Implementation of Key Provisions* (September 2004) of the U.S. Government Accountability Office (www.gao.gov/cgi-bin/getrpt?GAO-04-734). The report of the Commission on No Child Left Behind *Beyond NCLB—Fulfilling the Promise to Our Nation's Children* (The Aspen Institute, 2007) concludes that statutory changes are needed to improve NCLBA. It notes the need to improve data on student performance.

Testimony on improving the accountability of NCLBA before the Subcommittee on Early Childhood, Elementary and Secondary Education (April 27, 2007) is available at http://edlabor.house.gov/hearings/2007/04/improving-the-no-child-left-be.shtml. Testimony at the Full Committee Hearing on the "Miller/McKeon Discussion Draft of ESEA Reauthorization" (September 10, 2007) is found at http://edlabor.house.gov/hearings/2007/09/millermckeon-discussion-draft.shtml.

The Center on Education Policy's Web site http://www.cep-dc.org contains links to a number of its reports on NCLBA: see for example *Has Student Achievement Increased Since 2002? State Test Score Trends Through 2006–07*, available at http://www.cep-dc.org/document/docWindow.cfm?fuseaction=document.viewDocument&documentid=241&documentFormatId=3794 (June 2008). Of interest is *Standards-Based Accountability Under No Child Left Behind: Experiences of Teachers and Administrators in Three States*, by Laura S. Hamilton et al., http://www.rand.org/pubs/monographs/2007/RAND_MG589.pdf (2007). The biweekly newsletter *Straight A's: Public Education Policy and Progress* of the Alliance for Excellent Education (http://www.all4ed.org/) also contains NCLB news. Please see the 13th edition of *Taking Sides* for additional sources of information on NCLB.

A *Guide to Education and No Child Left Behind* available from the U.S. Department of Education (October 2004) provides an overview of NCLBA.

ISSUE 19

Is the Inequality in U.S. Income Distribution Surging?

YES: James M. Cypher, from "Slicing Up at the Long Barbeque," *dollars & sense* (January/February 2007)

NO: Diana Furchtgott-Roth, from Testimony before the Subcommittee on Workforce Protections of the House Committee on Education and Labor (July 31, 2008)

ISSUE SUMMARY

YES: Economist James M. Cypher believes that the U.S. economy is currently experiencing the largest shift in the distribution of income and wealth since the late nineteenth century with the share of income of the poorest 90 percent of the population falling from 67 percent in 1970 to 52 percent in 2000.

NO: Hudson Institute Scholar Diana Furchtgott-Roth does not deny that income inequality is rising but argues that by considering alternative measures of income and recognizing demographic changes, the shifts in income distribution are not a cause for alarm.

$\mathbf{N}$o one denies that income and wealth are distributed unequally in the United States. All except those on the very far left would argue that income and wealth should be distributed unequally. Indeed, income and wealth inequality are the logical consequences of a free enterprise, market economy, integral to the efficient operation of such an economy. More productive workers are expected to earn more than less productive workers, and the earnings differential should encourage the less productive workers to acquire the education and training that will allow them to become more productive and to earn higher wages. But how much inequality is enough to achieve this kind of efficiency and growth? When do considerations of social justice argue for a tempering of the market mechanisms?

As might be expected, one of the stating points for any general discussion of income inequality involves the actual measurement of the degree of economic inequality. To get a snapshot of income equality, economists use several different devices. One measure, referenced by both Cypher and Furchtgott-Roth, involves the quintile or decile distribution of income. For the former, households or families are divided into groups ranging from the poorest 20 percent (lowest quintile) to the richest 20 percent (highest quintile). For example, the Census Bureau estimates that there were 116,783,000 households in the United States in 2007. So a household quintile in 2007 would consist of 23,356,600 households (20 percent of 116,783,000), and the lowest quintile would consist of the 23,356,000 households with the lowest incomes. Having so divided the households in the country, the question then becomes, what percent of total household income does each of the quintiles receive? The Census Bureau collects and publishes these data each year (see *Income, Poverty, and Health Insurance Coverage in the United States: 2007* for the most recent data). For 2007, the numbers are as follows:

Quintile	Shares of Household Income
Lowest quintile	3.4%
Second quintile	8.7%
Third quintile	14.8%
Fourth quintile	23.4%
Highest quintile	49.7%

Thus, in 2007 the highest or richest quintile received about one-half of total household income. The Census Bureau also provides information on the average (mean) income for each quintile. In 2007, the average income in the lowest quintile was $11,551, while the average income for the richest quintile was $167,971.

Another device that is used to evaluate income distribution, also referenced by both Cypher and Furchtgott-Roth, is the Gini coefficient. One advantage of the Gini coefficient or Gini index is that it captures the distribution of income in a single number. According to the Census Bureau, "The Gini index ranges from 0, indicating perfect equality (where everyone receives an equal share), to 1, perfect inequality (where all the income is received by only one person or group of persons)." For 2007, the Census Bureau estimated the Gini index at 0.47. It should be noted that in arriving at both the quintile distribution of income and the Gini index the Census Bureau must establish definitions for both income and households (as opposed to, say, families). The Census Bureau provides detailed information about the definitions that it employs as well as detailed statistical information about the reliability of its estimates.

In his analysis of income distribution, Cypher uses a variety of data to confirm the surge in income inequality and to explain the surge. In one case, he quotes from a study that uses a broader definition of income than the Census Bureau. In another, he documents what he calls "Exploding Millionairism" between 1999 and 2005. Furchtgott-Roth does not deny a rise in income inequality but rejects the view that the United States is experiencing a surge of inequality.

YES

James M. Cypher

Slicing Up at the Long Barbeque: Who Gorges, Who Serves, and Who Gets Roasted?

Economic inequality has been on the rise in the United States for 30-odd years. Not since the Gilded Age of the late 19th century—during what Mark Twain referred to as "the Great Barbeque"—has the country witnessed such a rapid shift in the distribution of economic resources.

Still, most mainstream economists do not pay too much attention to the distribution of income and wealth—that is, how the value of current production (income) and past accumulated assets (wealth) is divided up among U.S. households. Some economists focus their attention on theory for theory's sake and do not work much with empirical data of any kind. Others who are interested in these on-the-ground data simply assume that each individual or group gets what it deserves from a capitalist economy. In their view, if the share of income going to wage earners goes up, that must mean that wage earners are more productive and thus deserve a larger slice of the nation's total income—and vice versa if that share goes down.

Heterodox economists, however, frequently look upon the distribution of income and wealth as among the most important shorthand guides to the overall state of a society and its economy. Some are interested in economic justice; others may or may not be, but nonetheless are convinced that changes in income distribution signal underlying societal trends and perhaps important points of political tension. And the general public appears to be paying increasing attention to income and wealth inequality. Consider the strong support voters have given to recent ballot questions raising state minimum wages and the extensive coverage of economic inequality that has suddenly begun to appear in mainstream news outlets like the New York Times, the Los Angeles Times, and the Wall Street Journal, all of which published lengthy article series on the topic in the past few years. Just last month, news outlets around the country spotlighted the extravagant bonuses paid out by investment firm Goldman Sachs, including a $53.4 million bonus to the firm's CEO.

By now, economists and others who do pay attention to the issue are aware that income and wealth inequality in the United States rose steadily during the last three decades of the 20th century. But now that we are several years into the 21st, what do we know about income and wealth distribution

From *Dollars & Sense*, January/February 2007. Reprinted by permission of Dollars & Sense, a progressive economics magazine. www.dollarsandsense.org.

today? Has the trend toward inequality continued, or are there signs of a reversal? And what can an understanding of the entire post-World War II era tell us about how to move again toward greater economic equality?

The short answers are: (1) Income distribution is even more unequal than we thought; (2) The newest data suggest the trend toward greater inequality continues, with no signs of a reversal; (3) We all do better when we all do better. During the 30 or so years after World War II the economy boomed and every stratum of society did better—pretty much at the same rate. When the era of shared growth ended, so too did much of the growth: the U.S. economy slowed down and recessions were deeper, more frequent, and harder to overcome. Growth spurts that did occur left most people out: the bottom 60% of U.S. households earned only 95 cents in 2004 for every dollar they made in 1979. A quarter century of falling incomes for the vast majority, even though average household income rose by 27% in real terms. Whew!

The Classless Society?

Throughout the 1950s, 1960s, and 1970s, sociologists preached that the United States was an essentially "classless" society in which everyone belonged to the middle class. A new "mass market" society with an essentially affluent, economically homogeneous population, they claimed, had emerged. Exaggerated as these claims were in the 1950s, there was some reason for their popular acceptance. Union membership reached its peak share of the private sector labor force in the early 1950s; unions were able to force corporations of the day to share the benefits of strong economic growth. The union wage created a target for nonunion workers as well, pulling up all but the lowest of wages as workers sought to match the union wage and employers often granted it as a tactic for keeping unions out. Under these circumstances, millions of families entered the lower middle class and saw their standard of living rise markedly. All of this made the distribution of income more equal for decades until the late 1970s. Of course there were outliers—some millions of poor, disproportionately blacks, and the rich family here and there.

Something serious must have happened in the 1970s as the trend toward greater economic equality rapidly reversed. Here are the numbers. The share of income received by the bottom 90% of the population was a modest 67% in 1970, but by 2000 this had shrunk to a mere 52%, according to a detailed study of U.S. income distribution conducted by Thomas Piketty and Emmanuel Saez, published by the prestigious National Bureau of Economic Research in 2002. Put another way, the top 10% increased their overall share of the nation's total income by 15 percentage points from 1970 to 2000. This is a rather astonishing jump—the gain of the top 10% in these years was equivalent to more than the total income received annually by the bottom 40% of households. To get on the bottom rung of the top 10% of households in 2000, it would have been necessary to have an adjusted gross income of $104,000 a year. The real money, though, starts on the 99th rung of the income ladder—the top 1% received an unbelievable 21.7% of all income in 2000. To get a handhold on the very bottom of this top rung took more than $384,000.

The Piketty–Saez study (and subsequent updates), which included in its measure of annual household income some data, such as income from capital gains, that generally are not factored in, verified a rising trend in income inequality which had been widely noted by others, and a degree of inequality which was far beyond most current estimates. The Internal Revenue Service has essentially duplicated the Piketty–Saez study. They find that in 2003, the share of total income going to the "bottom" four-fifths of households (that's 80% of the population!) was only slightly above 40%. Both of these studies show much higher levels of inequality than were previously thought to exist based on widely referenced Census Bureau studies. The Census studies still attribute 50% of total income to the top fifth for 2003, but this number appears to understate what the top fifth now receives—nearly 60%, according to the IRS.

A Brave New (Globalized) World for Workers

Why the big change from 1970 to 2000? That is too long a story to tell here in full. But briefly, we can say that beginning in the early 1970s, U.S. corporations and the wealthy individuals who largely own them had the means, the motive, and the opportunity to garner a larger share of the nation's income—and they did so.

Let's start with the motive. The 1970s saw a significant slowdown in U.S. economic growth, which made corporations and stockholders anxious to stop sharing the benefits of growth to the degree they had in the immediate post-war era.

Opportunity appeared in the form of an accelerating globalization of economic activity. Beginning in the 1970s, more and more U.S.-based corporations began to set up production operations overseas. The trend has only accelerated since, in part because international communication and transportation costs have fallen dramatically. Until the 1970s, it was very difficult—essentially unprofitable—for giants like General Electric or General Motors to operate plants offshore and then import their foreign-made products into the United States. So from the 1940s to the 1970s, U.S. workers had a geographic lever, one they have now almost entirely lost. This erosion in workers' bargaining power has undermined the middle class and decimated the unions that once managed to assure the working class a generally comfortable economic existence. And today, of course, the tendency to send jobs offshore is affecting many highly trained professionals such as engineers. So this process of gutting the middle class has not run its course.

Given the opportunity presented by globalization, companies took a two-pronged approach to strengthening their hand vis-à-vis workers: (1) a frontal assault on unions, with decertification elections and get-tough tactics during unionization attempts, and (2) a debilitating war of nerves whereby corporations threatened to move offshore unless workers scaled back their demands or agreed to givebacks of prior gains in wage and benefit levels or working conditions.

A succession of U.S. governments that pursued conservative—or pro-corporate—economic policies provided the means. Since the 1970s, both Republican and Democratic administrations have tailored their economic policies to benefit corporations and shareholders over workers. The laundry list of such policies includes:

- new trade agreements, such as NAFTA, that allow companies to cement favorable deals to move offshore to host nations such as Mexico;
- tax cuts for corporations and for the wealthiest households, along with hikes in the payroll taxes that represent the largest share of the tax burden on the working and middle classes;
- lax enforcement of labor laws that are supposed to protect the right to organize unions and bargain collectively.

Exploding Millionairism

Given these shifts in the political economy of the United States, it is not surprising that economic inequality in 2000 was higher than in 1970. But at this point, careful readers may well ask whether it is misleading to use data for the year 2000, as the studies reported above do, to demonstrate rising inequality. After all, wasn't 2000 the year the NASDAQ peaked, the year the dot-com bubble reached its maximum volume? So if the wealthiest households received an especially large slice of the nation's total income that year, doesn't that just reflect a bubble about to burst rather than an underlying trend?

To begin to answer this question, we need to look at the trends in income and wealth distribution since 2000. And it turns out that after a slight pause in 2000–2001, inequality has continued to rise. Look at household income, for example. According to the standard indicators, the U.S. economy saw a brief recession in 2000–2001 and has been in a recovery ever since. But the median household income has failed to recover. In 2000, the median household had an annual income of $49,133; by 2005, after adjusting for inflation, the figure stood at $46,242. This 6% drop in median household income occurred while the inflation-adjusted Gross Domestic Product expanded by 14.4%. When the Census Bureau released these data, it noted that median household income had gone up slightly between 2004 and 2005. This point was seized upon by Bush administration officials to bolster their claim that times are good for American workers. A closer look at the data, however, revealed a rather astounding fact: Only 23 million households moved ahead in 2005, most headed by someone aged 65 or above. In other words, subtracting out the cost-of-living increase in Social Security benefits and increases in investment income (such as profits, dividends, interest, capital gains, and rents) to the over-65 group, workers again suffered a decline in income in 2005.

Another bit of evidence is the number of millionaire households—those with net worth of $1 million or more excluding the value of a primary residence and any IRAs. In 1999, just before the bubbles burst, there were 7.1 million millionaire households in the United States. In 2005, there were 8.9 million, a record number. Ordinary workers may not have recovered from the 2000–2001 rough patch yet, but evidently the wealthiest households have!

Many economists pay scant attention to income distribution patterns on the assumption that those shifts merely reflect trends in the productivity of labor or the return to risk-taking. But worker productivity rose in the 2000–2005 period, by 27.1%. At the same time, from 2003 to 2005 average hourly pay fell by 1.2%. (Total compensation, including all forms of benefits, rose by 7.2% between 2000 and 2005. Most of the higher compensation spending merely reflects rapid increases in the health insurance premiums that employers have to pay just to maintain the same levels of coverage. But even if benefits are counted as part of workers' pay—a common and questionable practice—productivity growth outpaced this elastic definition of "pay" by 50% between 1972 and 2005.)

And at the macro level, recent data released by the Commerce Department demonstrate that the share of the country's GDP going to wages and salaries sank to its lowest postwar level, 45.4%, in the third quarter of 2006. And this figure actually overstates how well ordinary workers are doing. The "Wage & Salary" share includes all income of this type, not just production workers' pay. Corporate executives' increasingly munificent salaries are included as well. Workers got roughly 65% of total wage and salary income in 2005, according to survey data from the U.S. Department of Labor; the other 35% went to salaried professionals—medical doctors and technicians, managers, and lawyers—who comprised only 15.6% of the sample.

Moreover, the "Wage & Salary" share shown in the National Income and Product Accounts includes bonuses, overtime, and other forms of payment not included in the Labor Department survey. If this income were factored in, the share going to nonprofessional, nonmanagerial workers would be even smaller. Bonuses and other forms of income to top employees can be many times base pay in important areas such as law and banking. Goldman Sachs's notorious 2006 bonuses are a case in point; the typical managing director on Wall Street garnered a bonus ranging between $1 and $3 million.

So, labor's share of the nation's income is falling, but it is actually falling much faster than these data suggest. Profits, meanwhile, are at their highest level as a share of GDP since the booming 1960s.

These numbers should come as no surprise to anyone who reads the paper: story after story illustrates how corporations are continuing to squeeze workers. For instance, workers at the giant auto parts manufacturer Delphi have been told to prepare for a drop in wages from $27.50 an hour in 2006 to $16.50 an hour in 2007. In order to keep some of Caterpillar's manufacturing work in the United States, the union was cornered into accepting a contract in 2006 that limits new workers to a maximum salary of $27,000 a year—no matter how long they work there—compared to the $38,000 or more that long-time Caterpillar workers make today. More generally, for young women with a high school diploma, average entry-level pay fell to only $9.08 an hour in 2005, down by 4.9% just since 2001. For male college graduates, starter-job pay fell by 7.3% over the same period.

Aiding and Abetting

And the federal government is continuing to play its part, facilitating the transfer of an ever-larger share of the nation's income to its wealthiest households. George W. Bush once joked that his constituency was "the haves and the have-mores"—this may have been one of the few instances in which he was actually leveling with his audience. Consider aspects of the four tax cuts for individuals that Bush has implemented since taking office. The first two cut the top nominal tax rate from 39.6% to 35%. Then, in 2003, the third cut benefited solely those who hold wealth, reducing taxes on dividends from 39.6% to 15% and on capital gains from 20% to 15%. (Bush's fourth tax cut—in 2006—is expected to drop taxes by 4.8% percent for the top one-tenth of one percent of all households, while the median household will luxuriate with an extra nickel per day.)

So, if you make your money by the sweat of your brow and you earned $200,000 in 2003, you paid an effective tax rate of 21%. If you earned a bit more, say another $60,500, you paid an effective tax rate of 35% on the additional income. But if, with a flick of the wrist on your laptop, you flipped some stock you had held for six months and cleared $60,500 on the transaction, you paid the IRS an effective tax rate of only 15%. What difference does it make? Well, in 2003 the 6,126 households with incomes over $10 million saw their taxes go down by an average of $521,905 from this one tax cut alone.

These tax cuts represent only one of the many Bush administration policies that have abetted the ongoing shift of income away from most households and toward the wealthiest ones. And what do these top-tier households do with all this newfound money? For one thing, they save. This is in sharp contrast to most households. While the top fifth of households by income has a savings rate of 23%, the bottom 80% as a group dissave—in other words, they go into debt, spending more than they earn. Households headed by a person under 35 currently show a negative savings rate of 16% of income. Today overall savings—the savings of the top fifth minus the dis-savings of the bottom four-fifths—are slightly negative, for the first time since the Great Depression.

Here we find the crucial link between income and wealth accumulation. Able to save nearly a quarter of their income, the rich search out financial assets (and sometimes real assets such as houses and businesses) to pour their vast funds into. In many instances, sometimes with inside information, they are able to generate considerable future income from their invested savings. Like a snowball rolling downhill, savings for the rich can have a turbo effect—more savings generates more income, which then accumulates as wealth.

Lifestyles of the Rich

Make the rich even richer and the creative forces of market capitalism will be unleashed, resulting in more savings and consequently more capital investment, raising productivity and creating abundance for all. At any rate, that's the supply-side/neoliberal theory. However—and reminiscent of the false boom that defined the Japanese economy in the late 1980s—the big money has not gone into productive investments in the United States. Stripping out the money pumped into the residential real estate bubble, inflation-adjusted investment in machinery, equipment, technology, and structures increased only 1.4% from 1999 through 2005—an average of 0.23% per year. Essentially, productive investment has stagnated since the close of the dot-com boom.

Instead, the money has poured into high-risk hedge funds. These are vast pools of unregulated funds that are now generating 40% to 50% of the trades in the New York Stock Exchange and account for very large portions of trading in many U.S. and foreign credit and debt markets.

And where is the income from these investments going? Last fall media mogul David Geffen sold two paintings at record prices, a Jasper Johns ($80 million) and a Willem de Kooning ($63.5 million), to two of "today's crop of hedge-fund billionaires" whose cash is making the art market "red-hot," according to the New York Times.

Other forms of conspicuous consumption have their allure as well. Boeing and Lufthansa are expecting brisk business for the newly introduced 787 airplane. The commercial version of the new Boeing jet will seat 330, but the VIP version offered by Lufthansa Technik (for a mere $240 million) will have seating for 35 or fewer, leaving room for master bedrooms, a bar, and the transport of racehorses or Rolls Royces. And if you lose your auto assembly job? It should be easy to find work as a dog walker: High-end pet care services are booming, with sales more than doubling between 2000 and 2004. Opened in 2001, Just Dogs Gourmet expects to have 45 franchises in place by the end of 2006 selling hand-decorated doggie treats. And then there is Camp Bow Wow, which offers piped-in classical music for the dogs (oops, "guests") and a live Camper Cam for their owners. Started only three years ago, the company already has 140 franchises up and running.

According to David Butler, the manager of a premiere auto dealership outside of Detroit, sales of Bentleys, at $180,000 a pop, are brisk. But not many $300,000 Rolls Royces are selling. "It's not that they can't afford it," Butler told the New York Times, "it's because of the image it would give." Just what is the image problem in Detroit? Well, maybe it has something to do with those Delphi workers facing a 40% pay cut. Michigan's economy is one of the hardest-hit in the nation. GM, long a symbol of U.S. manufacturing prowess, is staggering, with rumors of possible bankruptcy rife. The best union in terms of delivering the goods for the U.S. working class, the United Auto Workers, is facing an implosion. Thousands of Michigan workers at Delphi, GM, and Ford will be out on the streets very soon. (The top three domestic car makers are determined to permanently lay off three-quarters of their U.S. assembly-line workers—nearly 200,000 hourly employees. If they do, then the number of autoworkers employed by the Big Three—Ford, Chrysler, and GM—will have shrunk by a staggering 900,000 since 1978.) So, this might not be the time to buy a Rolls. But a mere $180,000 Bentley—why not?

Had Enough of the "Haves"?

In the era Twain decried as the "great barbeque," the outrageous concentration of income and wealth eventually sparked a reaction and a vast reform movement. But it was not until the onset of the Great Depression, decades later, that massive labor/social unrest and economic collapse forced the country's political elite to check the growing concentration of income and wealth.

Today, it does not appear that there are, as yet, any viable forces at work to put the brakes on the current runaway process of rising inequality. Nor does it appear that this era's power elite is ready to accept any new social compact. In a recent report on the "new king of Wall Street" (a co-founder of the hedge fund/private-equity buyout corporation Blackstone Group) that seemed to typify elite perspectives on today's inequality, the New York Times gushed that "a crashing wave of capital is minting new billionaires each year." Naturally, the Times was too discreet to mention is that those same "crashing waves" have flattened the middle class. And their backwash has turned the working class every-which-way while pulling it down, down, down.

But perhaps those who decry the trend can find at least symbolic hope in the new boom in yet another luxury good. Private mausoleums, in vogue during that earlier Gilded Age, are back. For $650,000, one was recently constructed at Daytona Memorial Park in Florida—with matching $4,000 Medjool date palms for shade. Another, complete with granite patio, meditation room, and doors of hand cast bronze, went up in the same cemetery. Business is booming, apparently, with 2,000 private mausoleums sold in 2005, up from a single-year peak of 65 in the 1980s. Some cost "well into the millions," according to one the nation's largest makers of cemetery monuments. Who knows: maybe the mausoleum boom portends the ultimate (dead) end for the neo-Gilded Age.

Testimony before the Subcommittee on Workforce Protections

American workers are earning more today than they were a year ago. Real disposable personal income has increased steadily since 1996. Between January 1996 and May 2008, real disposable personal income increased 54.5 percent. Over past year, from May 2007 to May 2008, real disposable income increased by 7.3 percent. In addition, the Census Bureau reported a 0.7 percent increase in median household income from 2005 to 2006 (the 2007 numbers will come out next month).

With increases in income, what has happened to inequality? The popular perception of income inequality is dire. A quick search through the popular press will yield dozens of articles and speeches decrying the increasing excesses of the super-rich while the poor grow ever poorer. Robert Frank's best-selling book, *Richistan,* portrays the "new rich" who have multiple mansions and staffs of household helpers. David Shipler's *The Working Poor: Invisible in America* describes those in low-wage jobs, struggling to get by. Yet rather than relying on anecdotes, we should base our views of inequality on a firm understanding of the data.

Economists use a variety of measures to determine how equally the income "pie" is divided. These measures include inequality indices and earning shares. Common to all these measures, however, are certain challenges. All measures need a definition of income, and defining income is not as straightforward as it seems. Some researchers will use pre-tax income, while others will look post-tax income before transfer payments such as food stamps, Medicare, or Social Security. Others use post-tax, post-transfer income. What measure is used makes a significant difference.

For example, consider the Gini coefficient, as calculated by the Census Bureau. The Gini coefficient is a statistical index of inequality ranging from zero to one, calculated from the distribution of income throughout the population. Low values represent low levels of inequality, while values near one mean that income is concentrated among a few individuals. As can be seen from a Census Bureau table using alternate measures of income, the official Gini coefficient is consistently overestimated by about 5 percentage points,[1] after taxes and transfers are accounted for.

U.S. House of Representatives, July 31, 2008.

A report from the Census Bureau concludes that "there have not been any statistically significant annual changes in the Gini index over the last 10 years."[2] A Congressional Budget Office report found that, between 1991 and 2005, the quintile of households with children with the lowest earnings experienced the second greatest percentage increase in income, after the top quintile. The lowest quintile experienced the largest percentage growth in earnings.[3]

The Internal Revenue Service reports that the top 50 percent of earners paid 97 percent of income taxes in 2006, a percentage which increased in almost every year since 1992.[4] Meanwhile, personal current transfer receipts, as reported by the Bureau of Economic Analysis, have been steadily increasing. These transfer payments go disproportionately to lower-income individuals. The net effect of taxes and transfer programs is to bring greater equality to the purchasing power of individuals.

Additionally, we need to consider the spending power of American dollars. Low-income households spend a greater portion of their income on goods that have become cheaper with international trade, such as food. High-income households, on the other hand, spend for "high-end services like private secondary schools, college tuition, high-end spas, message therapists, landscape gardeners, and other service providers whose relative prices rise steadily relative to the overall consumer price level."[5] Jerry Hausman and Ephraim Leibtag found in 2004 that a Wal-Mart in a new market decreases food prices by 15 to 25 percent.[6]

Demographic changes can create potentially spurious increases in income inequality. Most inequality measures are calculated from household or family income. So the increasing tendency of high-income men to marry high-income women will boost the inequality among household incomes without changing inequality among individual earners.

Furthermore, not all households are the same size, and household size has diminished over time due to later marriages, fewer children, and divorce. There are 1.7 people in the average household in the lowest fifth of households, and this number rises steadily to 3.1 persons in the top fifth of households. Differences in household income, then, are larger than differences in income per person. Similarly, there are differences in the number of earners per household, with the top fifth averaging 2.1 earners compared to the bottom fifth's half an earner per household.[7] Since more people are working in the higher income households, it is hardly surprising that the household as a whole is earning more.

Besides the questions of determining the "true" Gini coefficient highlighted above, there are concerns when using the Gini coefficient for comparison. It is important to realize that the Gini coefficient represents a snapshot of inequality. As the working force population changes its average characteristics, the Gini coefficient likewise changes.

Consider an economy where workers have the same earnings experience over their lives. Younger workers earn less than older workers, and earnings rise throughout workers' careers. A snapshot of this economy will show income inequality between workers even though lifetime income is more equal. In this case, the Gini coefficient indicates less an egregious lack of income equality than a need for good credit markets.

But even more than properly understanding the nuances of the numbers used to track income inequality, we need to understand the data that are used to generate them. A study by Thomas Piketty and Emmanuel Saez is the basis, directly or indirectly, for many of the commentators warning of rising income inequality. This study uses individual income tax returns from 1913 to 1998 (updated to 2001) to chart changes in the top earners' income shares over the past century.

To calculate these shares, Piketty and Saez aggregate the reported income of the top percentage groups of interest (specifically, the top 1 percent) and divide this number by the total personal income reported in the National Income and Product Accounts by the Bureau of Economic Analysis.[8]

Unfortunately, this simple measure is wholly dependent on the consistency of the underlying data. Individual income tax returns provide complicated data to work with, especially over time, because income tax returns provide data on tax units, not individuals. A married couple filing together represent one tax unit, as does their teenage son who has earned $3,350 at his part-time and summer jobs.[9] These three represent one household, but two tax units: one relatively rich, the other relatively poor.

With the entry of greater numbers of women into the workforce over the past 25 years, the growing tendency towards dual income couples polarizes the income distribution without any change in individual income inequality. Two earners marrying, whether they be attorneys or automotive mechanics, results in an immediate change in the income distribution. A police officer married to a nurse, each at the top of their profession, can earn almost $200,000. If more teenagers take after-school jobs, the number of low-income tax "households" balloons and income inequality appears to rise.

The Tax Reform Act of 1986 lowered the top income rate from 50 percent to 28 percent, and raised the capital gains tax to equal the ordinary income rate.[10] Prior to the passage of the Tax Reform Act, it was advantageous for many small-business owners to file under the comparatively lower corporate tax rate. After the Act, the individual tax rate was more favorable than the corporate rate, so small businesses switched to filing individual tax returns. This explains that large jump in the inequality series of Piketty and Saez between 1986 and 1988. A mass switch from corporate to individual filings by small-business owners fits this pattern perfectly.[11] After correcting for this change and the effect of transfer payments, Cato Institute economist Alan Reynolds finds that "the *apparent* increase of 1.7 percentage points in the top 1 percent's share from 1988 to 2003 in the unadjusted Piketty–Saez estimates becomes no increase."[12]

As well as analyzing income inequality directly, we can consider consumption inequality. This provides a better view of how much citizens actually spend, and therefore how well Americans live. Consumption spending generally has fewer fluctuations than income, so consumption data will be influenced less by transitory shocks. Data from the Consumer Expenditure Survey of the Bureau of Labor Statistics adjusted for the number of people per household gives us insight into spending equality among Americans.[13]

In 2006, the last year for which data are available, Americans in the lowest quintile of pre-tax income spent $12,006 per person, compared to $16,572 per person in the middle fifth household, and $30,371 per person in the top quintile. On a per person basis, the top quintile spends only 2.5 times what the bottom quintile does, and 1.8 times what the middle fifth does.

When spending is broken down into categories, results are similar. The bottom quintile spends $874 per person for health costs, about 1.5 times as much as the top quintile's $1318 per person. For food, the bottom fifth paid $1,878 while the top fifth paid $3,304. The top 20 percent spend only 1.8 times as much. In housing, the lowest quintile spent $4,781 to the top's $9,700 – about two times as much. In all these categories, the middle quintiles are roughly in between.

The areas where the high-income quintile outspends the low-income quintile are personal insurance and pension, entertainment, and transportation. The top 20 percent spend 14.6 times more on personal insurance than the lowest fifth, but only three times more than the middle fifth. In both entertainment and transportation, the top quintile expends about three times as much as the bottom quintile. The top quintile outspends the middle quintile in entertainment and transportation by 2.2 times and 1.7 times, respectively. The pattern that emerges is not one of extreme inequality. The top income earners do not outspend the lowest earners by extreme amounts.

The demographic characteristics of the bottom fifth of households shed light on consumption patterns. The bottom income quintile has the highest average age, 52, while the top quintile has the second youngest age at 47 (the second-highest quintile has an average age of 46). Only 17 percent of the top 20 percent own homes mortgage-free, with 75 percent still paying off their mortgage; 30 percent of the bottom fifth own homes free of any mortgage, and only 13 percent have to spend for mortgages.[14]

These data support the conclusion that some households in the bottom income quintile are not truly poor. Instead, they are older citizens living off accumulated savings. Some of those in the top quintile are at the peak of their earning careers, and are saving up for their future.

Another important difference between income quintiles is in education. The percentage of reference people in each household with a college education rises to 83 percent in the top quintile, starting at 40 percent for the lowest 20 percent of households.[15]

Studies consistently find high returns to education. A study by economists Louis Jacobson, Robert LaLonde, and Daniel Sullivan on displaced workers in Washington State found that workers increased their incomes by 7 to 10 percent per year of community college, the same as students entering directly from high school.[16] Another study by economists Thomas Kane and Cecilia Rouse found that these returns, about a 5 to 10 percent improvement in earnings per year of education, are remarkably similar across community colleges and four-year colleges.[17]

Perhaps more importantly, the subjects studied make a difference. A related study by Jacobson, LaLonde, and Sullivan finds higher returns, 14 percent income improvement per year of education for men and 29 percent for women, when more technical or quantitative subjects are taken.[18]

Education gives Americans the skills they need to succeed in today's dynamic business world. Improvements to the education system focused on providing quality education in key areas will increase the human capital of America's citizens and help workers attain their potential in the workplace.

America's workforce is not in the midst of a surge of inequality as popularly portrayed. We should be wary of conclusions reached from dubious data, and keep in mind other ways of determining inequality, such as through consumption expenditures. To the extent that there is inequality in incomes, differences in education are an important factor. A better education system gives everyone a fairer shot in the workplace.

Putting in place more mandated employer-provided benefits to combat alleged problems of inequality would hurt those Americans that members of Congress are seeking to help. Many of the protections are aimed at women. Examples of such protections include paid maternity leave, government-provided child care, and "paycheck fairness"—mandating that women be paid the same as men not for equal work, as is the case now, but for jobs of equal worth.

Yet women in the United States have enjoyed a low unemployment rate, one comparable to men's, because low taxes and lack of employer mandates encourage women to work outside the home and be hired. This has remained true over the past year, as the economy has slowed. According to BLS data, the 2007 unemployment rate for American women was 4.5 percent and the rate for men was 4.7 percent. In June, 2008, the adult female unemployment rate in the United States was 4.7 percent, compared to the male rate of 5.1 percent. Of particular note is that the unemployment rate for American women moves closely to the rate for men.

In other countries, unemployment rates for women are higher than in the United States. In 2007, compared to the rate for American women of 4.5 percent, the rate for women in Canada was 4.8 percent; Australia, at 4.8 percent; France, at 9.1 percent; Italy, at 7.9 percent; Sweden, at 6.4 percent; and the UK, at 5 percent. In Italy, France, the Netherlands, and Sweden, women have a significantly higher unemployment rate than men.[19]

Not only do women in the United States have a lower unemployment rate, they also find jobs more quickly. According to the latest release from the OECD, only 9.2 percent of unemployed women in the United States had been unemployed for a year or more. This compares favorably to Australia, where 15.2 percent of unemployed women were unemployed for a year or more; France, where it was 43.3 percent; Germany, where it was 56.5 percent; Italy, where it was 54.8 percent; Japan, where it was 20.8 percent; the Netherlands, where it was 43.6 percent; Spain, where it was 32.2 percent; Sweden, where it was 12.2 percent; and the UK, where in 2006 14.9 percent of unemployed women had been unemployed for a year or more.[20]

The labor force participation rate for American women is also high. From 1980 to 1990, the participation rate rose 6 percentage points to 57.5 percent as large numbers of women entered the workforce. The rate peaked in 1999 at 60 percent, and in 2007 was only seven-tenths of a percentage point lower, at 59.3 percent. In April 2008, 59.6 percent of women were in the labor market.

The 2007 labor force participation rate for women was higher than in Australia at 59 percent; Japan, at 47.9 percent; France, at 51.3 percent; Italy, at 37.9 percent; the Netherlands, at 59 percent; and the UK, at 56.5 percent.

The way to reduce economic inequality is to provide more education and job opportunities for those in lower income groups. To that end, we need to focus not only on education, but also on how to spur economic growth and keep prices low. Members could consider keeping taxes low, making use of America's oil and gas reserves through oil drilling and exploration so that we have a reliable source of energy, and removal of the ethanol mandates that are driving up our food prices.

References

1. U.S. Census Bureau, Current Population Survey, Annual Social and Economic Supplements, Table RDI-5, "Index of Income Concentration (Gini Index), by Definition of Income: 1979 to 2003." . . .

2. Ibid.

3. Dahl, Molly, Congressional Budget Office, "Changes in the Economic Resources of Low-Income Households with Children" May 2007. . . .

4. Internal Revenue Service, SOI Tax Stats – Individual Income Tax Rates and Tax Shares, Table 1 "Number of Shares, Shares of AGI and Total Income Tax, AGI Floor on Percentiles in Current and Constant Dollars, and Average Tax Rates.". . .

5. Gordon, Robert and Ian Dew-Becker. "Controversies about the Rise of American Inequality: A Survey." NBER Working Paper No 13982 (May 2008), pg 33.

6. Hausman, Jerry and Ephraim Leibtag. "CPI Bias From Supercenters: Does the BLS Know that Wal-Mart Exists?" NBER Working Paper No 10712 (August 2004).

7. U.S. Department of Labor, Consumer Expenditure Survey, Table 55. . . .

8. Piketty, Thomas and Emmanuel Saez. "Income Inequality in the United States, 1913–1998." Quarterly Journal of Economics, Vol 118, Is 1 (Feb 2003) pp 1–39.

9. Internal Revenue Service, "2007 Inst 1040 Instructions for Form 1040 and Schedules A, B, C, D, E, F, J, and SE." Chart B, pg 7, for dependent children who are not blind or over 65 years of age.

10. Tax Reform Act of 1986, Pub. L. 99-514, 100 Stat. 2085, as reported by Stacey Kean and David Brumbaugh, Congressional Research Service, CRS Report for Congress No. 87-231E, "Tax Reform Act of 1986 (P.L. 99-514): Comparison of New with Prior Tax Law."

11. Reynolds, Alan. "Has U.S. Income Inequality *Really* Increased?" Policy Analysis No 586, Jan 8, 2007.

12. Ibid., at 11.

13. All calculations on per-person spending are performed using U.S. Department of Labor's Consumer Expenditure Survey, table 1, . . .

14. Ibid.

15. Ibid.

16. Jacobson, Louis, Robert J LaLonde and Daniel Sullivan. "The Impact of Community College Retraining on Older Displaced Workers: Should We Teach Old Dogs New Tricks?" Industrial and Labor Relations Review, Vol 58, No 3 (April 2005) pp 398–415.

17. Kane, Thomas J. and Cecilia Elena Rouse. "The Community College: Educating Students at the Margin Between College and Work," *Journal of Economic Perspectives,* 13, no. 1 (Winter 1999): 63–84.

18. Jacobson, Louis, Robert J LaLonde and Daniel Sullivan. "Is Retraining Displaced Workers a Good Investment?" FRB of Chicago Economic Perspectives, Vol 29, Is 2 (2nd Quarter 2005) pp 47–66.

19. Bureau of Labor Statistics, "Comparative Civilian Labor Force Statistics, 10 Countries, 1960–2007," Washington, DC: Department of Labor, Updated April 18, 2008.

20. OECD Employment Outlook 2007, Statistical Annex Table G, p 267.

POSTSCRIPT

Is the Inequality in U.S. Income Distribution Surging?

Economist James M. Cypher begins his analysis by contrasting the views of mainstream and heterodox economists on income and wealth distribution: the former do not pay much attention to this issue, while the latter believe it is a critical measure of the health of an economy. He then explores the notion of a classless society, something that sociologists, during the 1950s and 1960s, thought the United States was becoming. But the trend toward greater equality was reversed. He proceeds to offer data to document the increase in inequality over the 1970–2000 period. Cypher then examines the reasons for the increase in inequality. His list of factors includes accelerating globalization and the pursuit of "conservative—or pro-corporate economic policies" by both Democratic and Republican administrations. The latter include trade agreements like the North American Free Trade Agreement (NAFTA), tax cuts for the wealthy, and lax enforcement of labor laws. Next, Cypher examines income and wealth data for the first half of the current decade. Important here is labor's falling share of national income and profits, rising share of gross national product. After discussing tax policy under the Bush administration and the investment and consumption choices of the rich, Cypher concludes that there do not appear to be "any visible forces at work to put the brakes on the current runaway process of rising inequality."

Hudson Institute senior fellow Diana Furchtgott-Roth begins her testimony by recognizing the rise in real disposable income since 1996: between January 1996 and May 2006 it increased by more than 50 percent. She then turns to the distribution of this growing income. She offers a variety of data to show that alternative measures can be used to tell different stories about income distribution. She then considers how a number of factors, including demographic change and tax policy, can affect the measurement of inequality. For example, if high-income men marry high-income women with greater frequency, then this "will boost the inequality among household incomes without changing inequality among individual earners." In this context, she also notes that household size is higher in the higher quintiles (1.7 person per household in the lowest quintile versus 3.1 in the top quintile), and this means that differences in household income are greater than differences in income per person. She then explores consumption patterns among the rich and the poor: "these data support the conclusion that some households in the bottom income quintile are not truly poor." All these considerations and others lead Furchtgott-Roth to conclude that "America's workforce is not in the midst of a surge in inequality as popularly portrayed."

Probably the best place to start in reviewing the literature on income inequality, is the U.S. government data on income distribution; the most recent data are included in *Income, Poverty, and Health Insurance Coverage in the United States: 2007*. It is available at http://www.census.gov/prod/2008pubs/p60-235.pdf.

The hearings at which Furchtgott-Roth presented her testimony also included the testimony of three other individuals: Jared Bernstein of the Economic Policy Institute, Robert Greenstein of the Center on Budget & Policy Priorities, and Nell Minnow of the Corporate Library. The hearings are available at http://edlabor.house.gov/hearings/2008/07/growing-middle-class-income-ga.shtml. Both Furchtgott-Roth and Cypher provide a number of additional sources. Finally, see the article by Thomas A. Garrett entitled "U.S. Income Inequality: It's Not So Bad" in the St. Louis Federal Reserve's *The Regional Economist* (October 2008).

ISSUE 20

Is the Treasury's $700 Billion Bailout the Solution to the Credit Crisis?

YES: George W. Bush, from "President's Address to the Nation," http://www.whitehouse.gov/news/releases/2008/09/20080924 (September 24, 2008)

NO: Newt Gingrich, from "Before D.C. Gets Our Money, It Owes Us Some Answers," nationalreviewonline (September 21, 2008)

ISSUE SUMMARY

YES: President George W. Bush maintains that the rescue will reduce the risk posed by troubled assets and allow banks to resume credit flows to families and businesses.

NO: Newt Gingrich contends that the bailout will become a long-term mess and that there is a nonbureaucratic solution to the multiple crises affecting the economy.

T he collapse of the housing industry contributed to an economic slowdown and left banks and other institutions holding financial assets (based on the now-infamous "subprime mortgages") that were fast losing value and becoming increasingly difficult to sell. When signs of a credit crunch appeared in August 2007, the Federal Reserve Bank responded with conventional and nontraditional policy measures to increase liquidity in the banking system. The Fed also extended currency swap lines to foreign central banks so that they could, in turn, provide dollars in international financial markets.

Financial market stresses, however, continued to grow and intensified significantly in September 2008, spreading rapidly in domestic and global financial markets. The cases of Lehman Brothers, Merrill Lynch, AIG, Washington Mutual, and Wachovia, following earlier action on Bear Stearns and Fannie Mae and Freddie Mac, are now well known, as are the record losses registered on stock markets. As Fed Chair Bernanke noted later, "at the root of the problem is a loss of confidence by investors and the public in the strength of key financial institutions and markets, which has had cascading and unwelcome effects on the availability of credit and the value of savings."

Faced with this unfolding scenario, in a press conference on September 19, 2008, Treasury Secretary Henry Paulson proposed for immediate implementation "a comprehensive approach to address market instability." His three-page $700 billion plan would give the Treasury the authority to buy mortgage-related assets from financial institutions.

The Fed supported the Treasury plan and the need for immediate action. The Group of Seven Finance Ministers and Central Bank Governors welcomed the plan on September 22. President George W. Bush voiced his support for the bailout package on September 23, 2008, tracing the causes of the financial crisis, defending the urgent need for the "rescue" plan, and explaining how it would work and what it meant for the economic future of Americans.

Others, including former Republican Speaker of the House Newt Gingrich, however, questioned the need to pass the "bailout" bill without debate and without taxpayer protection, called the plan fundamentally flawed for a number of reasons, and offered alternative analyses of causes and different solutions based, for example, on private capital rather than taxpayer money.

On September 29, 2008, Congress rejected (by a vote of 228 to 205) a 110-page bailout bill, and the Dow Jones Industrial Average posted its largest decline. On October 1, 2008, the Senate passed a 450-page bill, and the next day the House approved it by a vote of 263 to 171. On October 3, the President signed into law the Emergency Economic Stabilization Act of 2008, saying that it would take time for the legislation to have its full impact on the economy.

The legislation includes three divisions: the Emergency Economic Stabilization Act (EESA) of 2008, the Energy Improvement and Extension Act of 2008, and Tax Extenders and Alternative Minimum Tax Relief. In addition to the troubled assets relief program (TARP), there are provisions for insurance of troubled assets, oversight, an increase in the amount of deposits insured by the Federal Deposit Insurance Corporation to $250,000, and provisions for transparency and protection of taxpayers, as well as incentives for energy production (including incentives for renewable energy), and $150 billion in tax breaks for families and businesses.

In a vivid analogy, the turmoil in financial markets has been likened to a tsunami. Its effects are far from over at home and continue to spread over the globe.

YES

George W. Bush

President's Address to the Nation

The President: Good evening. This is an extraordinary period for America's economy. Over the past few weeks, many Americans have felt anxiety about their finances and their future. I understand their worry and their frustration. We've seen triple-digit swings in the stock market. Major financial institutions have teetered on the edge of collapse, and some have failed. As uncertainty has grown, many banks have restricted lending. Credit markets have frozen. And families and businesses have found it harder to borrow money.

We're in the midst of a serious financial crisis, and the federal government is responding with decisive action. We've boosted confidence in money market mutual funds, and acted to prevent major investors from intentionally driving down stocks for their own personal gain.

Most importantly, my administration is working with Congress to address the root cause behind much of the instability in our markets. Financial assets related to home mortgages have lost value during the housing decline. And the banks holding these assets have restricted credit. As a result, our entire economy is in danger. So I've proposed that the federal government reduce the risk posed by these troubled assets, and supply urgently-needed money so banks and other financial institutions can avoid collapse and resume lending.

This rescue effort is not aimed at preserving any individual company or industry – it is aimed at preserving America's overall economy. It will help American consumers and businesses get credit to meet their daily needs and create jobs. And it will help send a signal to markets around the world that America's financial system is back on track.

I know many Americans have questions tonight: How did we reach this point in our economy? How will the solution I've proposed work? And what does this mean for your financial future? These are good questions, and they deserve clear answers.

First, how did our economy reach this point?

Well, most economists agree that the problems we are witnessing today developed over a long period of time. For more than a decade, a massive amount of money flowed into the United States from investors abroad, because our country is an attractive and secure place to do business. This large influx of money to U.S. banks and financial institutions – along with low interest rates – made it easier for Americans to get credit. These developments allowed more families to borrow money for cars and homes and college tuition – some

September 24, 2008. http://www.whitehouse.gov/news/releases/2008/09/20080924

for the first time. They allowed more entrepreneurs to get loans to start new businesses and create jobs.

Unfortunately, there were also some serious negative consequences, particularly in the housing market. Easy credit – combined with the faulty assumption that home values would continue to rise – led to excesses and bad decisions. Many mortgage lenders approved loans for borrowers without carefully examining their ability to pay. Many borrowers took out loans larger than they could afford, assuming that they could sell or refinance their homes at a higher price later on.

Optimism about housing values also led to a boom in home construction. Eventually the number of new houses exceeded the number of people willing to buy them. And with supply exceeding demand, housing prices fell. And this created a problem: Borrowers with adjustable rate mortgages who had been planning to sell or refinance their homes at a higher price were stuck with homes worth less than expected – along with mortgage payments they could not afford. As a result, many mortgage holders began to default.

These widespread defaults had effects far beyond the housing market. See, in today's mortgage industry, home loans are often packaged together, and converted into financial products called "mortgage-backed securities." These securities were sold to investors around the world. Many investors assumed these securities were trustworthy, and asked few questions about their actual value. Two of the leading purchasers of mortgage-backed securities were Fannie Mae and Freddie Mac. Because these companies were chartered by Congress, many believed they were guaranteed by the federal government. This allowed them to borrow enormous sums of money, fuel the market for questionable investments, and put our financial system at risk.

The decline in the housing market set off a domino effect across our economy. When home values declined, borrowers defaulted on their mortgages, and investors holding mortgage-backed securities began to incur serious losses. Before long, these securities became so unreliable that they were not being bought or sold. Investment banks such as Bear Stearns and Lehman Brothers found themselves saddled with large amounts of assets they could not sell. They ran out of the money needed to meet their immediate obligations. And they faced imminent collapse. Other banks found themselves in severe financial trouble. These banks began holding on to their money, and lending dried up, and the gears of the American financial system began grinding to a halt.

With the situation becoming more precarious by the day, I faced a choice: To step in with dramatic government action, or to stand back and allow the irresponsible actions of some to undermine the financial security of all.

I'm a strong believer in free enterprise. So my natural instinct is to oppose government intervention. I believe companies that make bad decisions should be allowed to go out of business. Under normal circumstances, I would have followed this course. But these are not normal circumstances. The market is not functioning properly. There's been a widespread loss of confidence. And major sectors of America's financial system are at risk of shutting down.

The government's top economic experts warn that without immediate action by Congress, America could slip into a financial panic, and a distressing scenario would unfold:

More banks could fail, including some in your community. The stock market would drop even more, which would reduce the value of your retirement account. The value of your home could plummet. Foreclosures would rise dramatically. And if you own a business or a farm, you would find it harder and more expensive to get credit. More businesses would close their doors, and millions of Americans could lose their jobs. Even if you have a good credit history, it would be more difficult for you to get the loans you need to buy a car or send your children to college. And ultimately, our country could experience a long and painful recession.

Fellow citizens: We must not let this happen. I appreciate the work of leaders from both parties in both houses of Congress to address this problem – and to make improvements to the proposal my administration sent to them. There is a spirit of cooperation between Democrats and Republicans, and between Congress and this administration. In that spirit, I've invited Senators McCain and Obama to join congressional leaders of both parties at the White House tomorrow to help speed our discussions toward a bipartisan bill.

I know that an economic rescue package will present a tough vote for many members of Congress. It is difficult to pass a bill that commits so much of the taxpayers' hard-earned money. I also understand the frustration of responsible Americans who pay their mortgages on time, file their tax returns every April 15th, and are reluctant to pay the cost of excesses on Wall Street. But given the situation we are facing, not passing a bill now would cost these Americans much more later.

Many Americans are asking: How would a rescue plan work?

After much discussion, there is now widespread agreement on the principles such a plan would include. It would remove the risk posed by the troubled assets – including mortgage-backed securities – now clogging the financial system. This would free banks to resume the flow of credit to American families and businesses. Any rescue plan should also be designed to ensure that taxpayers are protected. It should welcome the participation of financial institutions large and small. It should make certain that failed executives do not receive a windfall from your tax dollars. It should establish a bipartisan board to oversee the plan's implementation. And it should be enacted as soon as possible.

In close consultation with Treasury Secretary Hank Paulson, Federal Reserve Chairman Ben Bernanke, and SEC Chairman Chris Cox, I announced a plan on Friday. First, the plan is big enough to solve a serious problem. Under our proposal, the federal government would put up to $700 billion taxpayer dollars on the line to purchase troubled assets that are clogging the financial system. In the short term, this will free up banks to resume the flow of credit to American families and businesses. And this will help our economy grow.

Second, as markets have lost confidence in mortgage-backed securities, their prices have dropped sharply. Yet the value of many of these assets will likely be higher than their current price, because the vast majority of Americans will ultimately pay off their mortgages. The government is the one institution with the patience and resources to buy these assets at their current low prices and hold them until markets return to normal. And when that happens, money will flow back to the Treasury as these assets are sold. And we expect that much, if not all, of the tax dollars we invest will be paid back.

A final question is: What does this mean for your economic future?

The primary steps – purpose of the steps I have outlined tonight is to safeguard the financial security of American workers and families and small businesses. The federal government also continues to enforce laws and regulations protecting your money. The Treasury Department recently offered government insurance for money market mutual funds. And through the FDIC, every savings account, checking account, and certificate of deposit is insured by the federal government for up to $100,000. The FDIC has been in existence for 75 years, and no one has ever lost a penny on an insured deposit – and this will not change.

Once this crisis is resolved, there will be time to update our financial regulatory structures. Our 21st century global economy remains regulated largely by outdated 20th century laws. Recently, we've seen how one company can grow so large that its failure jeopardizes the entire financial system.

Earlier this year, Secretary Paulson proposed a blueprint that would modernize our financial regulations. For example, the Federal Reserve would be authorized to take a closer look at the operations of companies across the financial spectrum and ensure that their practices do not threaten overall financial stability. There are other good ideas, and members of Congress should consider them. As they do, they must ensure that efforts to regulate Wall Street do not end up hampering our economy's ability to grow.

In the long run, Americans have good reason to be confident in our economic strength. Despite corrections in the marketplace and instances of abuse, democratic capitalism is the best system ever devised. It has unleashed the talents and the productivity and entrepreneurial spirit of our citizens. It has made this country the best place in the world to invest and do business. And it gives our economy the flexibility and resilience to absorb shocks, adjust, and bounce back.

Our economy is facing a moment of great challenge. But we've overcome tough challenges before – and we will overcome this one. I know that Americans sometimes get discouraged by the tone in Washington, and the seemingly endless partisan struggles. Yet history has shown that in times of real trial, elected officials rise to the occasion. And together, we will show the world once again what kind of country America is – a nation that tackles problems head on, where leaders come together to meet great tests, and where people of every background can work hard, develop their talents, and realize their dreams.

Thank you for listening. May God bless you.

Newt Gingrich  **NO**

Before D.C. Gets Our Money, It Owes Us Some Answers

Watching Washington rush to throw taxpayer money at Wall Street has been sobering and a little frightening.

We are being told Treasury Secretary Henry Paulson has a plan which will shift $700 billion in obligations from private companies to the taxpayer.

We are being warned that this $700 billion bailout is the only answer to a crisis.

We are being reassured that we can trust Secretary Paulson "because he knows what he is doing."

Congress had better ask a lot of questions before it shifts this much burden to the taxpayer and shifts this much power to a Washington bureaucracy.

Imagine that the political balance of power in Washington were different.

If this were a Democratic administration the Republicans in the House and Senate would be demanding answers and would be organizing for a "no" vote.

If a Democratic administration were proposing this plan, Republicans would realize that having Connecticut Democratic Senator Chris Dodd (the largest recipient of political funds from Fannie Mae and Freddie Mac) as chairman of the Banking Committee guarantees that the Obama-Reid-Pelosi-Paulson plan that will emerge will be much worse as legislation than it started out as the Paulson proposal.

If this were a Democratic proposal, Republicans would remember that the Democrats wrote a grotesque housing bailout bill this summer that paid off their left-wing allies with taxpayer money, which despite its price tag of $300 billion has apparently failed as of last week, and could expect even more damage in this bill.

But because this gigantic power shift to Washington and this avalanche of taxpayer money is being proposed by a Republican administration, the normal conservative voices have been silent or confused.

It's time to end the silence and clear up the confusion.

Congress has an obligation to protect the taxpayer.

Congress has an obligation to limit the executive branch to the rule of law.

Congress has an obligation to perform oversight.

Congress was designed by the Founding Fathers to move slowly, precisely to avoid the sudden panic of a one-week solution that becomes a 20-year mess.

There are four major questions that have to be answered before Congress adopts a new $700 billion burden for the American taxpayer. On each of these questions, I believe Congress's answer will be "no" if it slows down long enough to examine the facts.

Question One: Is the current financial crisis the only crisis affecting the economy?

Answer: There are actually multiple crises hurting the economy.

There is an immediate crisis of liquidity on Wall Street.

There is a longer term crisis of a bad energy policy transferring $700 billion a year to foreign countries (so foreign sovereign capital funds are now using our energy payments to buy our companies).

There is a longer term crisis of Sarbanes-Oxley (the last "crisis"-inspired congressional disaster) crippling entrepreneurial start ups, driving public companies private, driving smart business people off public boards, and driving offerings from New York to London.

There is a long term crisis of a high corporate tax rate driving business out of the United States.

No solution to the immediate liquidity crisis should further cripple the American economy for the long run. Instead, the liquidity solution should be designed to strengthen the economy for competition in the world market.

Question Two: Is a big bureaucracy solution the only answer?

Answer: There is a non-bureaucratic solution that would stop the liquidity crisis almost overnight and do it using private capital rather than taxpayer money.

Four reform steps will have capital flowing with no government bureaucracy and no taxpayer burden.

First, suspend the mark-to-market rule which is insanely driving companies to unnecessary bankruptcy. If short selling can be suspended on 799 stocks (an arbitrary number and a warning of the rule by bureaucrats which is coming under the Paulson plan), the mark-to-market rule can be suspended for six months and then replaced with a more accurate three year rolling average mark-to-market.

Second, repeal Sarbanes-Oxley. It failed with Freddie Mac. It failed with Fannie Mae. It failed with Bear Stearns. It failed with Lehman Brothers. It failed with AIG. It is crippling our entrepreneurial economy. I spent three days this week in Silicon Valley. Everyone agreed Sarbanes-Oxley was crippling the economy. One firm told me they would bring more than 20 companies public in the next year if the law was repealed. Its Sarbanes-Oxley's $3 million per startup annual accounting fee that is keeping these companies private.

Third, match our competitors in China and Singapore by going to a zero capital gains tax. Private capital will flood into Wall Street with zero capital gains and it will come at no cost to the taxpayer. Even if you believe in a static analytical model in which lower capital gains taxes mean lower revenues for the Treasury, a zero capital gains tax costs much less than the Paulson plan. And if you believe in a historic model (as I do), a zero capital gains tax would lead to a dramatic increase in federal revenue through a larger, more competitive and more prosperous economy.

Fourth, immediately pass an "all of the above" energy plan designed to bring home $500 billion of the $700 billion a year we are sending overseas. With that much energy income the American economy would boom and government revenues would grow.

Question Three: Will the Paulson plan be implemented with transparency and oversight?

Answer: Implementation of the Paulson plan is going to be a mess. It is going to be a great opportunity for lobbyists and lawyers to make a lot of money. Who are the financial magicians Paulson is going to hire? Are they from Wall Street? If they're from Wall Street, aren't they the very people we are saving? And doesn't that mean that we're using the taxpayers' money to hire people to save their friends with even more taxpayer money? Won't this inevitably lead to crony capitalism? Who is going to do oversight? How much transparency is there going to be? We still haven't seen the report which led to bailing out Fannie Mae and Freddie Mac. It is "secret." Is our $700 billion going to be spent in "secret" too? In practical terms, will a bill be written in public so people can analyze it? Or will it be written in a closed room by the very people who have been collecting money from the institutions they are now going to use our money to bail out?

Question Four: In two months we will have an election and then there will be a new administration. Is this plan something we want to trust to a post-Paulson Treasury?

Answer: We don't know who will inherit this plan.

The balance of power on election day will shift to either McCain or Obama. Who will they pick for Treasury Secretary? What will their allies want done? We are about to give the next administration a level of detailed control over big companies on a scale even FDR did not exercise during the Great Depression. Is this really wise?

For these reasons I hope Congress will slow down and have an open debate.

And in the course of that debate, I hope someone will introduce an economic recovery act that makes America a better place to grow jobs. I hope the details will be made public before the vote.

For more details on my action plan for getting the American economy back on track and building long-term economic prosperity, you can read this *message* recorded yesterday to American Solutions members.

This is a very important week for the integrity of the Congress.

This is a very important week for the future of America.

If Washington wants our money, then it owes us some answers.

POSTSCRIPT

Is the Treasury's $700 Billion Bailout the Solution to the Credit Crisis?

The Treasury Department's original TARP underwent a metamorphosis as financial market stresses intensified and spread. In the relatively brief time it took to enact the EESA, the financial turmoil was so severe and was spreading so rapidly that the Treasury decided a quick $250 billion capital injection program was a better strategy than buying illiquid troubled assets from banks. Consequently, it disbursed $172.5 billion under its Capital Purchase Program (CPP) for healthy banks and thrifts between October 28 and December 22, 2008. The Treasury has also put EESA funds to a number of other uses. On November 23, 2008, it announced an investment of $20 billion in Citigroup under its new Targeted Investment Program (used on a case-by-case basis). On November 25, 2008, it committed $20 billion of EESA funds to a new Federal Reserve Bank facility, the Term Asset-Backed Securities Loan Facility, designed to meet the credit needs of households and small businesses. The Treasury also announced guidelines for a new Systemically Failing Institutions Program (funded under EESA) to prevent the disorderly failure of a financial institution that is significant enough to threaten the financial system and adversely affect jobs, savings, and retirement security. On December 19, 2008, Treasury announced it would loan up to $13.4 billion to GM and $4 billion to Chrysler to stabilize the automotive industry. On December 29, 2008, Treasury announced an investment of $5 billion in GMAC and a (further) loan of $1 billion to General Motors so that GM can participate in a rights offering at GMAC in support of GMAC's reorganization as a bank holding company. The Treasury's Web site http://www.ustreas.gov/initiatives/eesa/ contains a range of information, including data on its use of the bailout monies, new programs, the Secretary's testimonies to Congress, other press releases, reports of the Financial Stability Oversight Board, and Treasury's December 30, 2008, response to questions posed by the Congressional Oversight Panel (COP) for Economic Stabilization (both established under EESA). The Treasury's Web site is constantly updated for new developments.

The first COP report (December 10, 2008) "Questions About the $700 Billion Emergency Economic Stabilization Funds" on the Treasury's conduct of the bailout is found at http://www.house.gov/apps/list/hearing/financialsvcs_dem/hr121008.shtml. It contains 10 questions and the discussion they generated; the Treasury responded to the questions on December 30, 2008. A statement by House Financial Services Committee Chairman Barney Frank on the Government Accountability Office (GAO) report on the Treasury Department's

implementation of the Troubled Asset Relief Program is available at http://www
.house.gov/apps/list/press/financialsvcs_dem/press120308.shtml (as is a link to the
GAO report).

The Federal Reserve Bank's Web site www.federalreserve.gov contains
valuable, detailed, and timely information and data on its new liquidity programs and other policy actions, as well as Chairman Bernanke's speeches on
the credit crisis—which provide a clear account of the causes and consequences
of the crisis and the rationale for its policies. See, for example, "Federal Reserve
Policies in the Financial Crisis," http://www.federalreserve.gov/newsevents/speech/
bernanke20081201a.htm. Of interest is Anthony Karydakis's article "In Saving the
World, the Fed Beats Treasury," http://money.cnn.com/2009/01/02/news/economy/fed_
treasury.fortune/index.htm?postversion=2009010210 (*Fortune,* January 2, 2009).

The FDIC's Web site www.fdic.gov provides information on its Temporary
Liquidity Guarantee Program and mortgage modification.

Many segments of the PBS *The News Hour with Jim Lehrer* contain discussions on the credit crisis and the bailout; see, for example, Episode
9306H (November 25, 2008) with economists Kenneth Rogoff and James
Galbraith on the Fed's role in managing the financial crisis at www.pbs
.org/newshour/bb/business/july-dec08/fedrole_25.html.

In his testimony to Congress in October 2008, former Federal Reserve
Chairman Alan Greenspan voices his "state of shocked disbelief" at the failure
of a free market to regulate itself and calls for regulatory policies to address
credit market problems (http://oversight.house.gov/documents/20081023100438
.pdf). Also read Joseph E. Stiglitz's "Commentary: How to Prevent the Next
Wall Street Crisis," at http://www.cnn.com/2008/POLITICS/09/17/stiglitz.crisis/index.
html (September 2007) for his view of the causes of the crisis and the preventive
measures he recommends.

The congressional hearing on the Treasury's initial proposal to buy troubled assets is accessible at http://www.house.gov/apps/list/hearing/financialsvcs_dem/
hr092408.shtml.

For those interested in a chronology of events up to the end of October
2008, "TIMELINE: 2008 a year of global financial turbulence" is available at
http://www.reuters.com/article/gc06/idUSTRE4927NC20081004?sp=true.

Contributors to This Volume

CO-EDITORS

FRANK J. BONELLO received his B.S. and his M.A. degrees from the University of Detroit and his Ph.D. from Michigan State University. He is currently associate professor of economics at the University of Notre Dame, where he also served as Arts and Letters College Fellow. He writes in the areas of monetary economics and economic education. This is his sixth book. He is the author of *The Formulation of Expected Interest Rates* and co-author of *Computer-Assisted Instruction in Economic Education*. In addition to *Taking Sides,* he has co-edited, with T.R. Swartz, *Alternative Directions in Economic Policy* (Notre Dame Press, 1978); *The Supply Side: Debating Current Economic Policies* (Dushkin, 1983); and *Urban Finance Under Siege* (M.E. Sharpe, 1993).

ISOBEL LOBO received her M.A., M.S.A., and Ph.D. from the University of Notre Dame. She is currently associate professor of economics in the International Business and Economics Department at Benedictine University. She has also taught at the University of Notre Dame and Saint Joseph's College in Rensselaer, Indiana. This is her first book. She writes in the areas of general economics and economic education and has presented papers at the Academy of International Business Conference, the Association for Global Business Conference, and the Hawaii Conference on International Business.

AUTHORS

ROBERT ALMEDER is a professor of philosophy at Georgia State University. He is the editor of the *American Philosophical Quarterly,* co-editor of the annual book series *Biomedical Ethic Reviews,* and former member of the editorial board of the *Journal of Business Ethics.* He earned his Ph.D. in philosophy at the University of Pennsylvania, and he is the author of *Harmless Naturalism: The Limits of Science and the Nature of Philosophy* (Open Court, 1998).

AMERICAN BENEFITS COUNCIL is a national trade association representing principally Fortune 500 companies and other organizations that either sponsor or administer health and retirement benefit plans covering more than 100 million Americans.

MARK H. AYERS is the president of the Building and Construction Trades Department of the AFL-CIO. He is also a trustee of the AFL-CIO.

DEAN BAKER is the co-director of the Center for Economic and Policy Research. His books include *Social Security: The Phony Crisis,* co-authored with Mark Weisbrot (University of Chicago Press, 1999), *Getting Prices Right: The Battle Over the Consumer Price Index* (M.E. Sharpe Press, 1997), and *Globalization and Progressive Economic Policy,* edited with Jerry Epstein and Bob Pollin (Cambridge University Press, 1998). He holds a Ph.D. in economics from the University of Michigan.

REBECCA BLANK is Robert V. Kerr visiting fellow at the Brookings Institution. She is also Henry Carter Adams Professor of Public Policy and Professor of Economics at the University of Michigan, where she also serves as co-director of the National Policy Center. She has also served as a member of the President's Council of Economic Advisors.

LINDA J. BLUMBERG is principal research associate at the Urban Institute. She holds a Ph.D. in economics from the University of Michigan.

ALEX BRILL is a research fellow at the American Enterprise Institute for Public Policy Research. He has served as chief economist to the House Committee on Ways and Means and on the staff of the President's Council of Economic Advisors.

GEORGE W. BUSH, the 43rd President of the United States, was elected in 2000 and then again in 2004. He also served as the 46th Governor of Texas, from January 1995 through December 2000. He is also the son of George H.W. Bush, the 41st President of the United States.

JOHN P. CAREY is the Chief Administrative Officer of Citi Cards, a leading provider of credit cards with approximately 45 million active bank card customer accounts in the United States.

JAMES M. CYPHER is professor-investigador, Programa de Doctorado en Estudios del Desarrollo, Universidad Autonoma de Zacatecas, Mexico, and a *Dollars & Sense* associate. He holds a Ph.D. in economics from the University of California, Riverside.

DEMOCRATIC STAFF OF THE HOUSE COMMITTEE ON EDUCATION AND THE WORKFORCE. The names of the individuals who serve as members can be found at http://edworkforce.house.gov/about/members/

BOB DINNEEN is president and chief executive officer of the Renewable Fuels Association, the national trade association for the U.S. ethanol industry.

CHARLES T. DREVNA is president of the National Petrochemical and Refiners Association, a national trade association with more than 450 members. The association includes virtually all U.S. refiners and petrochemical manufacturers who supply building block chemicals necessary to produce products ranging from plastics to pharmaceuticals, clothing, and computers. He previously served as director of Environmental Affairs for the National Coal Association.

CHRIS EDWARDS is the director of Tax Policy Studies at the Cato Institute. He has also been an economist with the Tax Foundation, a consultant and manager with PriceWaterhouseCoopers, and senior economist with the congressional Joint Economic Committee. He holds an M.A. in economics from George Mason University.

EDWIN G. FOULKE, JR., at the time of his testimony was assistant secretary in the Occupational Safety and Health Administration in the U.S. Department of Labor. He left that position in 2008 to join the firm of Fisher & Phillips, LLP.

MILTON FRIEDMAN received the 1976 Nobel Prize in Economic Science for his work in consumption analysis, monetary history and theory, and for demonstrating the complexity of economic stabilization policy. In 1998, he received both the Presidential Medal of Freedom and the National Medal of Science. He and his wife co-authored several publications, including *Two Lucky People* (University of Chicago Press, 1998) and *Free to Choose: A Personal Statement* (Harcourt Brace, 1990). He served as a senior research fellow at the Stanford University Hoover Institution on War, Revolution, and Peace from 1977 up to his passing in November 2006.

DIANA FURCHTGOTT-ROTH is a senior fellow at the Hudson Institute and director of Hudson's Center for Employment Policy. She is a former chief economist at the U.S. Department of Labor and has also served as chief of staff of the President's Council of Economic Advisors. She is the co-author of *Women's Figures: An Illustrated Guide to the Economics of Women in America*. She has appeared on a number of radio and television shows, including C-SPAN'S Washington Journal and The News Hour with Jim Lehrer.

NEWT GINGRICH is a former congressman representing the Sixth District of Georgia for 20 years. He was first elected in 1978 and in 1995 was selected Speaker of the House, where he served until 1999. He is currently chairman of the Gingrich Group, a communications and consulting firm that specializes in transformational change. He is also a news and political analyst for the Fox News Channel.

JAGADEESH GOKHALE is a senior fellow at the Cato Institute, where he works with Cato's Project on Social Security Choice. His previous positions include consultant to the U.S. Department of Treasury, senior economic adviser to the Federal Reserve Bank of Cleveland, and visiting scholar with the American Enterprise Institute. He is co-author of *Fiscal and Generational Imbalances: New Budget Measures for New Budget Priorities*. He holds a Ph.D. in economics from Boston University.

JULIA GORDON is the policy counsel at the Center for Responsible Lending, a not-for-profit, nonpartisan research and policy organization dedicated to protecting homeownership and family wealth by working to eliminate abusive financial practices.

GARY HUFBAUER is the Reginald Jones Senior Fellow at the Peterson Institute for International Economics. He has served as deputy assistant secretary for International Trade and Investment Policy of the U.S. Treasury.

IRA T. KAY is global practice director for executive compensation at Watson Wyatt Worldwide and co-author of the book *Myths and Realities of Executive Pay*. His previous publications include *CEO Pay and Shareholder Value: Helping the U.S. Win the Global Economic War* and *Value at the Top: Solutions to the Executive Compensation Crisis*. He earned his undergraduate degree in industrial and labor relations from Cornell University and his Ph.D. in economics from Wayne State University.

DAVID G. KITTLE, CMB, was installed in 2008 as the chairman of the Mortgage Bankers Association, a national association representing the real estate finance industry. He is also Executive Vice President of Vision Mortgage Capital.

LOS ANGELES COUNTY ECONOMIC DEVELOPMENT CORPORATION is a private nonprofit organization established in 1981 with the mission to attract, retain, and grow business and jobs in the Los Angeles region.

D.W. MACKENZIE teaches economics at the State University of New York at Plattsburgh.

STEVEN MALANGA is a contributing editor of *City Journal* and a senior fellow at the Manhattan Institute. He previously held the position of executive editor of *Crain's New York Business*. His articles have also appeared in such publications as *The Wall Street Journal, New York Daily News,* and the *New York Post*. His education includes an M.A. in English literature and language from the University of Maryland.

MARK McCLELLAN is currently visiting senior fellow at the AEI-Brookings Joint Center. His previous positions include Administrator for the Centers for Medicare and Medicaid Services in the U.S. Department of Health and Human Services and Commissioner for the Food and Drug Administration. He holds an M.D. degree from the Harvard-MIT Division of Health Sciences and Technology, a Ph.D. in economics from Massachusetts Institute of Technology, and an M.P.A. from the Harvard University Kennedy School of Government.

JOHN M. MELLE is deputy assistant U.S. Trade Representative for North America. At USTR since 1987, his previous positions include senior director for North American Affairs and deputy director of the Generalized System of Preferences. He holds an M.A. degree in Public Policy from the University of Michigan.

GEORGE MILLER is a Democratic congressman representing the Seventh District of California. He was first elected to the House in 1974, and he currently chairs the House Committee on Education and Labor.

TRAVIS B. PLUNKETT is Legislative Director of the Consumer Federation of America, a nonprofit association of over 280 pro-consumer groups, with a combined membership of 50 million people.

SANDRA POLASKI is a senior associate with the Carnegie Endowment for International Peace, serving as the director of the Trade, Equity, and Development Project. Before moving to her current position, she served as the U.S. Secretary of State's special representative for international labor affairs. She holds M.S. degrees from both the University of Wisconsin and Johns Hopkins University.

RAYMOND SIMON was appointed to the position of deputy secretary in the U.S. Department of Education in 2005. He previously served as Chief State School Officer for Arkansas and as superintendent of the Conway, Arkansas, School District.

CHARLIE STENHOLM is a former member of the U.S. House of Representatives, serving the Seventeenth District in Texas for 13 terms, from 1979 to 2005. He has two degrees from Texas Tech University and has operated a cotton farm in Texas. He is currently a senior policy advisor at a Washington, D.C., law firm and is a member of the board of directors of the Committee for a Responsible Federal Budget and the Concord Coalition.

JOSEPH E. STIGLITZ is University Professor at Columbia University. He served as the chief economist of the World Bank from 1997 to 2000. He is the author of *Making Globalization Work* (W.W. Norton, 2006) and most recently, with Linda Biles of Harvard's Kennedy School, *The Three Trillion Dollar War: The True Costs of the Iraq Conflict* (W.W. Norton, 2008). Along with two others, he received the Nobel Prize in Economic Science in 2001.

U.S. DEPARTMENT OF HEALTH AND HUMAN SERVICES is the "U.S. government's principal agency for protecting the health of all Americans and providing essential human services, especially for those who are least able to help themselves." For fiscal year 2005, it had a budget of $581 billion and over 67,000 employees.

JEANNETTE WICKS-LIM is an economist and research fellow at the Political Economy Research Institute at the University of Massachusetts-Amherst. She holds an undergraduate from the University of Michigan and earned her Ph.D. in economics from the University of Massachusetts-Amherst.

JACKSON WILLIAMS, at the time he wrote his essay, was the legal counsel for Public Citizen's Congress Watch, concentrating on civil justice issues.

Previously, he was manager of public affairs for Defense Research Institute, the bar association of insurance defense counsel, where he also specialized in civil justice policy issues. He is a graduate of Loyola University of Chicago School of Law.

EDGAR WOOLARD, JR., was the CEO and chairman of the board of directors of Dupont. He is the current chairman of the New York Stock Exchange's Compensation Committee. He is also a former director of Citigroup Inc., IBM, Apple Computer, Inc., and Bell Atlantic Delaware. He received his undergraduate degree in industrial engineering from North Carolina State University.